Disney

BIG HERO 6

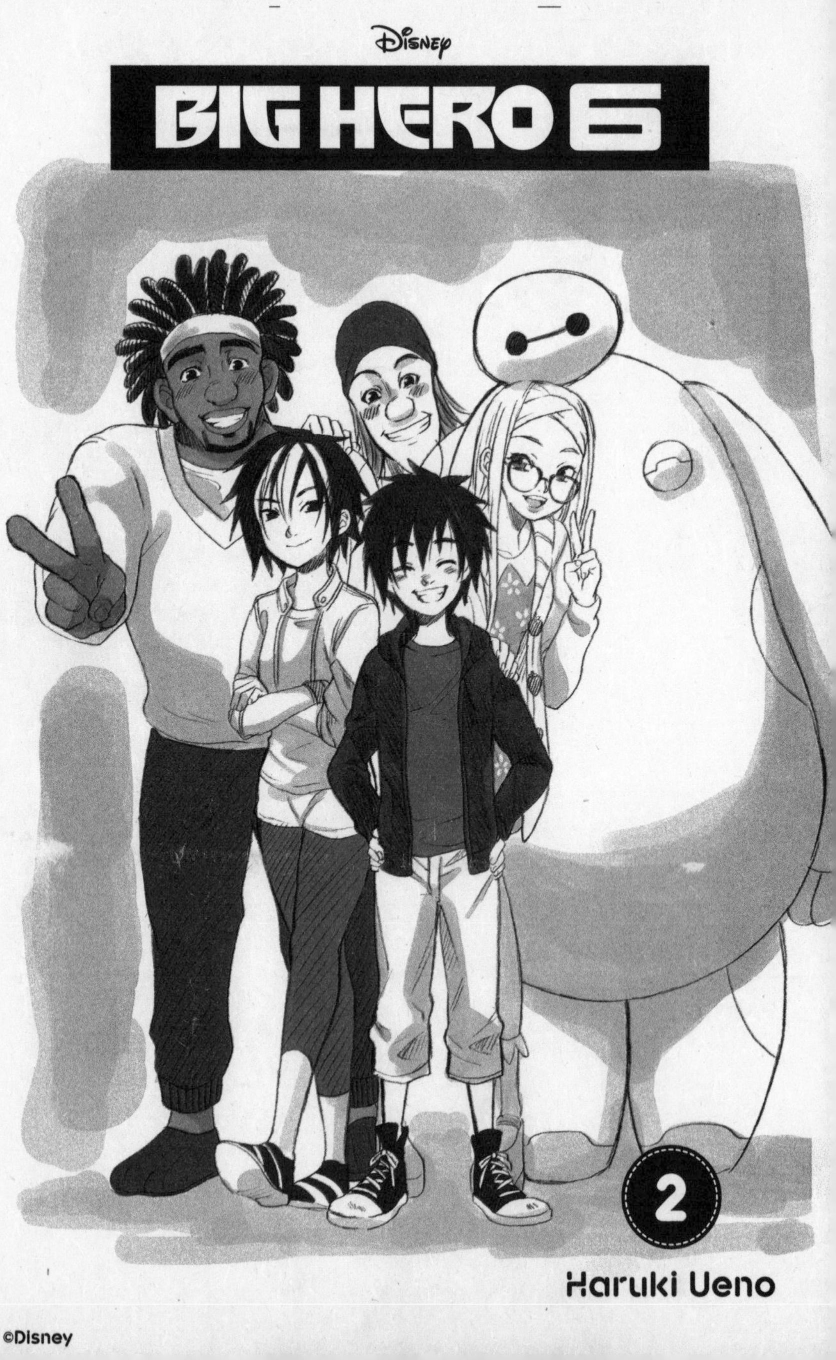

2

Haruki Ueno

CHARACTERS

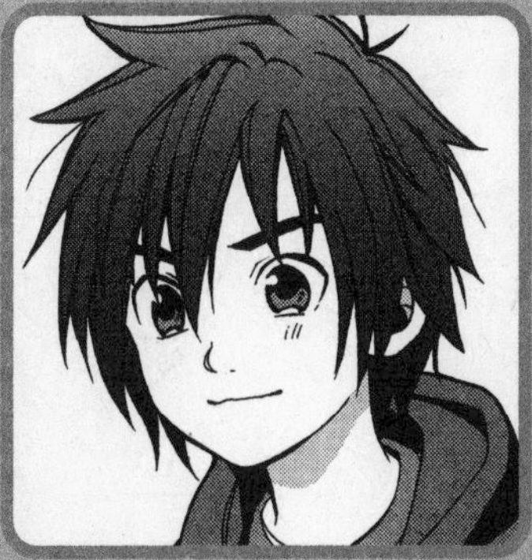

Hiro (Hiro Hamada)

A child prodigy who started college at age fourteen. He dreams of becoming the world's greatest inventor, following in the footsteps of his brother, Tadashi. He is trying to resolve the incident that led to Tadashi's disappearance.

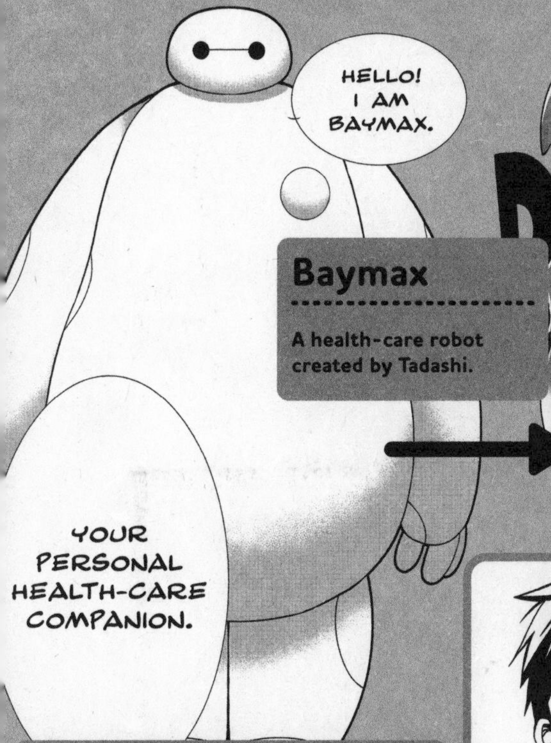
HELLO! I AM BAYMAX.
YOUR PERSONAL HEALTH-CARE COMPANION.

Baymax

A health-care robot created by Tadashi.

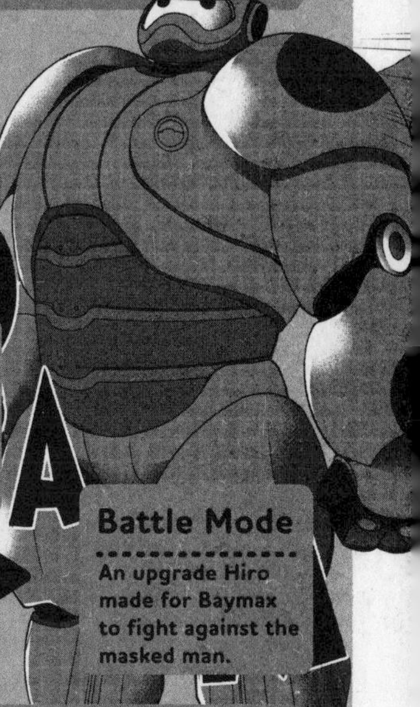

Battle Mode

An upgrade Hiro made for Baymax to fight against the masked man.

Tadashi (Tadashi Hamada)

Hiro's older brother. A college student and inventor. Creator of Baymax.

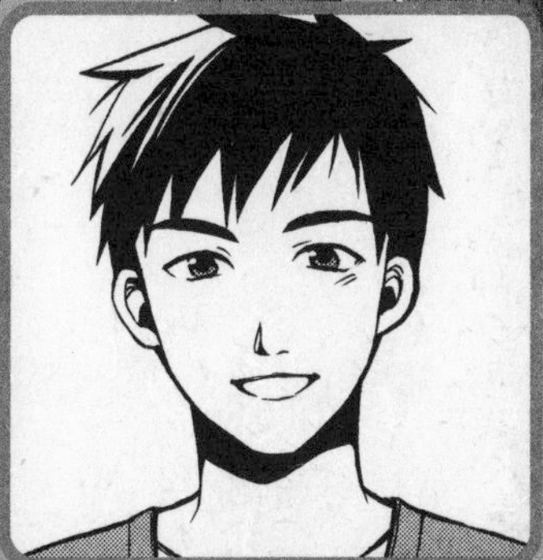

The Masked Man

He was at the scene when Tadashi disappeared. He is plotting something and is using Hiro's invention, the microbots, to carry it out.

Tadashi was the emotional support for the lonely boy Hiro, as well as everything Hiro wanted to be...before he was sucked into a mysterious dimension and disappeared. All Hiro had left was Baymax, the health-care robot invented by Tadashi. To investigate the truth of what happened, Hiro, Baymax, and four friends go to confront the mysterious phantom they saw at the scene of the crime!

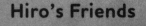

Hiro's Friends

GoGo

Fred

Wasabi

Honey Lemon

CONTENTS

2

By Haruki Ueno

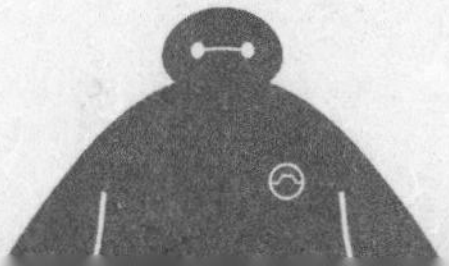

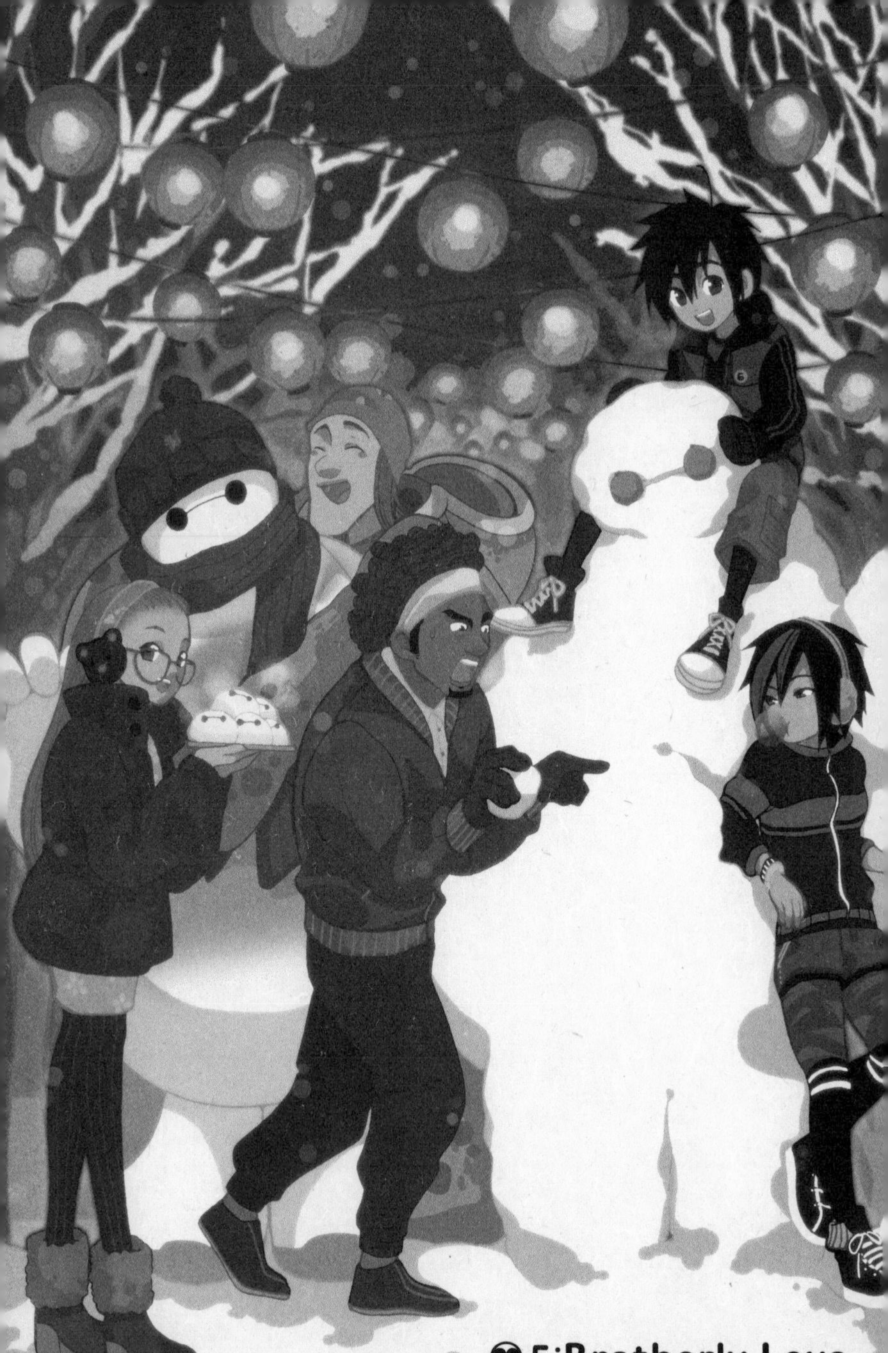

5: Brotherly Love

Disney
BIG HERO 6

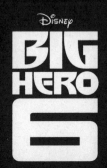

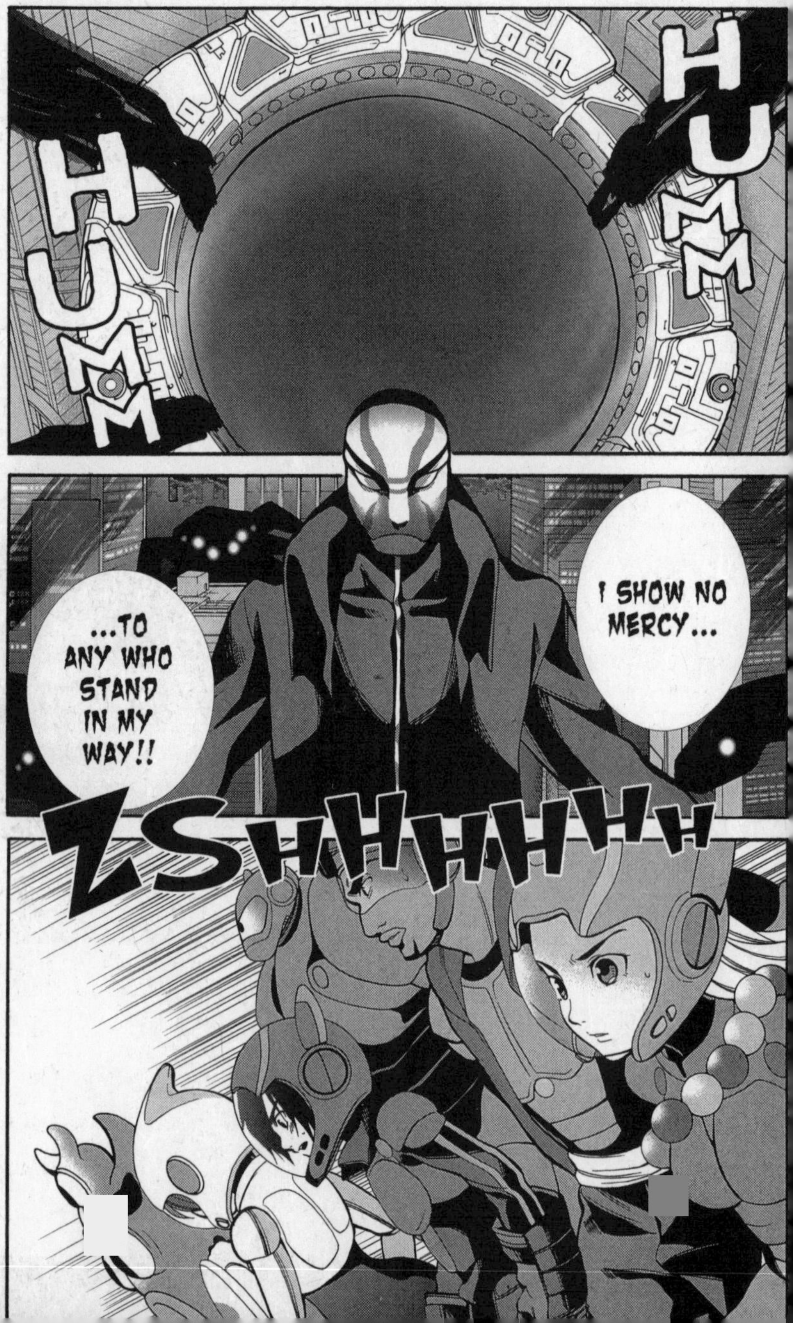
HUMM
HUMM
I SHOW NO MERCY...
...TO ANY WHO STAND IN MY WAY!!
ZSHHHHHH

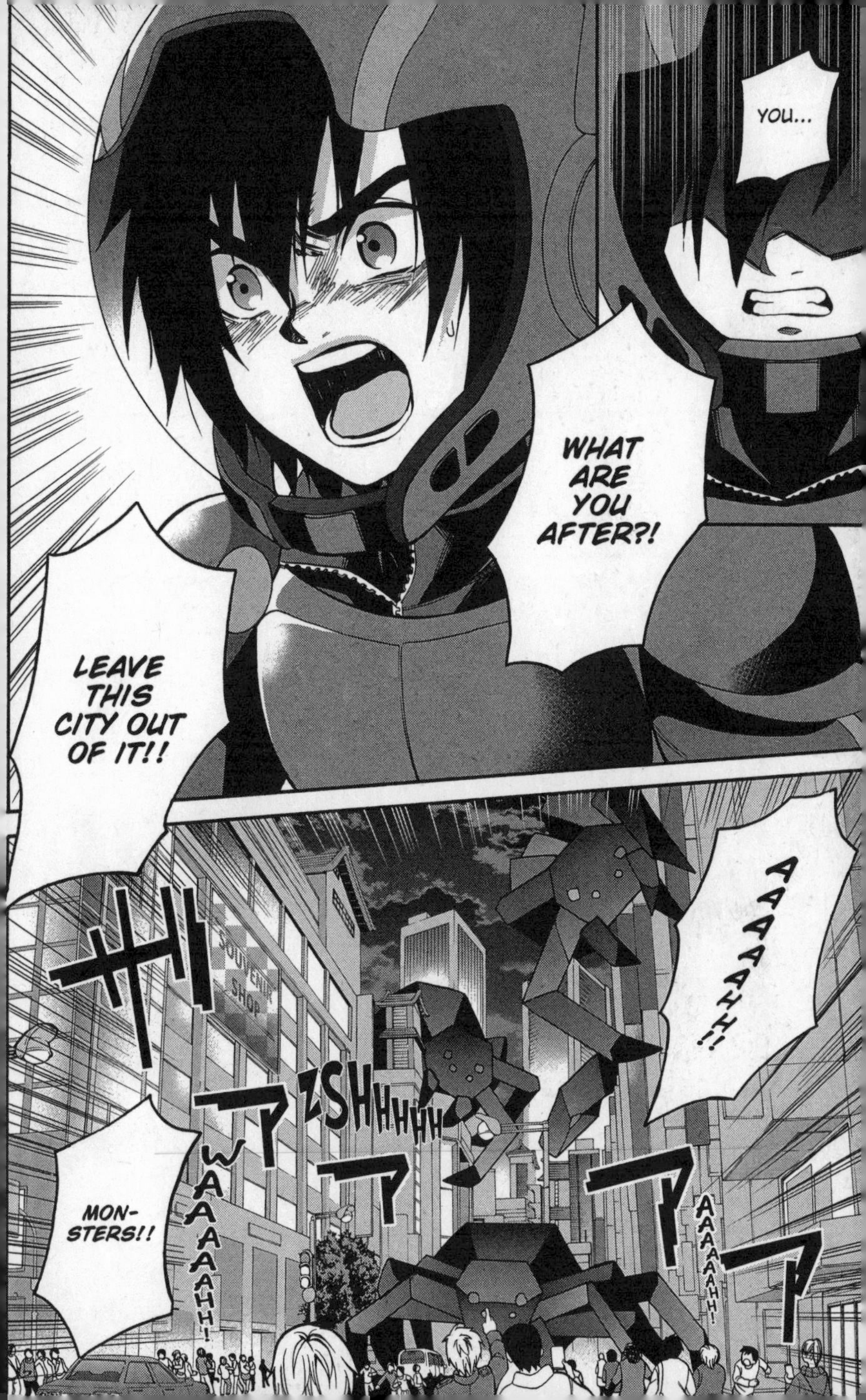
YOU...
WHAT ARE YOU AFTER?!
LEAVE THIS CITY OUT OF IT!!
AAAAAAAHH!!
ZSHHHHHH
AAAAAAAH!
WAAAAAAAAHH!
MON-STERS!!

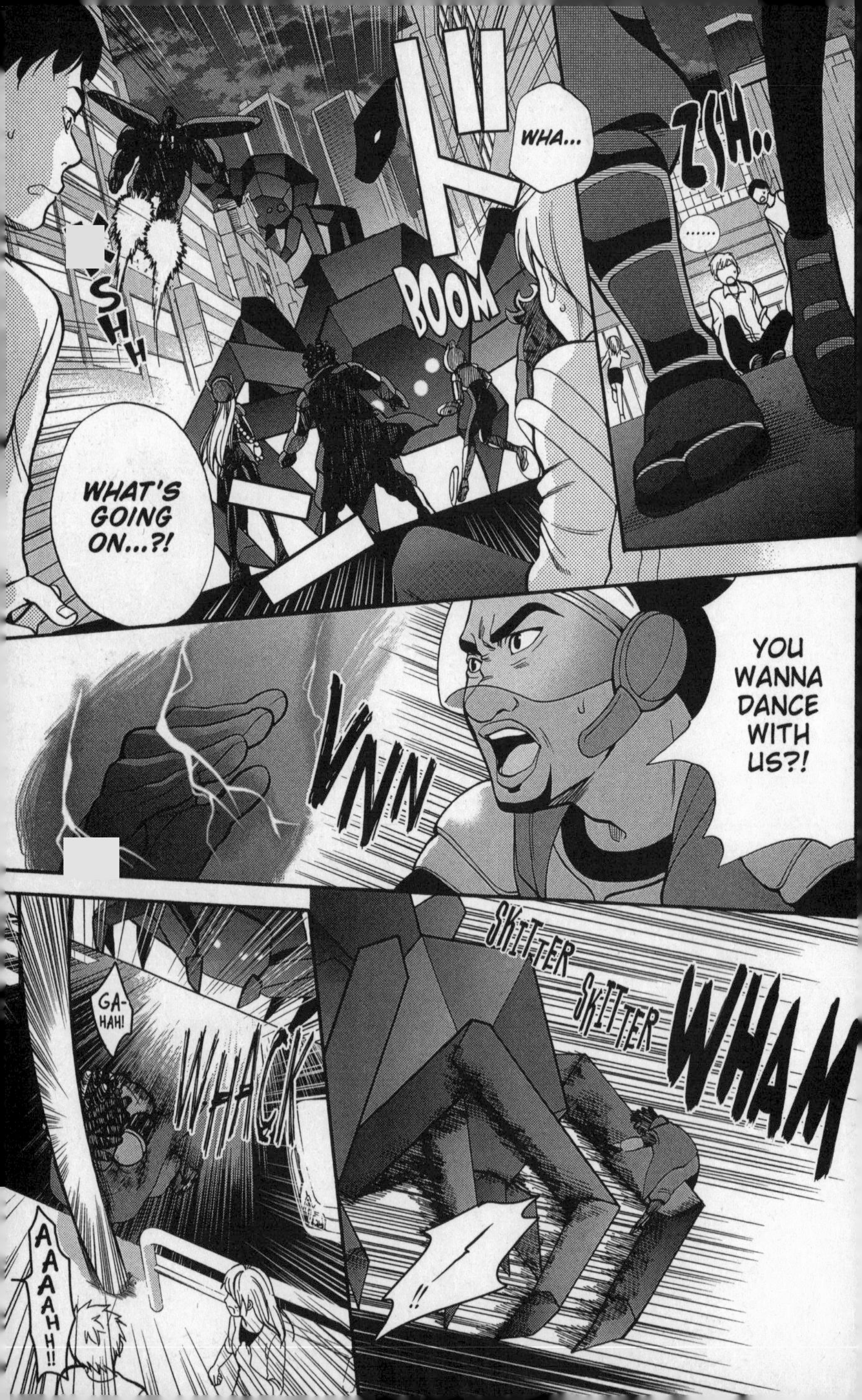
ZSH..
......
WHA...
BOOM
SHH
WHAT'S GOING ON...?!
YOU WANNA DANCE WITH US?!
VNN
WHAM
SKITTER
SKITTER
!!
WHACK
GA-HAH!
AAAAAH!!

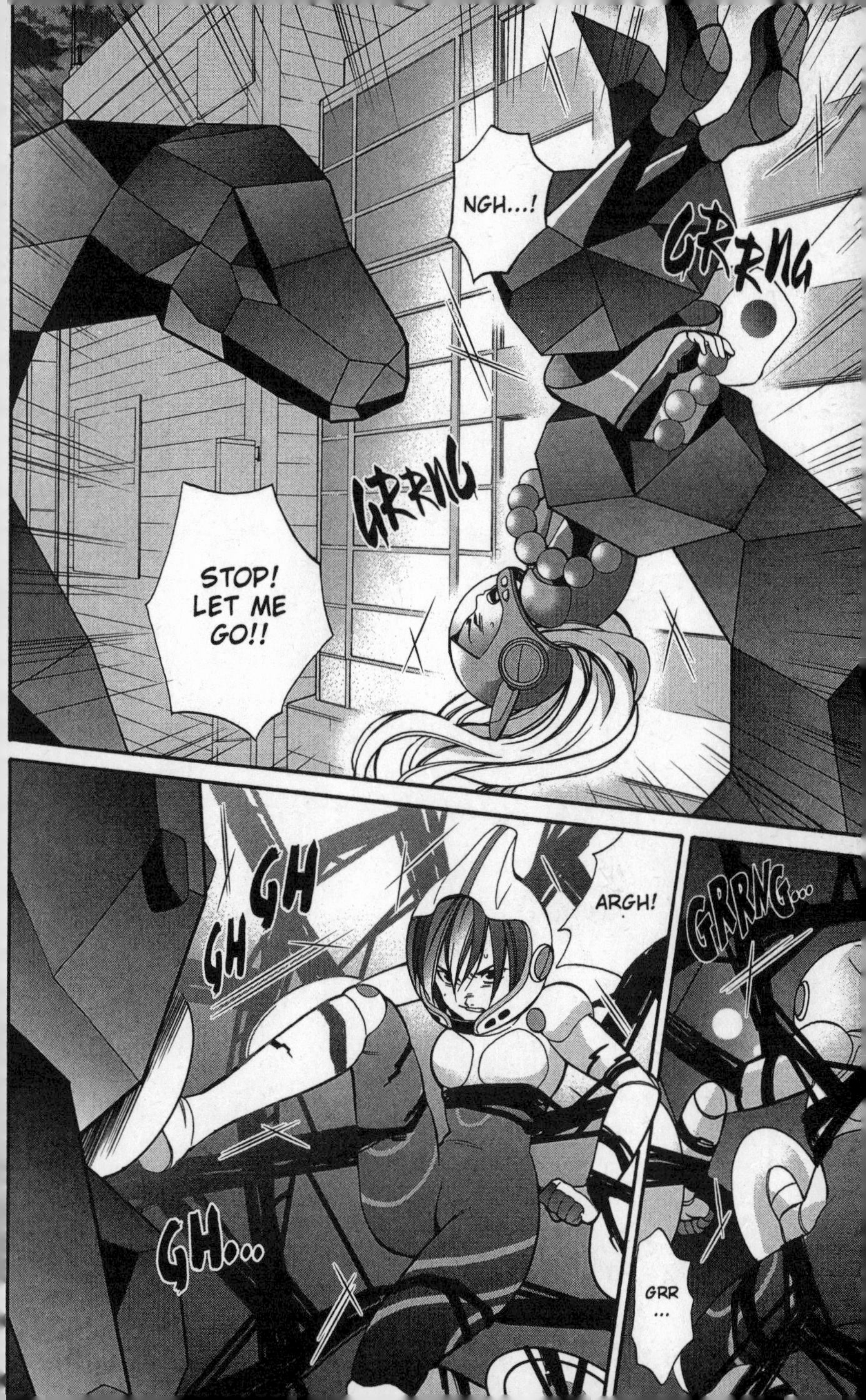
NGH...!
GRRNG
GRRNG
STOP! LET ME GO!!
GRRNG...
GRR...
ARGH!
GH GH
GH...

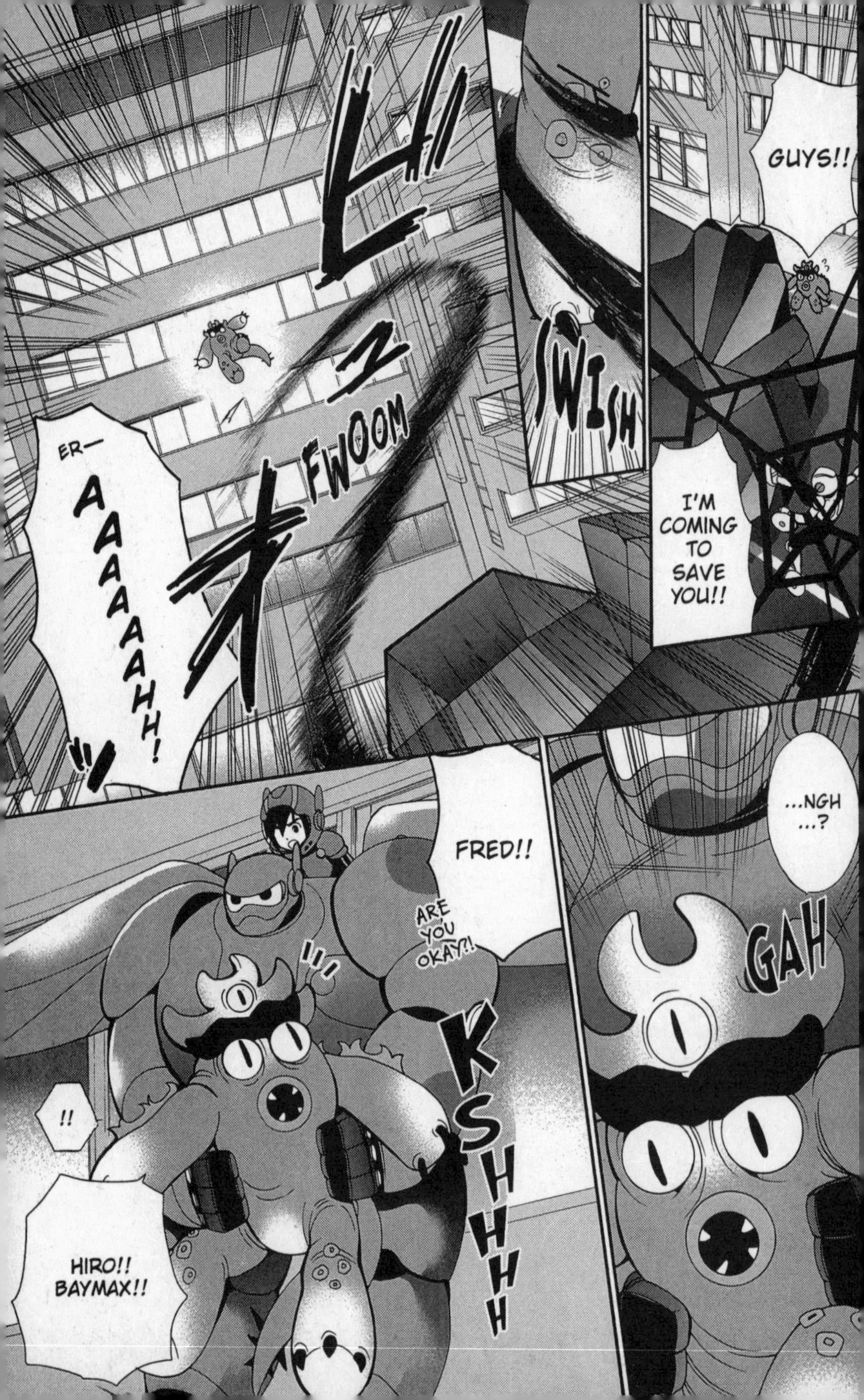
GUYS!!
I'M COMING TO SAVE YOU!!
SWISH
FWOOM
ER—
AAAAAAHH!
!!
...NGH ...?
GAH
FRED!!
ARE YOU OKAY?!
!!
KSHHHHH
!!
HIRO!! BAYMAX!!

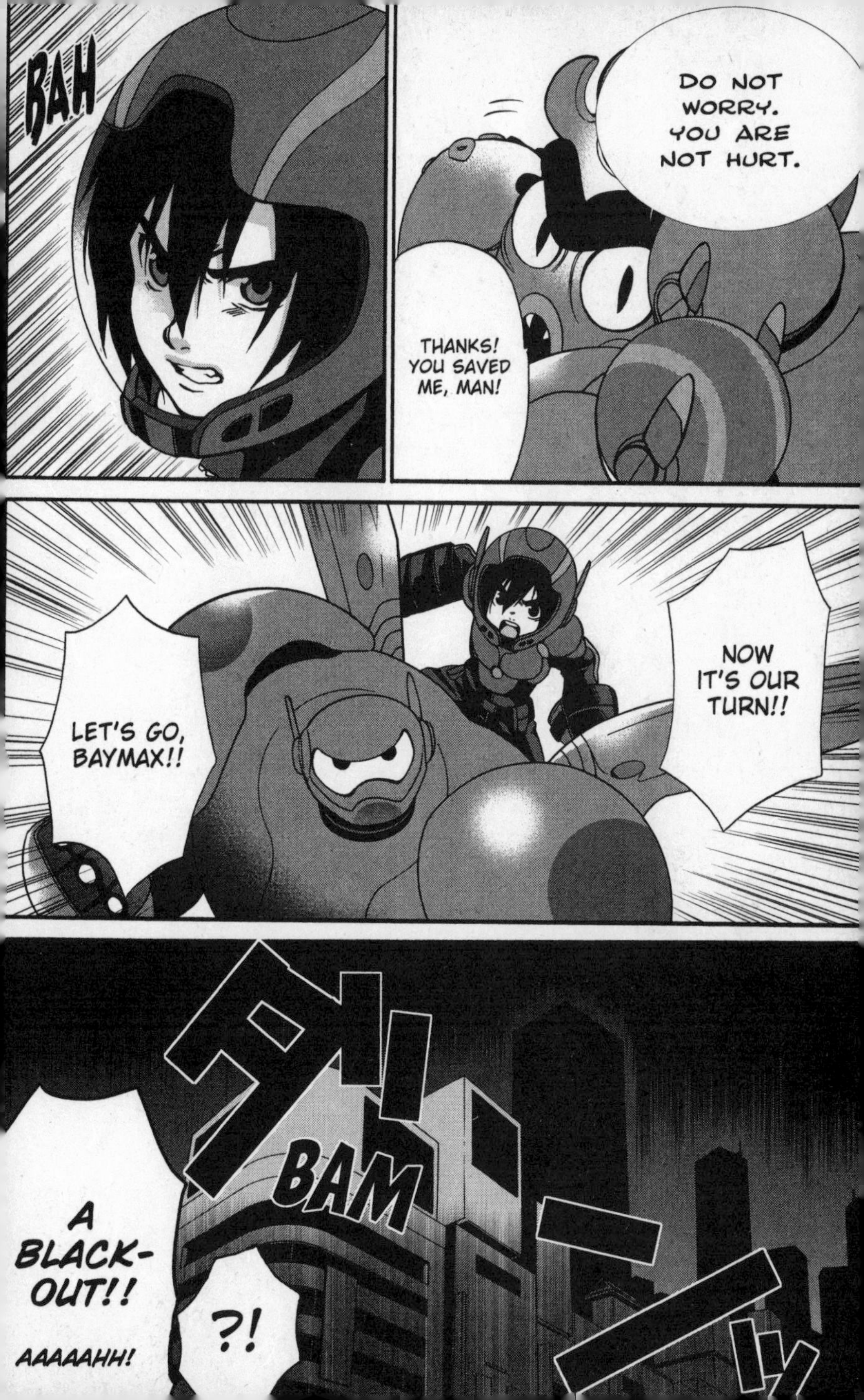
DO NOT WORRY. YOU ARE NOT HURT.
THANKS! YOU SAVED ME, MAN!
BAH
NOW IT'S OUR TURN!!
LET'S GO, BAYMAX!!
BAM
A BLACK-OUT!!
?!
AAAAAHH!

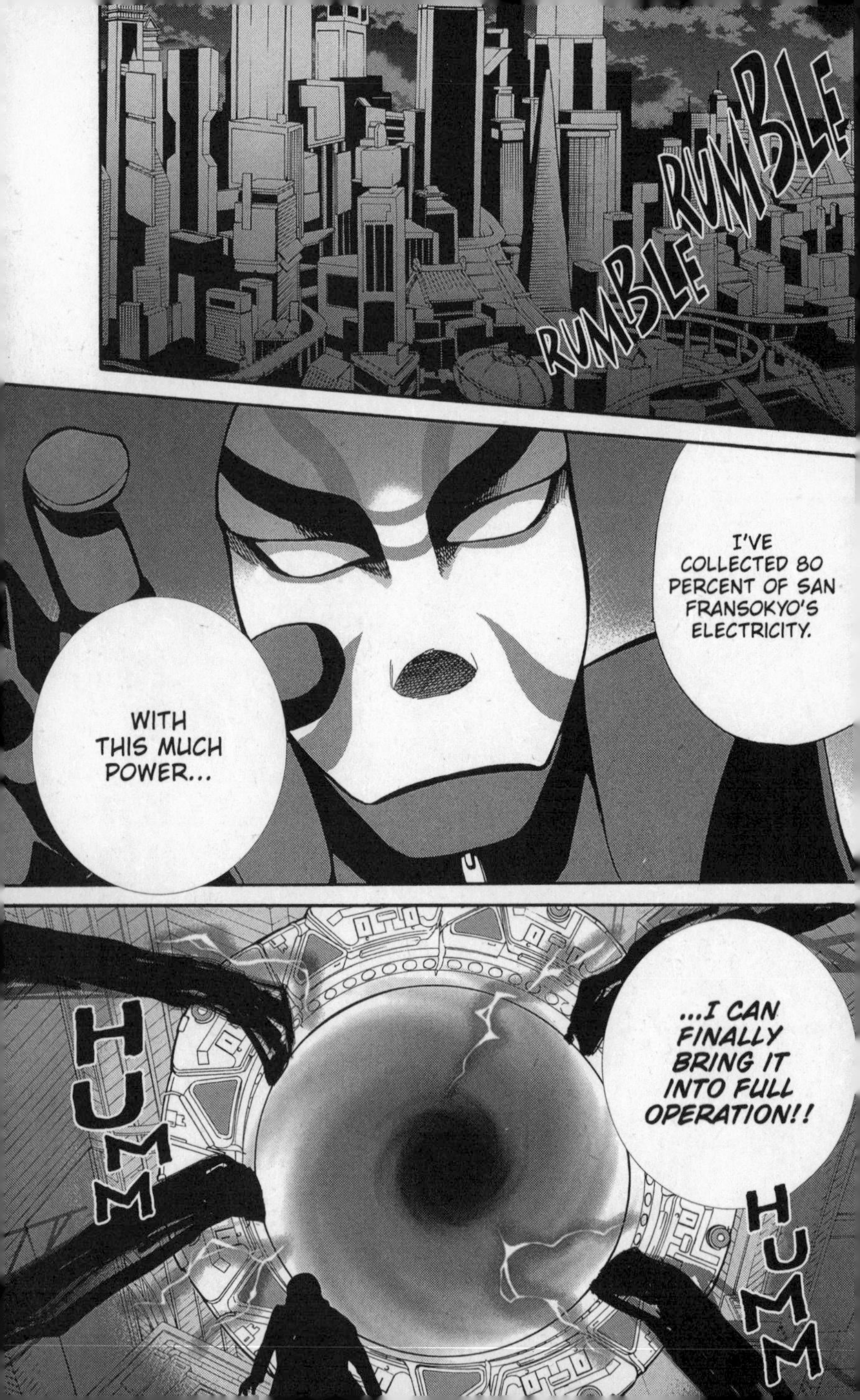
RUMBLE RUMBLE
I'VE COLLECTED 80 PERCENT OF SAN FRANSOKYO'S ELECTRICITY.
WITH THIS MUCH POWER...
...I CAN FINALLY BRING IT INTO FULL OPERATION!!
HUMM
HUMM

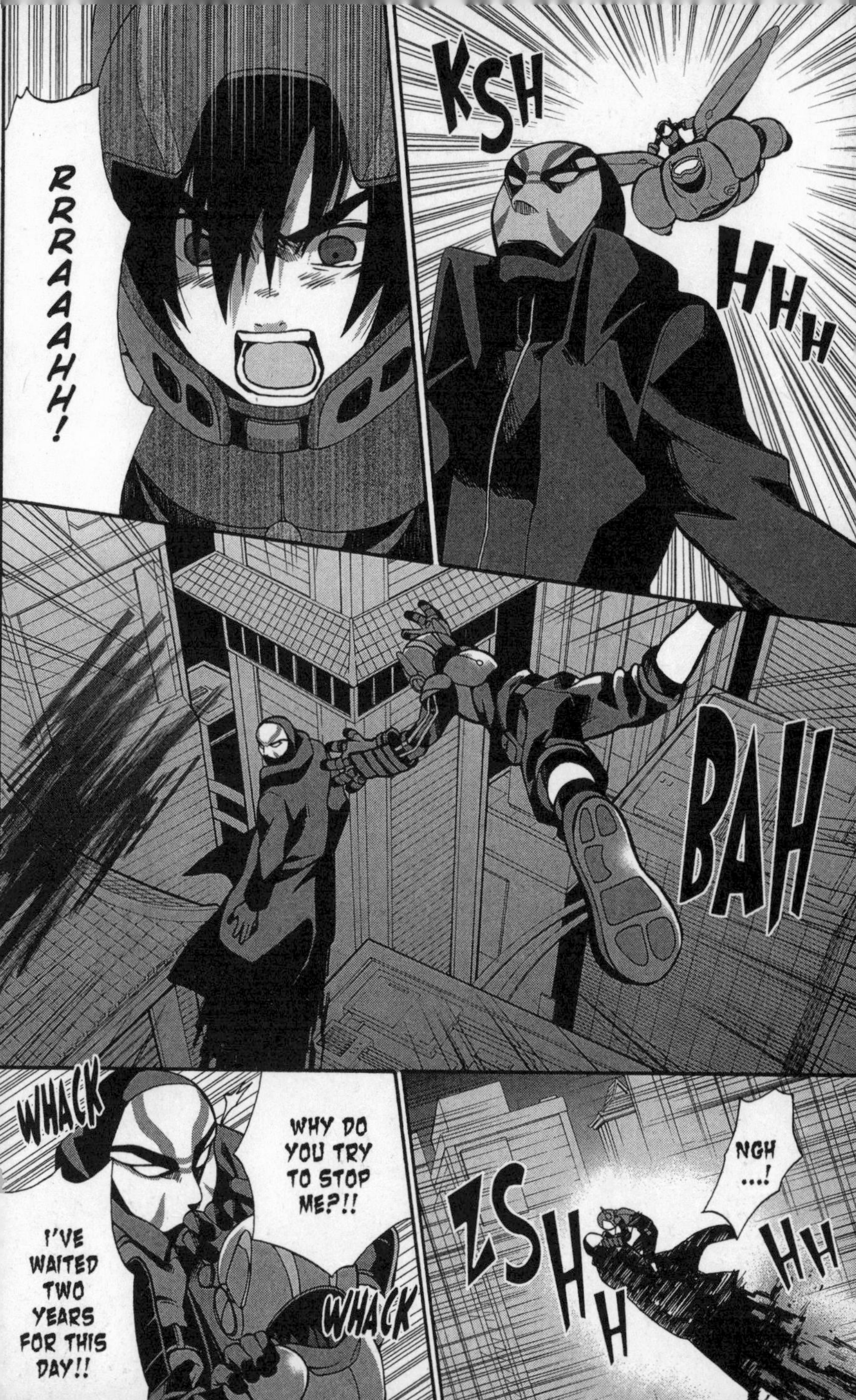
KSH
HHH
RRRAAAHH!
BAH
NGH ...!
ZSHHH HH
WHY DO YOU TRY TO STOP ME?!!
WHACK
WHACK
I'VE WAITED TWO YEARS FOR THIS DAY!!

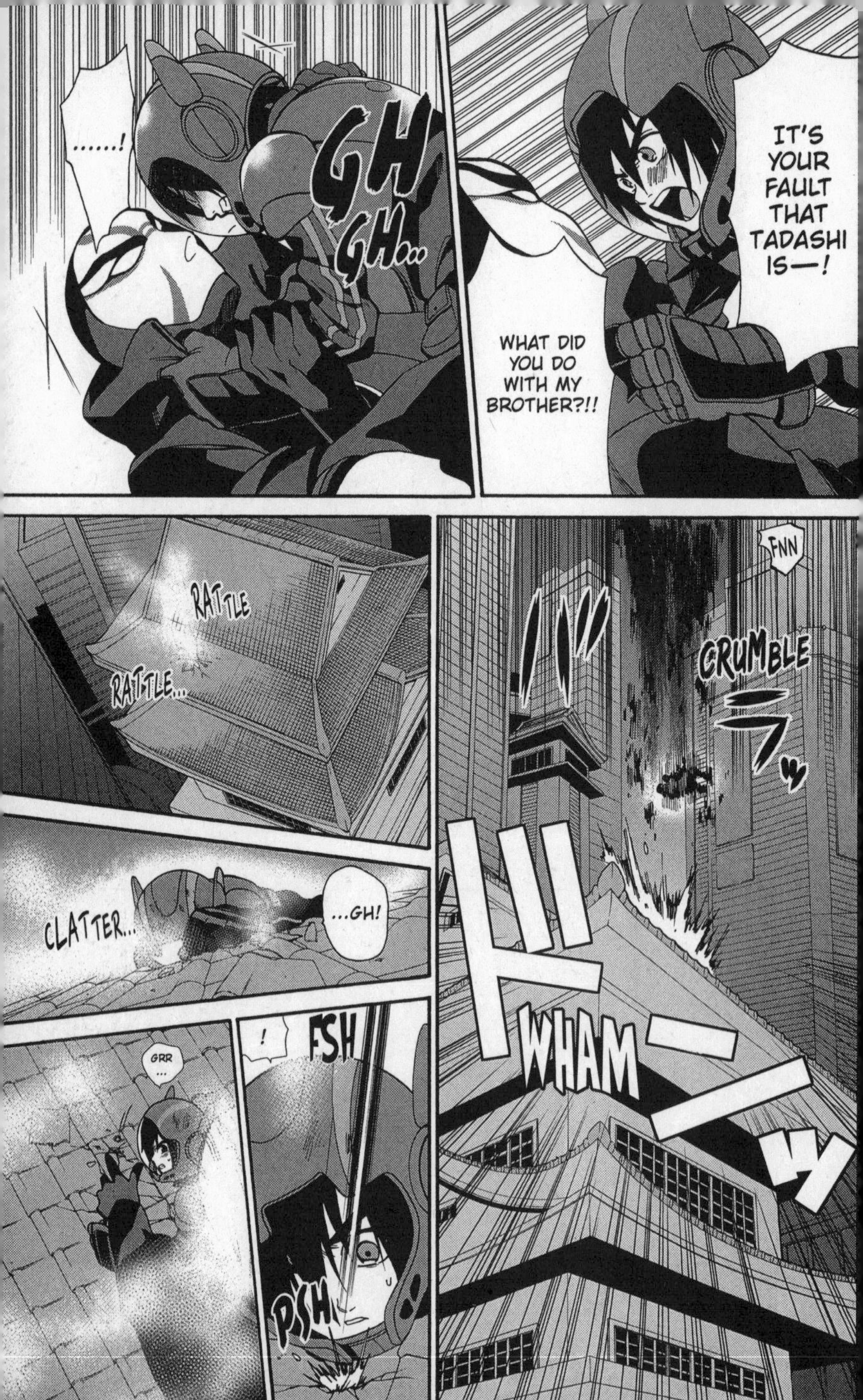
IT'S YOUR FAULT THAT TADASHI IS—!
WHAT DID YOU DO WITH MY BROTHER?!!
GH GH..
......!
FNN
CRUMBLE
WHAM
RATTLE
RATTLE...
...GH!
CLATTER...
FSH
!
PSH
GRR ...

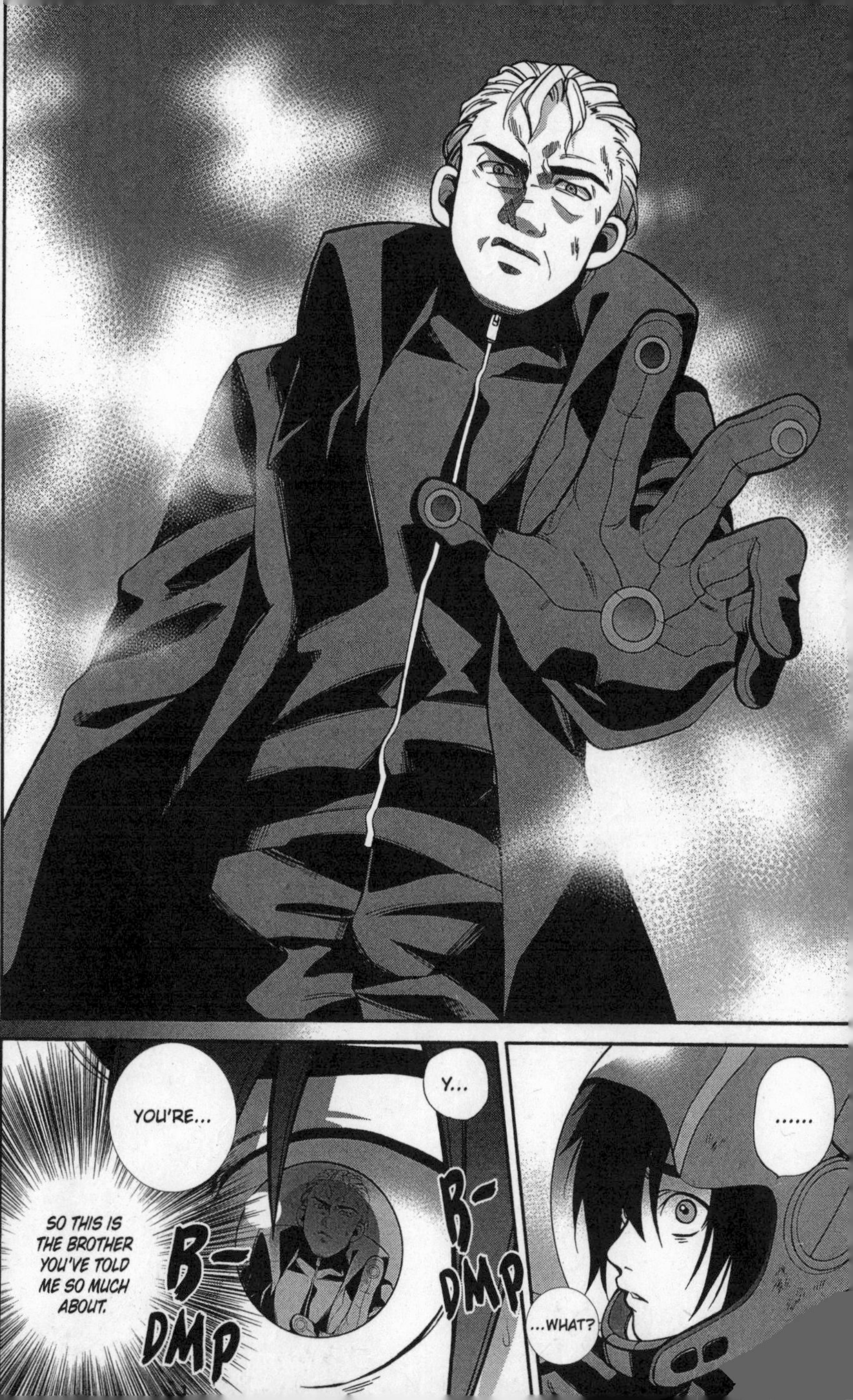
......
...WHAT?
Y...
YOU'RE...
B-DMP
SO THIS IS THE BROTHER YOU'VE TOLD ME SO MUCH ABOUT.
B-DMP

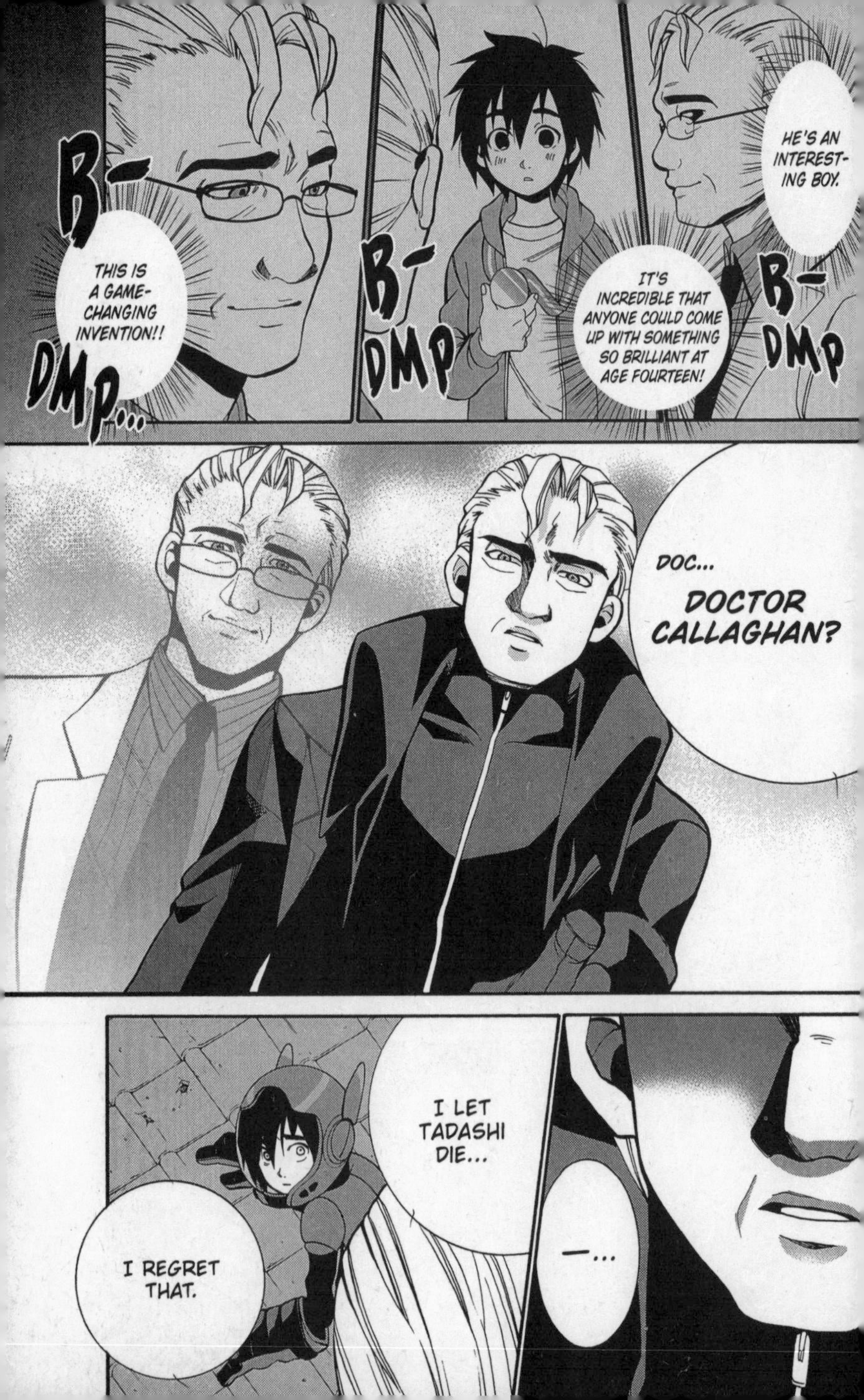

HE'S AN INTERESTING BOY.
B-DMP
IT'S INCREDIBLE THAT ANYONE COULD COME UP WITH SOMETHING SO BRILLIANT AT AGE FOURTEEN!
B-DMP
THIS IS A GAME-CHANGING INVENTION!!
B-DMP...
DOC...
DOCTOR CALLAGHAN?
—...
I LET TADASHI DIE...
I REGRET THAT.

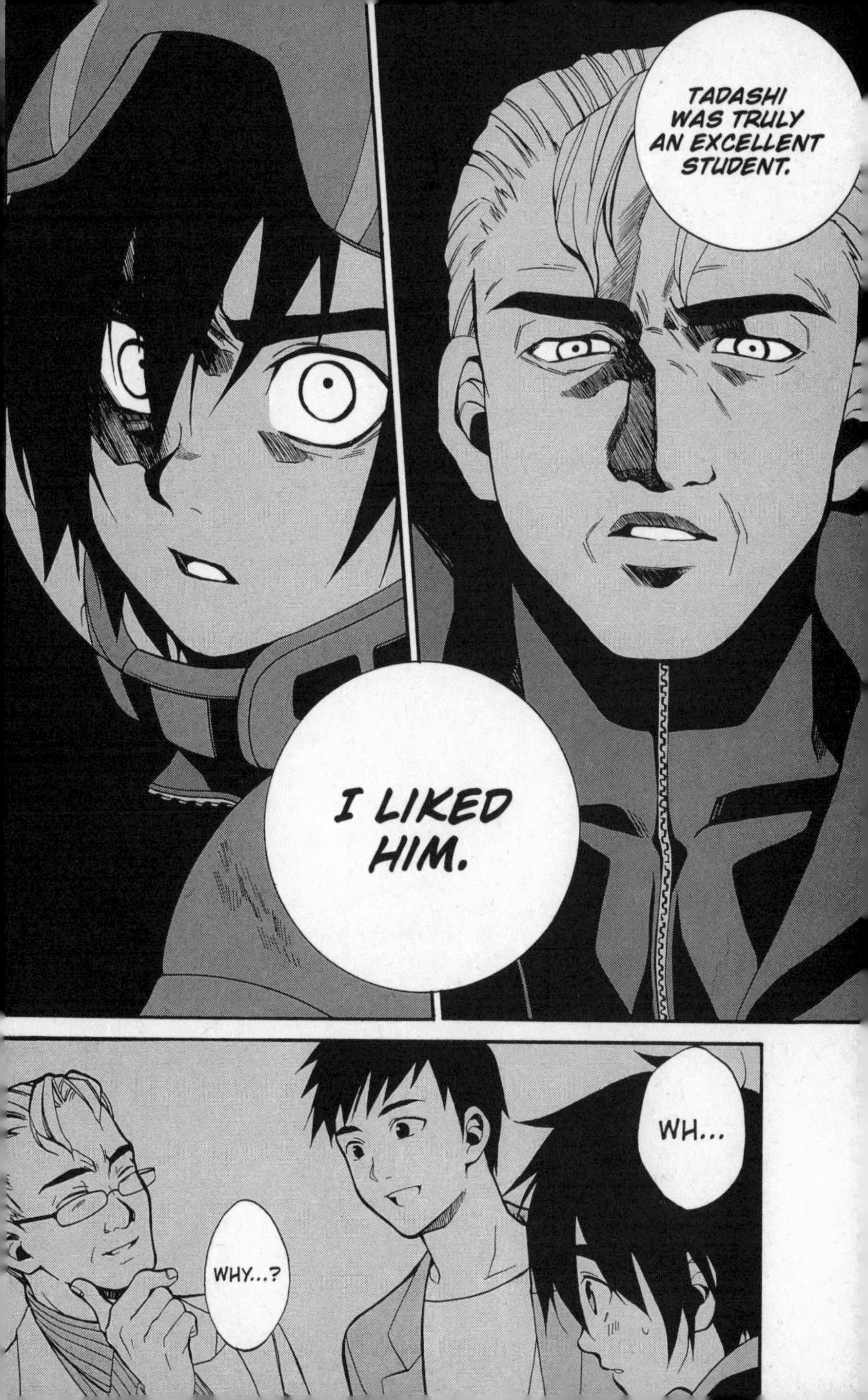
TADASHI WAS TRULY AN EXCELLENT STUDENT.
I LIKED HIM.
WH...
WHY...?

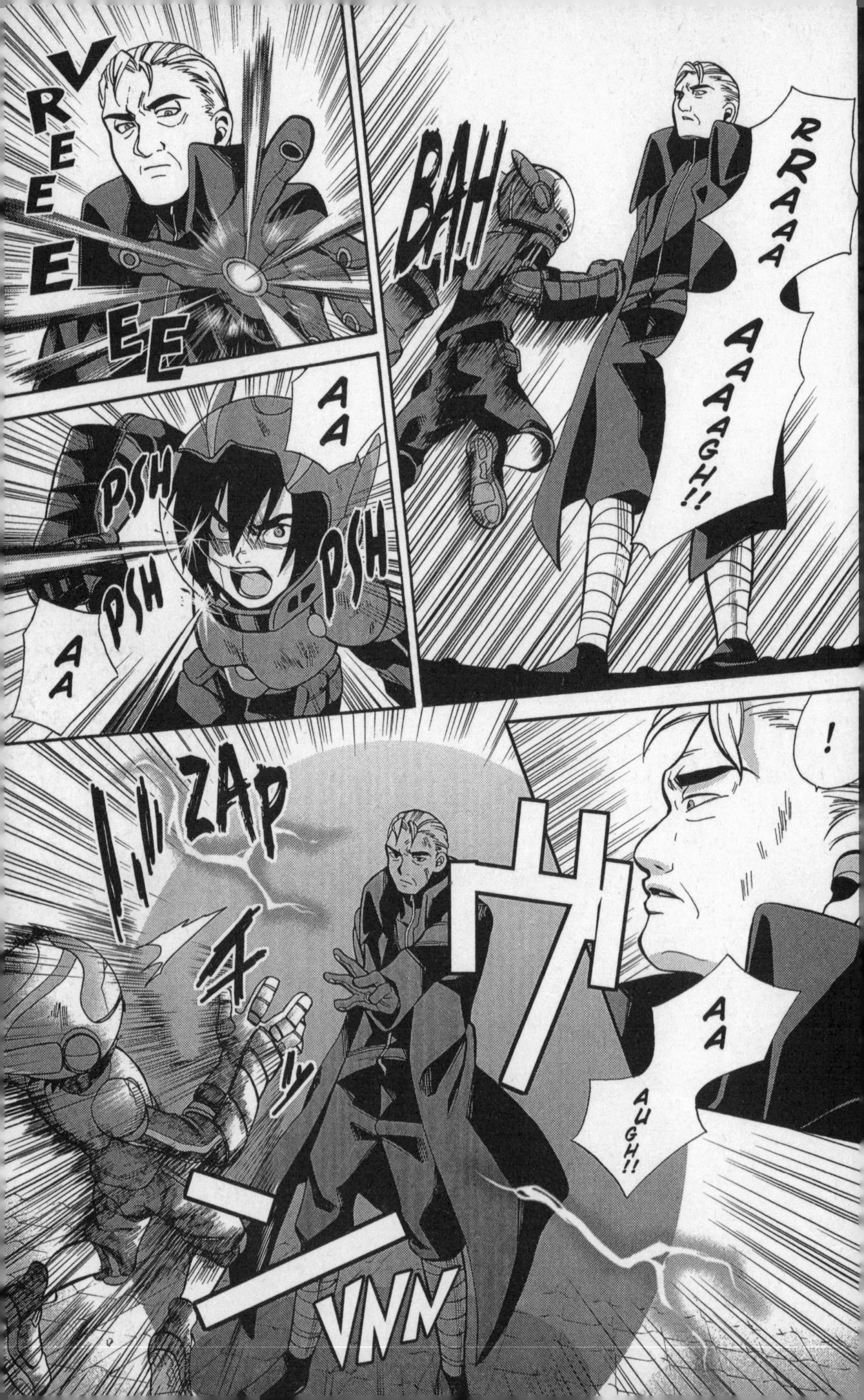

RRAAAA AAAAAGH!!
BAH BAH
VREEEE
EE
AA
PSH
PSH
PSH
PSH
AA
!
AA AUGH!!
ZAP
VNN

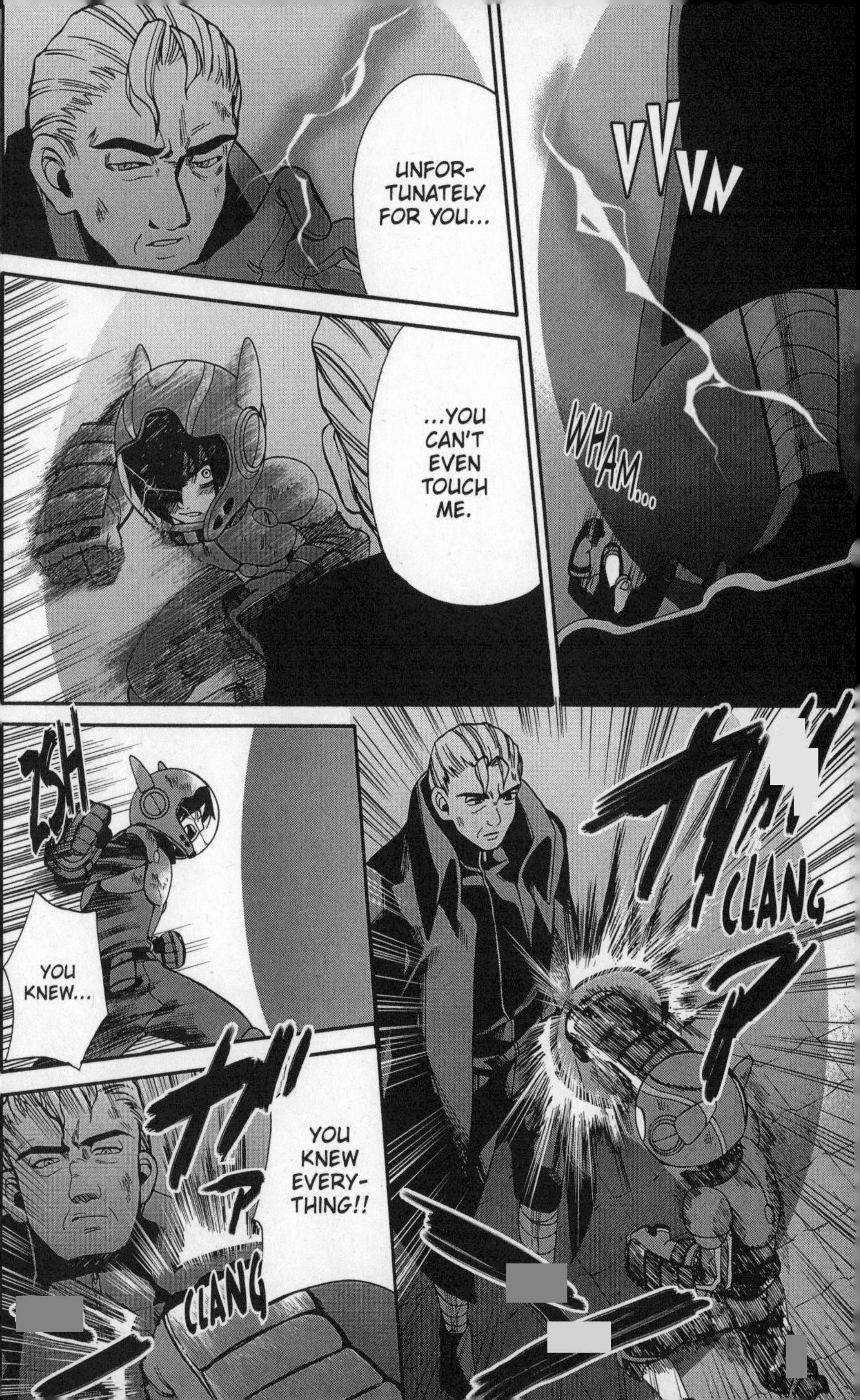
VVVN
WHAM...
UNFOR-TUNATELY FOR YOU...
...YOU CAN'T EVEN TOUCH ME.
CLANG
ZSH
YOU KNEW...
YOU KNEW EVERY-THING!!
CLANG

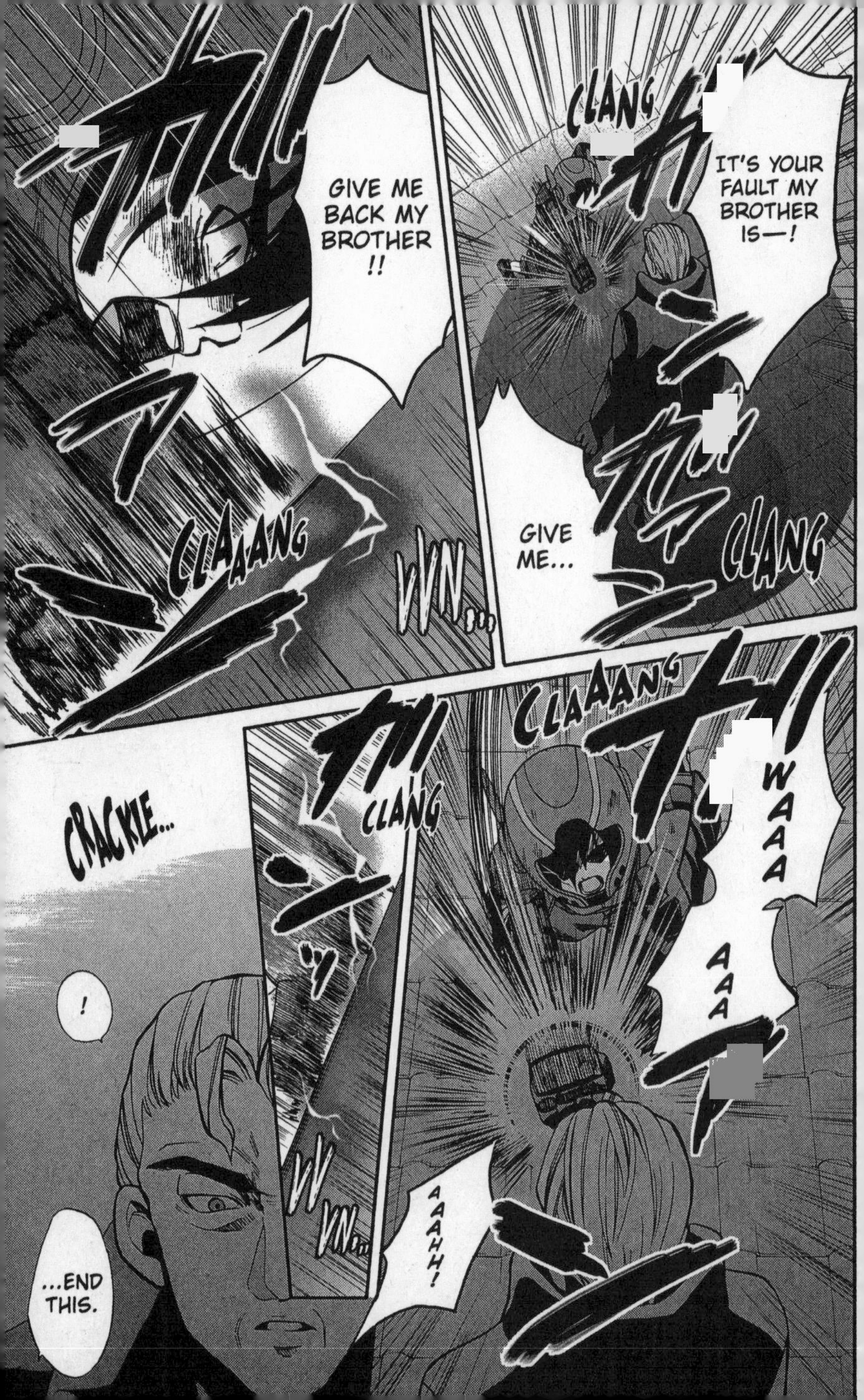
CLANG
IT'S YOUR FAULT MY BROTHER IS—!
GIVE ME...
CLANG
GIVE ME BACK MY BROTHER !!
CLAAANG
VVN...
CLAAANG
WAAA
AAA
AAAAH!
CLANG
VVN...
CRACKLE...
!
...END THIS.

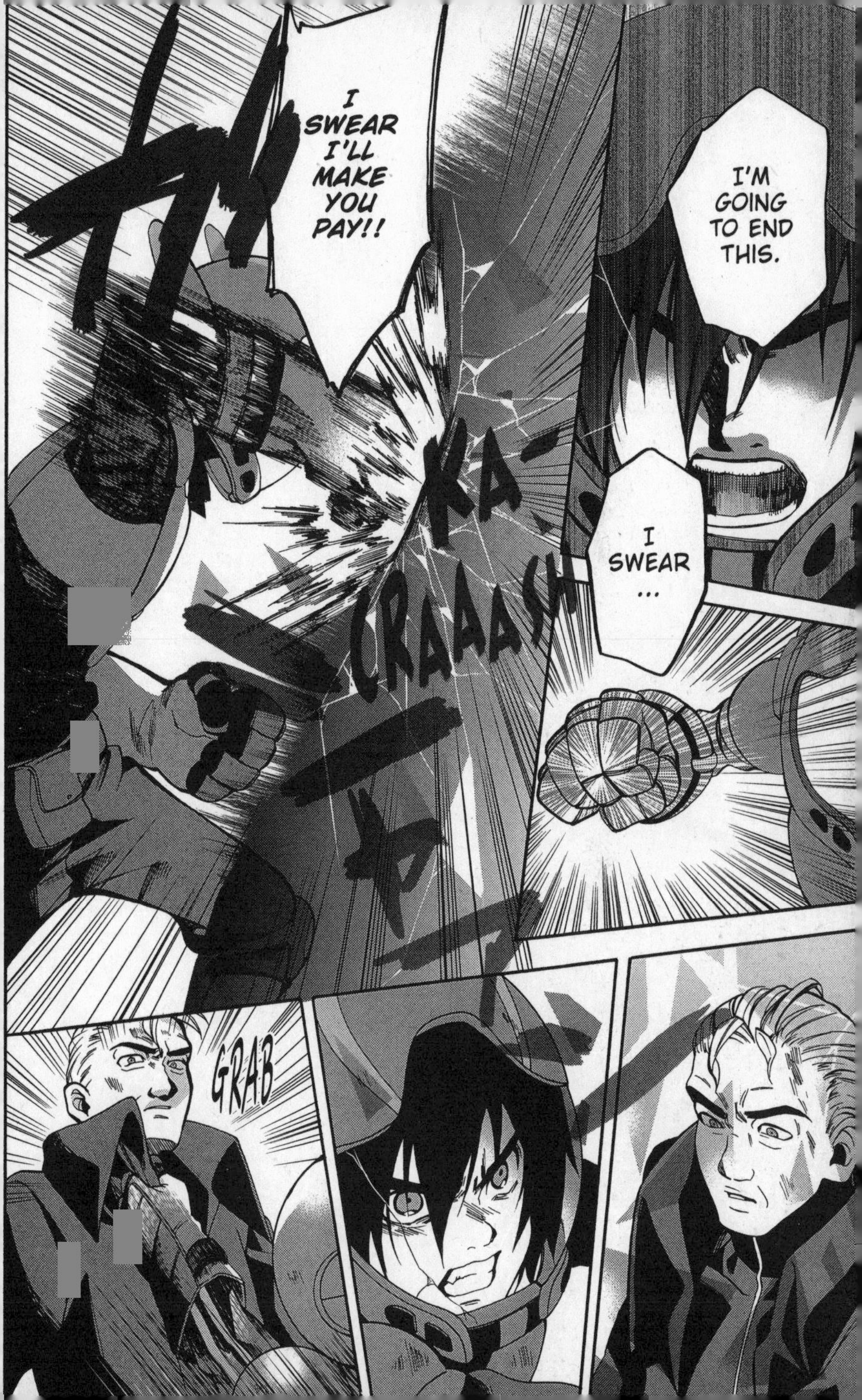
I'M GOING TO END THIS.
I SWEAR ...
I SWEAR I'LL MAKE YOU PAY!!
KA-CRAAASH
GRAB

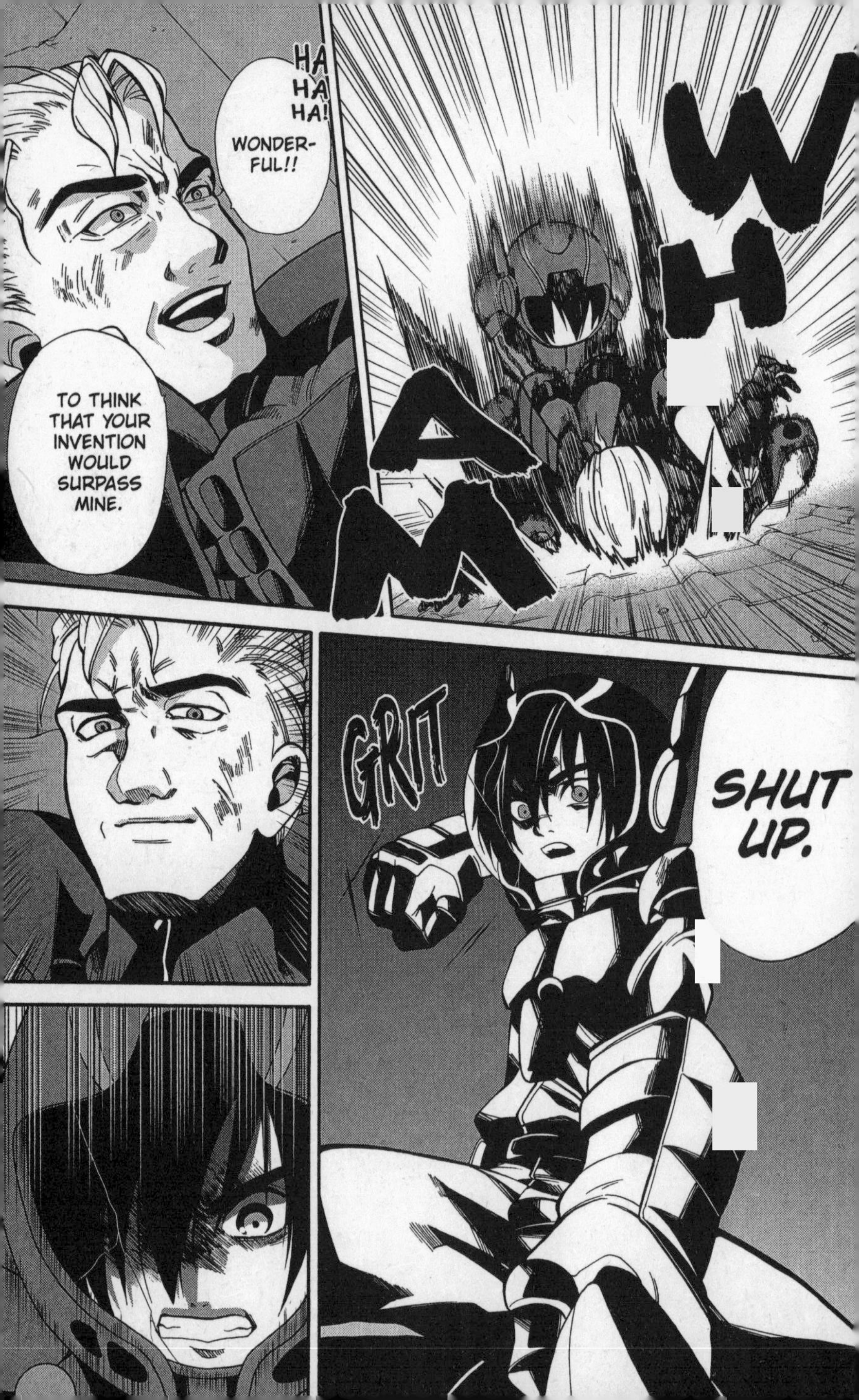
WHAM
HA HA HA!
WONDERFUL!!
TO THINK THAT YOUR INVENTION WOULD SURPASS MINE.
SHUT UP.
GRIT

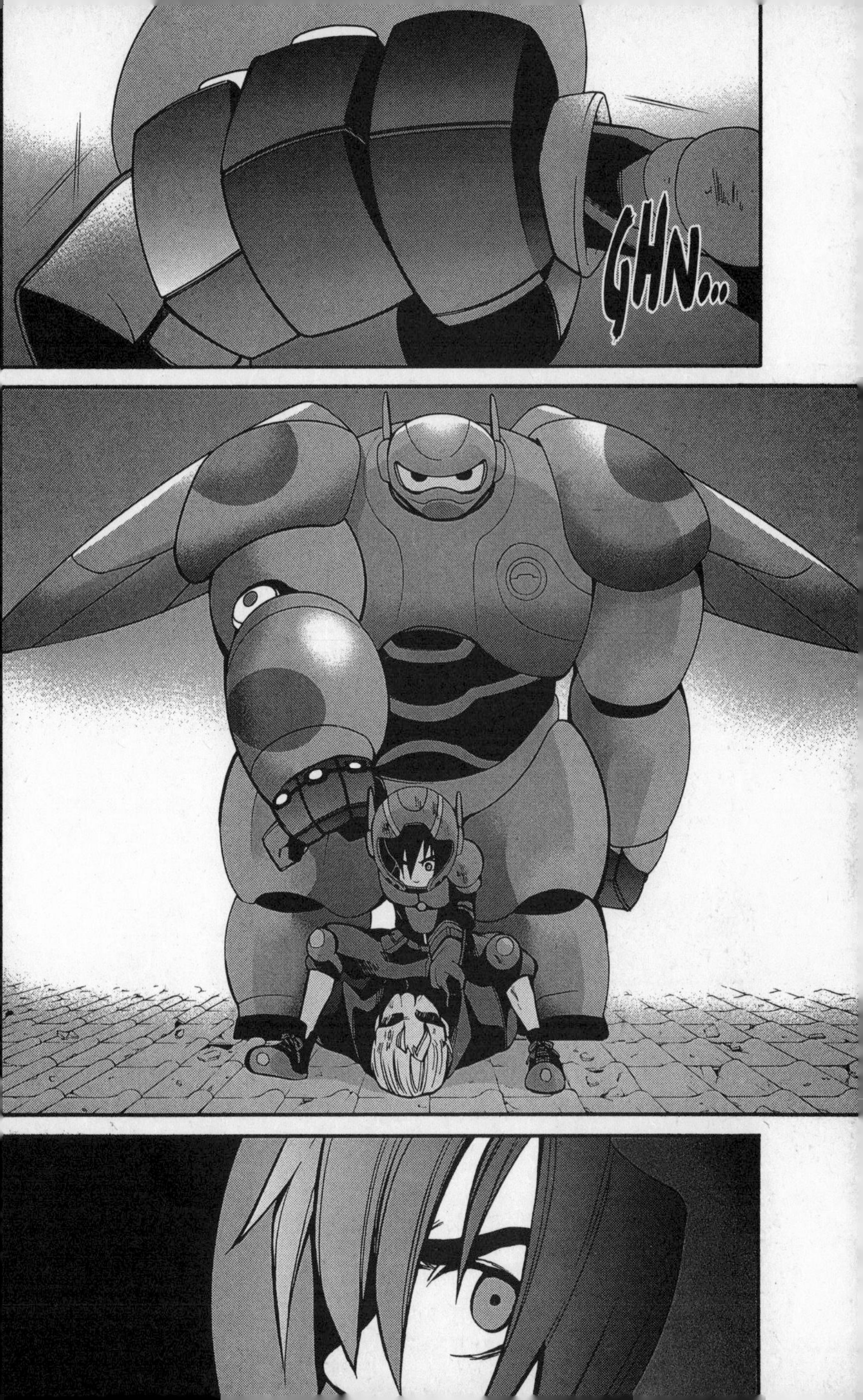
GHN...

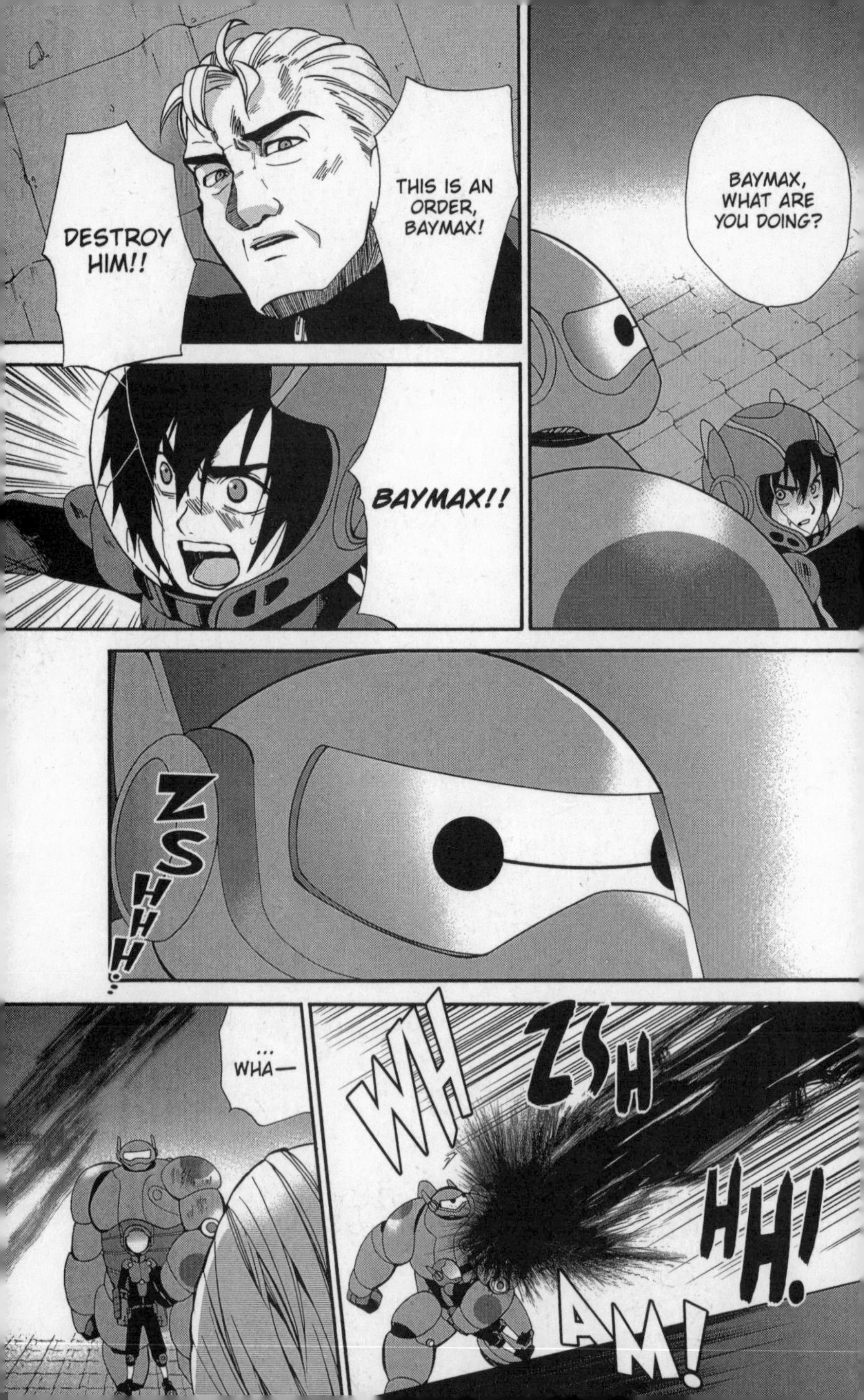
BAYMAX, WHAT ARE YOU DOING?
THIS IS AN ORDER, BAYMAX!
DESTROY HIM!!
BAYMAX!!
ZSHHHH!
ZSHHH!
WHAM!
... WHA—

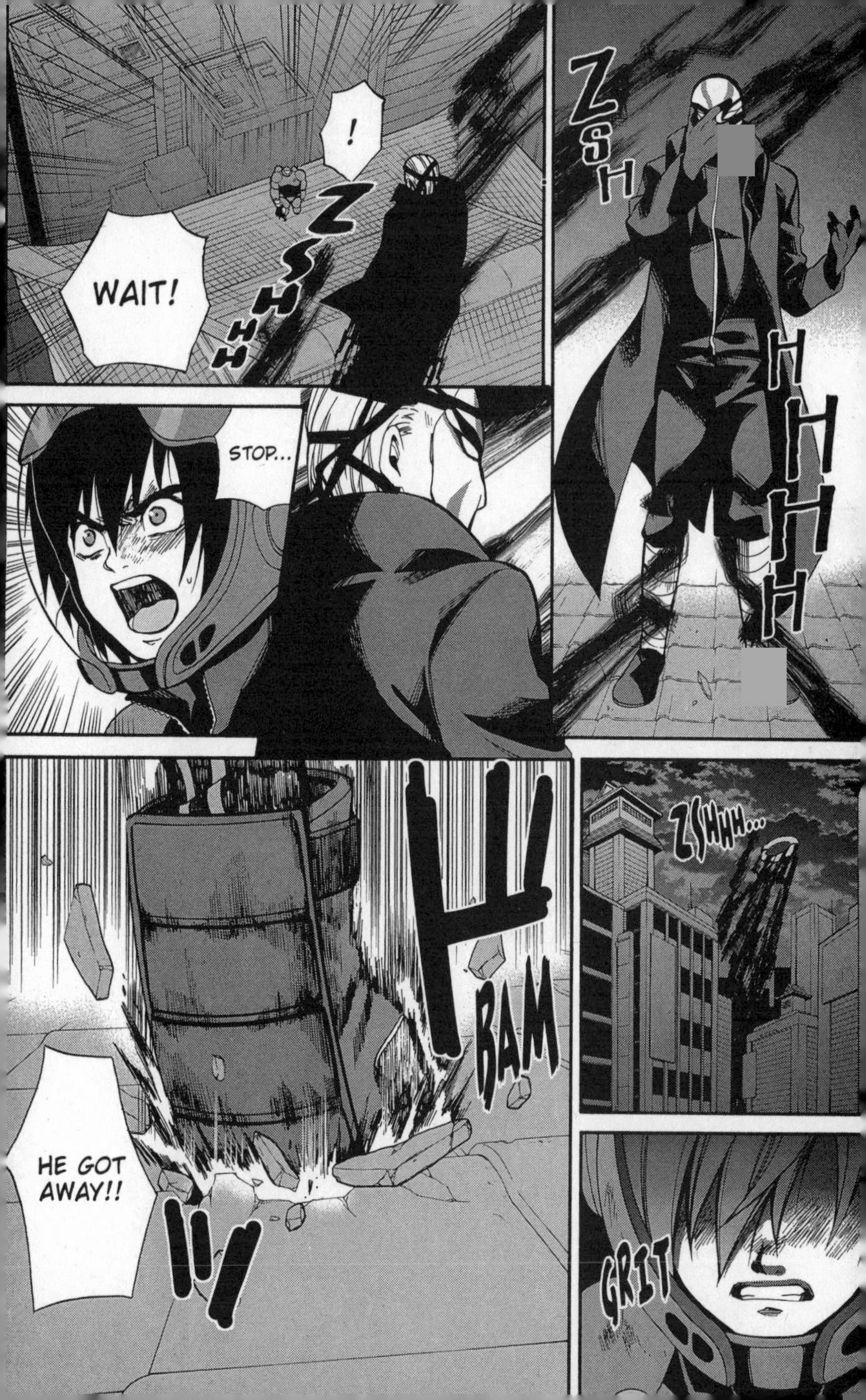
ZSH
HHHHHH
!
ZSHHHH
WAIT!
STOP...
ZSHHH...
GRIT
BAM
HE GOT AWAY!!

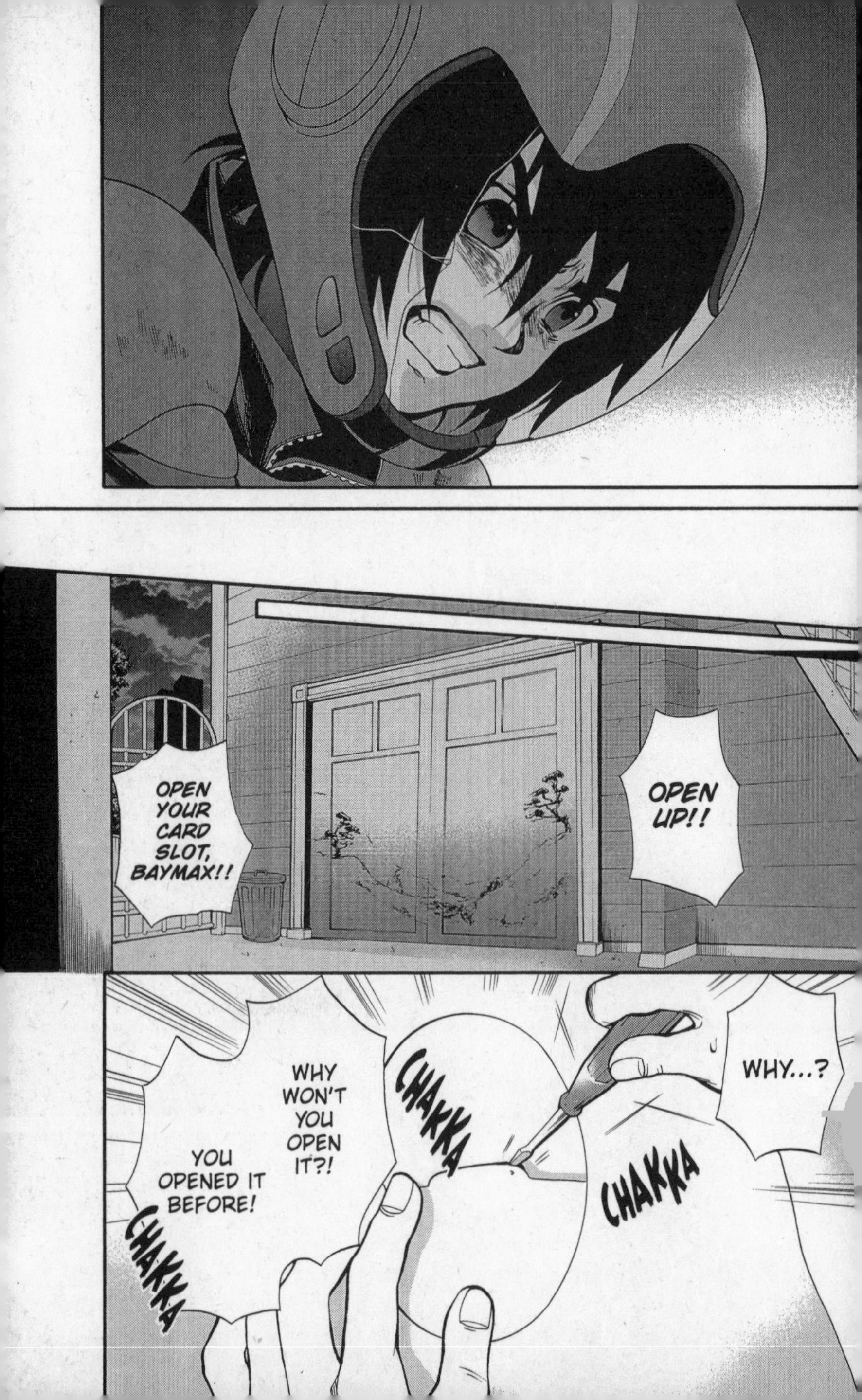
OPEN UP!!
OPEN YOUR CARD SLOT, BAYMAX!!
WHY...?
CHAKKA
CHAKKA
WHY WON'T YOU OPEN IT?!
YOU OPENED IT BEFORE!
CHAKKA

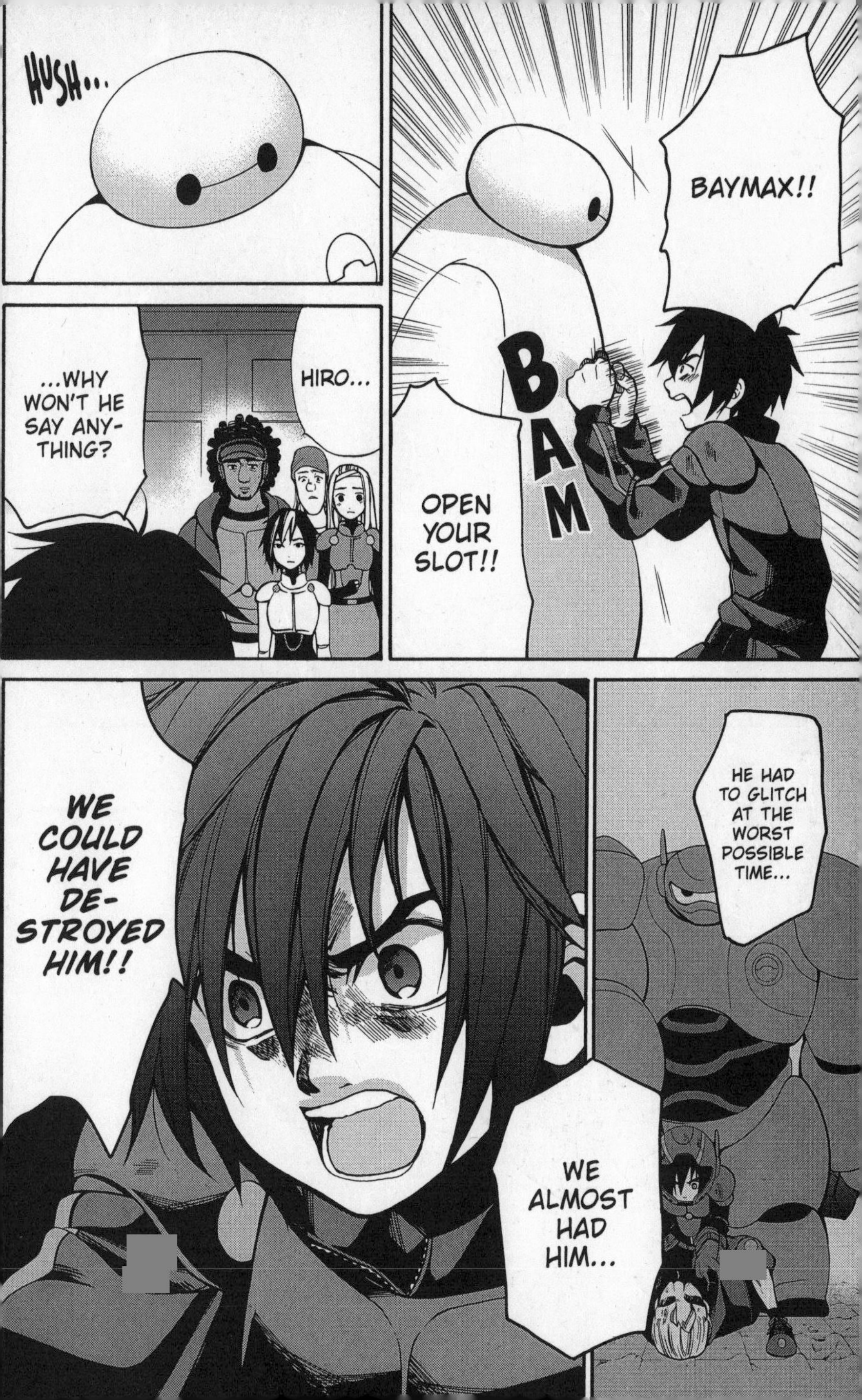
BAYMAX!!
BAM
OPEN YOUR SLOT!!
HUSH...
HIRO...
...WHY WON'T HE SAY ANY-THING?
HE HAD TO GLITCH AT THE WORST POSSIBLE TIME...
WE ALMOST HAD HIM...
WE COULD HAVE DE-STROYED HIM!!

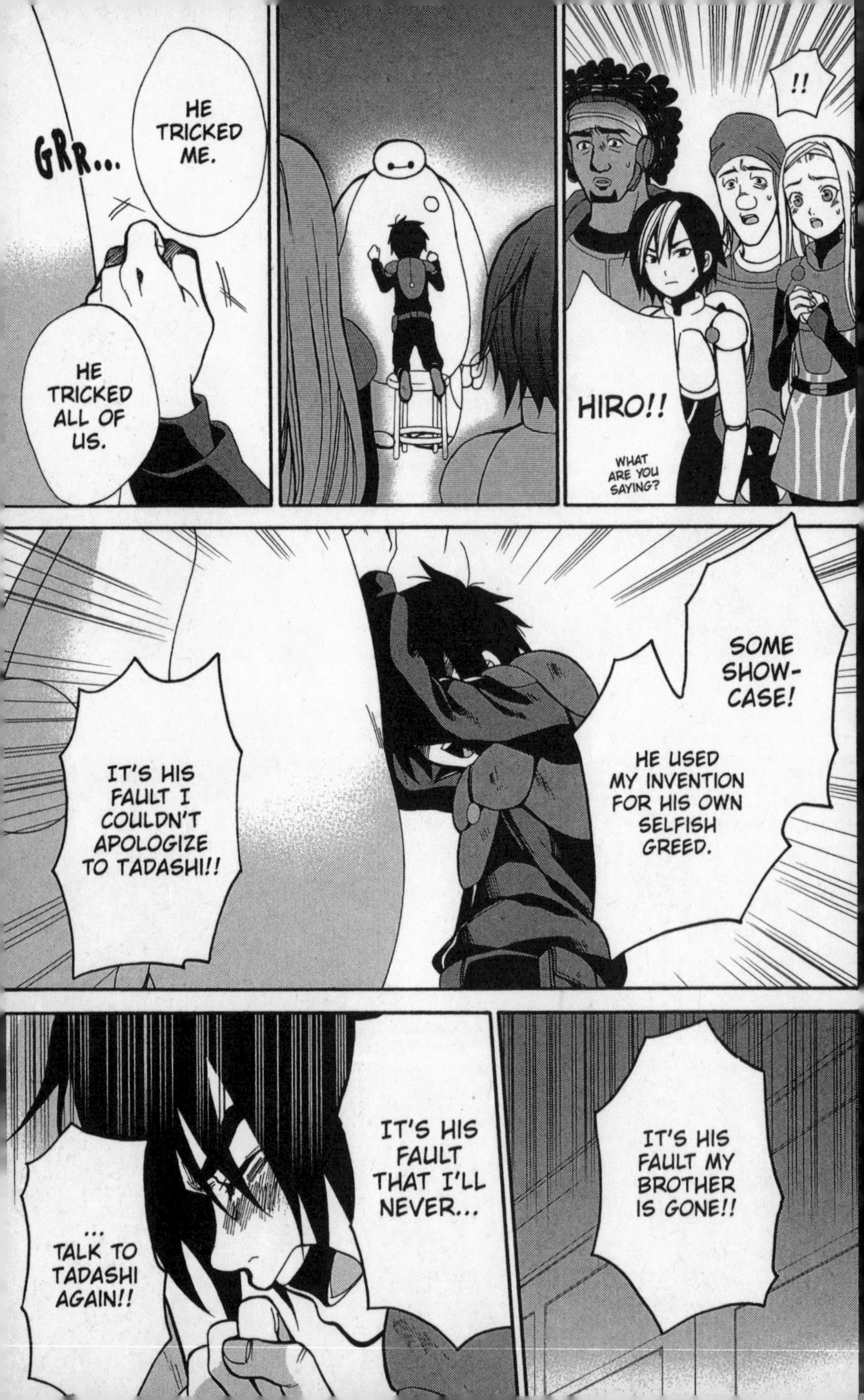
!!
HIRO!!
WHAT ARE YOU SAYING?
GRR...
HE TRICKED ME.
HE TRICKED ALL OF US.
SOME SHOW-CASE!
HE USED MY INVENTION FOR HIS OWN SELFISH GREED.
IT'S HIS FAULT I COULDN'T APOLOGIZE TO TADASHI!!
IT'S HIS FAULT MY BROTHER IS GONE!!
IT'S HIS FAULT THAT I'LL NEVER...
... TALK TO TADASHI AGAIN!!

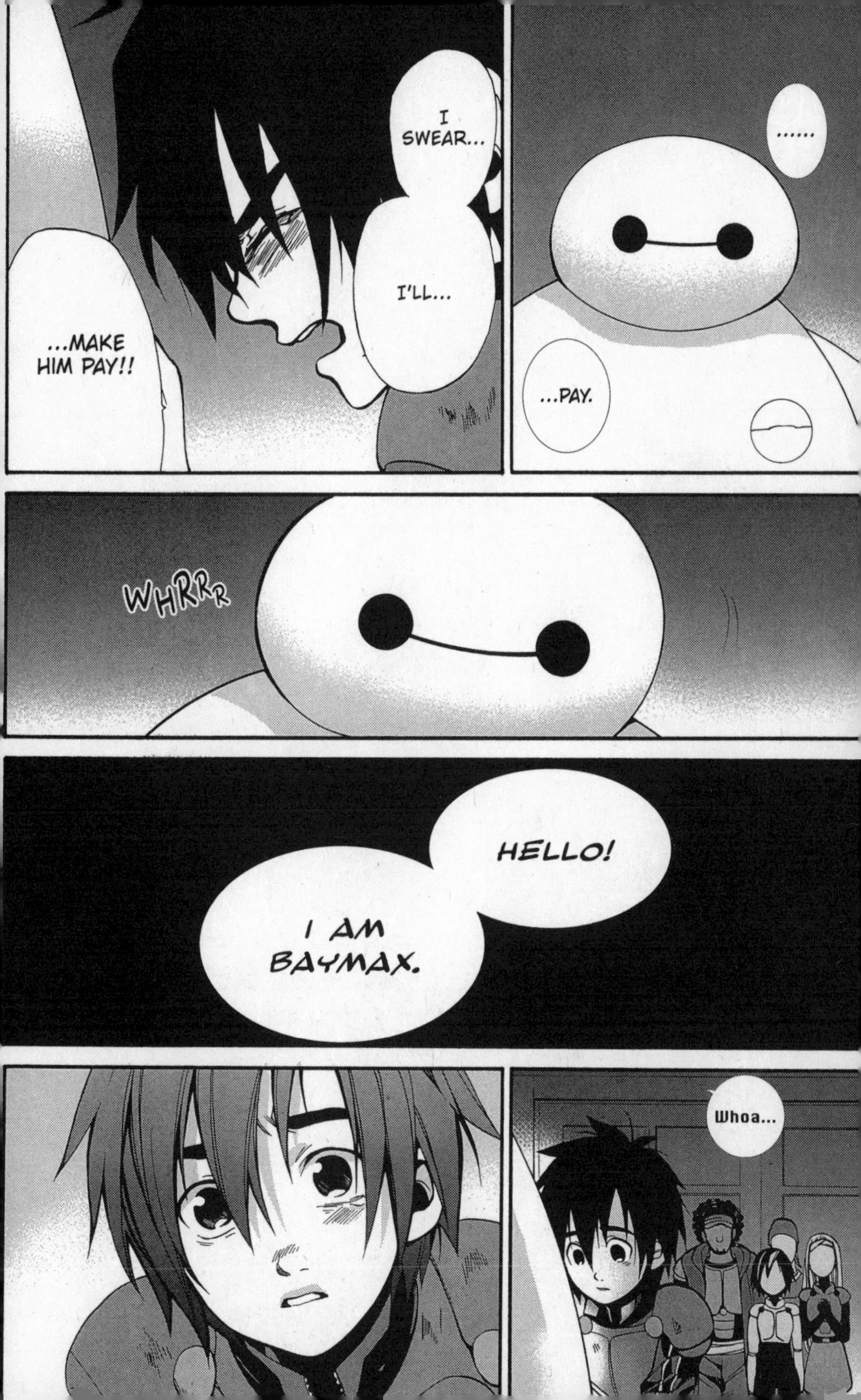
......
...PAY.
I SWEAR...
I'LL...
...MAKE HIM PAY!!
WHRRR
HELLO!
I AM BAYMAX.
Whoa...

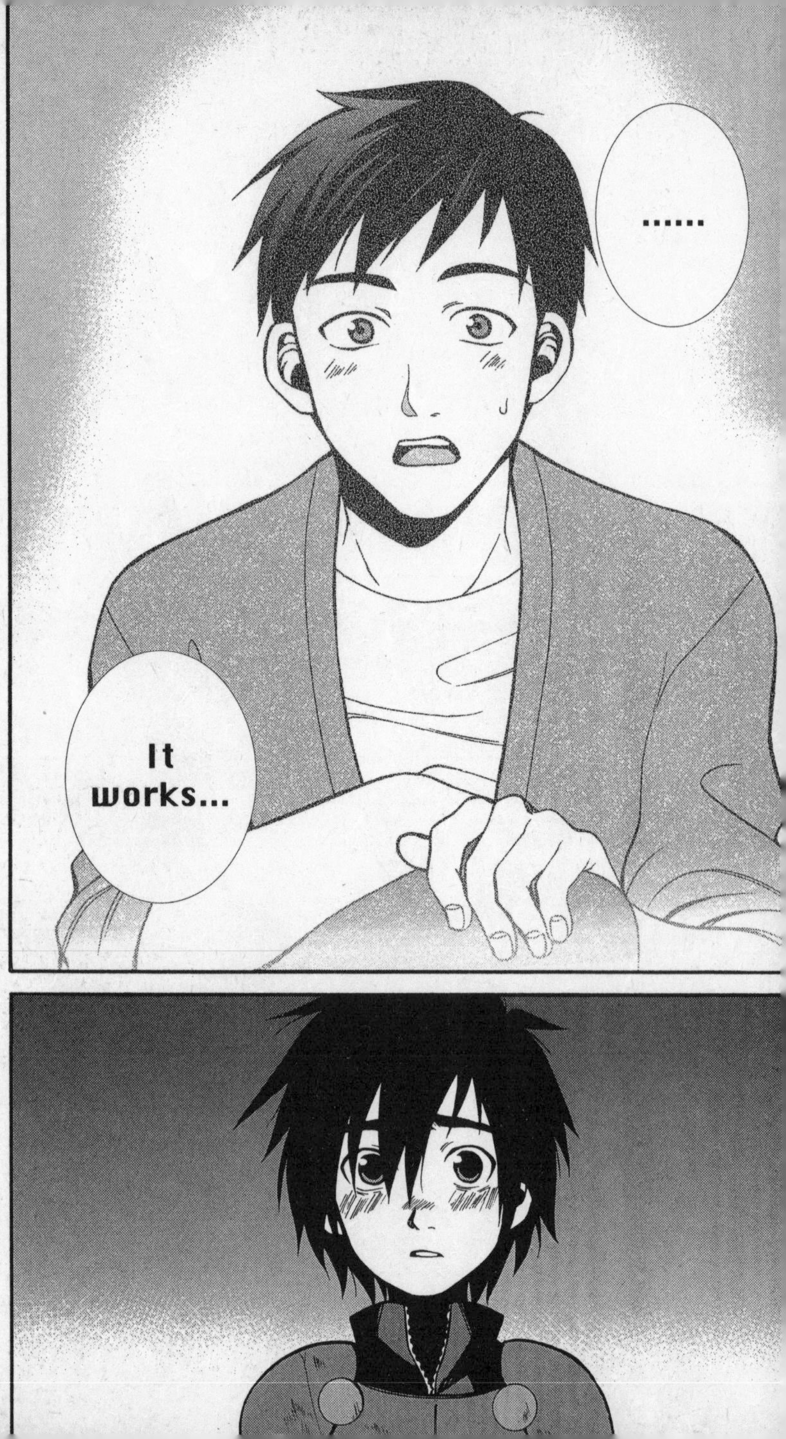
......
It works...

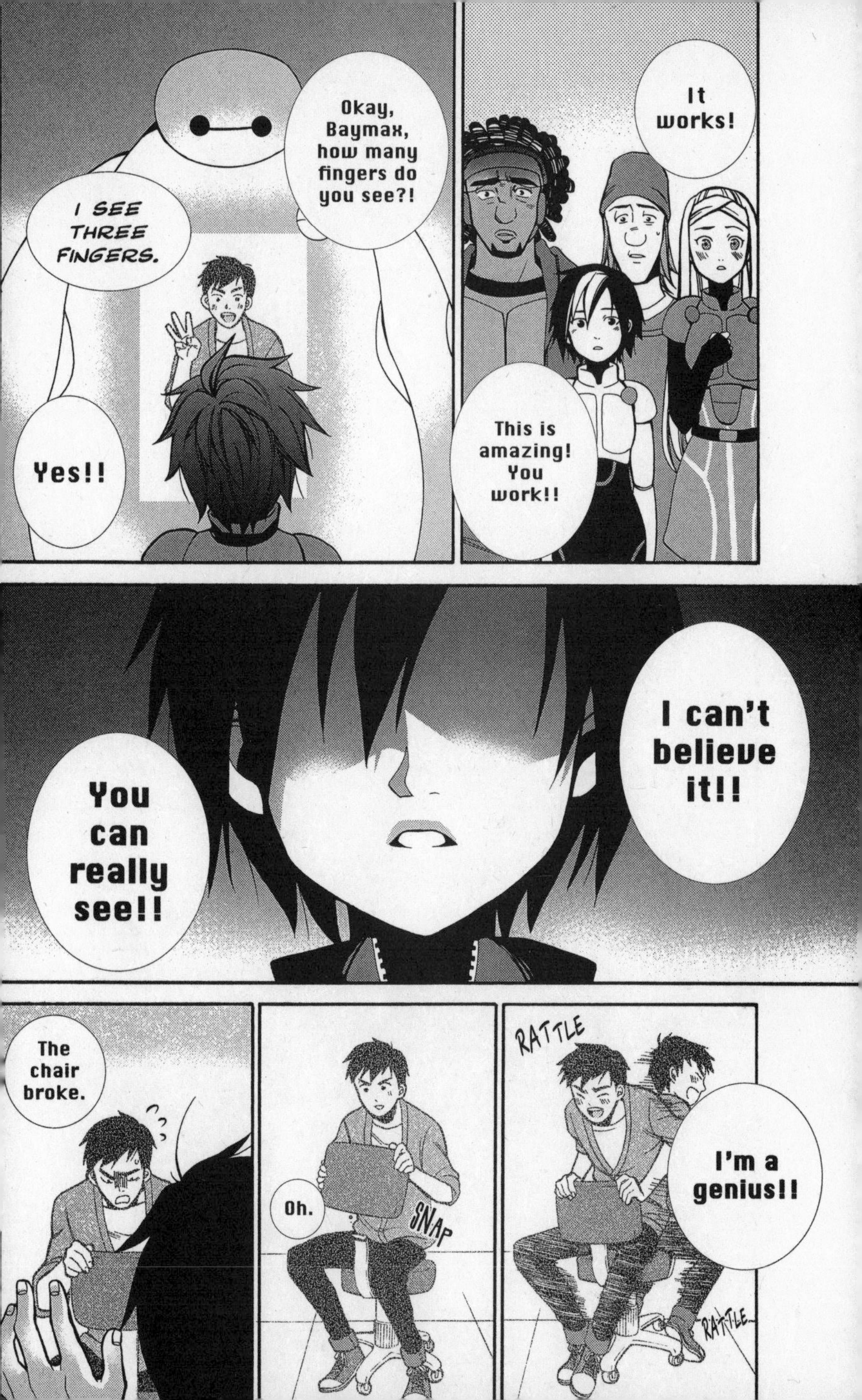
It works!
This is amazing! You work!!
Okay, Baymax, how many fingers do you see?!
I SEE THREE FINGERS.
Yes!!
I can't believe it!!
You can really see!!
RATTLE
I'm a genius!!
RATTLE
SNAP
Oh.
The chair broke.

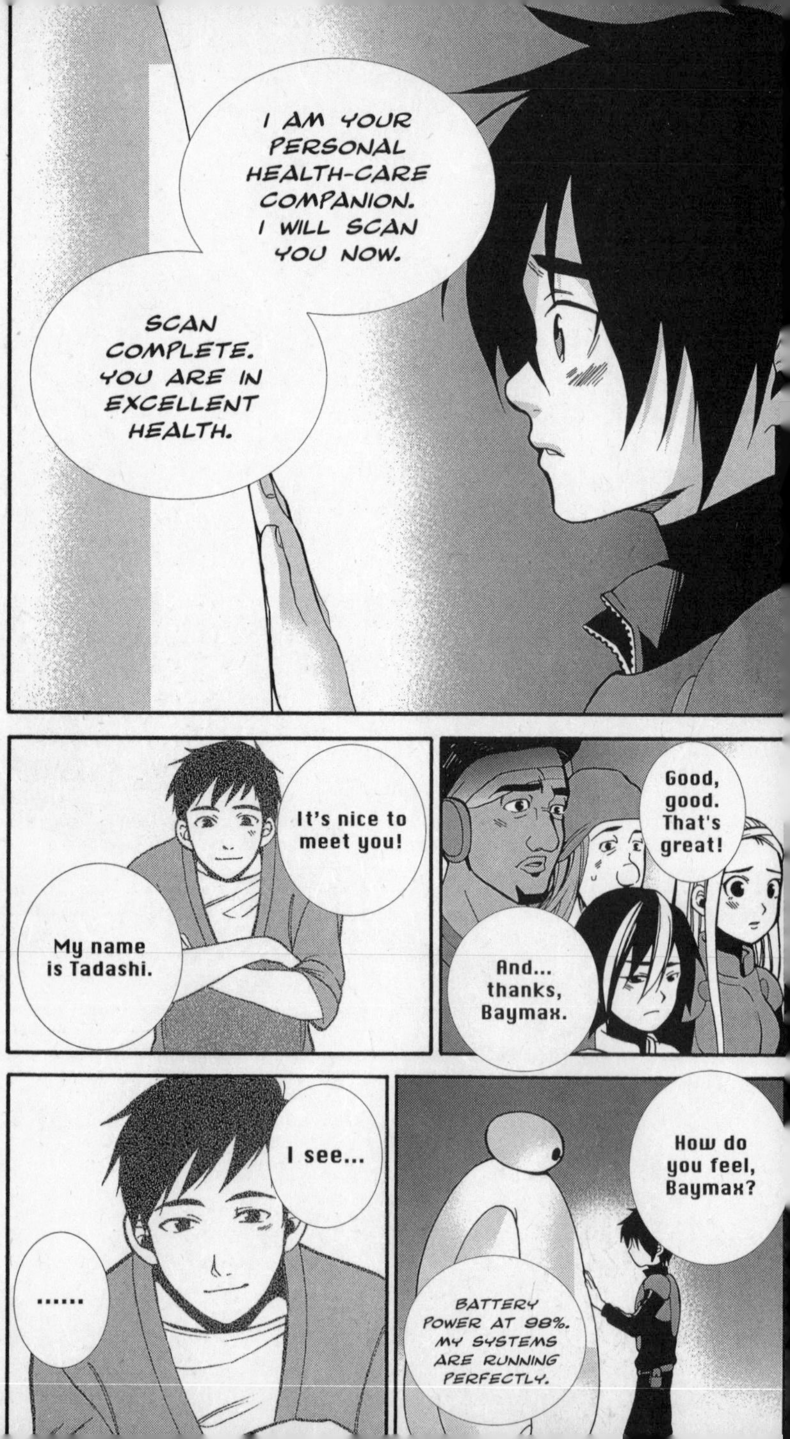
I AM YOUR PERSONAL HEALTH-CARE COMPANION. I WILL SCAN YOU NOW.
SCAN COMPLETE. YOU ARE IN EXCELLENT HEALTH.
Good, good. That's great!
And... thanks, Baymax.
It's nice to meet you!
My name is Tadashi.
How do you feel, Baymax?
BATTERY POWER AT 98%. MY SYSTEMS ARE RUNNING PERFECTLY.
I see...
......

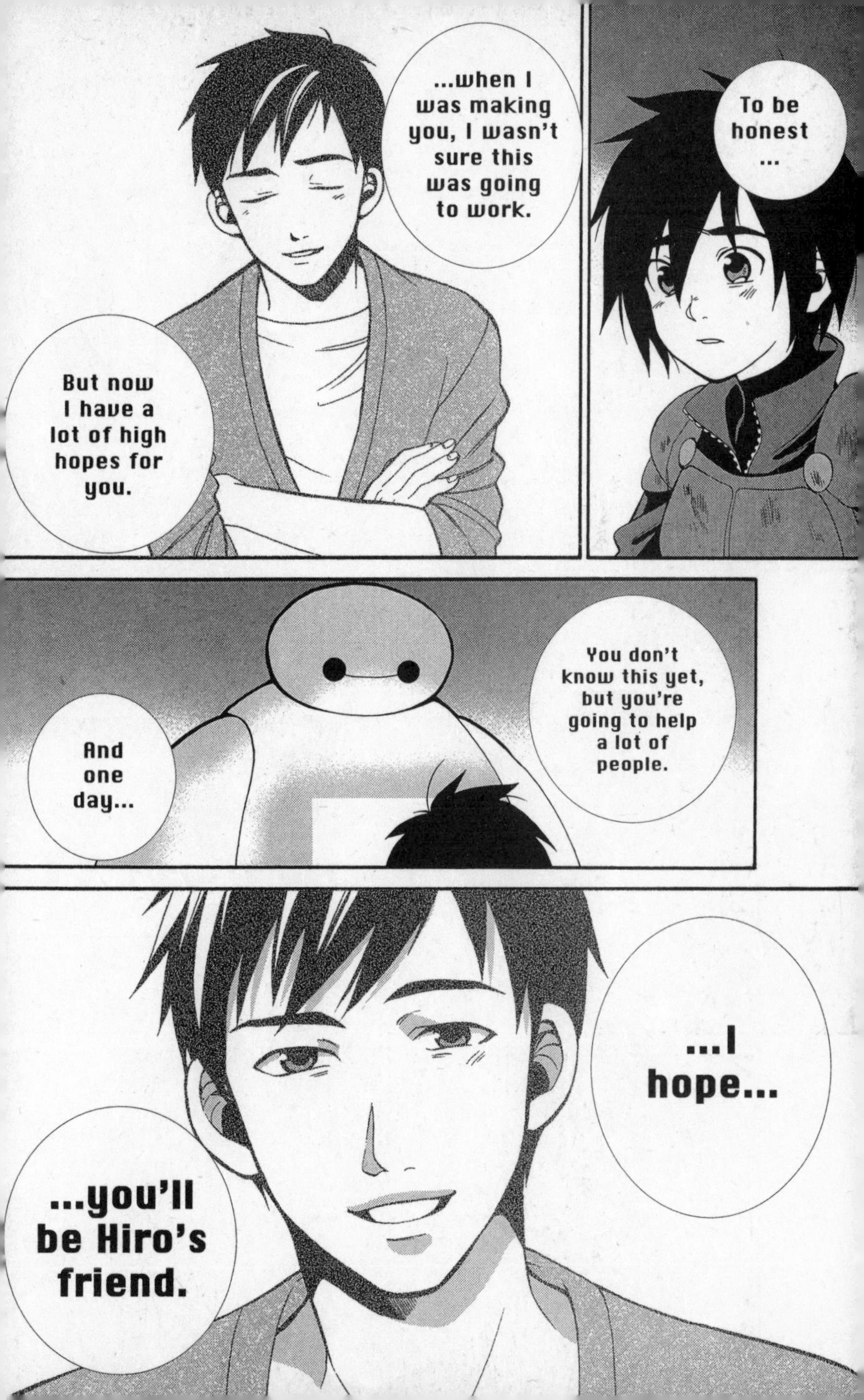
To be honest ...
...when I was making you, I wasn't sure this was going to work.
But now I have a lot of high hopes for you.
You don't know this yet, but you're going to help a lot of people.
And one day...
...I hope...
...you'll be Hiro's friend.

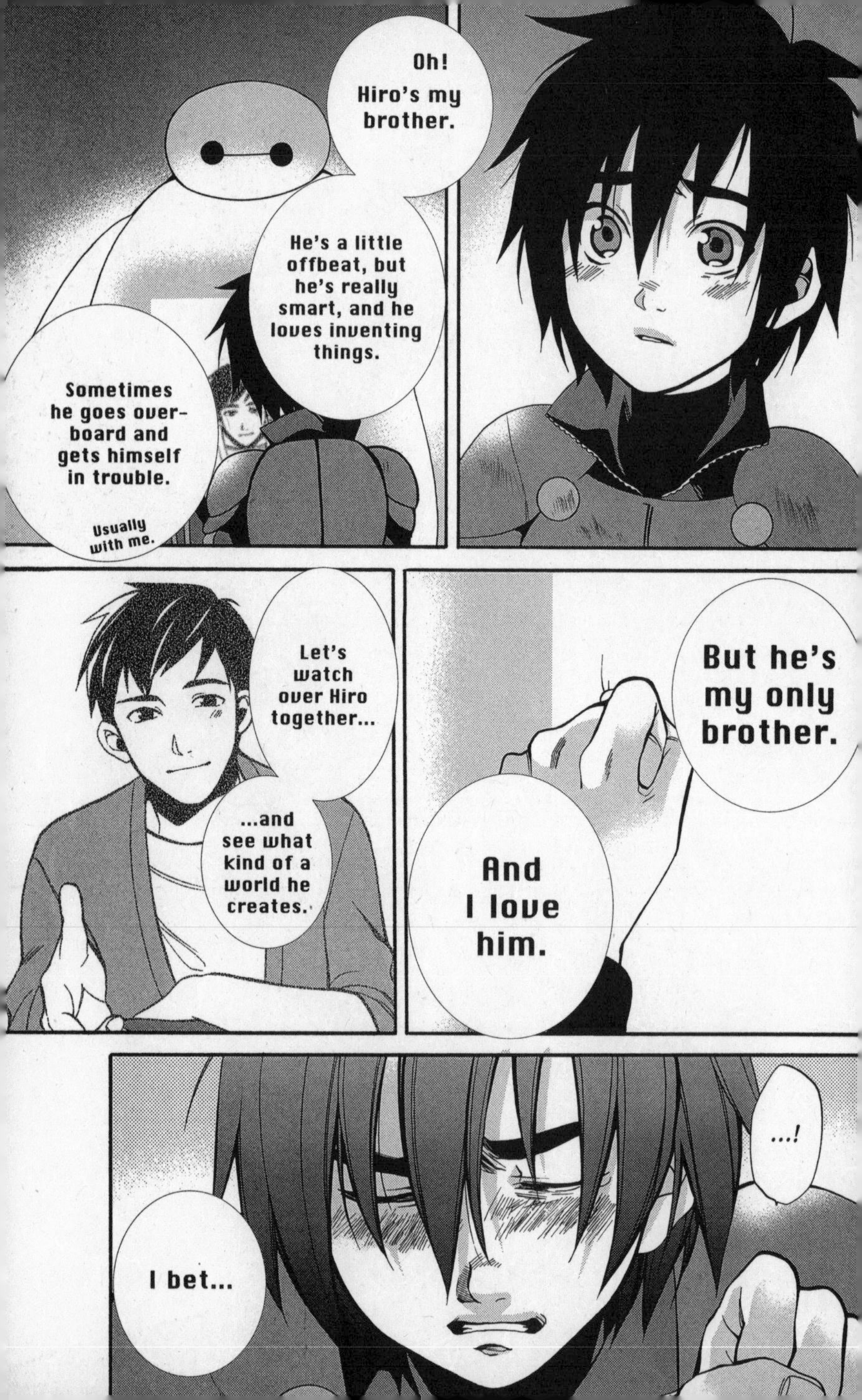
Oh! Hiro's my brother.
He's a little offbeat, but he's really smart, and he loves inventing things.
Sometimes he goes over-board and gets himself in trouble.
Usually with me.
But he's my only brother.
And I love him.
Let's watch over Hiro together...
...and see what kind of a world he creates.
...!
I bet...

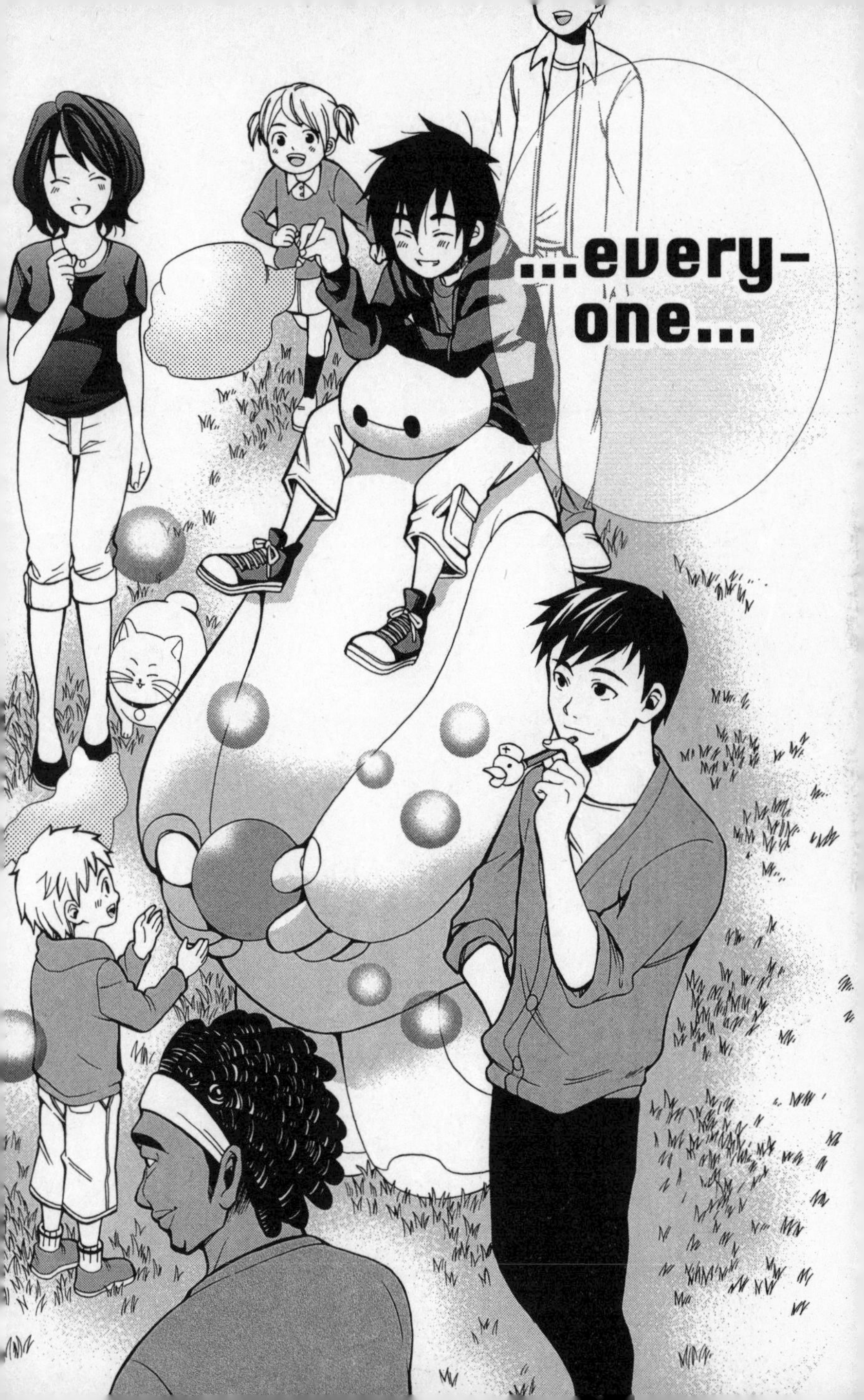
...every-
one...

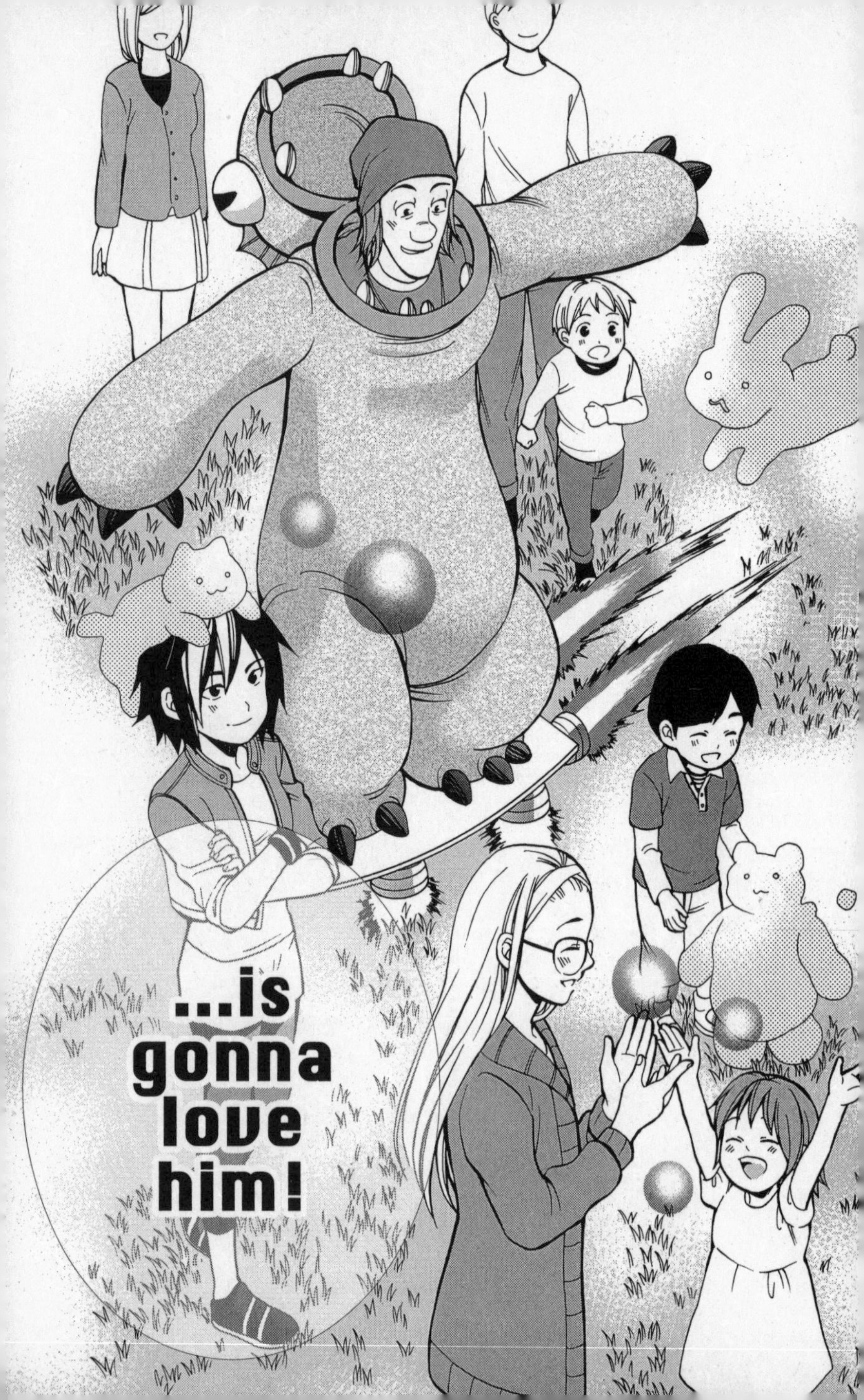
...is gonna love him!

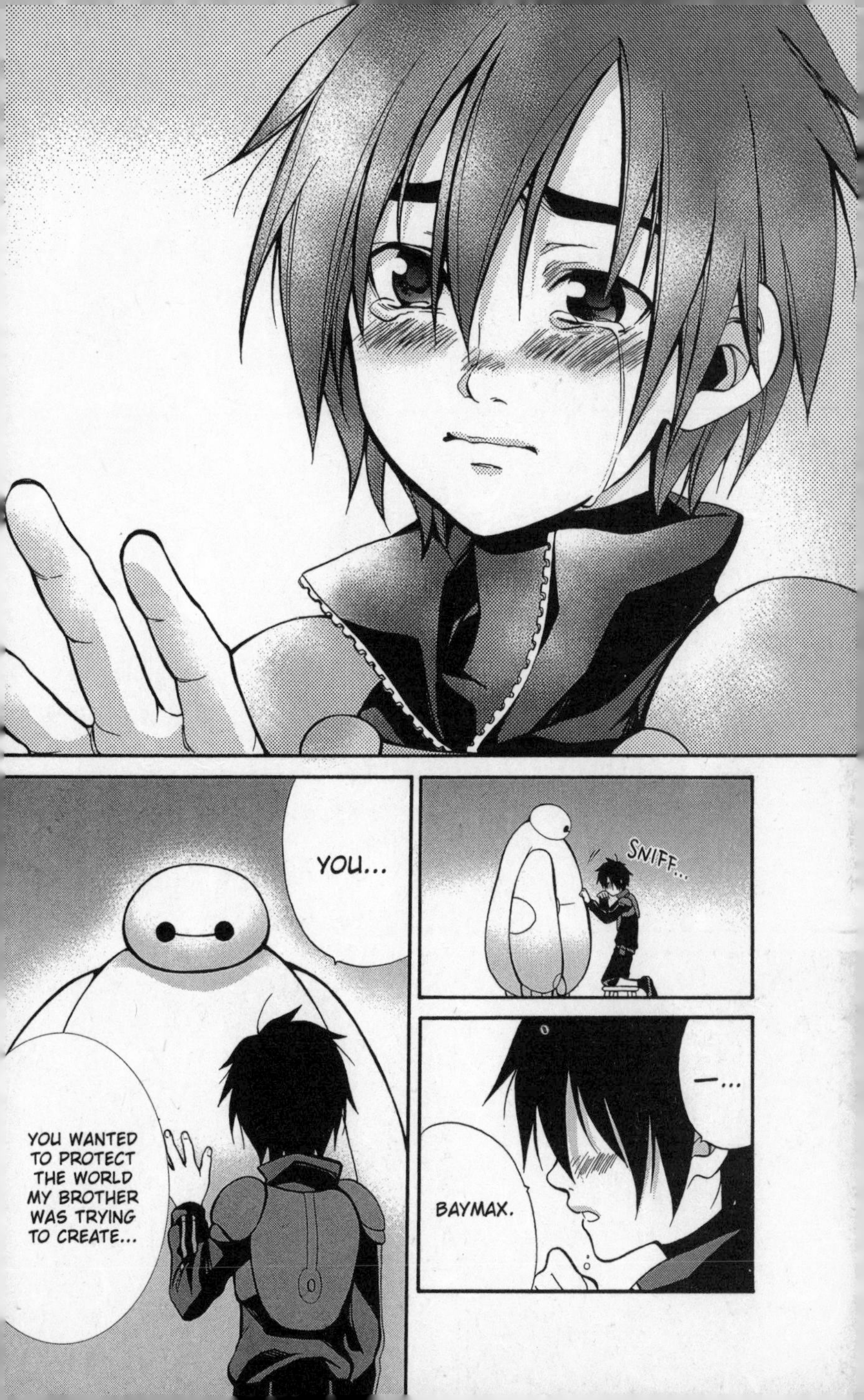
SNIFF...
—...
BAYMAX.
YOU...
YOU WANTED TO PROTECT THE WORLD MY BROTHER WAS TRYING TO CREATE...

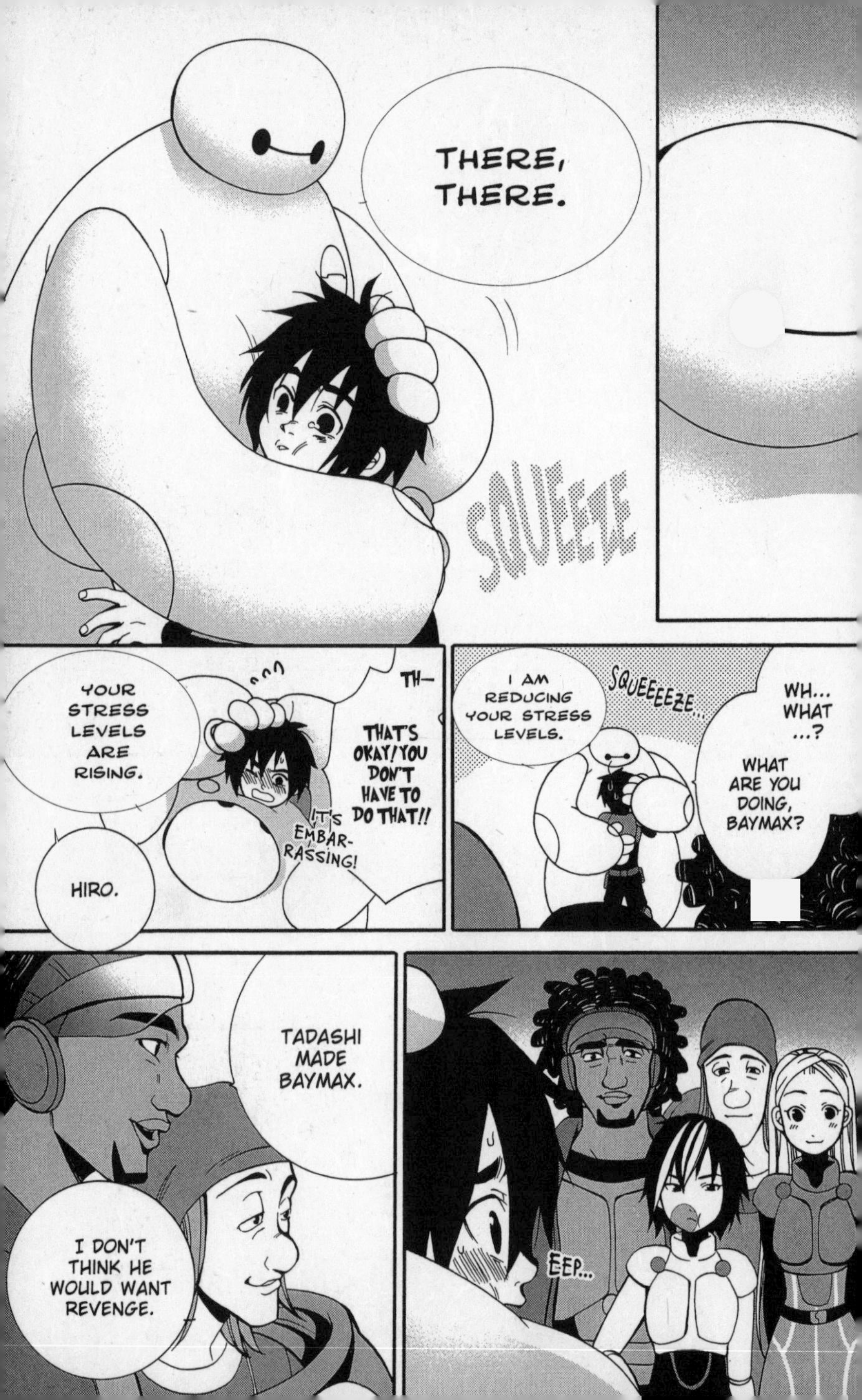
THERE, THERE.
SQUEEZE
WH... WHAT ...?
WHAT ARE YOU DOING, BAYMAX?
SQUEEEEEZE...
I AM REDUCING YOUR STRESS LEVELS.
TH—
THAT'S OKAY! YOU DON'T HAVE TO DO THAT!!
IT'S EMBAR-RASSING!
YOUR STRESS LEVELS ARE RISING.
HIRO.
EEP...
TADASHI MADE BAYMAX.
I DON'T THINK HE WOULD WANT REVENGE.

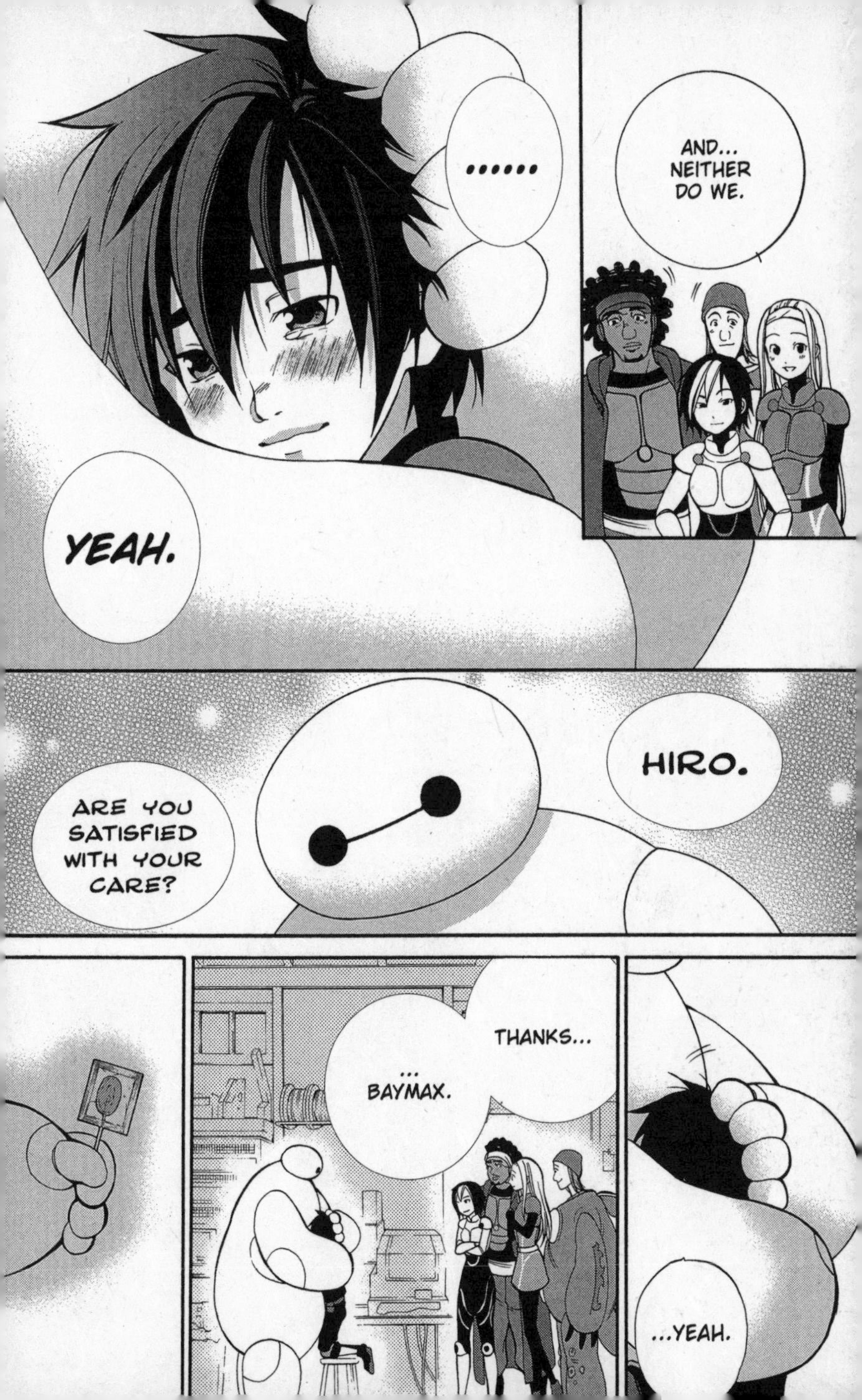
AND... NEITHER DO WE.
......
YEAH.
HIRO.
ARE YOU SATISFIED WITH YOUR CARE?
...YEAH.
THANKS...
...BAYMAX.

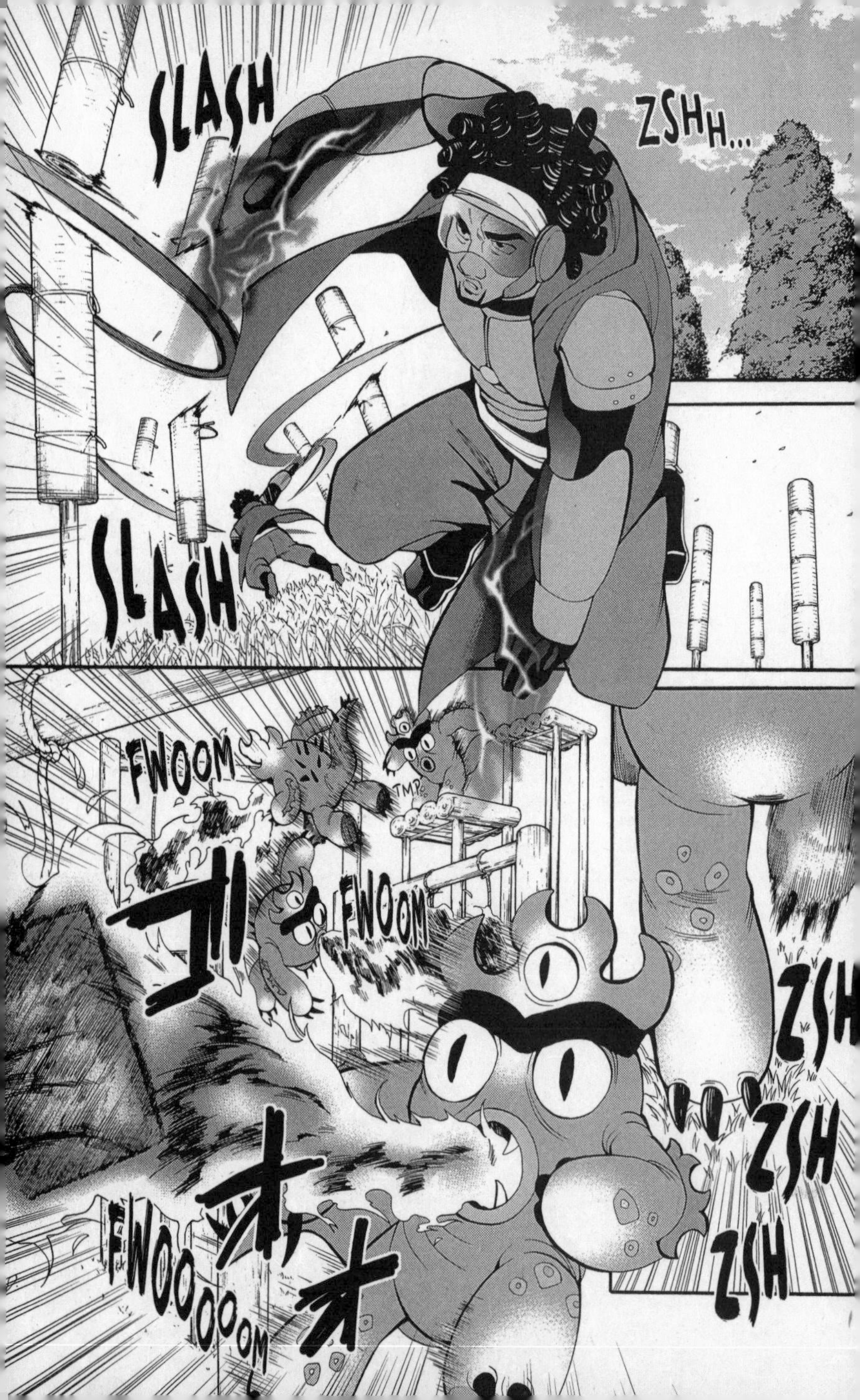
ZSHH...
SLASH
SLASH
ZSH
ZSH
ZSH
TMP
FWOOM
FWOOM
FWOOOOOM

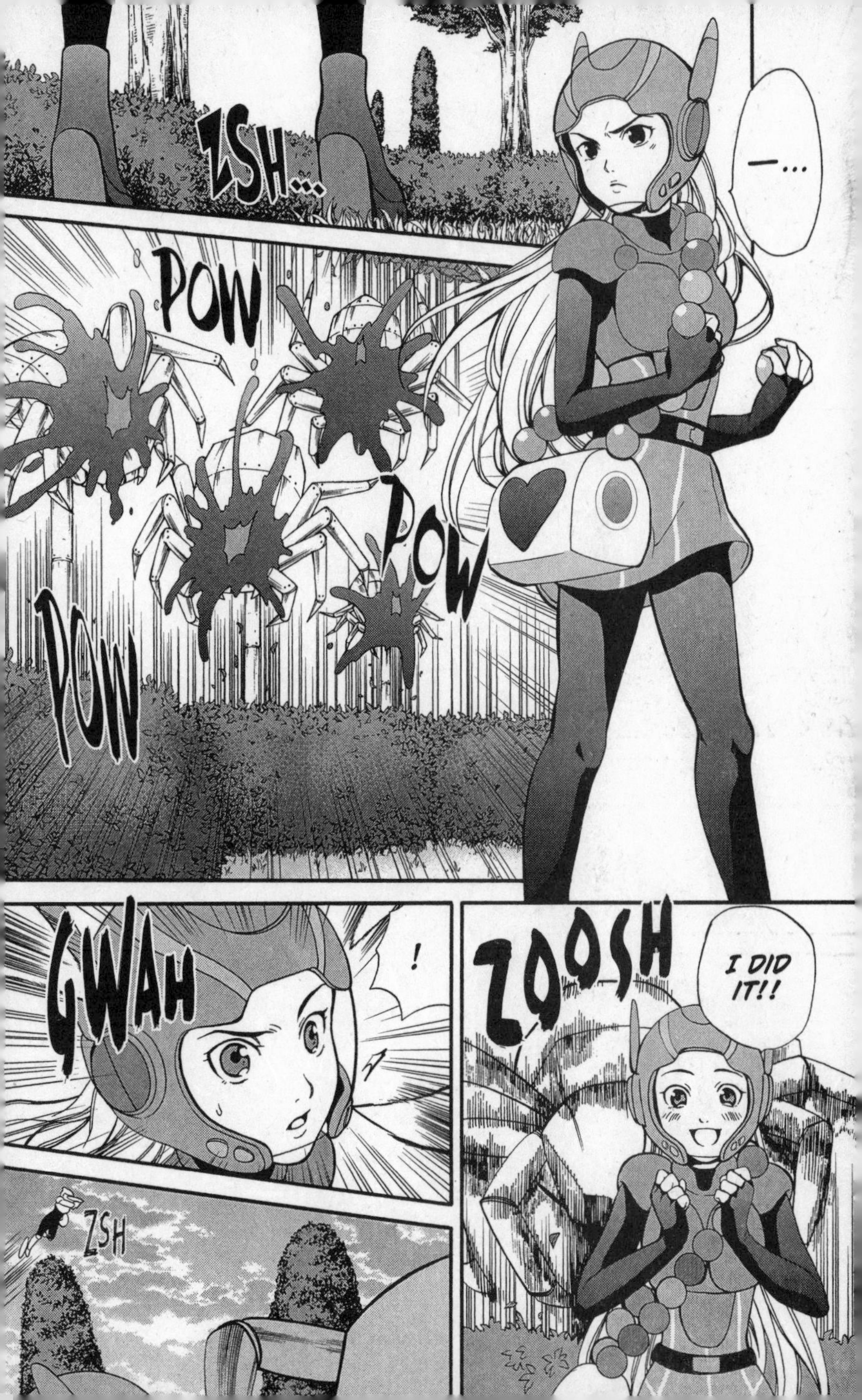
—...
ZSH...
POW
POW
POW
ZOOSH
I DID IT!!
GWAH
!
ZSH

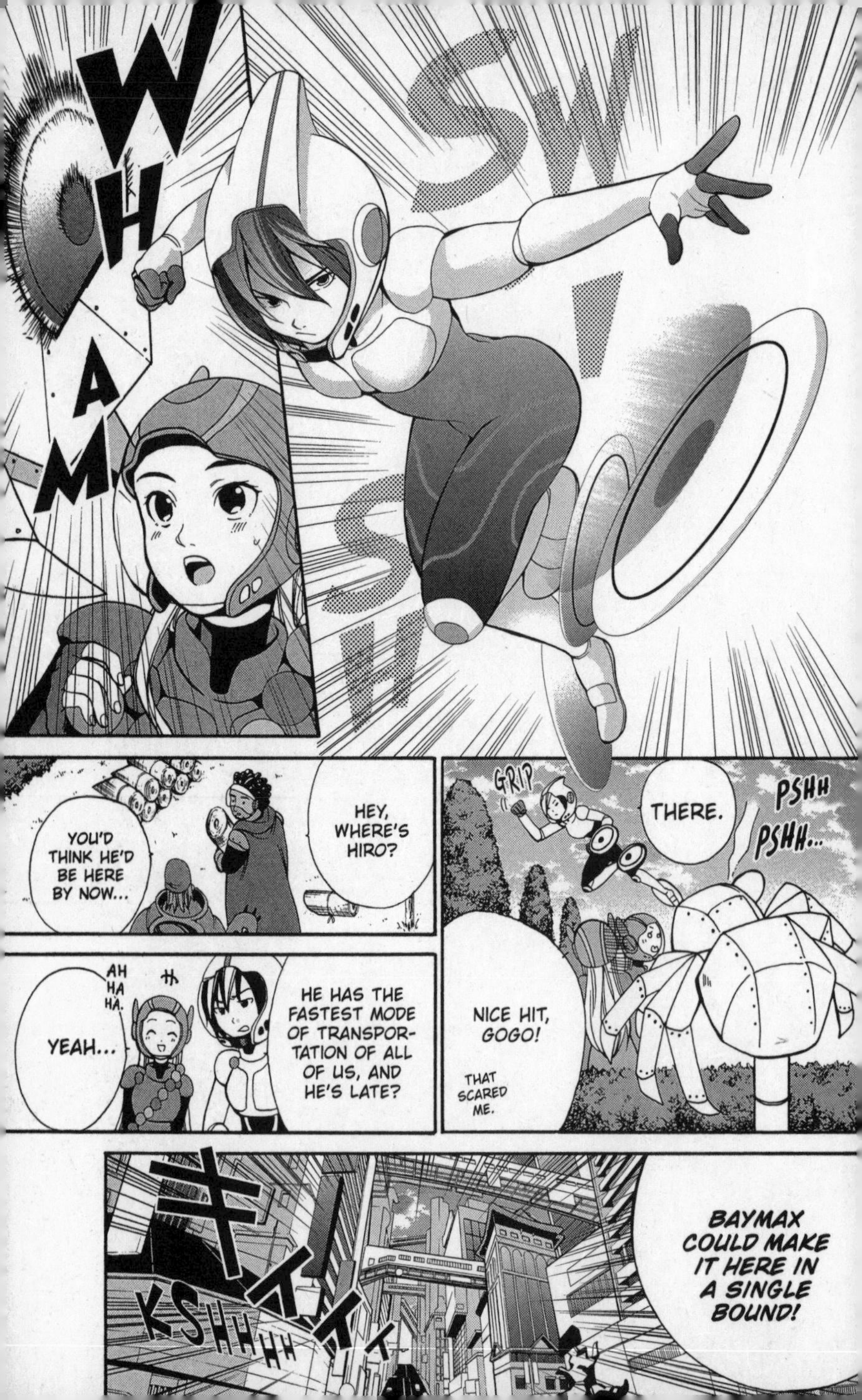
WHAM
SWISH
GRIP
THERE.
PSHH PSHH...
NICE HIT, GOGO!
THAT SCARED ME.
HEY, WHERE'S HIRO?
YOU'D THINK HE'D BE HERE BY NOW...
HE HAS THE FASTEST MODE OF TRANSPORTATION OF ALL OF US, AND HE'S LATE?
AH HA HA.
YEAH...
KSHHHHH
BAYMAX COULD MAKE IT HERE IN A SINGLE BOUND!

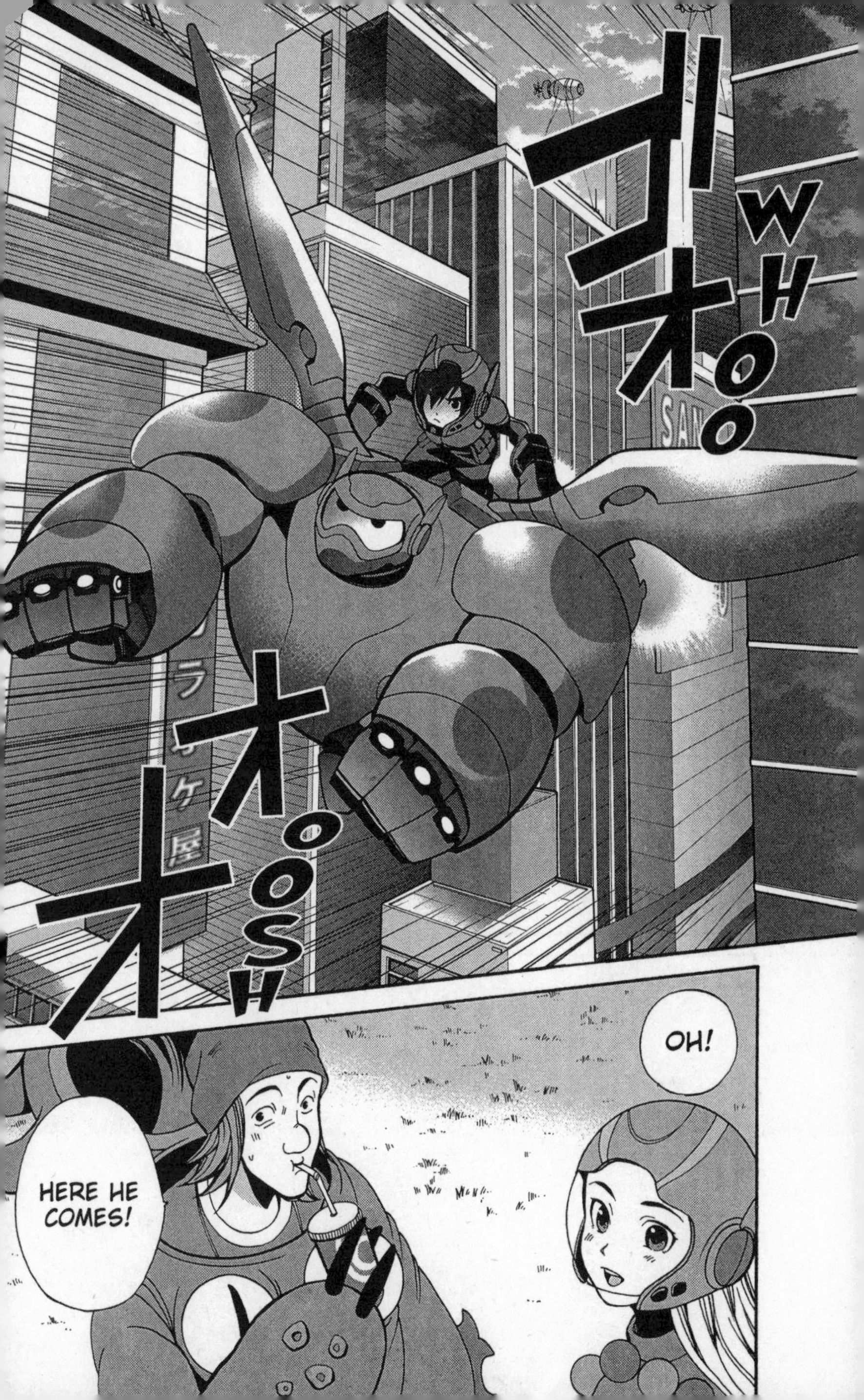
ゴオ
WHOO
オオ
OOSH
OH!
HERE HE COMES!

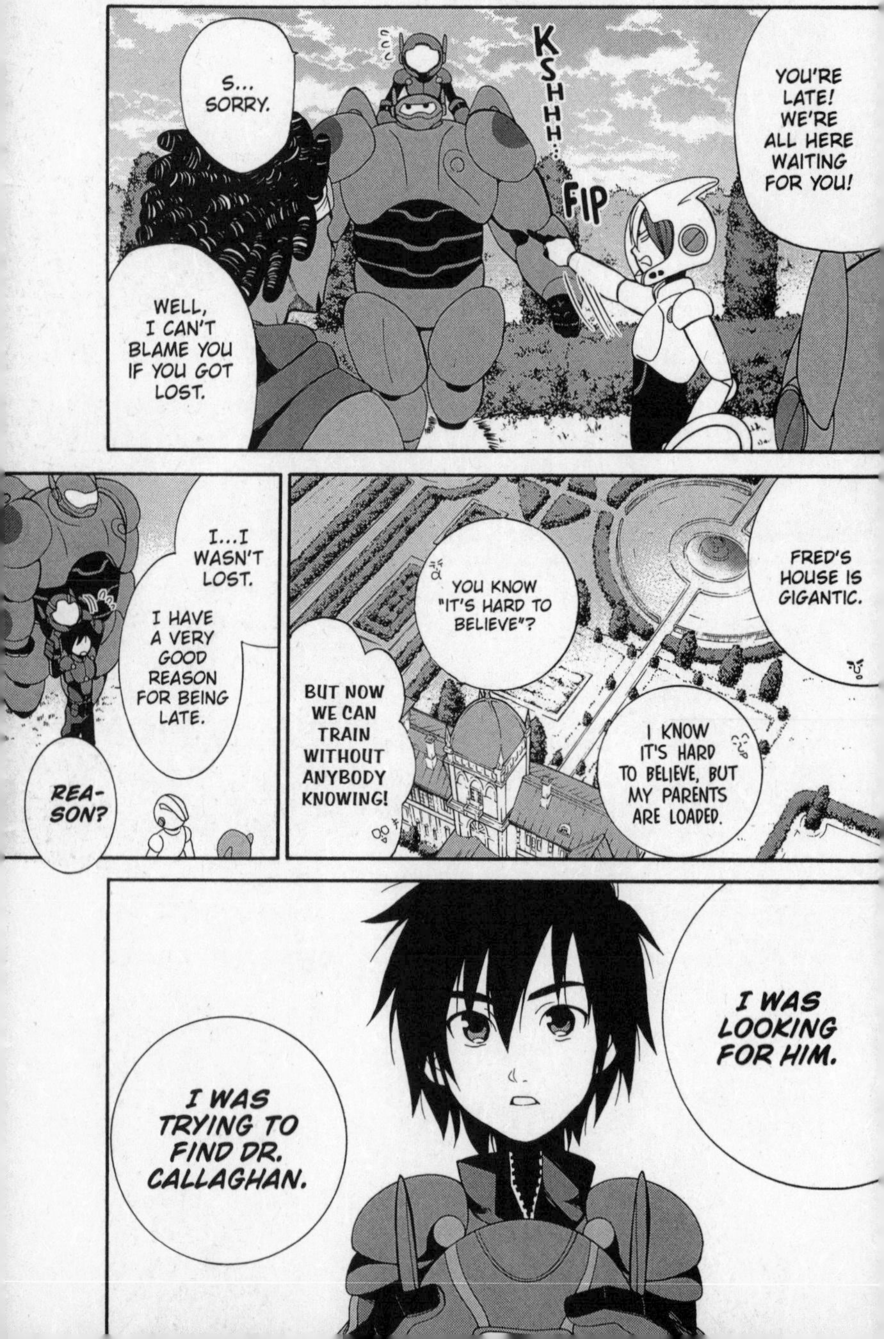
YOU'RE LATE! WE'RE ALL HERE WAITING FOR YOU!
KSHHH...
FIP
S... SORRY.
WELL, I CAN'T BLAME YOU IF YOU GOT LOST.
FRED'S HOUSE IS GIGANTIC.
YOU KNOW "IT'S HARD TO BELIEVE"?
I KNOW IT'S HARD TO BELIEVE, BUT MY PARENTS ARE LOADED.
BUT NOW WE CAN TRAIN WITHOUT ANYBODY KNOWING!
I...I WASN'T LOST.
I HAVE A VERY GOOD REASON FOR BEING LATE.
REA-SON?
I WAS LOOKING FOR HIM.
I WAS TRYING TO FIND DR. CALLAGHAN.

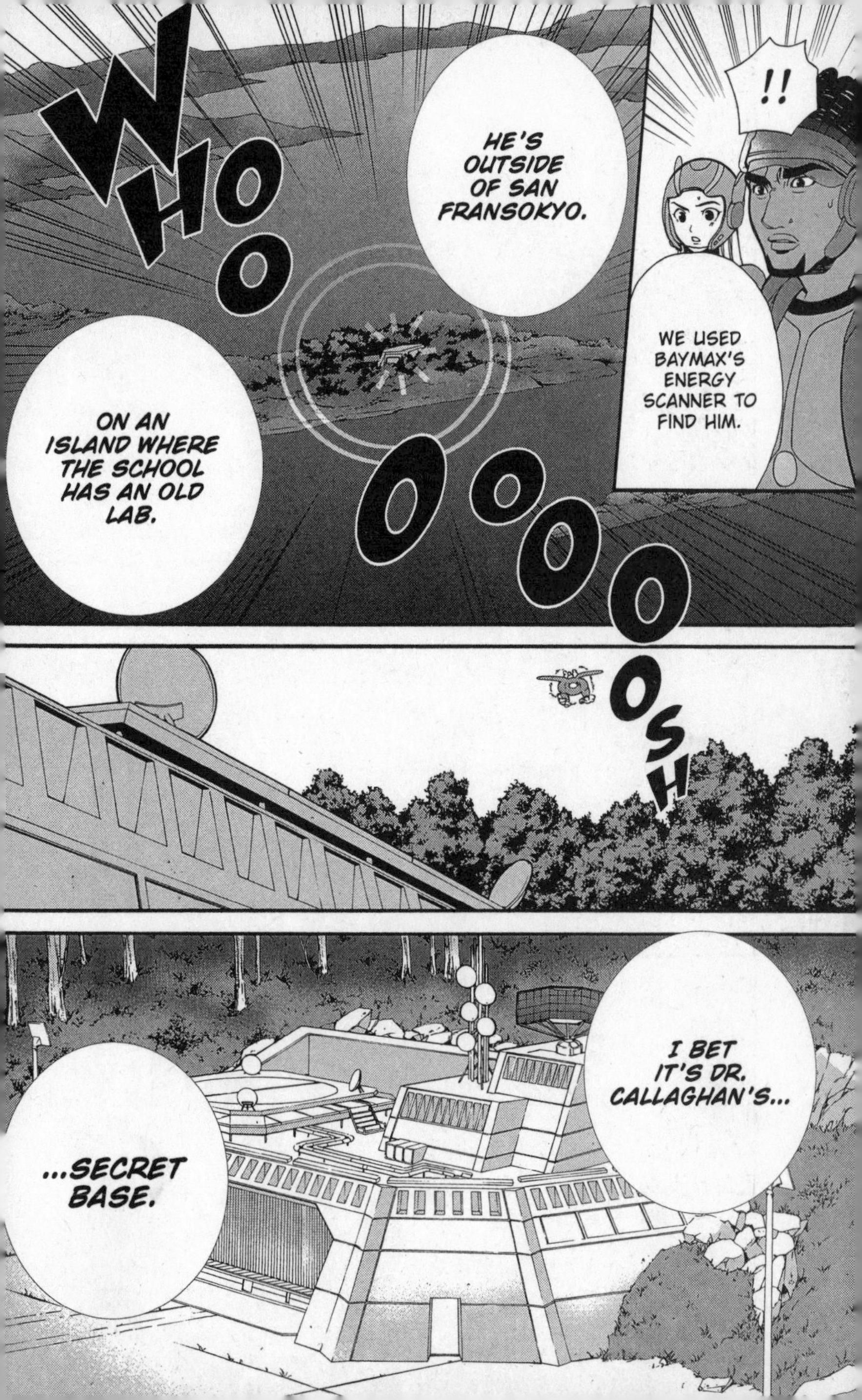
!!
WE USED BAYMAX'S ENERGY SCANNER TO FIND HIM.
HE'S OUTSIDE OF SAN FRANSOKYO.
ON AN ISLAND WHERE THE SCHOOL HAS AN OLD LAB.
WHOOOOOOOOSH
I BET IT'S DR. CALLAGHAN'S...
...SECRET BASE.

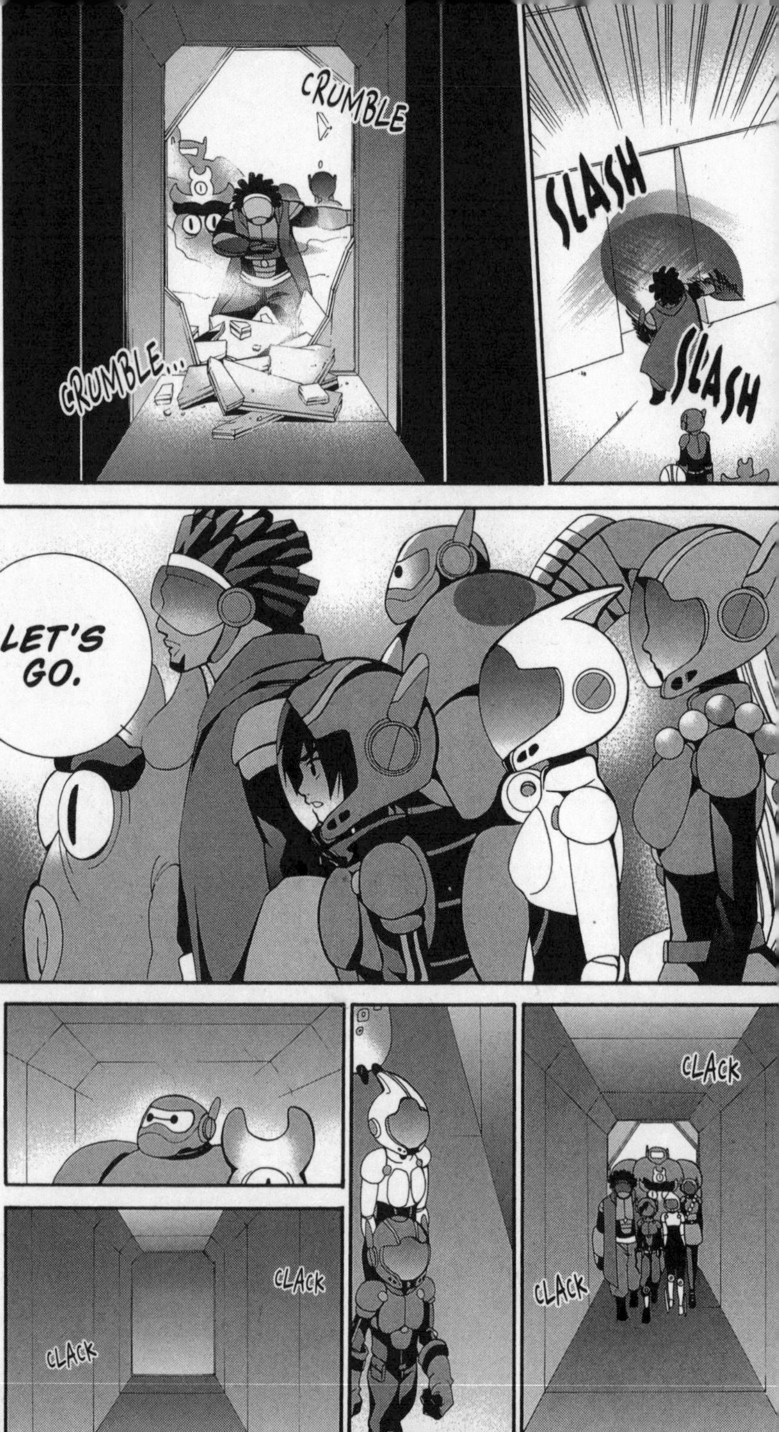
SLASH
SLASH
CRUMBLE
CRUMBLE...
LET'S GO.
CLACK
CLACK
CLACK
CLACK

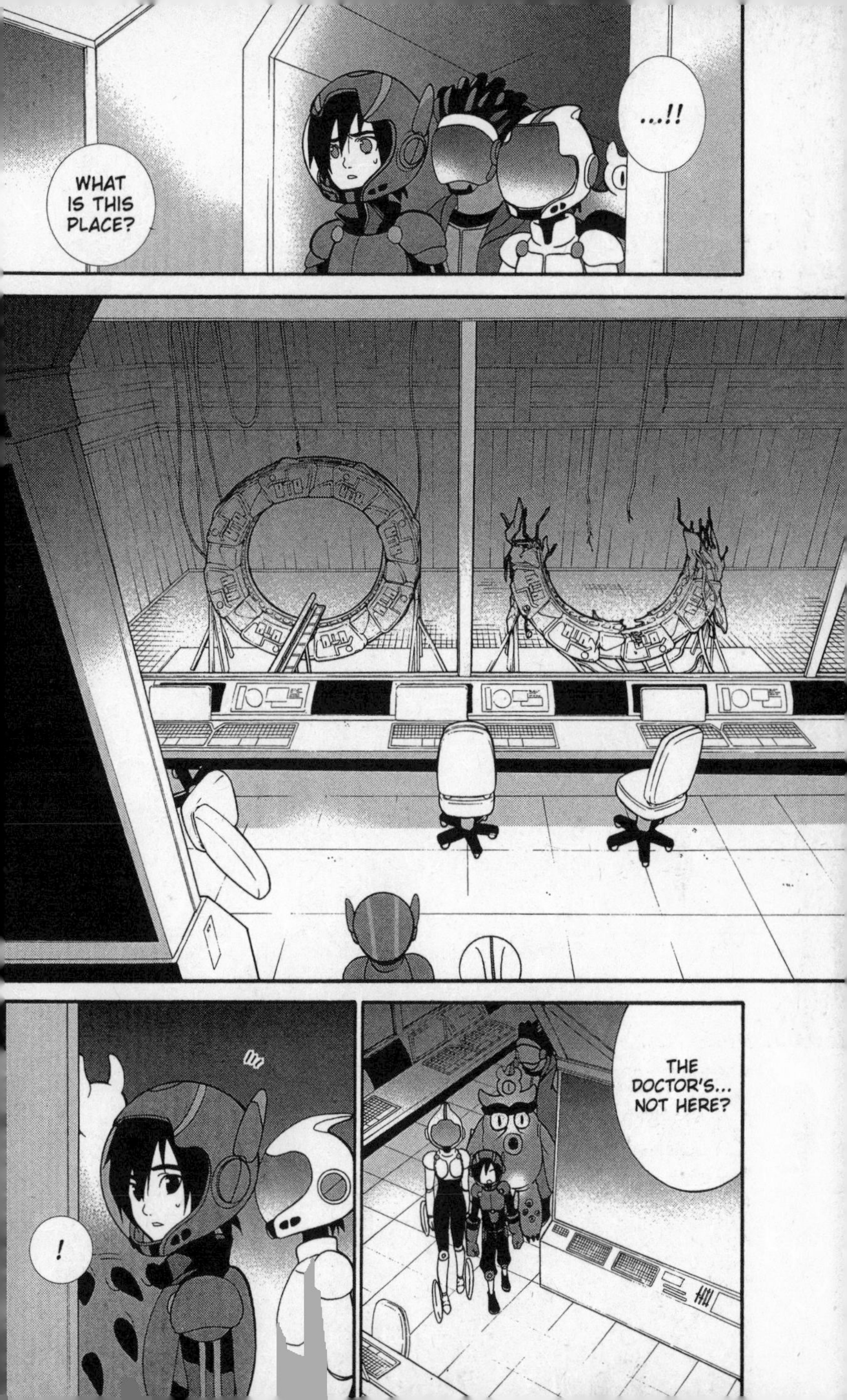
...!!
WHAT IS THIS PLACE?
THE DOCTOR'S... NOT HERE?
!

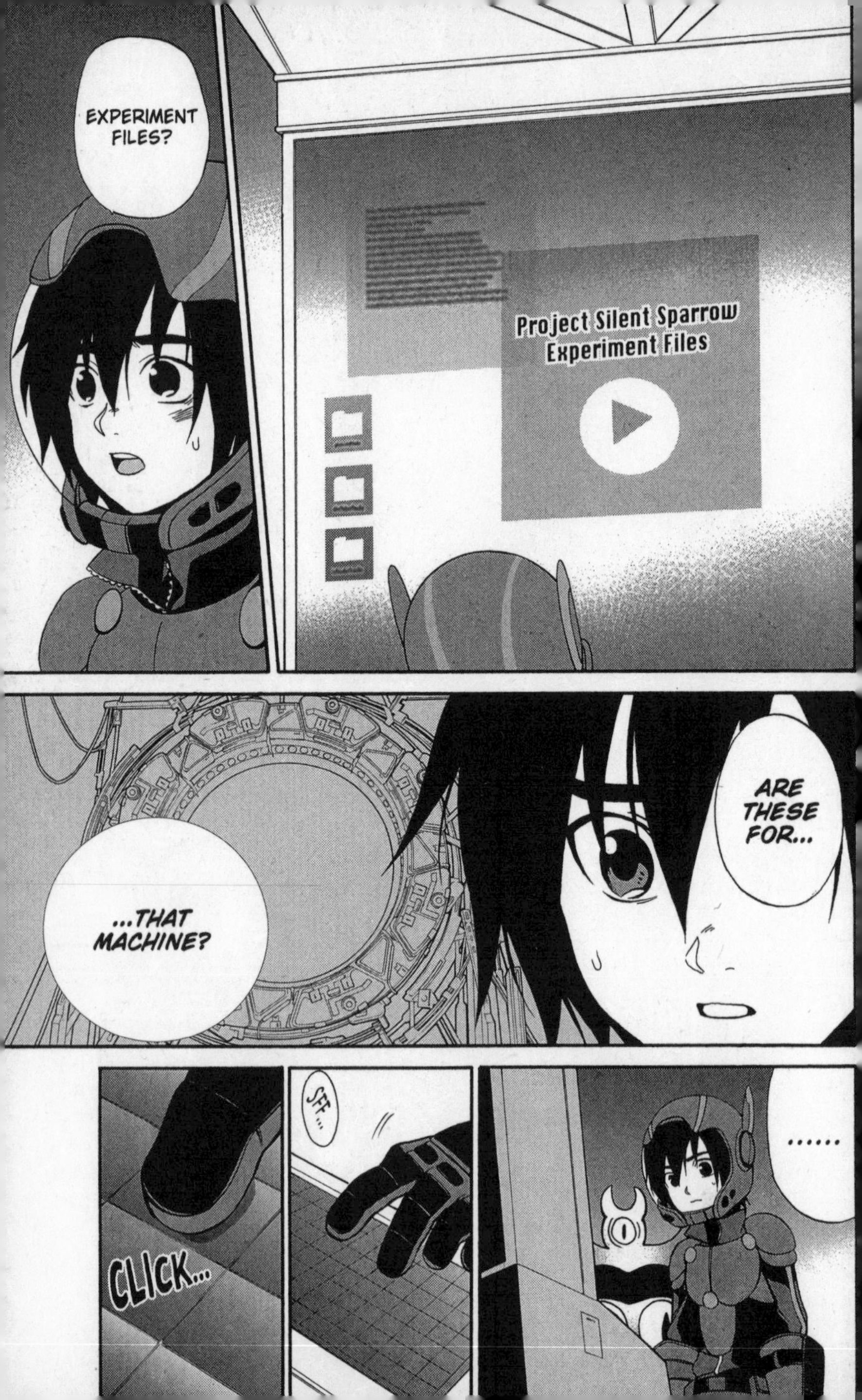
Project Silent Sparrow
Experiment Files
EXPERIMENT FILES?
ARE THESE FOR...
...THAT MACHINE?
......
SFF...
CLICK...

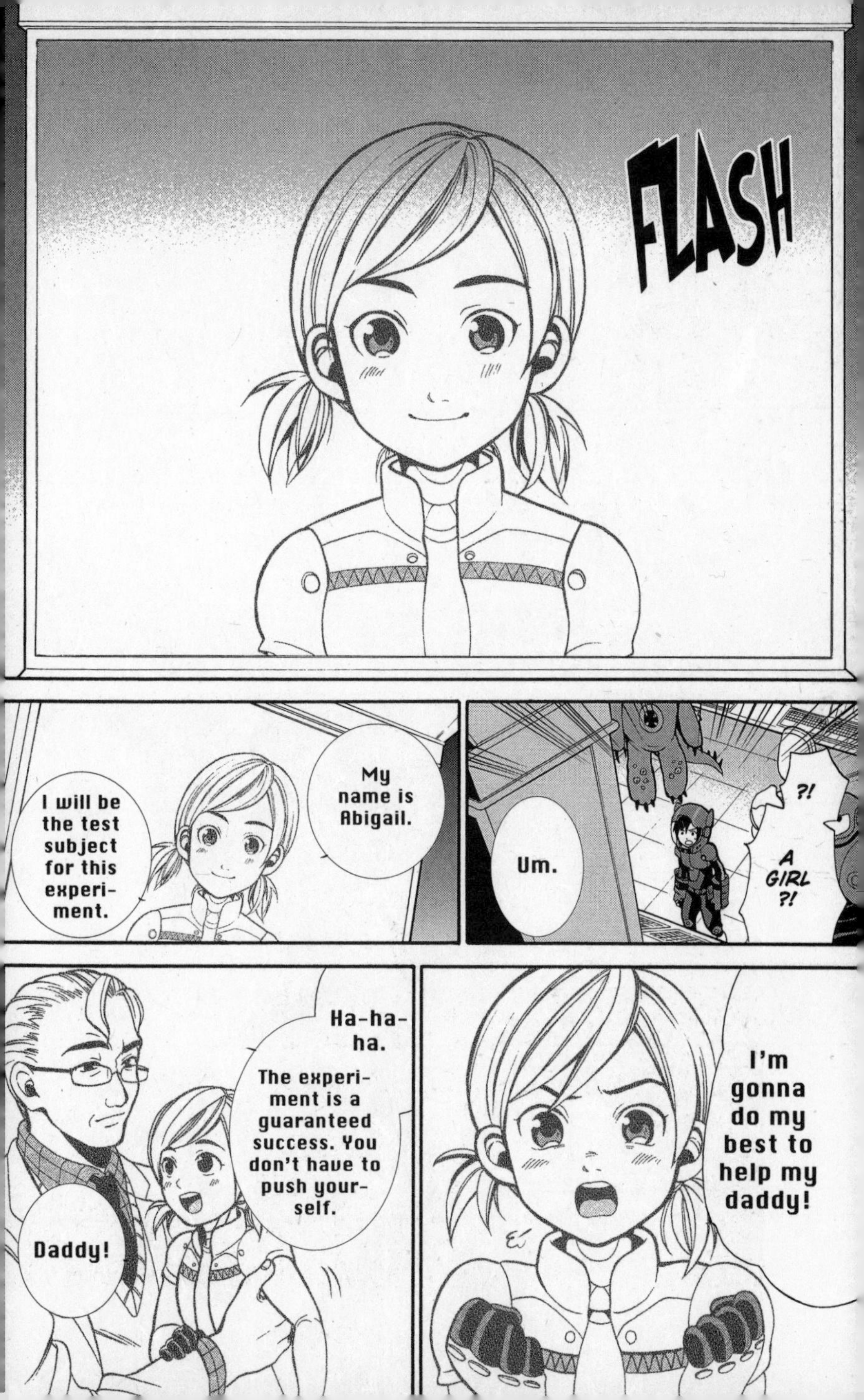
FLASH
?!
A GIRL ?!
Um.
My name is Abigail.
I will be the test subject for this experiment.
I'm gonna do my best to help my daddy!
Ha-ha-ha.
The experiment is a guaranteed success. You don't have to push yourself.
Daddy!

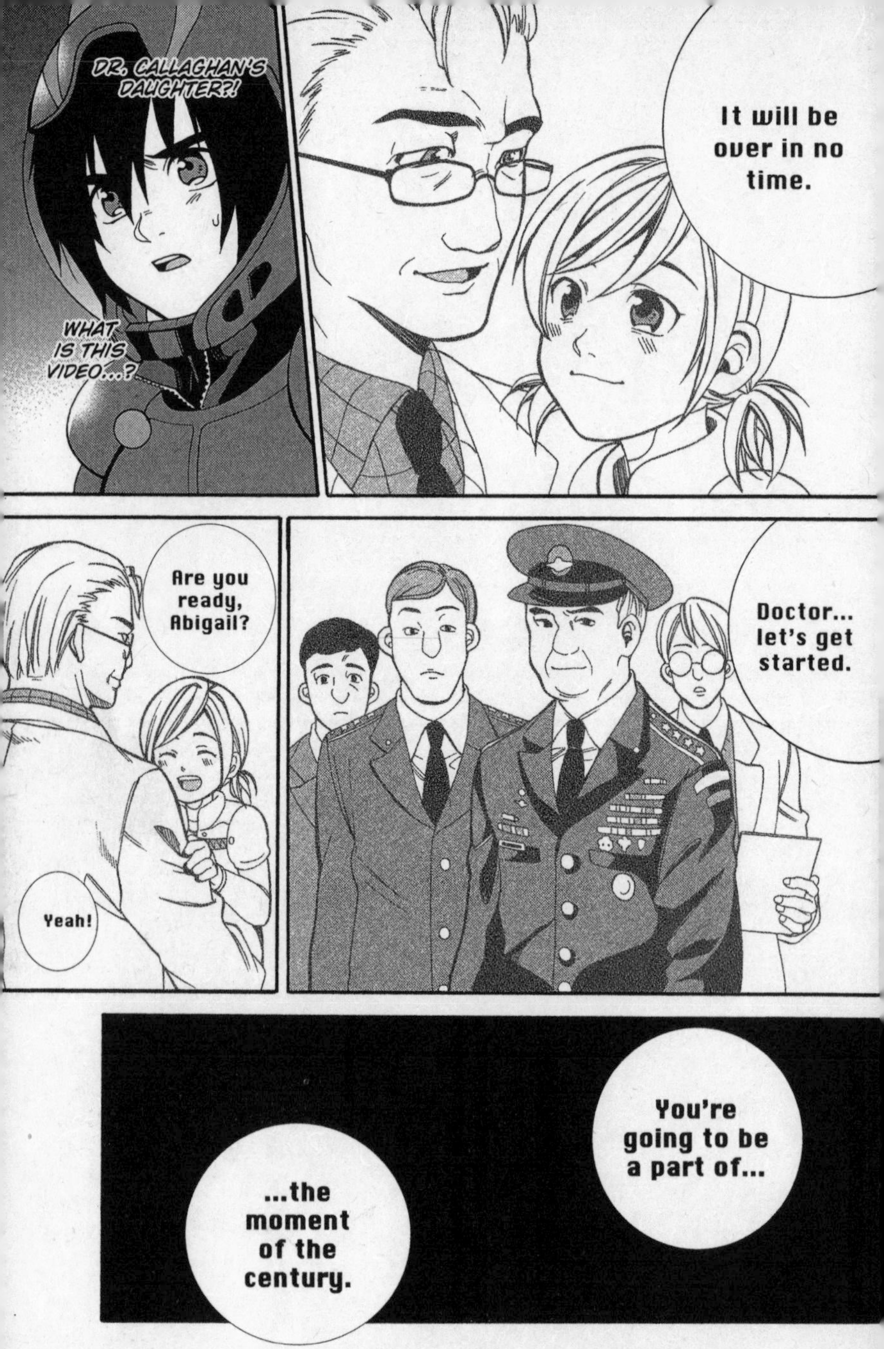
It will be over in no time.
DR. CALLAGHAN'S DAUGHTER?!
WHAT IS THIS VIDEO...?
Doctor... let's get started.
Are you ready, Abigail?
Yeah!
You're going to be a part of...
...the moment of the century.

Disney

BIG
HERO
6

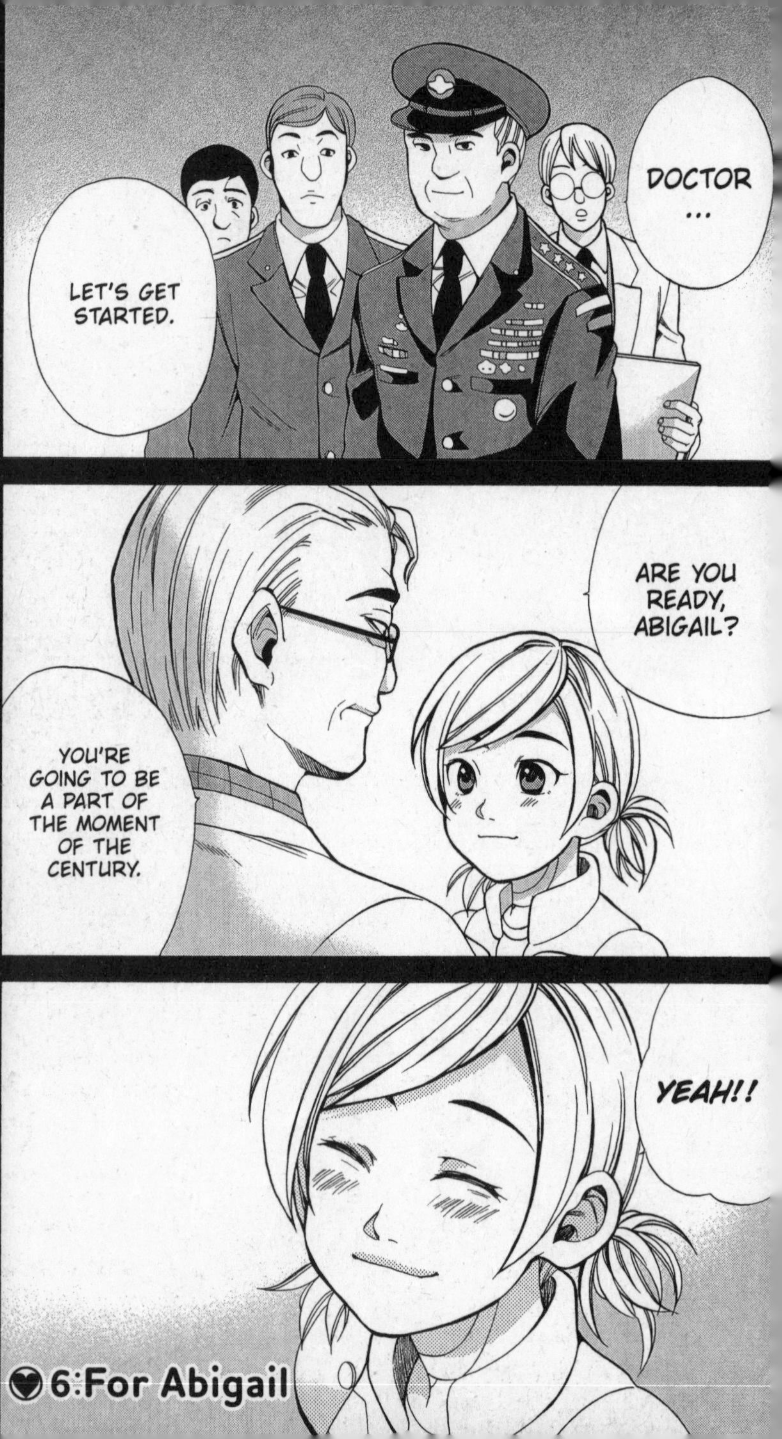
DOCTOR ...
LET'S GET STARTED.
ARE YOU READY, ABIGAIL?
YOU'RE GOING TO BE A PART OF THE MOMENT OF THE CENTURY.
YEAH!!

6:For Abigail

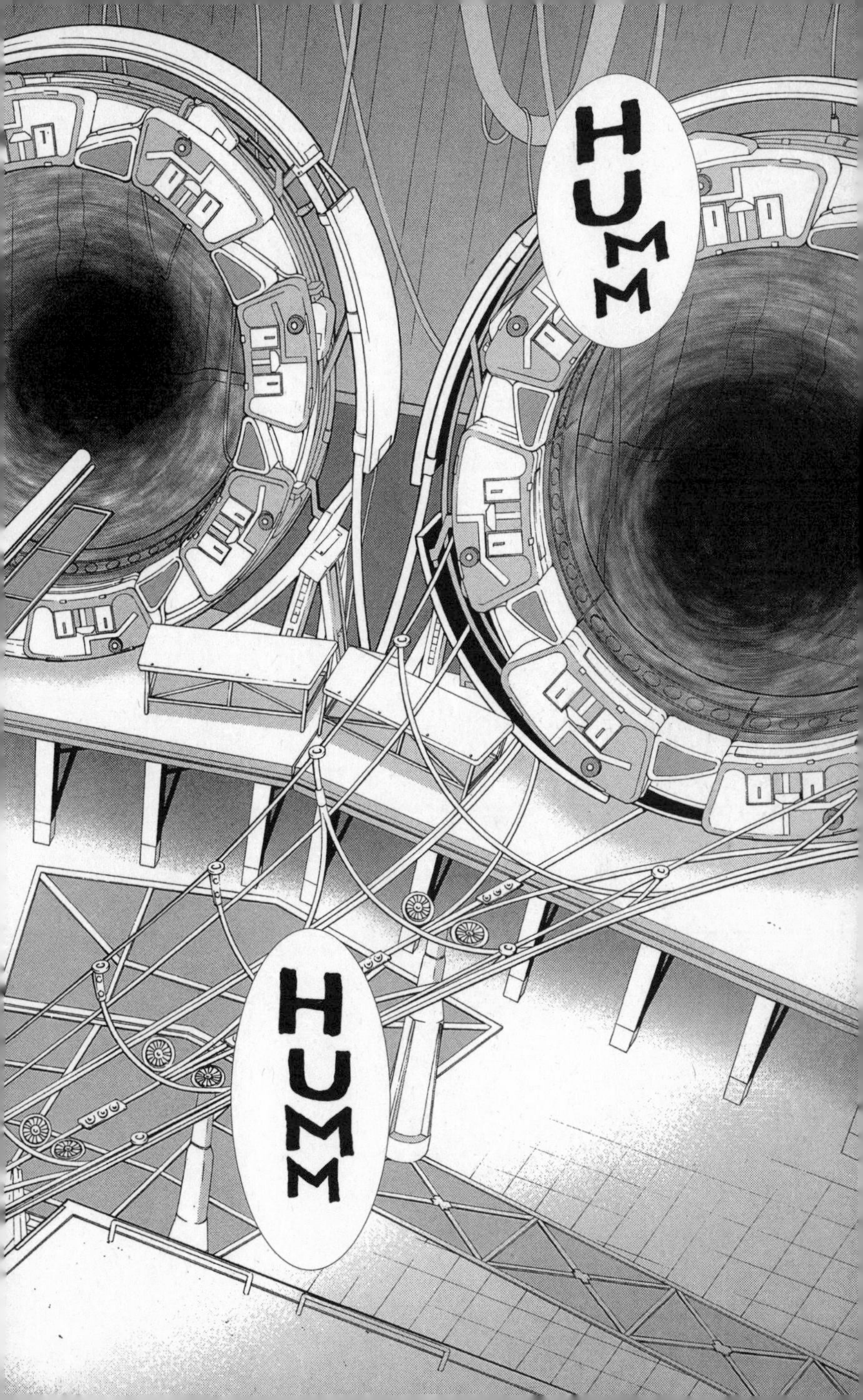
HUMM
HUMM

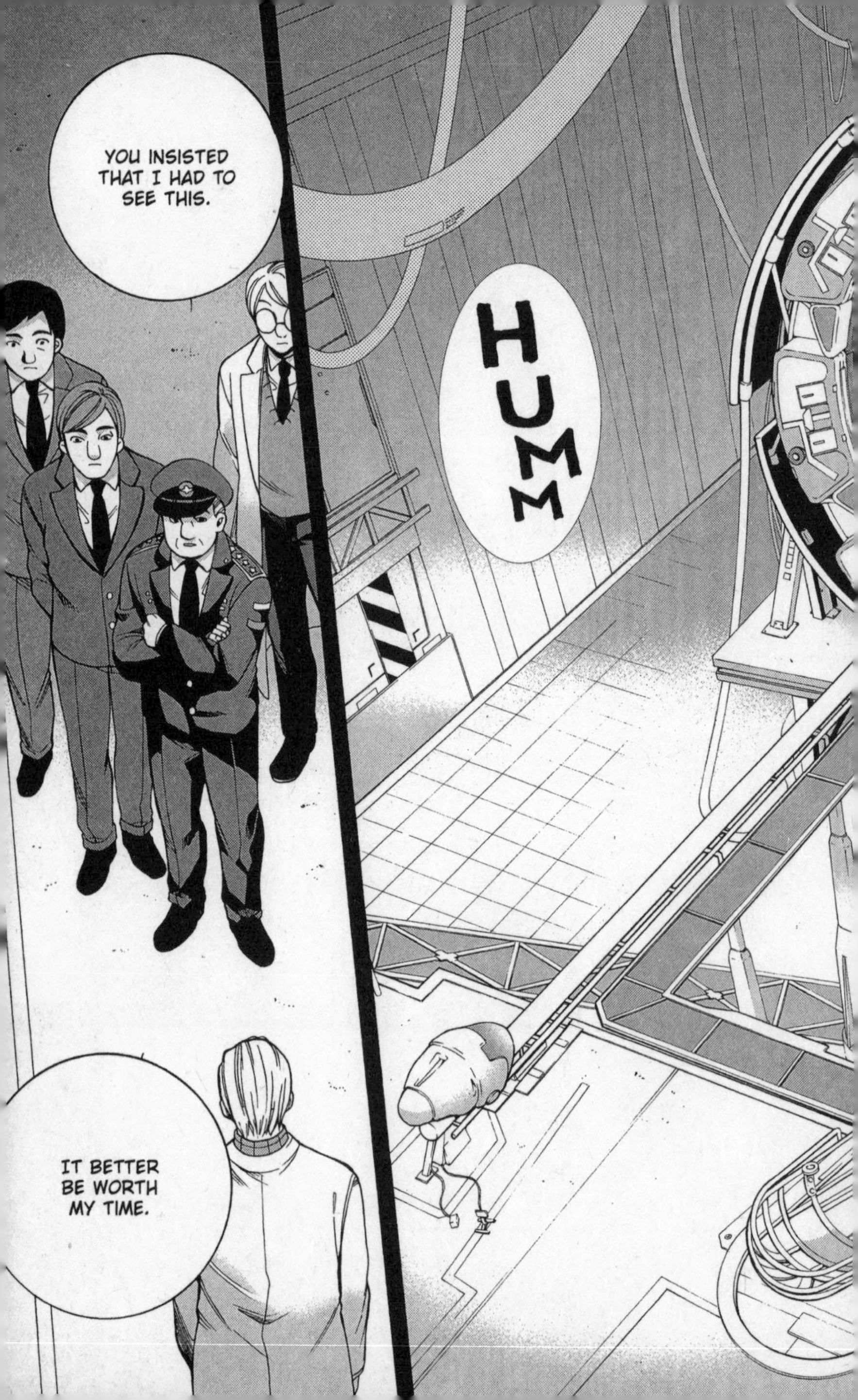
HUMM
YOU INSISTED THAT I HAD TO SEE THIS.
IT BETTER BE WORTH MY TIME.

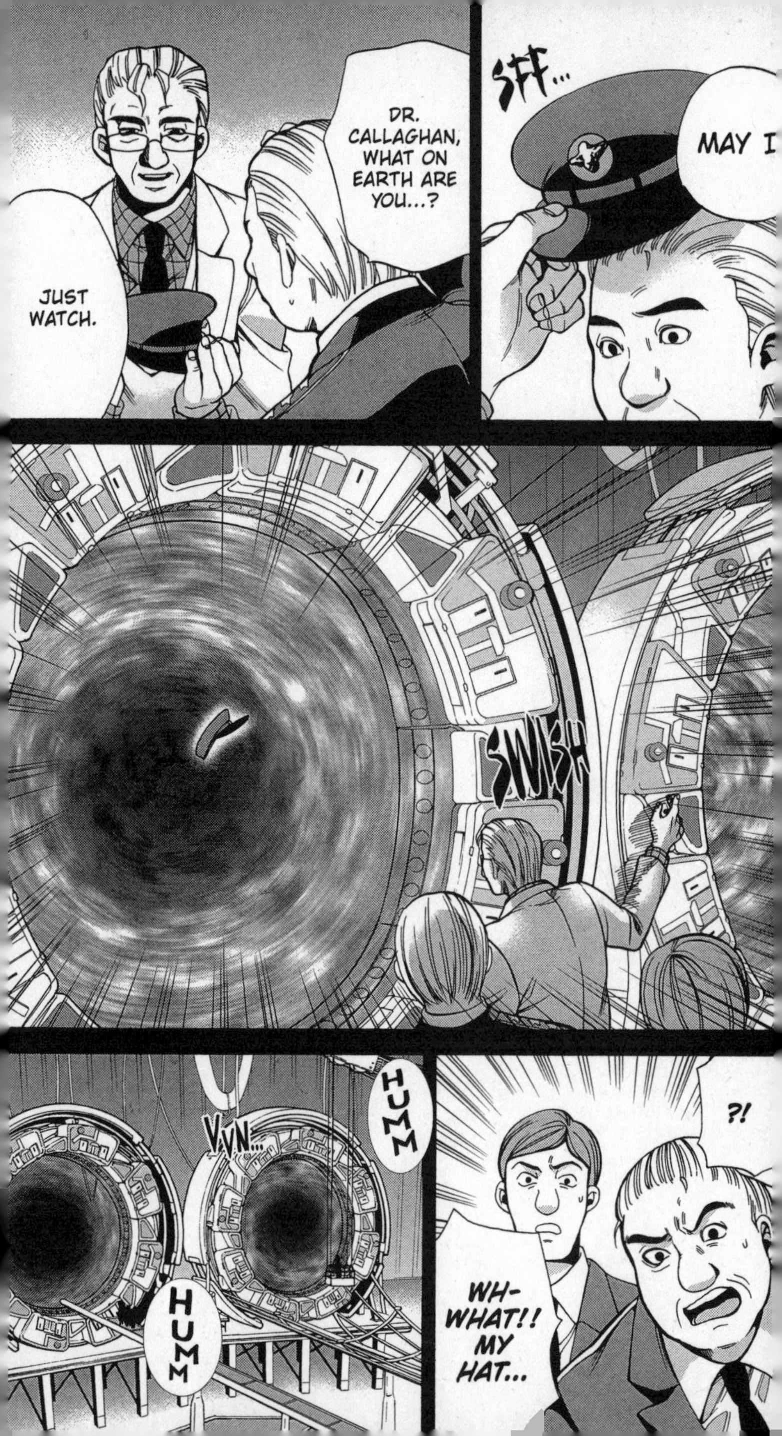
SFF...
MAY I
DR. CALLAGHAN, WHAT ON EARTH ARE YOU...?
JUST WATCH.
SWISH
?!
WH-WHAT!! MY HAT...
HUMM
VVN...
HUMM

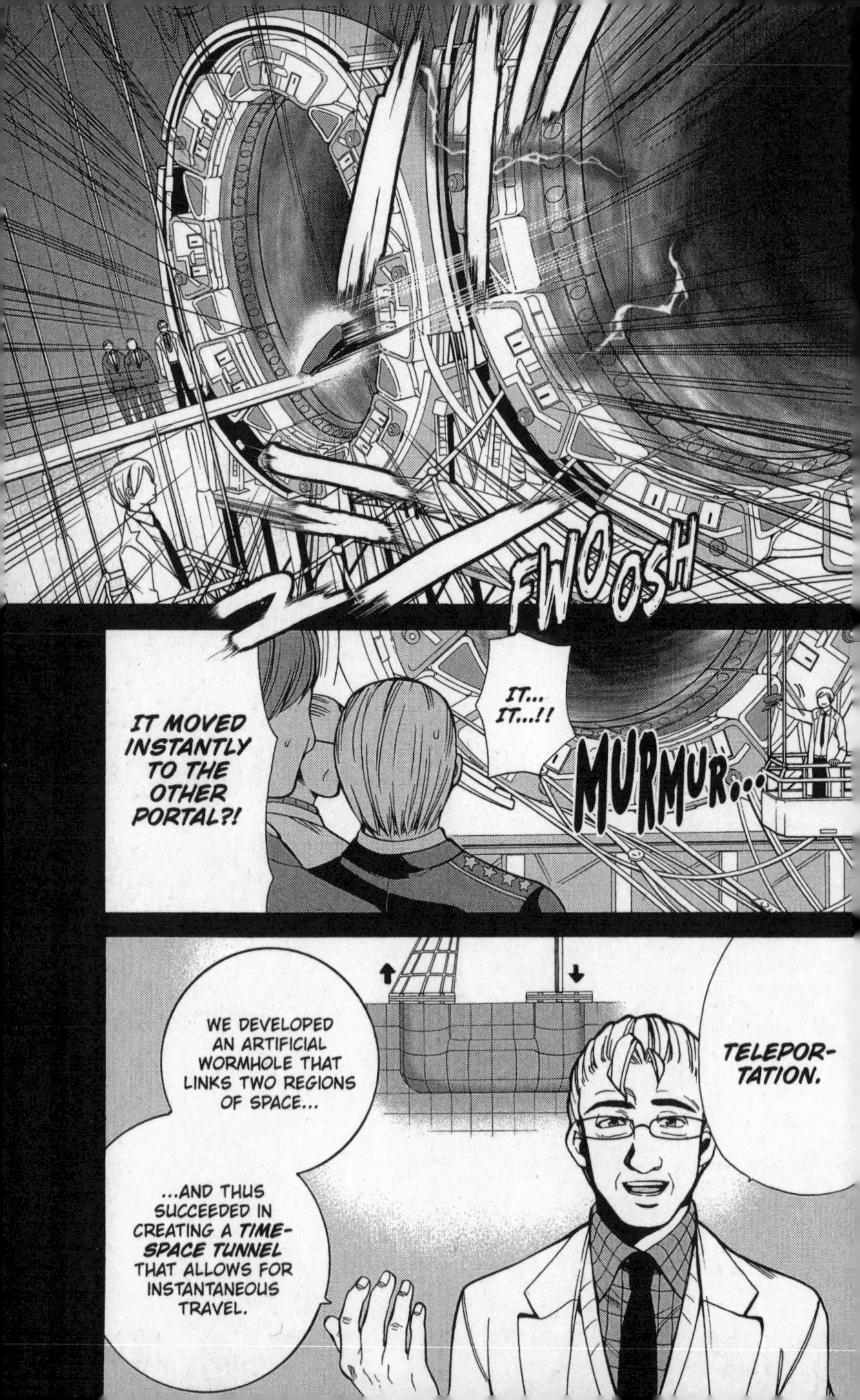
FWOOSH
IT... IT...!!
IT MOVED INSTANTLY TO THE OTHER PORTAL?!
MURMUR...
TELEPOR-TATION.
WE DEVELOPED AN ARTIFICIAL WORMHOLE THAT LINKS TWO REGIONS OF SPACE...
...AND THUS SUCCEEDED IN CREATING A TIME-SPACE TUNNEL THAT ALLOWS FOR INSTANTANEOUS TRAVEL.

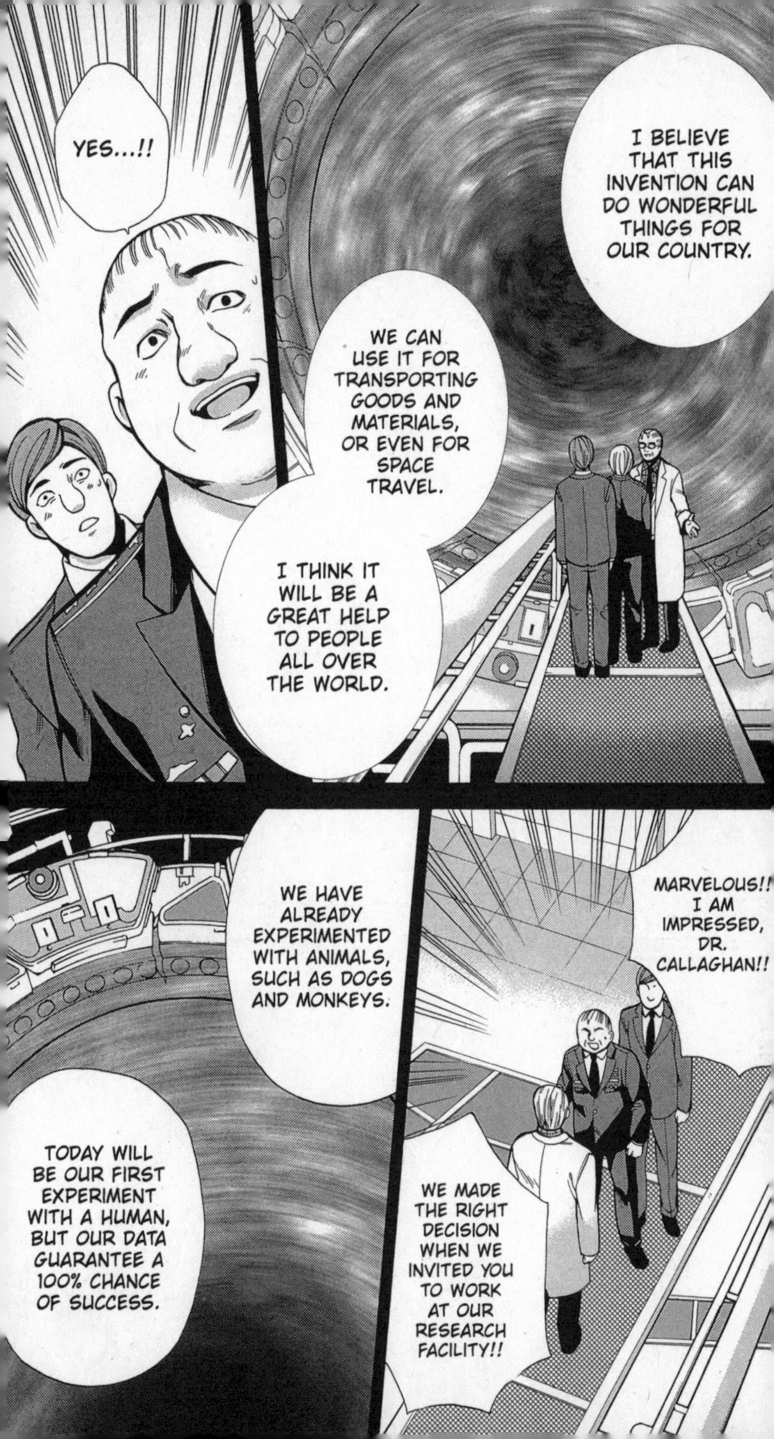
I BELIEVE THAT THIS INVENTION CAN DO WONDERFUL THINGS FOR OUR COUNTRY.
WE CAN USE IT FOR TRANSPORTING GOODS AND MATERIALS, OR EVEN FOR SPACE TRAVEL.
I THINK IT WILL BE A GREAT HELP TO PEOPLE ALL OVER THE WORLD.
YES...!!
MARVELOUS!! I AM IMPRESSED, DR. CALLAGHAN!!
WE MADE THE RIGHT DECISION WHEN WE INVITED YOU TO WORK AT OUR RESEARCH FACILITY!!
WE HAVE ALREADY EXPERIMENTED WITH ANIMALS, SUCH AS DOGS AND MONKEYS.
TODAY WILL BE OUR FIRST EXPERIMENT WITH A HUMAN, BUT OUR DATA GUARANTEE A 100% CHANCE OF SUCCESS.

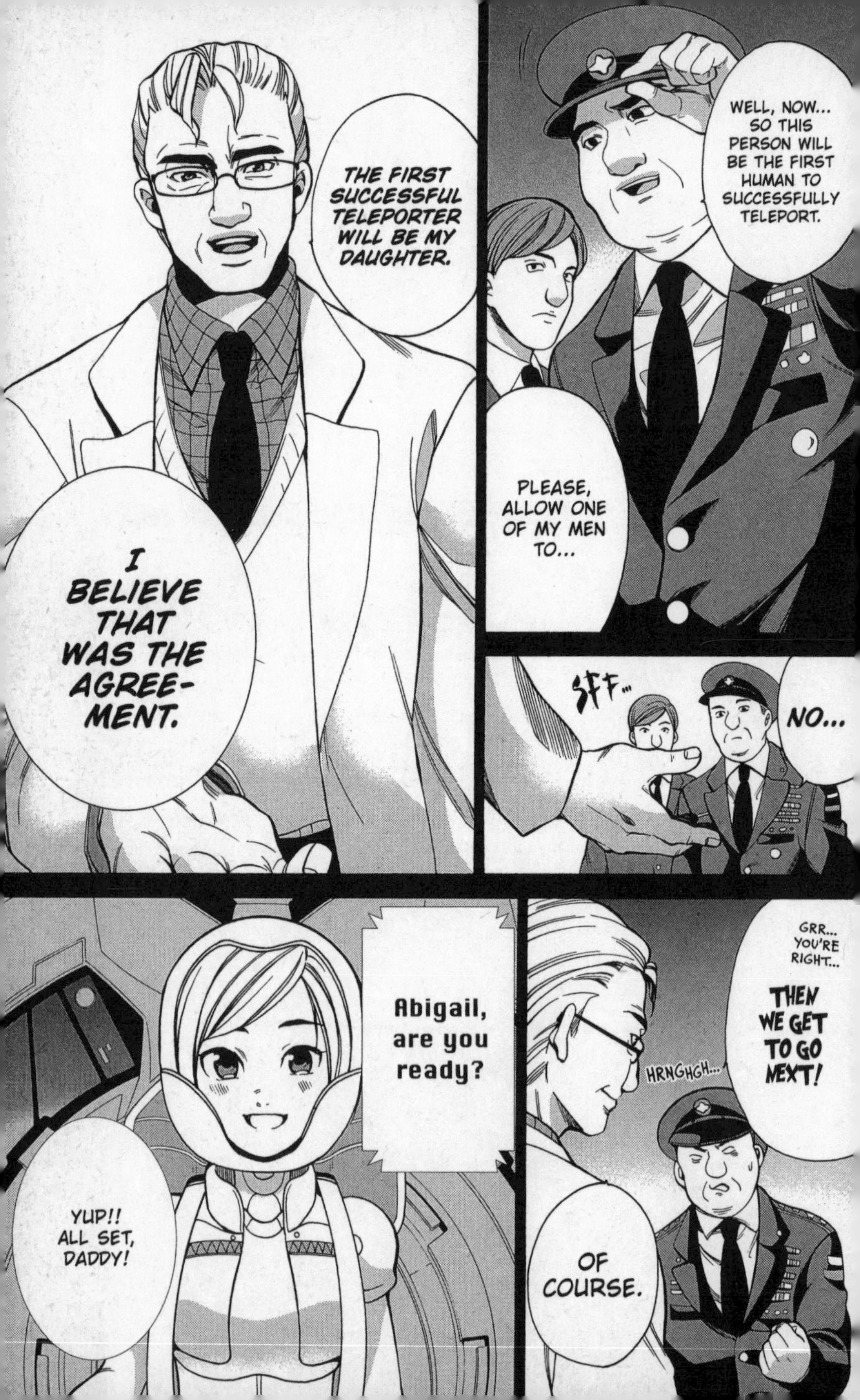
WELL, NOW... SO THIS PERSON WILL BE THE FIRST HUMAN TO SUCCESSFULLY TELEPORT.
PLEASE, ALLOW ONE OF MY MEN TO...
NO...
SFF...
THE FIRST SUCCESSFUL TELEPORTER WILL BE MY DAUGHTER.
I BELIEVE THAT WAS THE AGREE-MENT.
GRR... YOU'RE RIGHT...
THEN WE GET TO GO NEXT!
HRNGHGH...
OF COURSE.
Abigail, are you ready?
YUP!! ALL SET, DADDY!

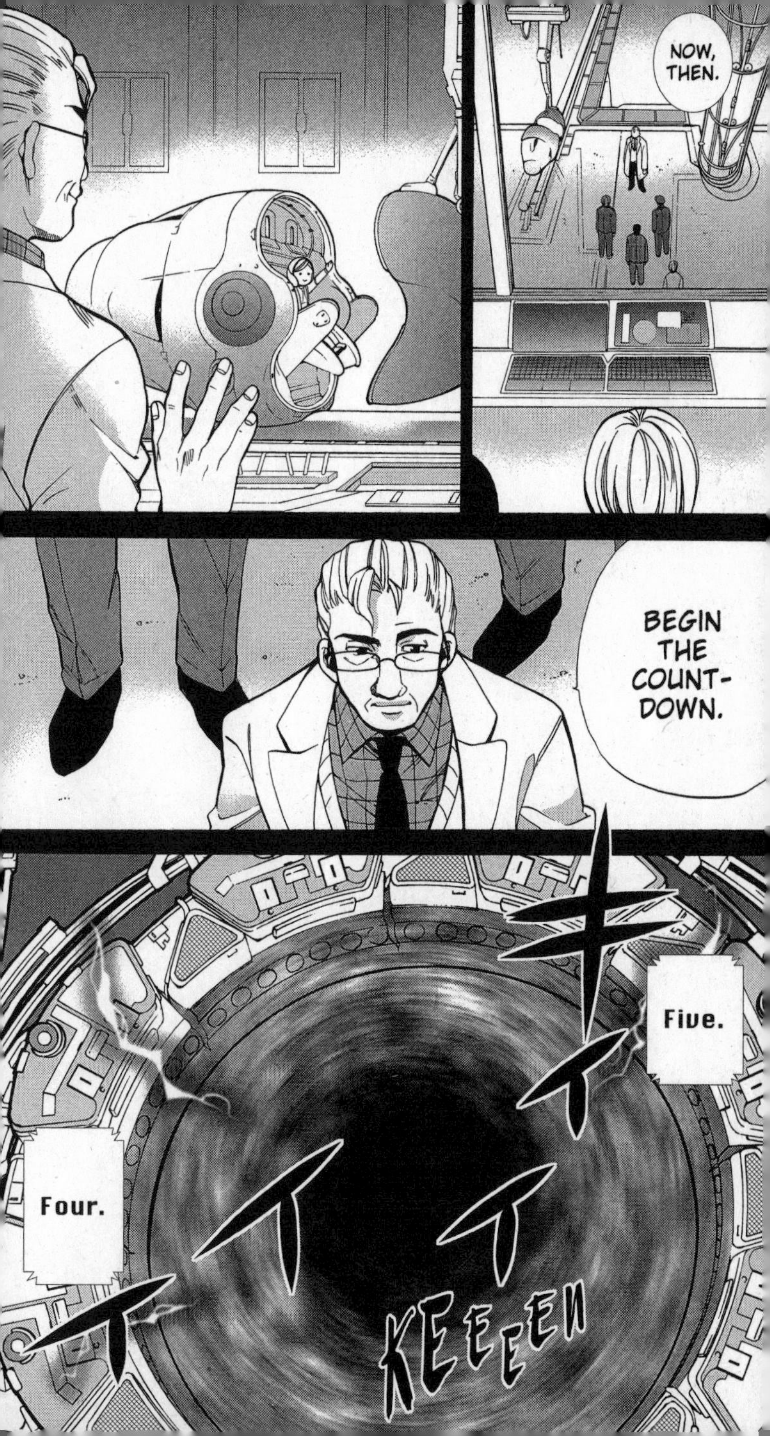
NOW, THEN.
BEGIN THE COUNT-DOWN.
Five.
Four.
KEEEEEN

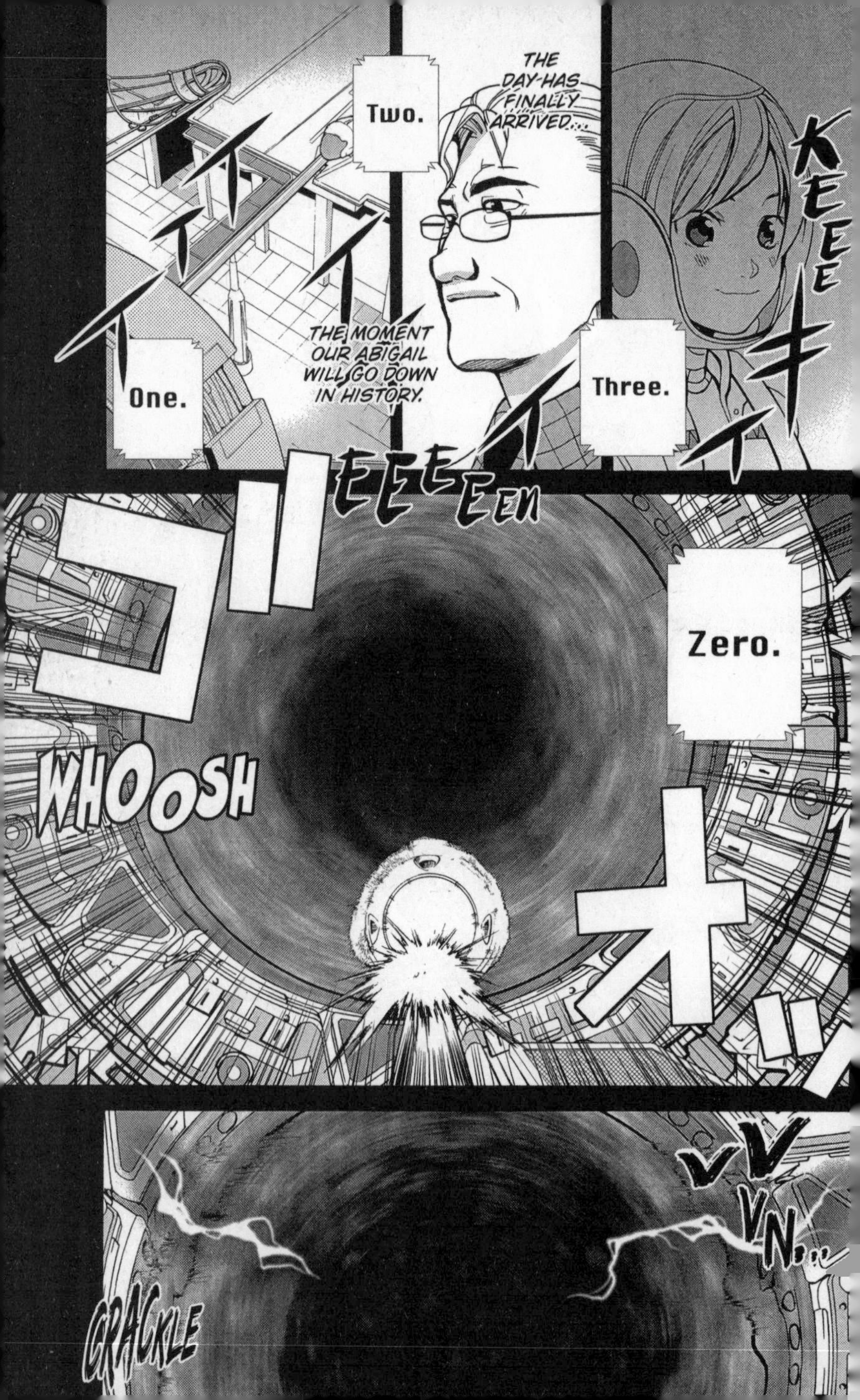
KEEEE
Three.
THE DAY HAS FINALLY ARRIVED...
Two.
THE MOMENT OUR ABIGAIL WILL GO DOWN IN HISTORY.
One.
EEEEEen
Zero.
WHOOSH
VVVN...
CRACKLE

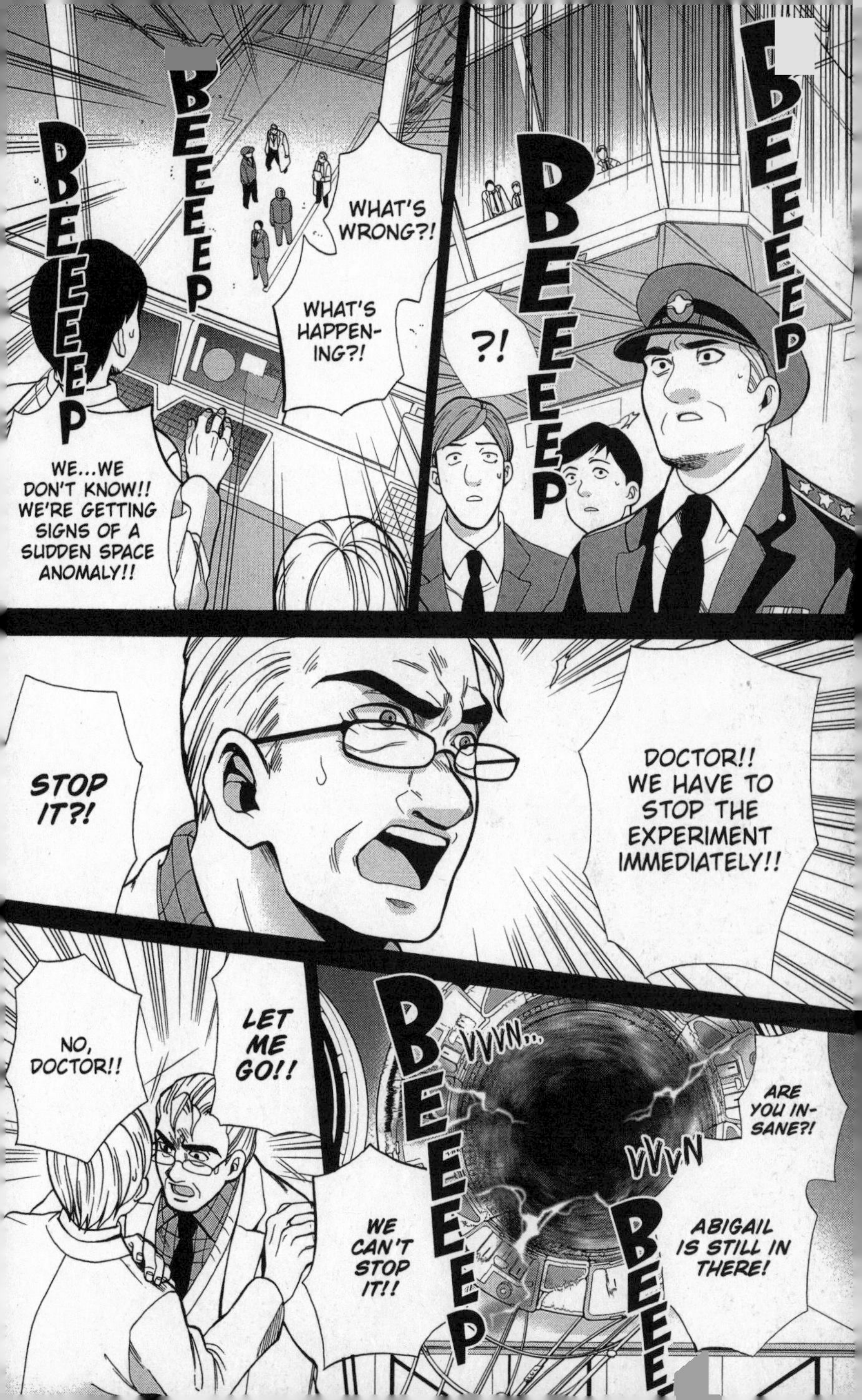
BEEEEP
BEEEEP
?!
WHAT'S WRONG?!
WHAT'S HAPPEN-ING?!
BEEEEP
BEEEEP
WE...WE DON'T KNOW!! WE'RE GETTING SIGNS OF A SUDDEN SPACE ANOMALY!!
DOCTOR!! WE HAVE TO STOP THE EXPERIMENT IMMEDIATELY!!
STOP IT?!
ARE YOU IN-SANE?!
VVVN
ABIGAIL IS STILL IN THERE!
BEEE...
VVVN..
BEEEEP
WE CAN'T STOP IT!!
LET ME GO!!
NO, DOCTOR!!

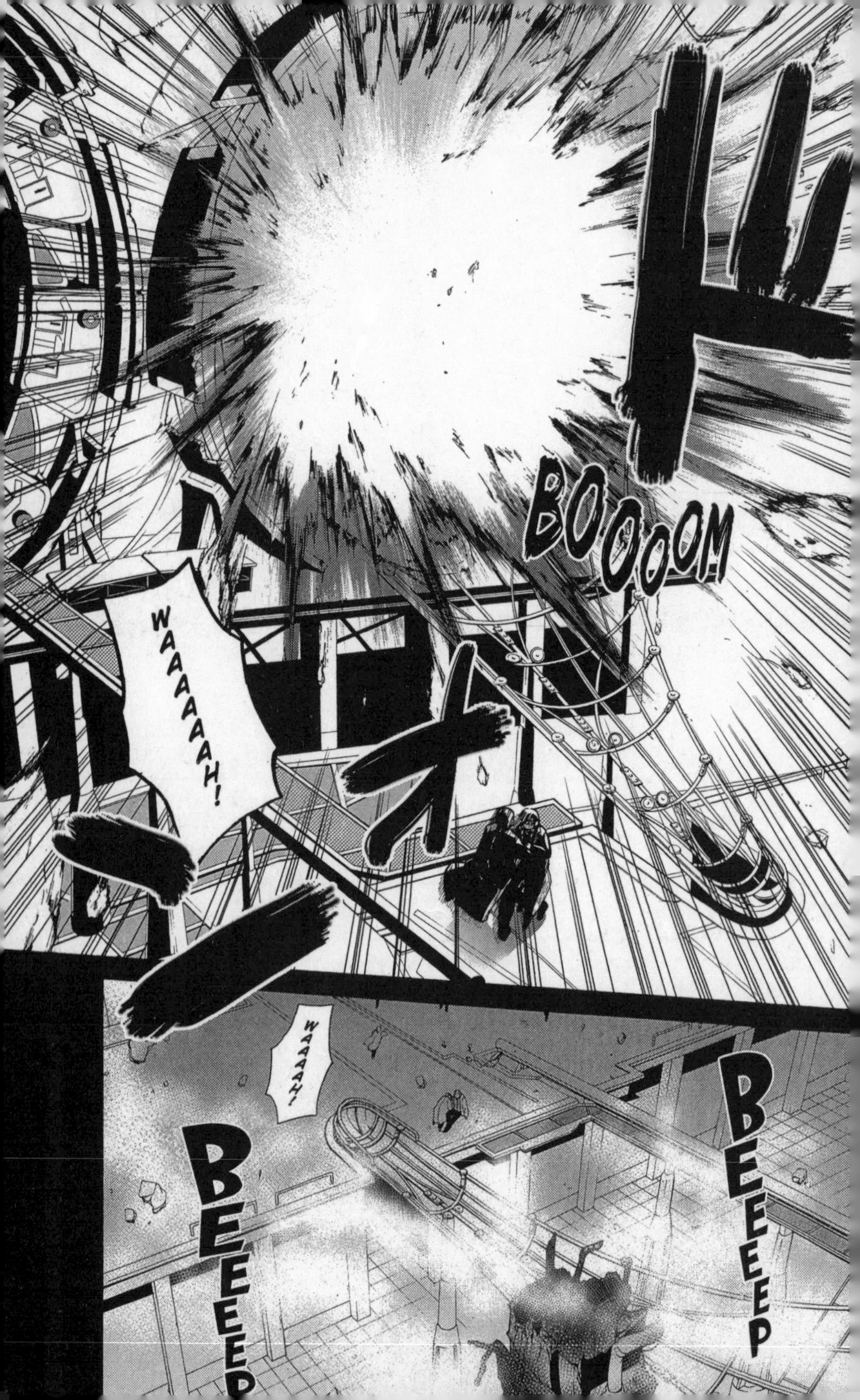
BOOOOM
WAAAAAAAH!
BEEEEP
WAAAAH!
BEEEE

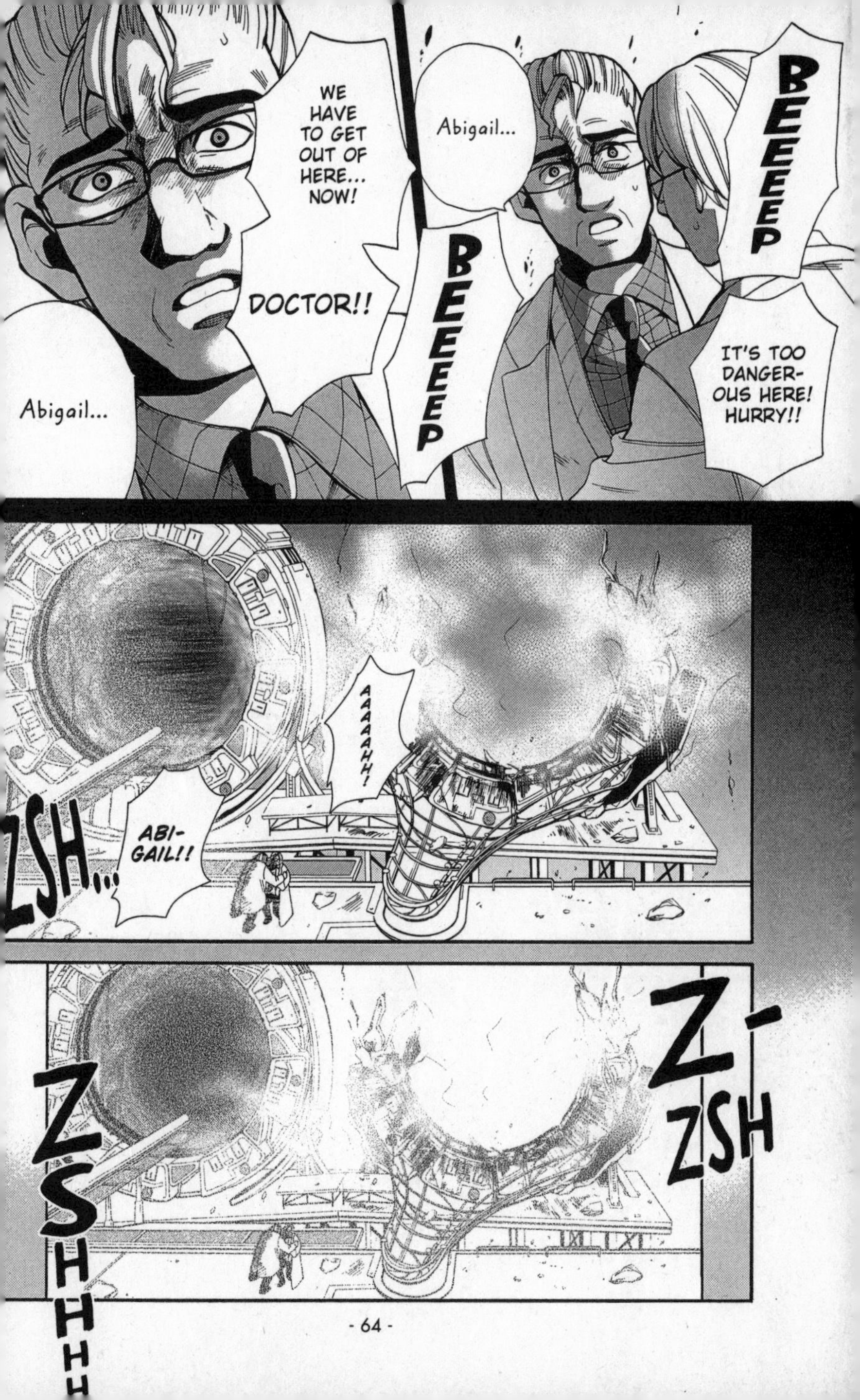
BEEEEP
Abigail...
BEEEEP
IT'S TOO DANGER-OUS HERE! HURRY!!
WE HAVE TO GET OUT OF HERE... NOW!
DOCTOR!!
Abigail...
AAAAAAHH!
ABI-GAIL!!
ZSH...
Z-ZSH
ZSHHHHH

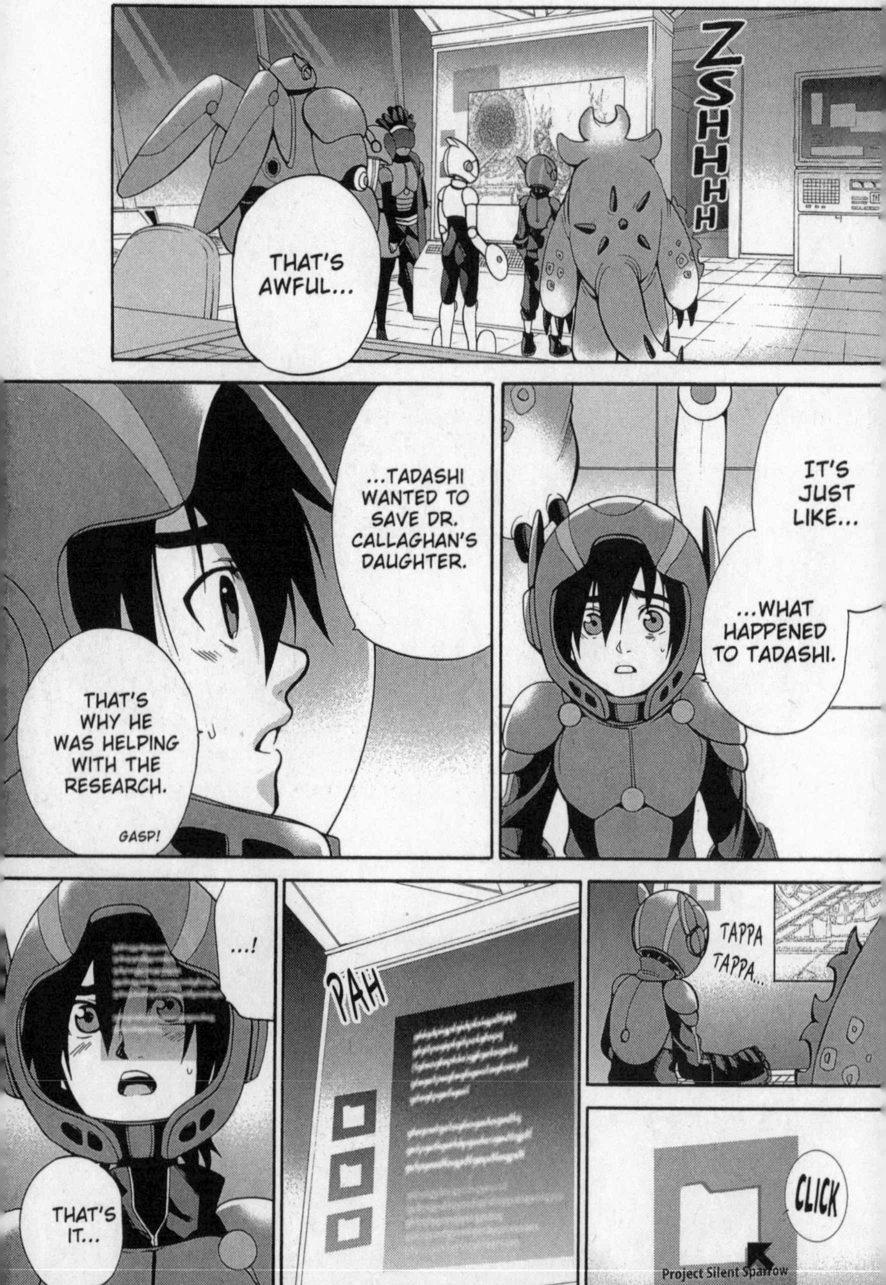
ZSHHHH
THAT'S AWFUL...
IT'S JUST LIKE...
...WHAT HAPPENED TO TADASHI.
...TADASHI WANTED TO SAVE DR. CALLAGHAN'S DAUGHTER.
THAT'S WHY HE WAS HELPING WITH THE RESEARCH.
GASP!
TAPPA TAPPA...
CLICK
Project Silent Sparrow programming
PAH
...!
THAT'S IT...

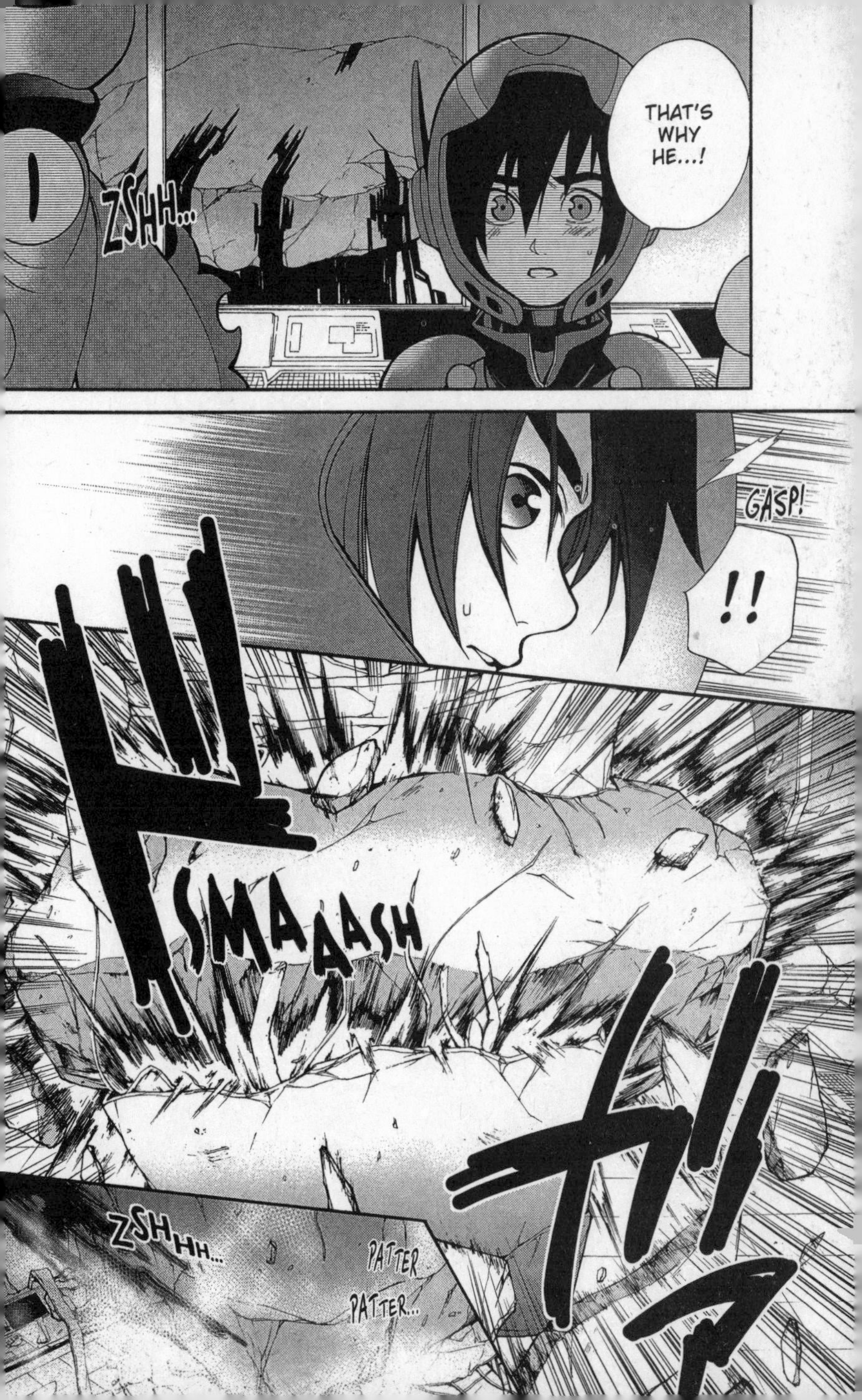
THAT'S WHY HE...!
ZSHH...
GASP!
!!
SMAAASH
PATTER PATTER...
ZSHHH...

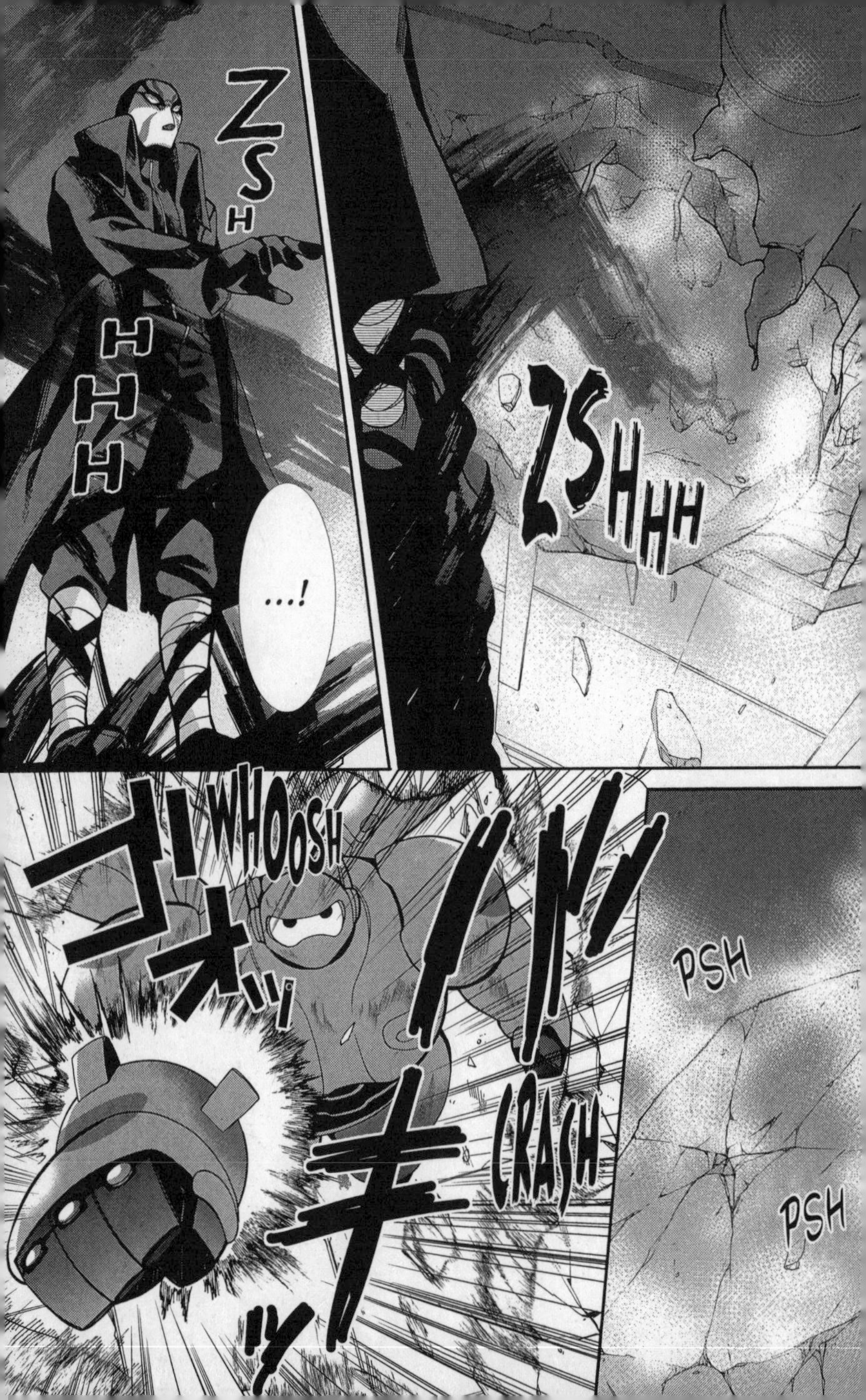
ZSHHH
ZSH
HHHH
...!
PSH
PSH
WHOOSH
CRASH

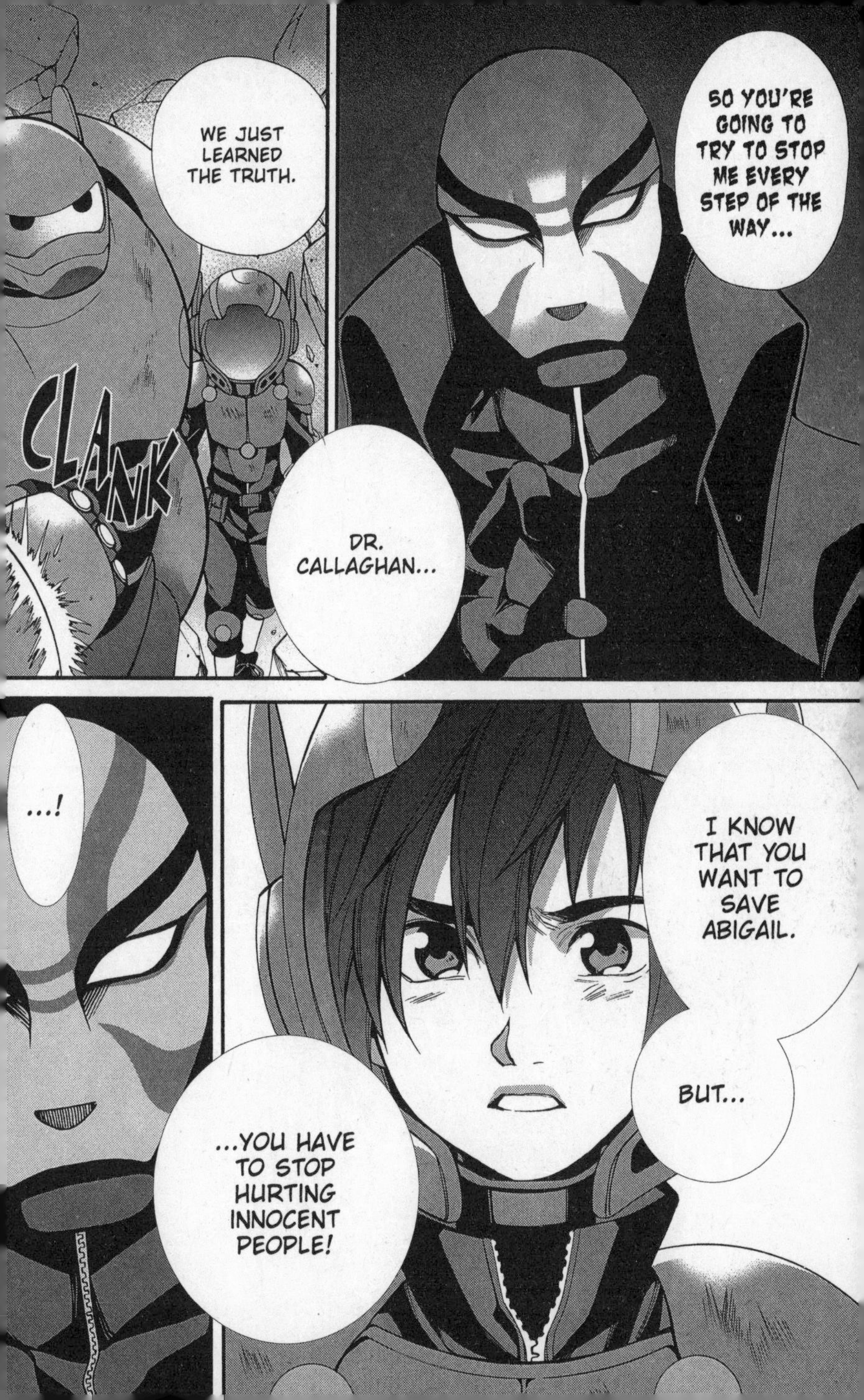
SO YOU'RE GOING TO TRY TO STOP ME EVERY STEP OF THE WAY...
DR. CALLAGHAN...
WE JUST LEARNED THE TRUTH.
CLANK
I KNOW THAT YOU WANT TO SAVE ABIGAIL.
BUT...
...YOU HAVE TO STOP HURTING INNOCENT PEOPLE!
...!

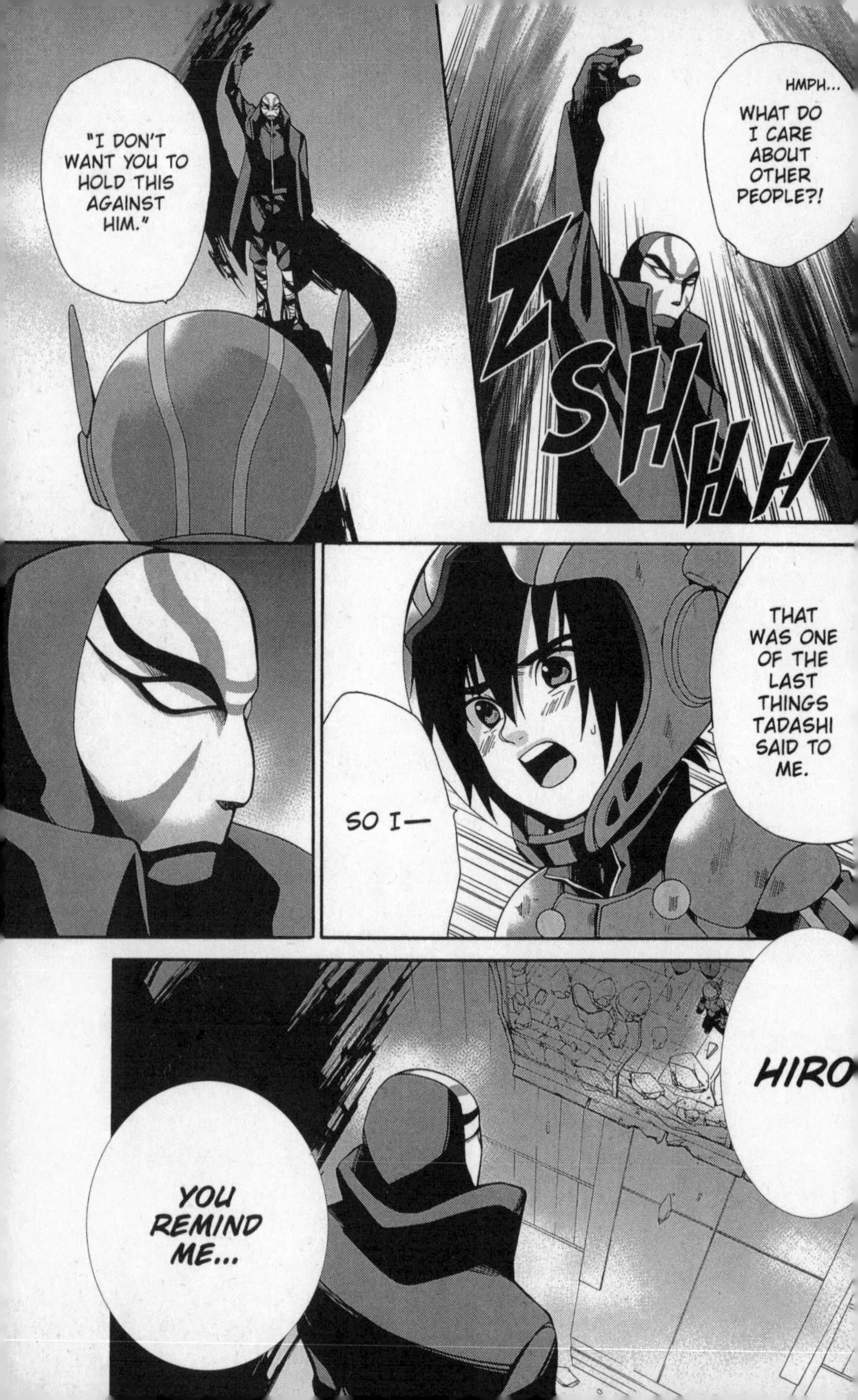

HMPH... WHAT DO I CARE ABOUT OTHER PEOPLE?!
ZSHHHH
"I DON'T WANT YOU TO HOLD THIS AGAINST HIM."
THAT WAS ONE OF THE LAST THINGS TADASHI SAID TO ME.
SO I—
HIRO
YOU REMIND ME...

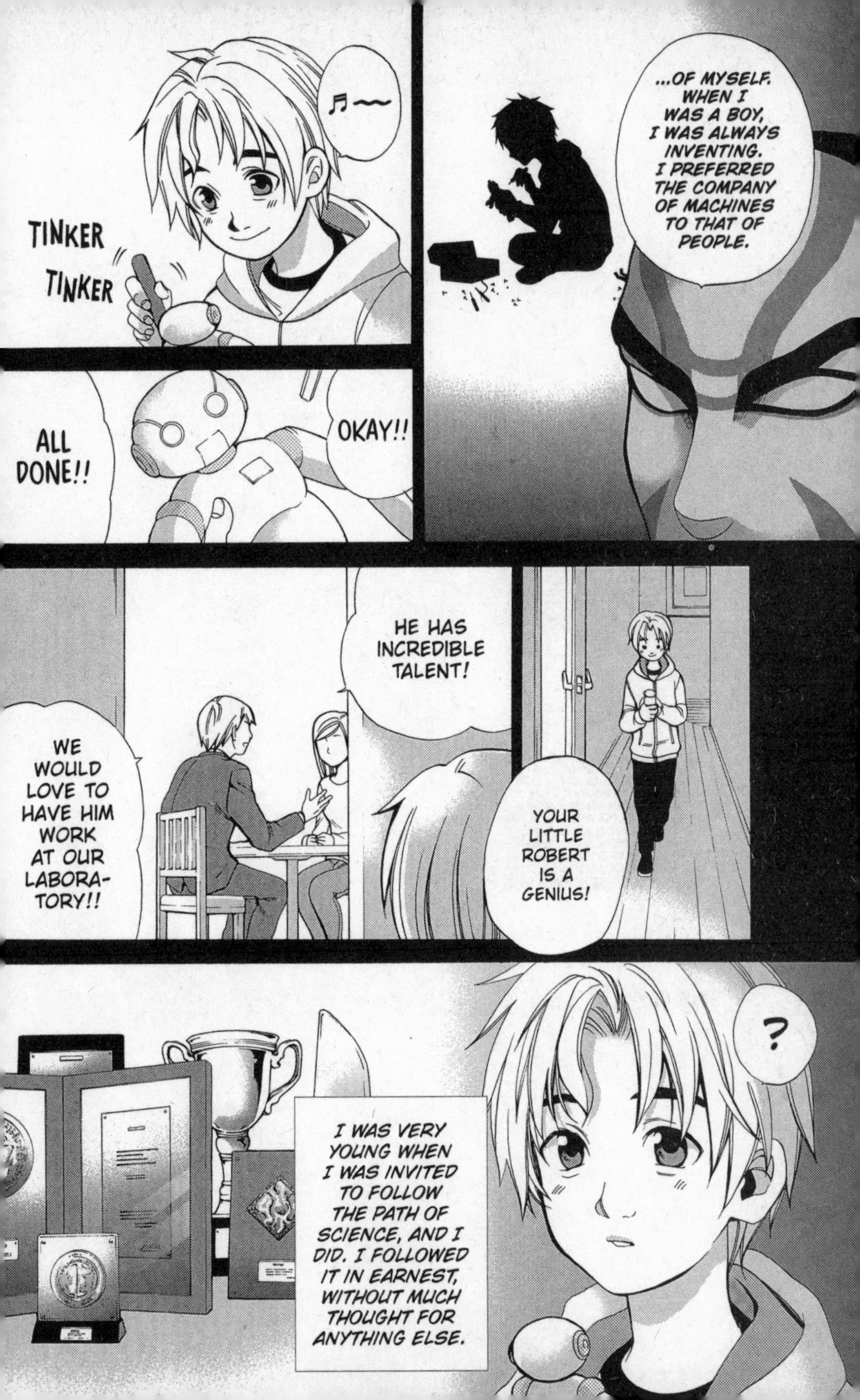
...OF MYSELF. WHEN I WAS A BOY, I WAS ALWAYS INVENTING. I PREFERRED THE COMPANY OF MACHINES TO THAT OF PEOPLE.
♪~~
TINKER TINKER
OKAY!!
ALL DONE!!
YOUR LITTLE ROBERT IS A GENIUS!
HE HAS INCREDIBLE TALENT!
WE WOULD LOVE TO HAVE HIM WORK AT OUR LABORATORY!!
?
I WAS VERY YOUNG WHEN I WAS INVITED TO FOLLOW THE PATH OF SCIENCE, AND I DID. I FOLLOWED IT IN EARNEST, WITHOUT MUCH THOUGHT FOR ANYTHING ELSE.

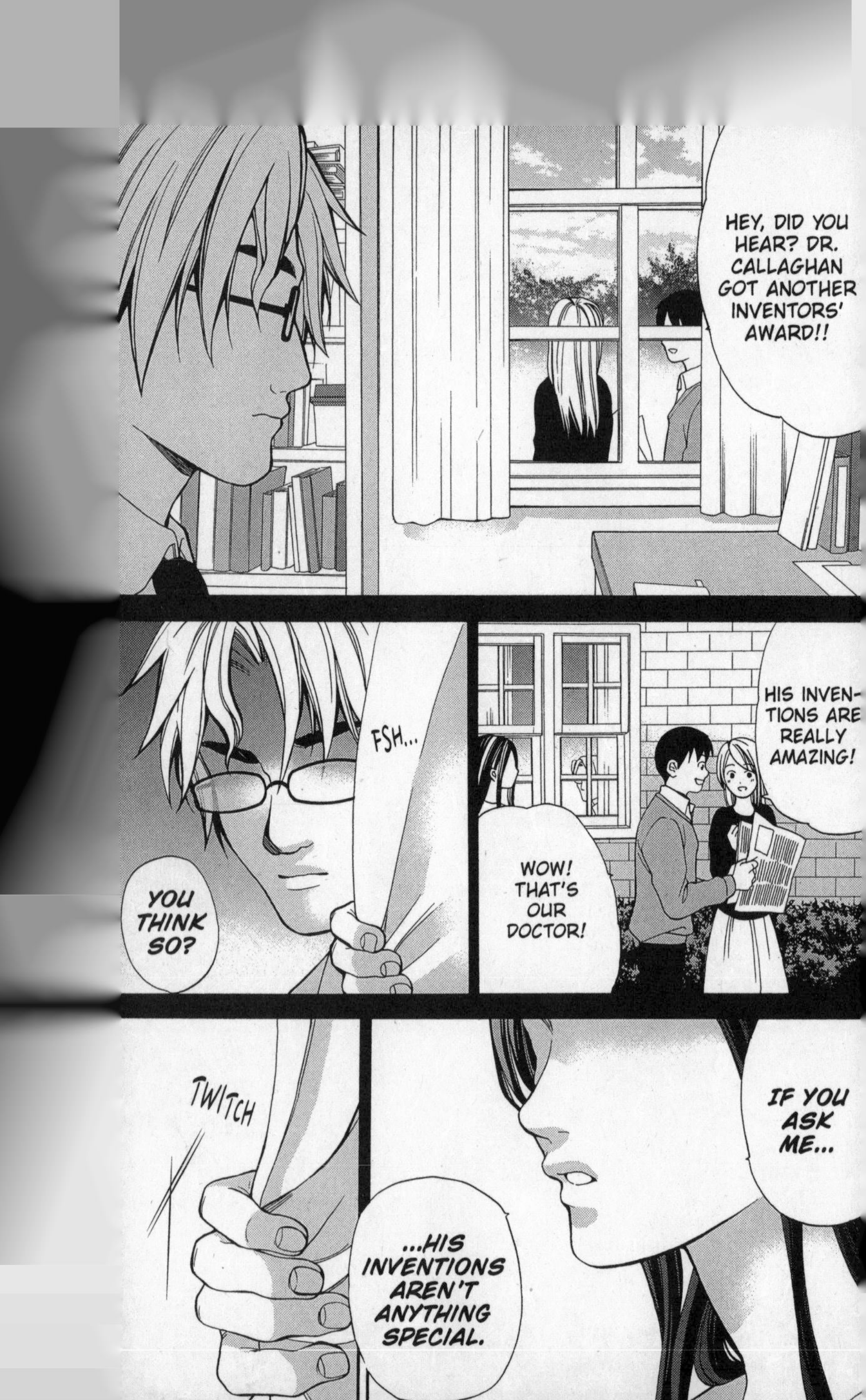
HEY, DID YOU HEAR? DR. CALLAGHAN GOT ANOTHER INVENTORS' AWARD!!
HIS INVEN-TIONS ARE REALLY AMAZING!
WOW! THAT'S OUR DOCTOR!
FSH...
YOU THINK SO?
IF YOU ASK ME...
...HIS INVENTIONS AREN'T ANYTHING SPECIAL.
TWITCH

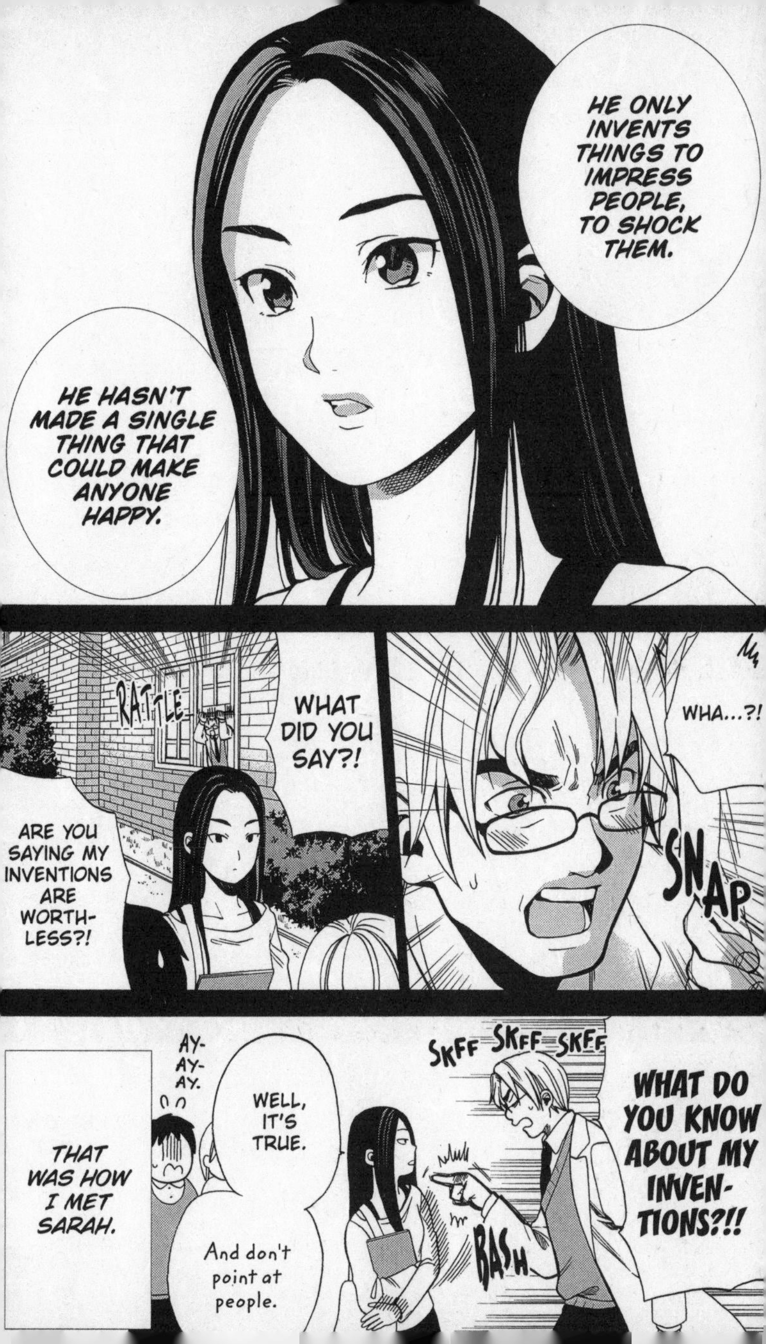
HE ONLY INVENTS THINGS TO IMPRESS PEOPLE, TO SHOCK THEM.
HE HASN'T MADE A SINGLE THING THAT COULD MAKE ANYONE HAPPY.
WHA...?!
SNAP
RATTLE
WHAT DID YOU SAY?!
ARE YOU SAYING MY INVENTIONS ARE WORTHLESS?!
WHAT DO YOU KNOW ABOUT MY INVEN-TIONS?!!
SKFF SKFF SKFF
BASH
WELL, IT'S TRUE.
And don't point at people.
AY-AY-AY.
THAT WAS HOW I MET SARAH.

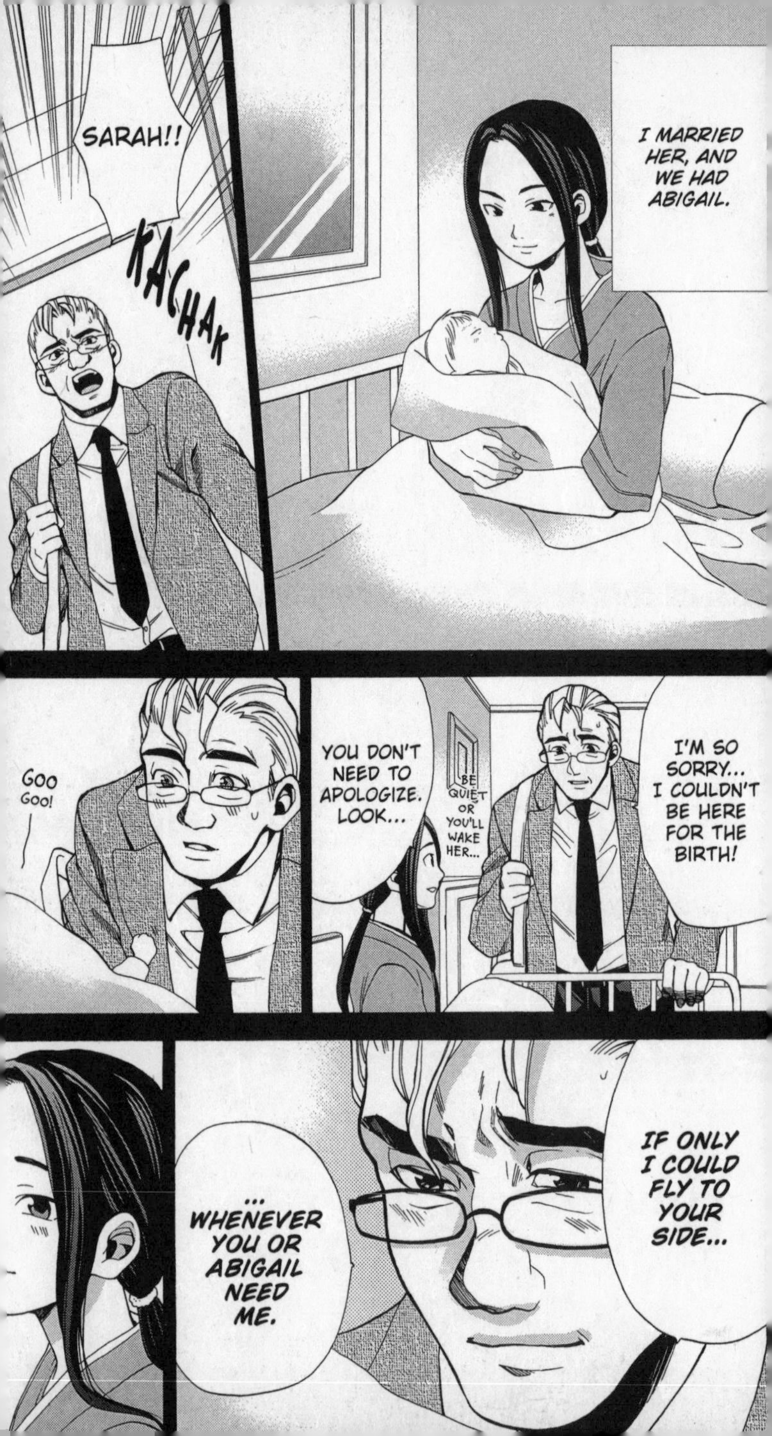
I MARRIED HER, AND WE HAD ABIGAIL.
SARAH!!
KACHAK
I'M SO SORRY... I COULDN'T BE HERE FOR THE BIRTH!
BE QUIET OR YOU'LL WAKE HER...
YOU DON'T NEED TO APOLOGIZE. LOOK...
GOO GOO!
IF ONLY I COULD FLY TO YOUR SIDE...
...WHENEVER YOU OR ABIGAIL NEED ME.

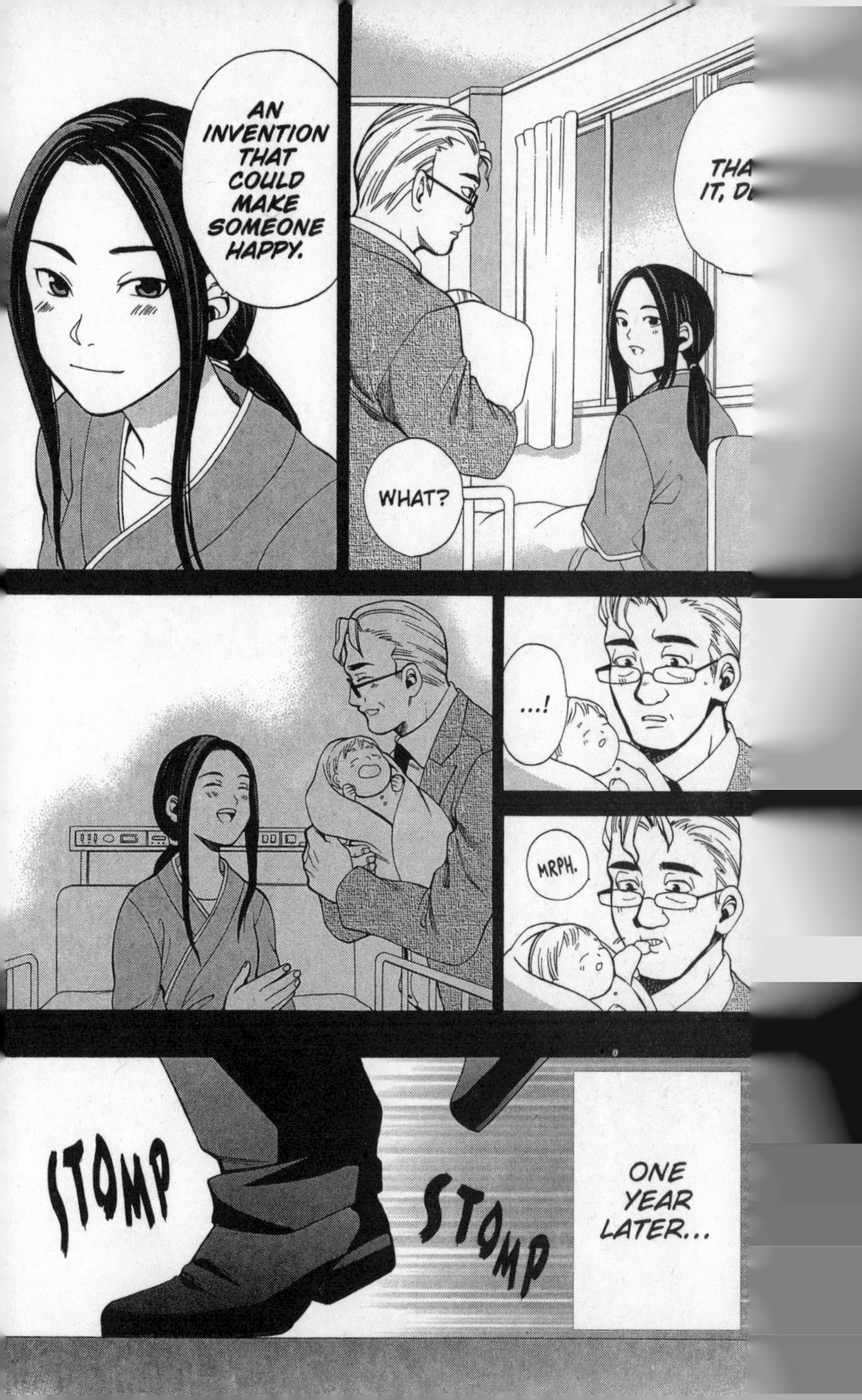
THA IT, D
WHAT?
AN INVENTION THAT COULD MAKE SOMEONE HAPPY.
...!
MRPH.
ONE YEAR LATER...
STOMP
STOMP

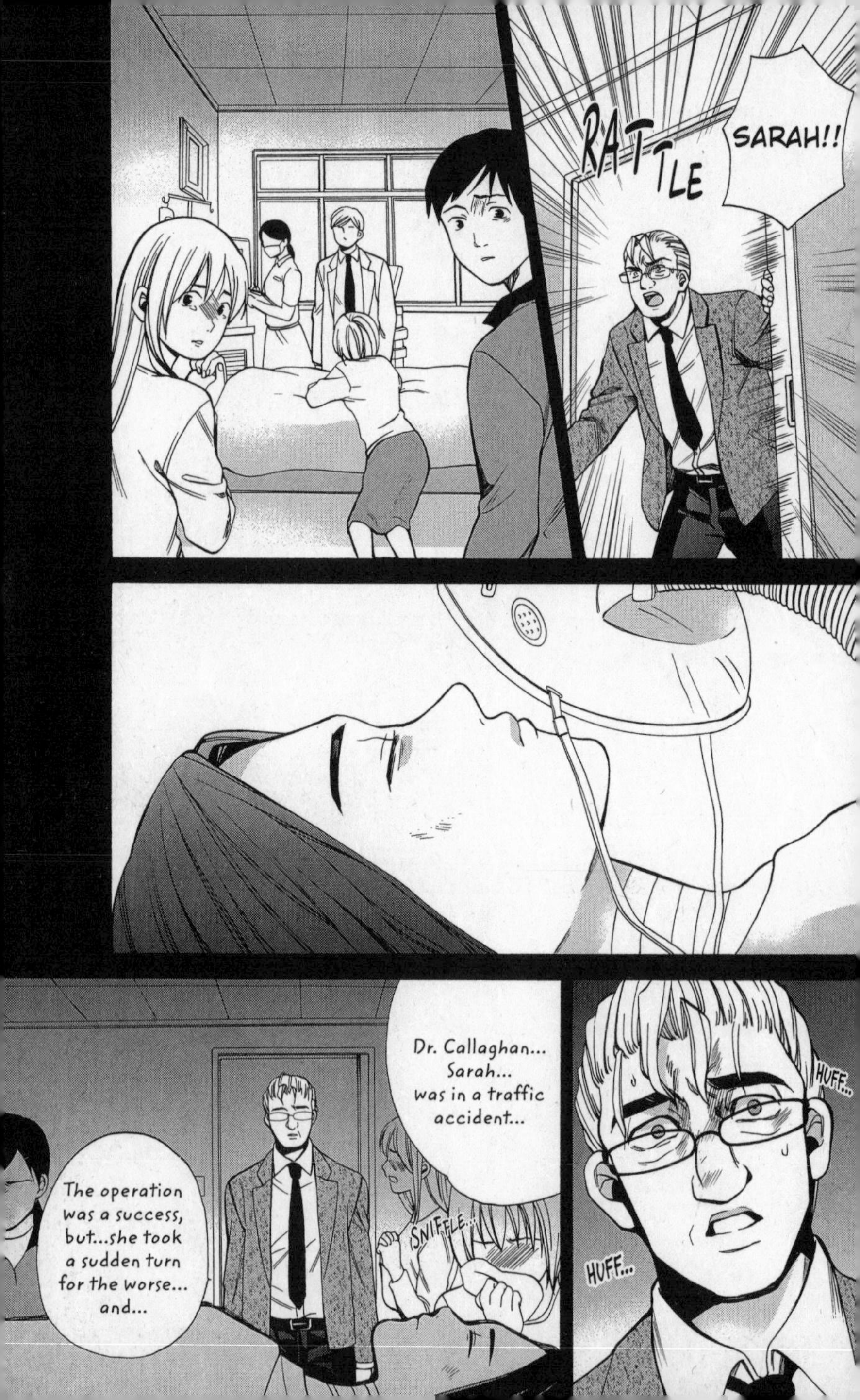
RATTLE
SARAH!!
HUFF...
HUFF...
Dr. Callaghan... Sarah... was in a traffic accident...
The operation was a success, but...she took a sudden turn for the worse... and...
SNIFFLE...

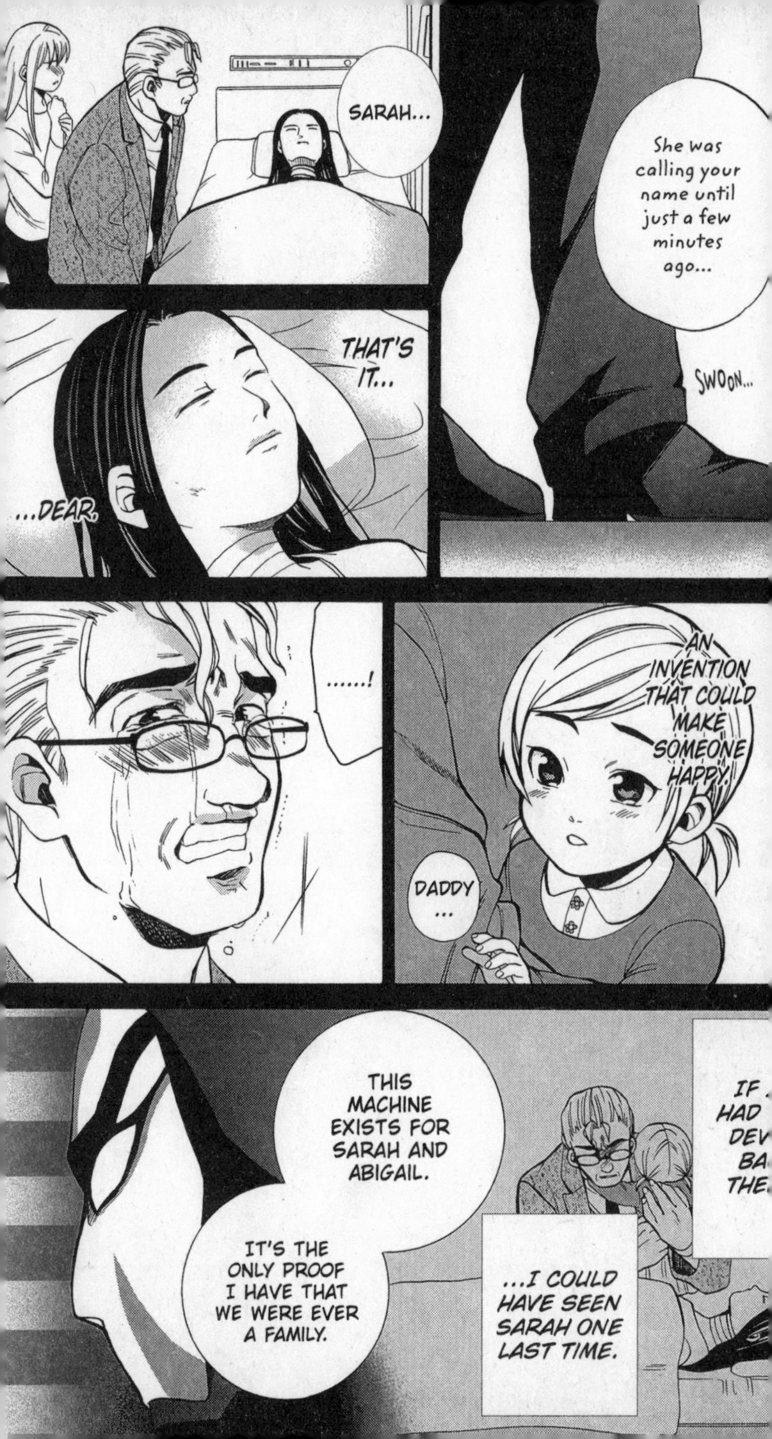
She was calling your name until just a few minutes ago...
SWOON...
SARAH...
THAT'S IT...
...DEAR.
AN INVENTION THAT COULD MAKE SOMEONE HAPPY.
DADDY...
......!
IF HAD
...I COULD HAVE SEEN SARAH ONE LAST TIME.
THIS MACHINE EXISTS FOR SARAH AND ABIGAIL.
IT'S THE ONLY PROOF I HAVE THAT WE WERE EVER A FAMILY.

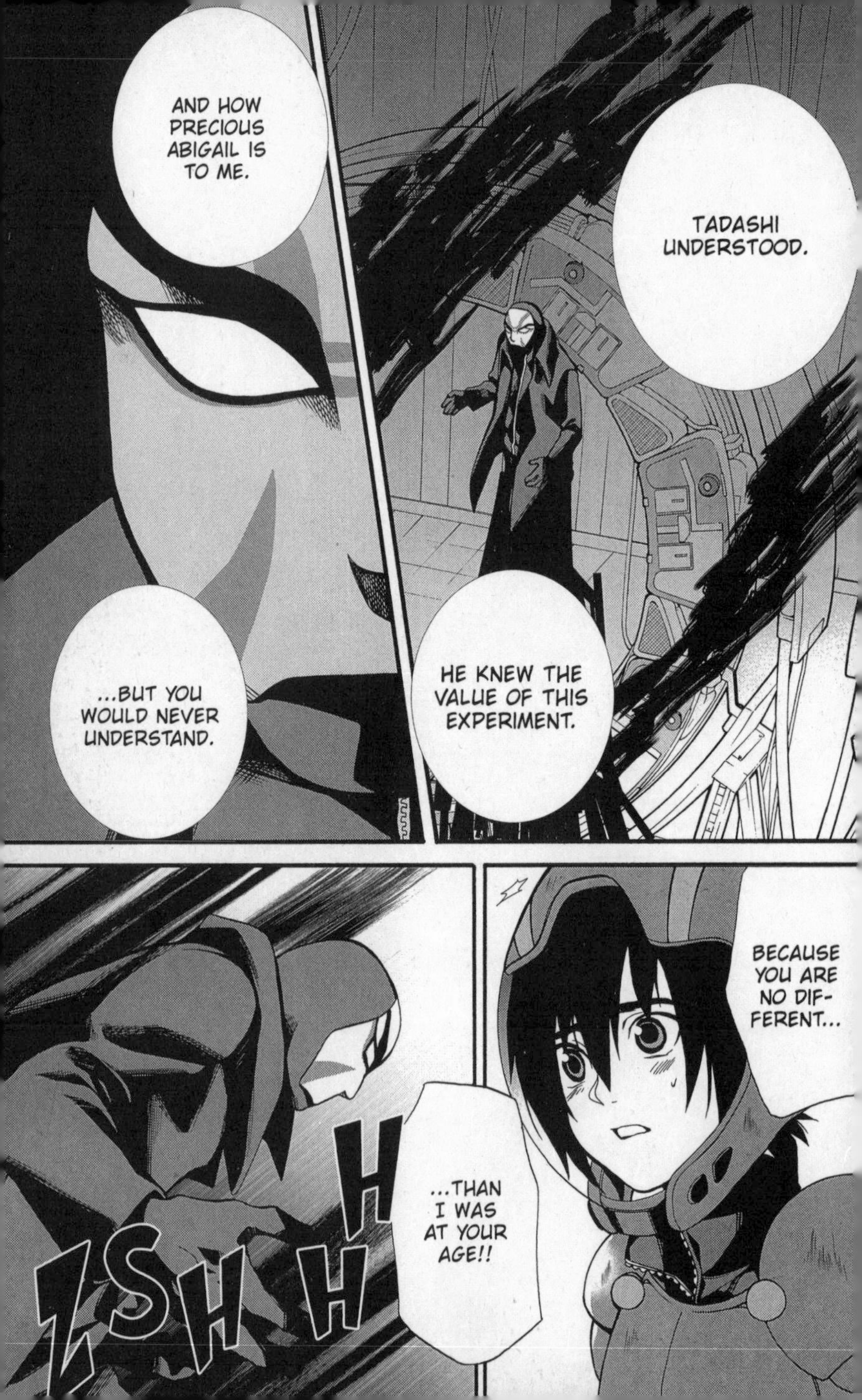
TADASHI UNDERSTOOD.
HE KNEW THE VALUE OF THIS EXPERIMENT.
AND HOW PRECIOUS ABIGAIL IS TO ME.
...BUT YOU WOULD NEVER UNDERSTAND.
BECAUSE YOU ARE NO DIF- FERENT...
...THAN I WAS AT YOUR AGE!!
ZSHHH

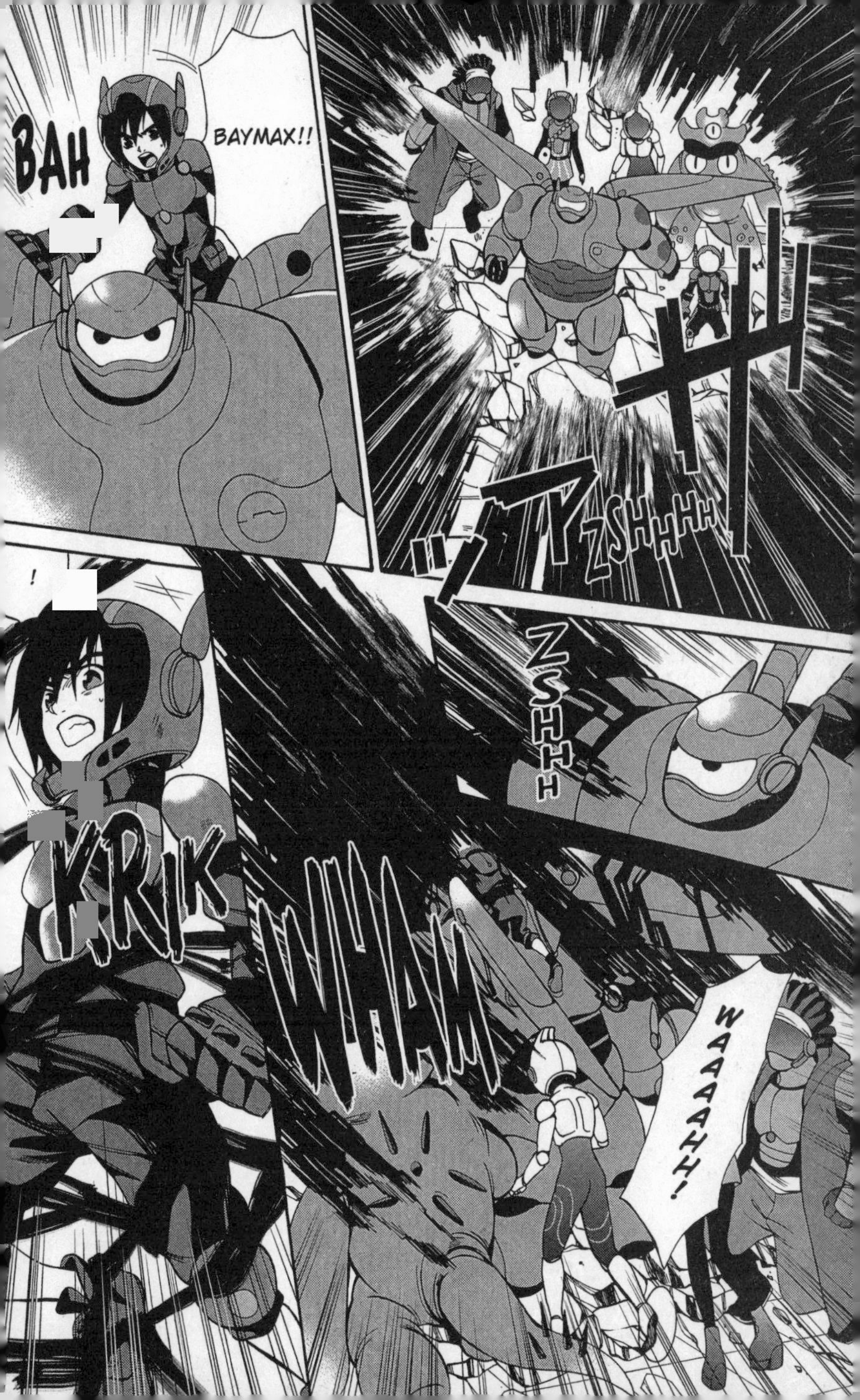
ZSHHHHH
BAYMAX!!
BAH
ZSHHHH
WAAAAAHH!
!
KRIK
WHAM

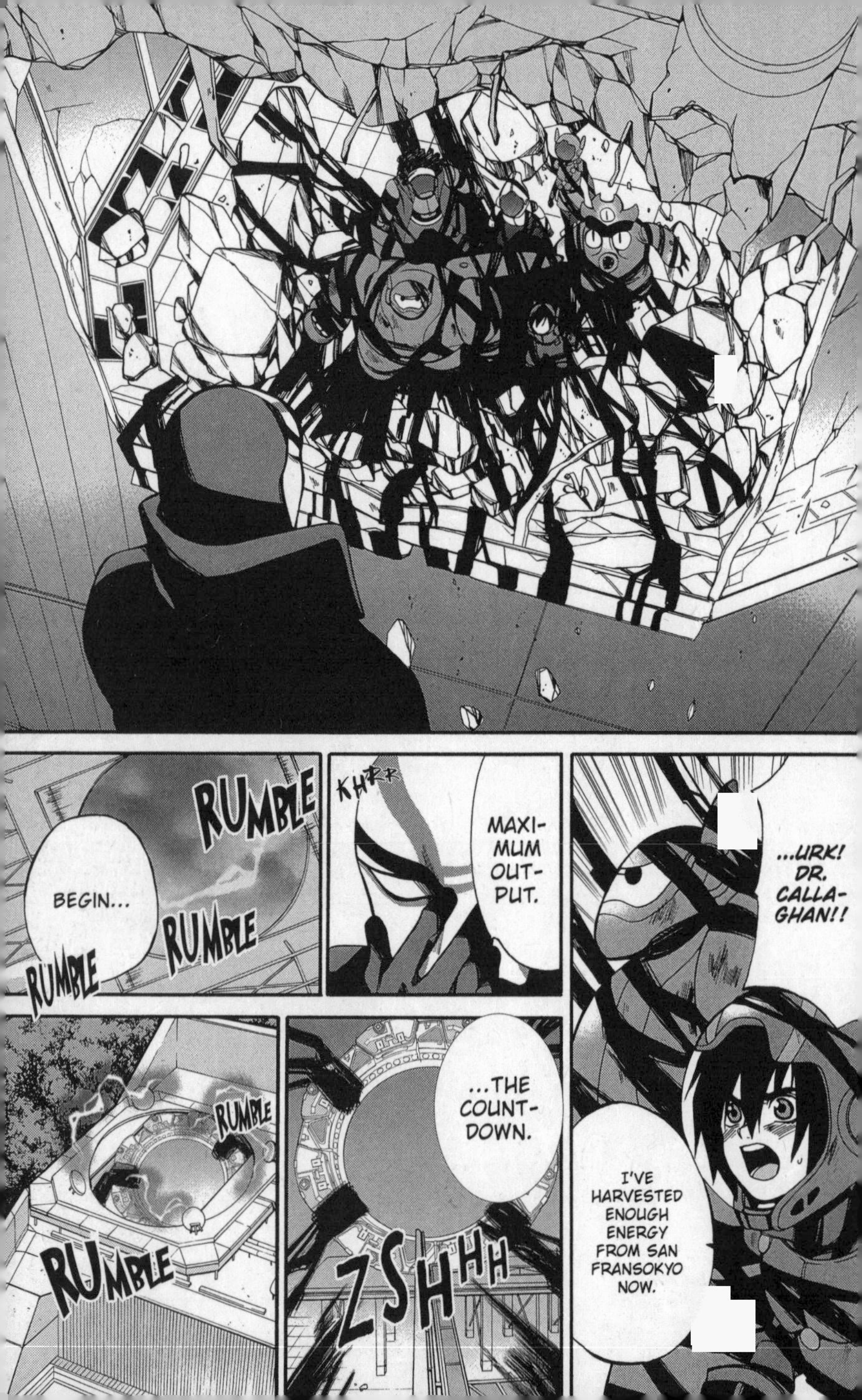
...URK! DR. CALLAGHAN!!
I'VE HARVESTED ENOUGH ENERGY FROM SAN FRANSOKYO NOW.
KHRR
MAXIMUM OUTPUT.
RUMBLE
BEGIN...
RUMBLE
RUMBLE
...THE COUNTDOWN.
ZSHHH
RUMBLE
RUMBLE

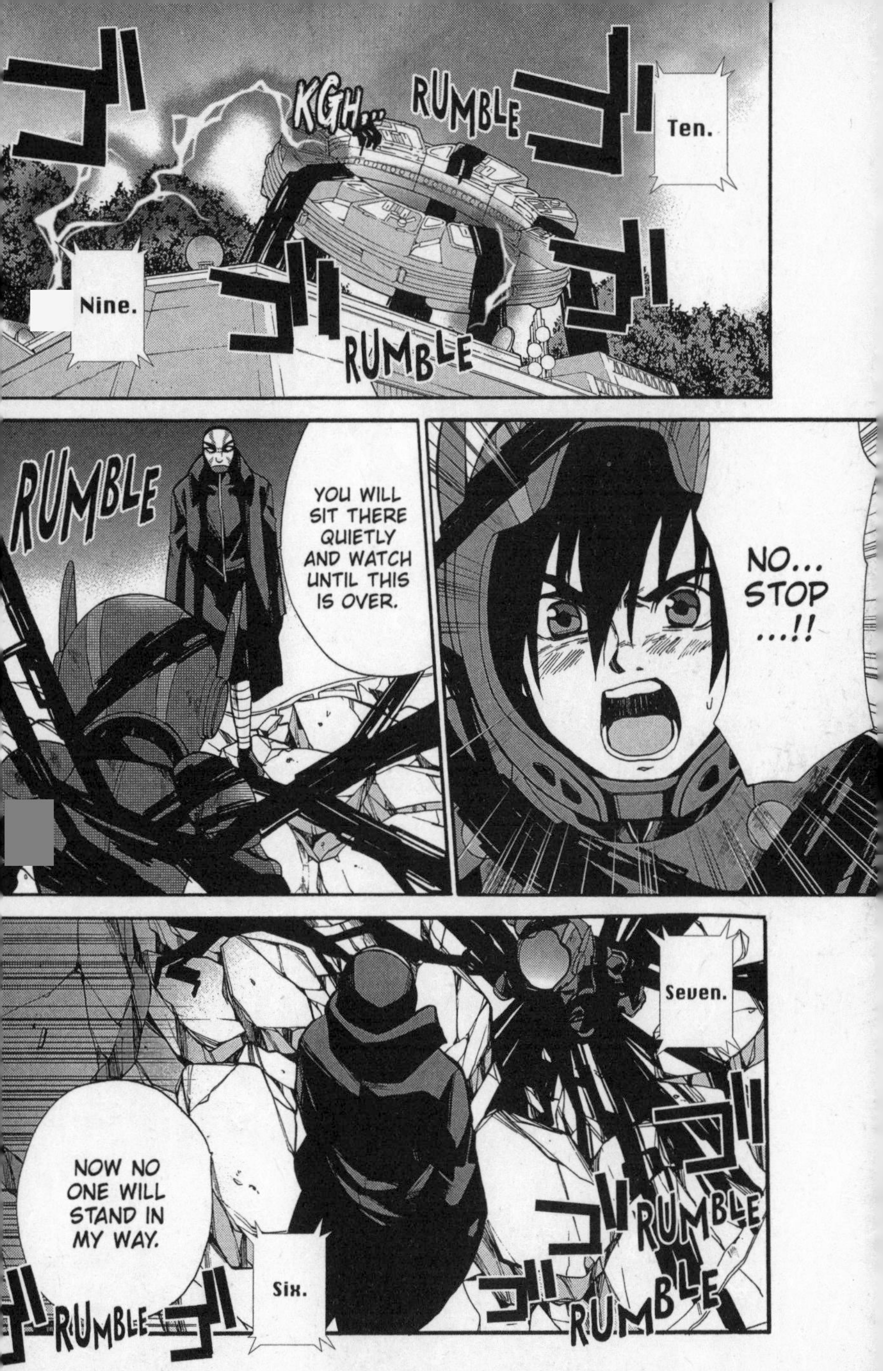
Ten.
RUMBLE
KGH...
Nine.
RUMBLE
NO... STOP ...!!
YOU WILL SIT THERE QUIETLY AND WATCH UNTIL THIS IS OVER.
RUMBLE
Seven.
RUMBLE
RUMBLE
NOW NO ONE WILL STAND IN MY WAY.
Six.
RUMBLE

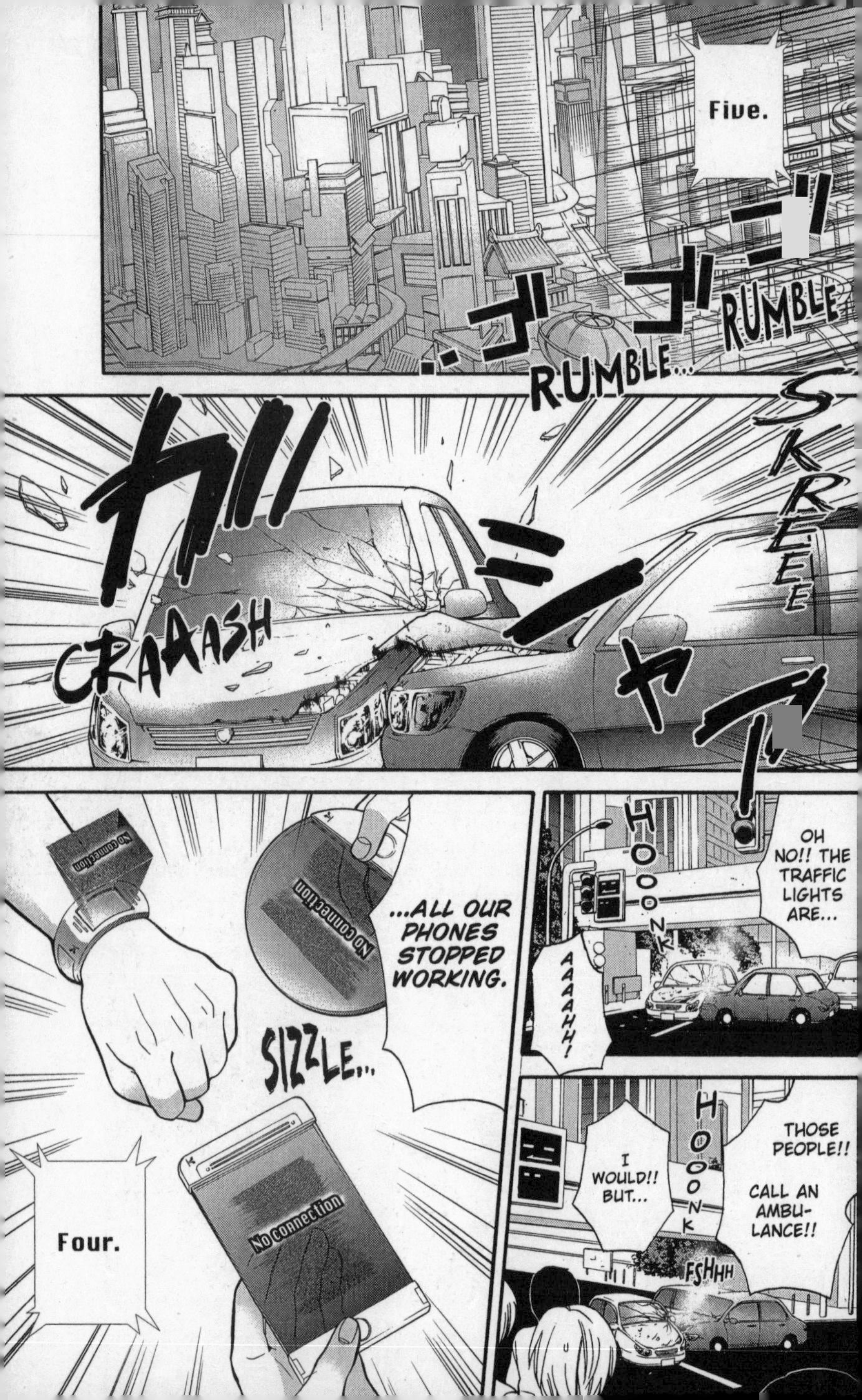
Five.
RUMBLE
RUMBLE...
SKREEE
CRAAASH
OH NO!! THE TRAFFIC LIGHTS ARE...
HOOONK
AAAAAHH!
THOSE PEOPLE!!
CALL AN AMBULANCE!!
HOOONK
I WOULD!! BUT...
FSHHH
...ALL OUR PHONES STOPPED WORKING.
No connection
No connection
SIZZLE...
No connection
Four.

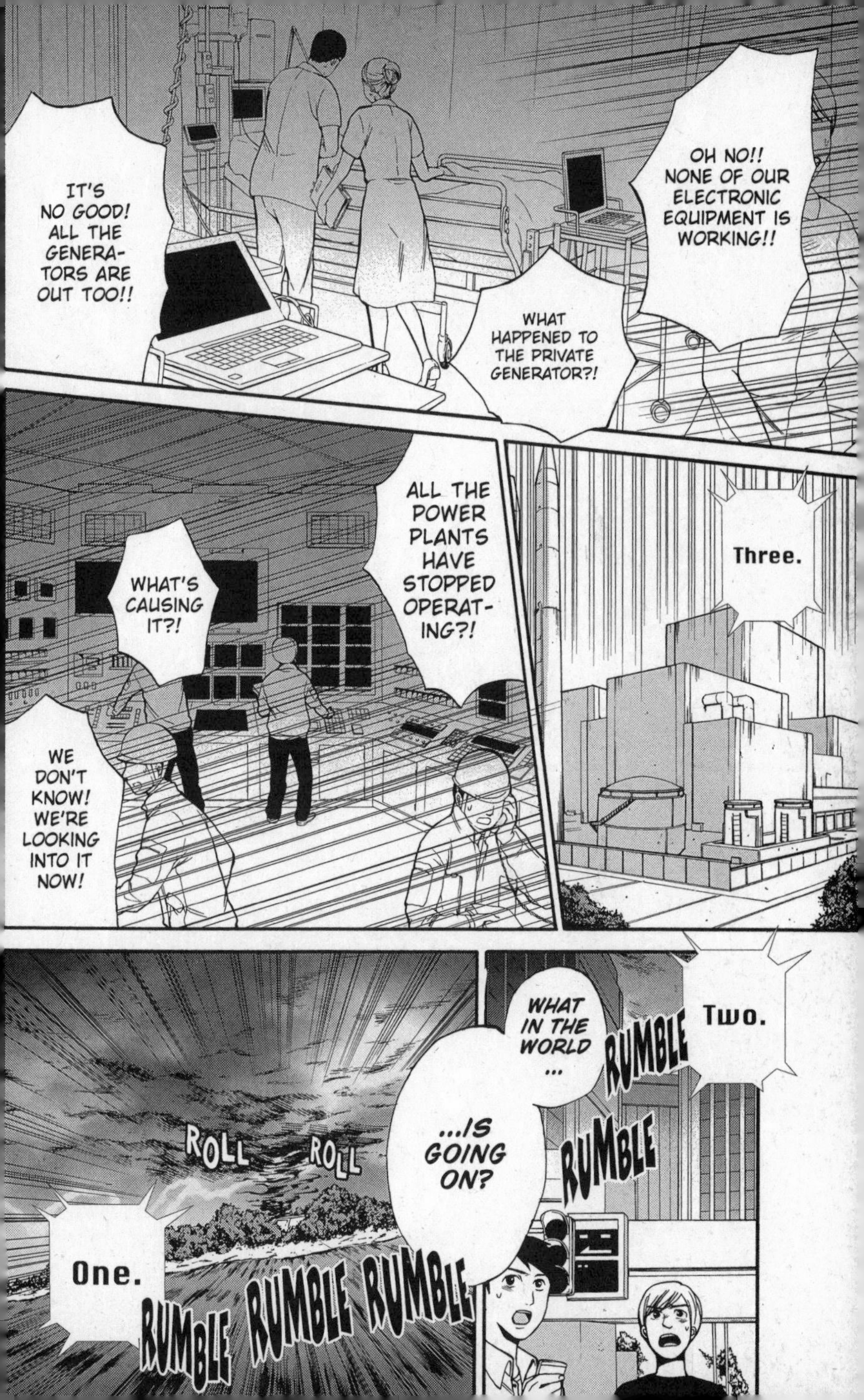
OH NO!! NONE OF OUR ELECTRONIC EQUIPMENT IS WORKING!!
WHAT HAPPENED TO THE PRIVATE GENERATOR?!
IT'S NO GOOD! ALL THE GENERATORS ARE OUT TOO!!
Three.
ALL THE POWER PLANTS HAVE STOPPED OPERATING?!
WHAT'S CAUSING IT?!
WE DON'T KNOW! WE'RE LOOKING INTO IT NOW!
Two.
RUMBLE
WHAT IN THE WORLD ...
RUMBLE
...IS GOING ON?
ROLL ROLL
One.
RUMBLE RUMBLE RUMBLE

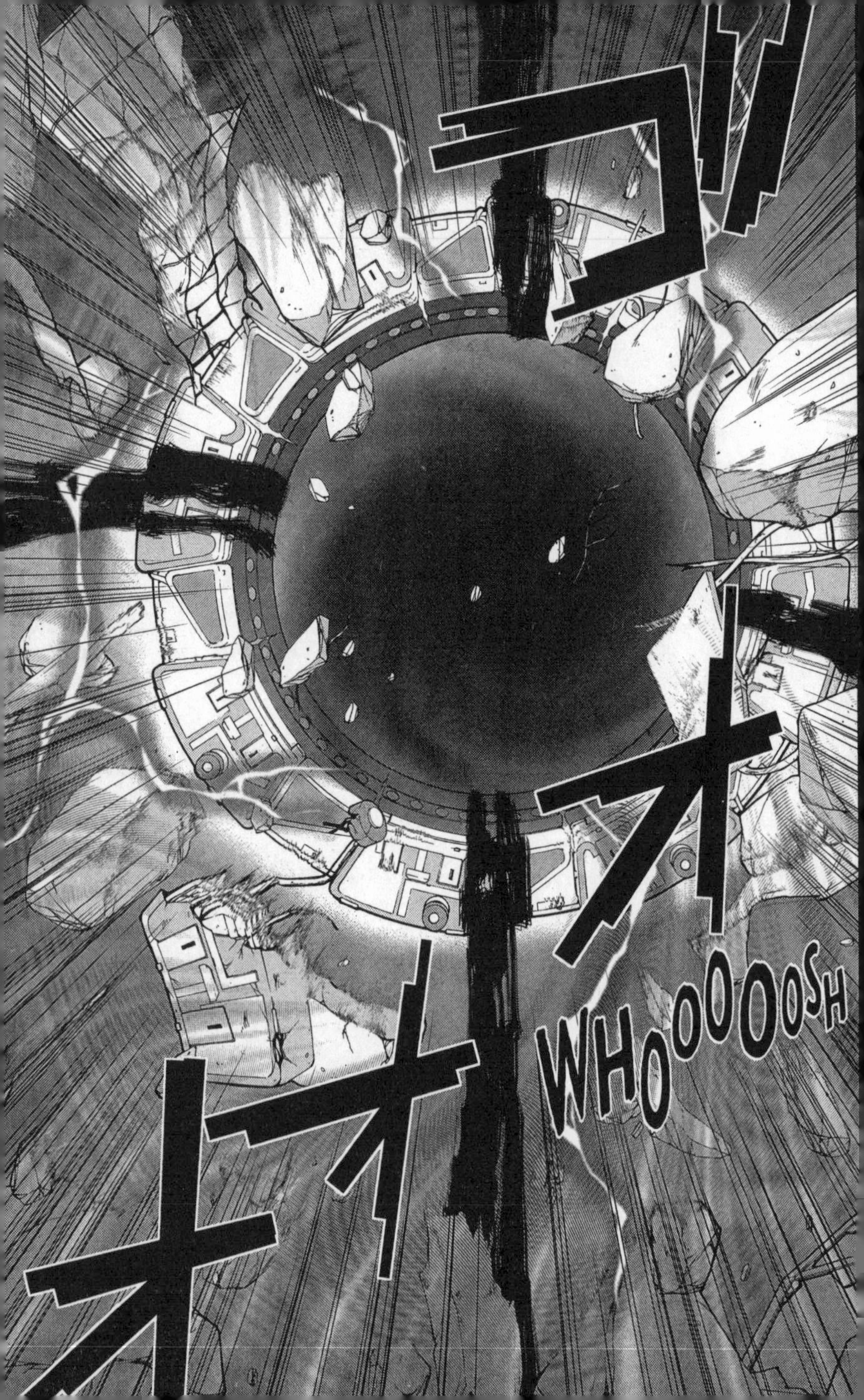
ゴオオ
WHOOOOOSH

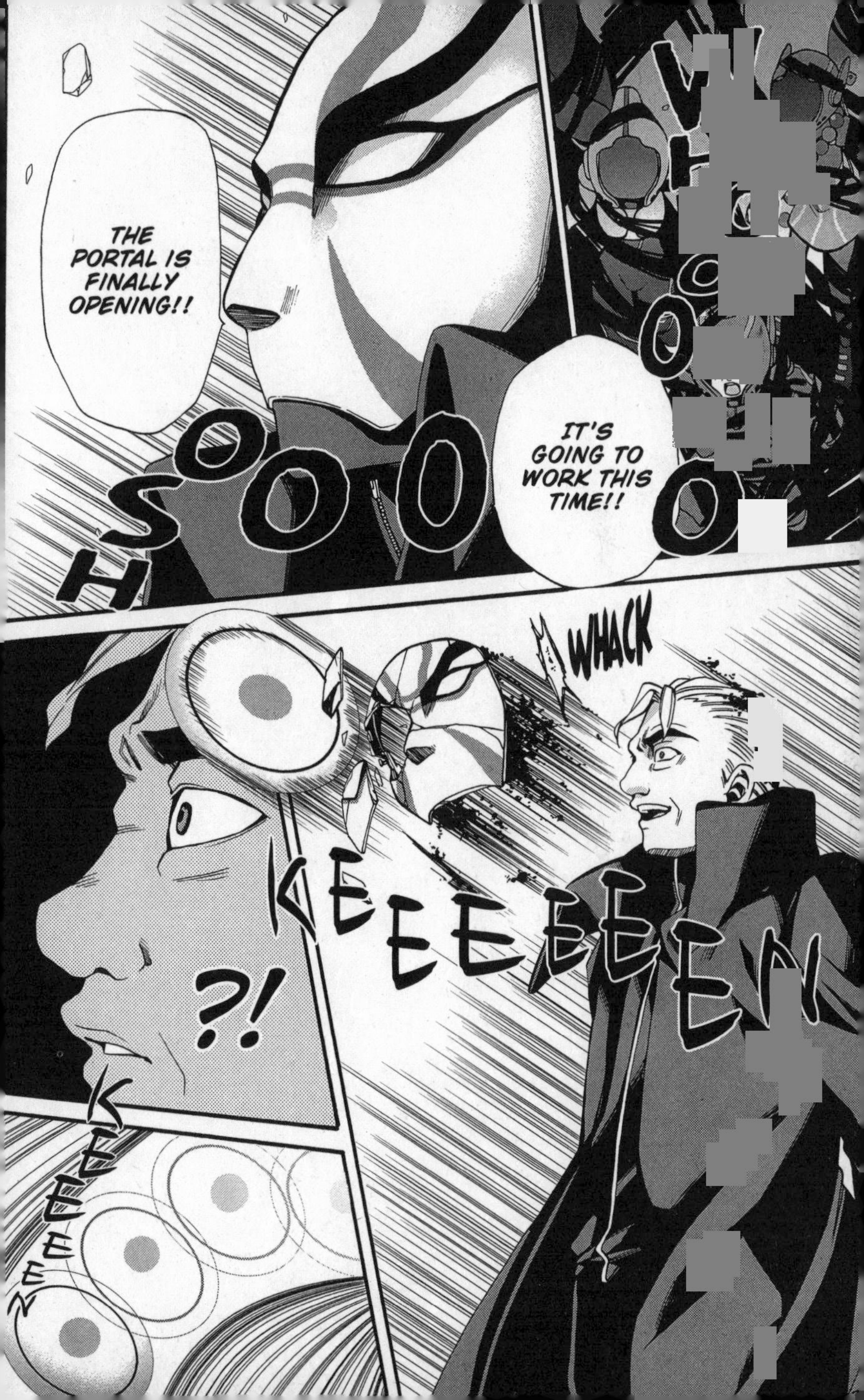

IT'S GOING TO WORK THIS TIME!!
THE PORTAL IS FINALLY OPENING!!
SHOOOOO
WHACK
KEEEEEEN
?!
KEEEEEN

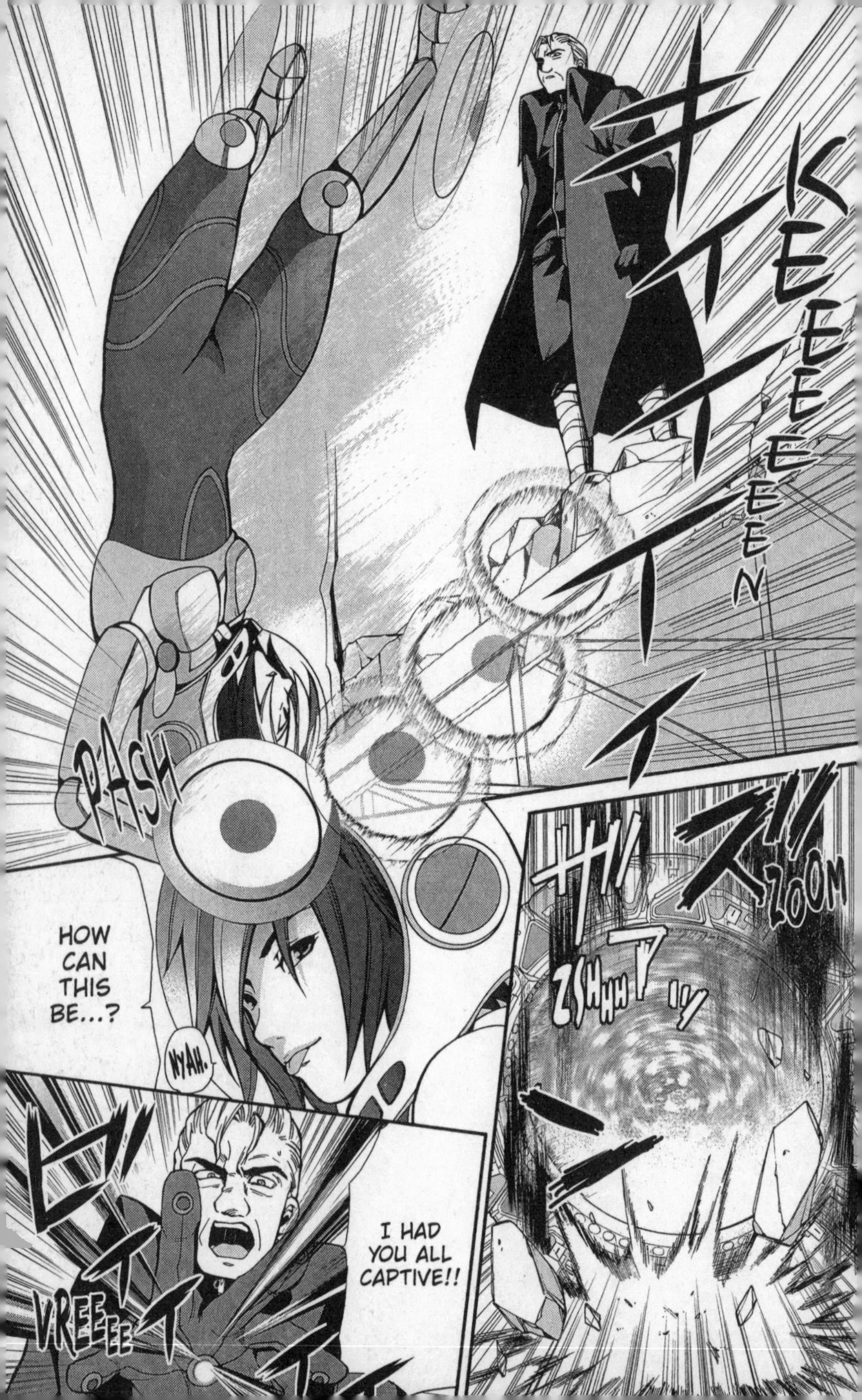
KEEEEEEEEN
PASH
ZOOM
ZSHHH
HOW CAN THIS BE...?
NYAH.
I HAD YOU ALL CAPTIVE!!
VREEEEE

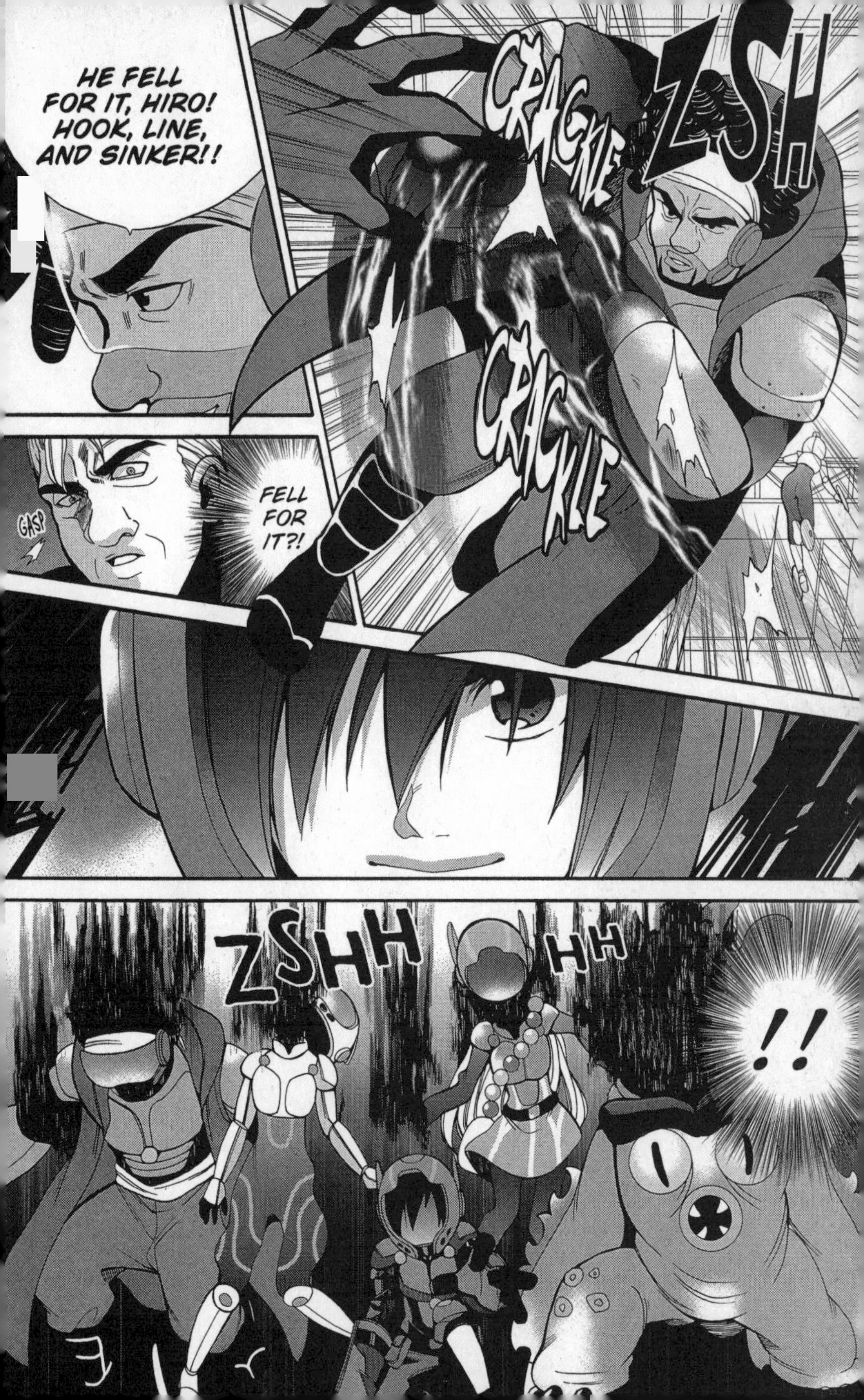
ZSH
CRACKLE
CRACKLE
HE FELL FOR IT, HIRO! HOOK, LINE, AND SINKER!!
FELL FOR IT?!
GASP
ZSHH HH
!!

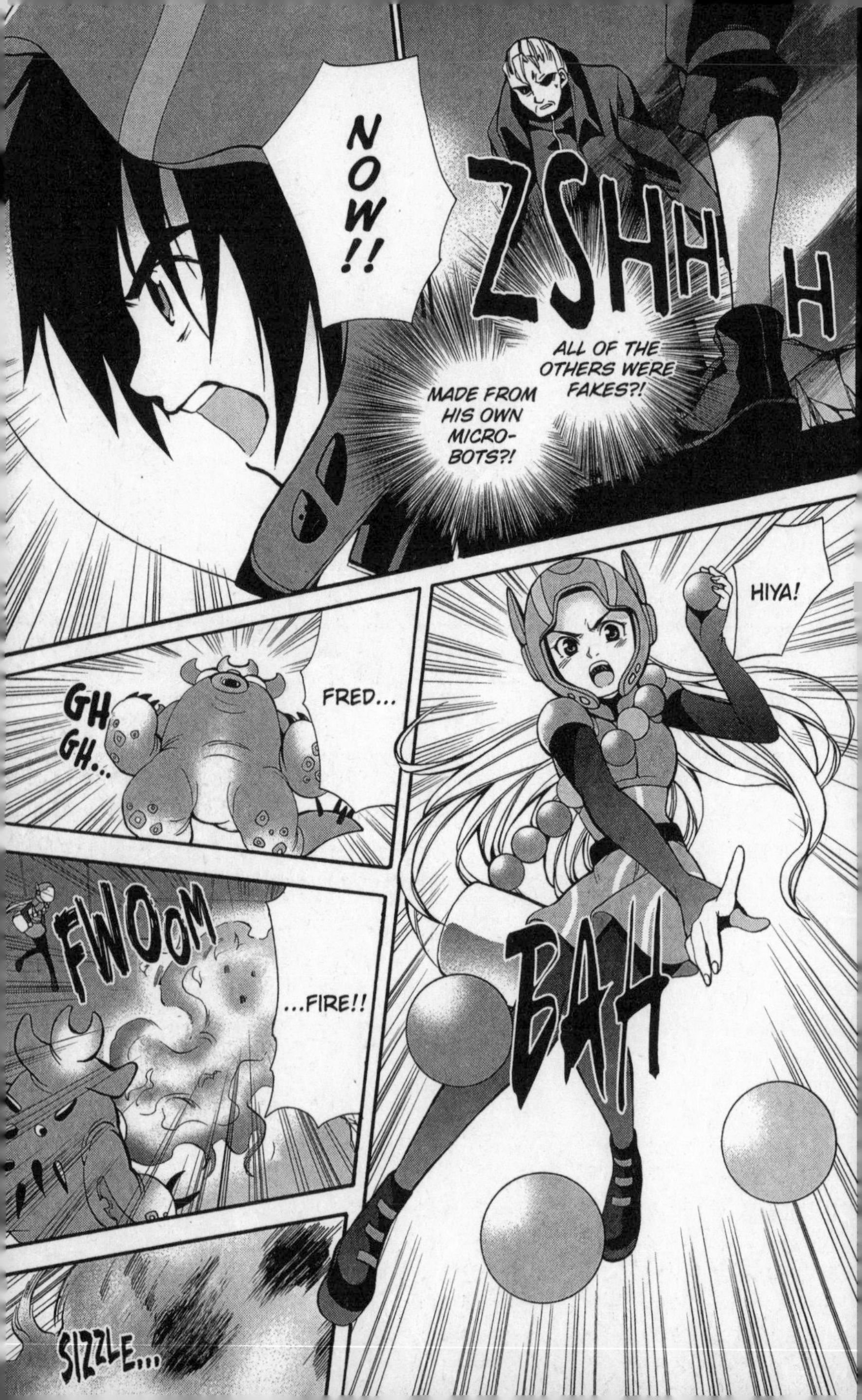
ZSHHH H
NOW!!
ALL OF THE OTHERS WERE FAKES?!
MADE FROM HIS OWN MICRO-BOTS?!
HIYA!
BAH
FRED...
GH GH...
...FIRE!!
FWOOM
SIZZLE...

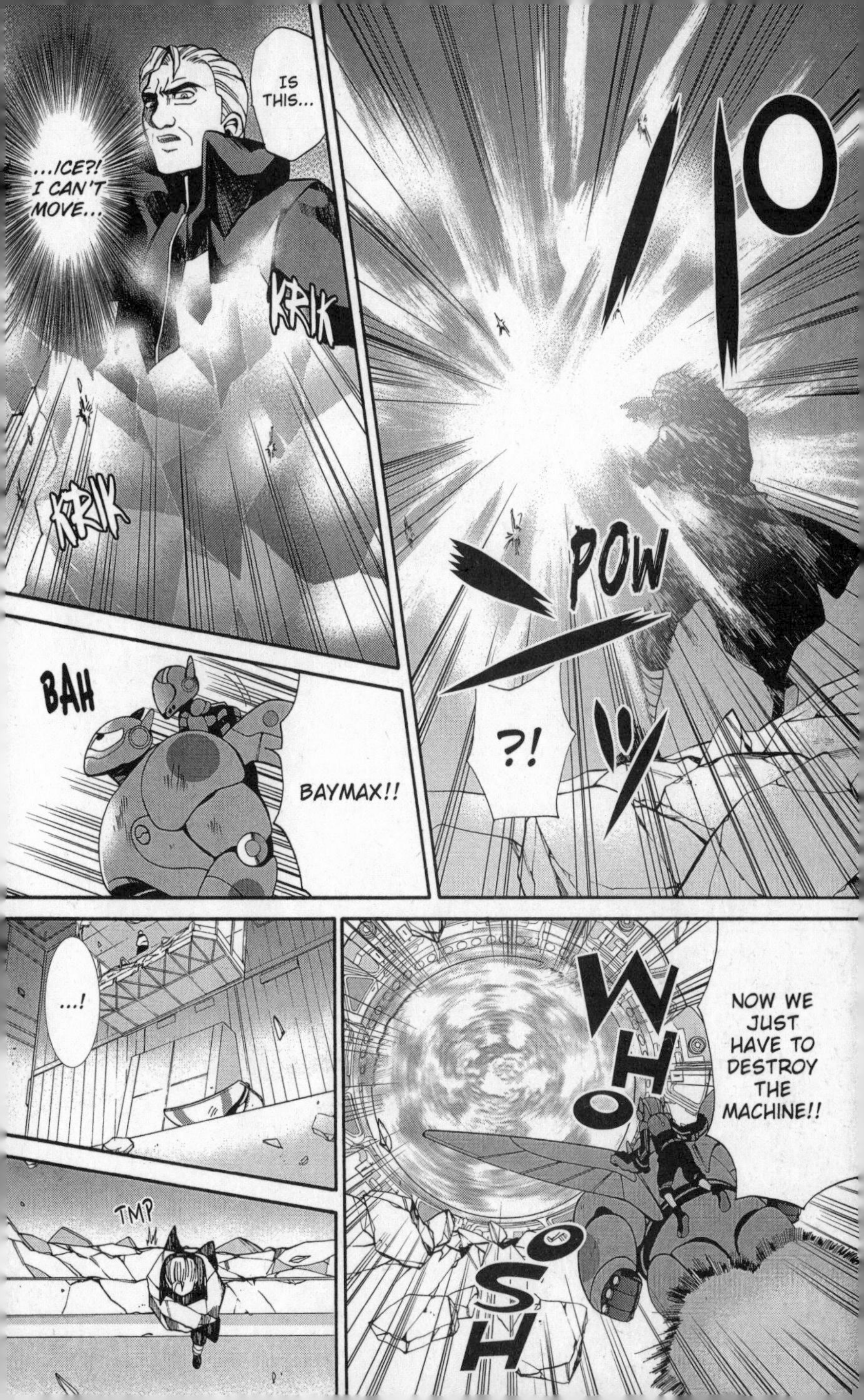
POW
?!
IS THIS...
...ICE?! I CAN'T MOVE...
KRIK
KRIK
BAH
BAYMAX!!
WHOOSH
NOW WE JUST HAVE TO DESTROY THE MACHINE!!
...!
TMP

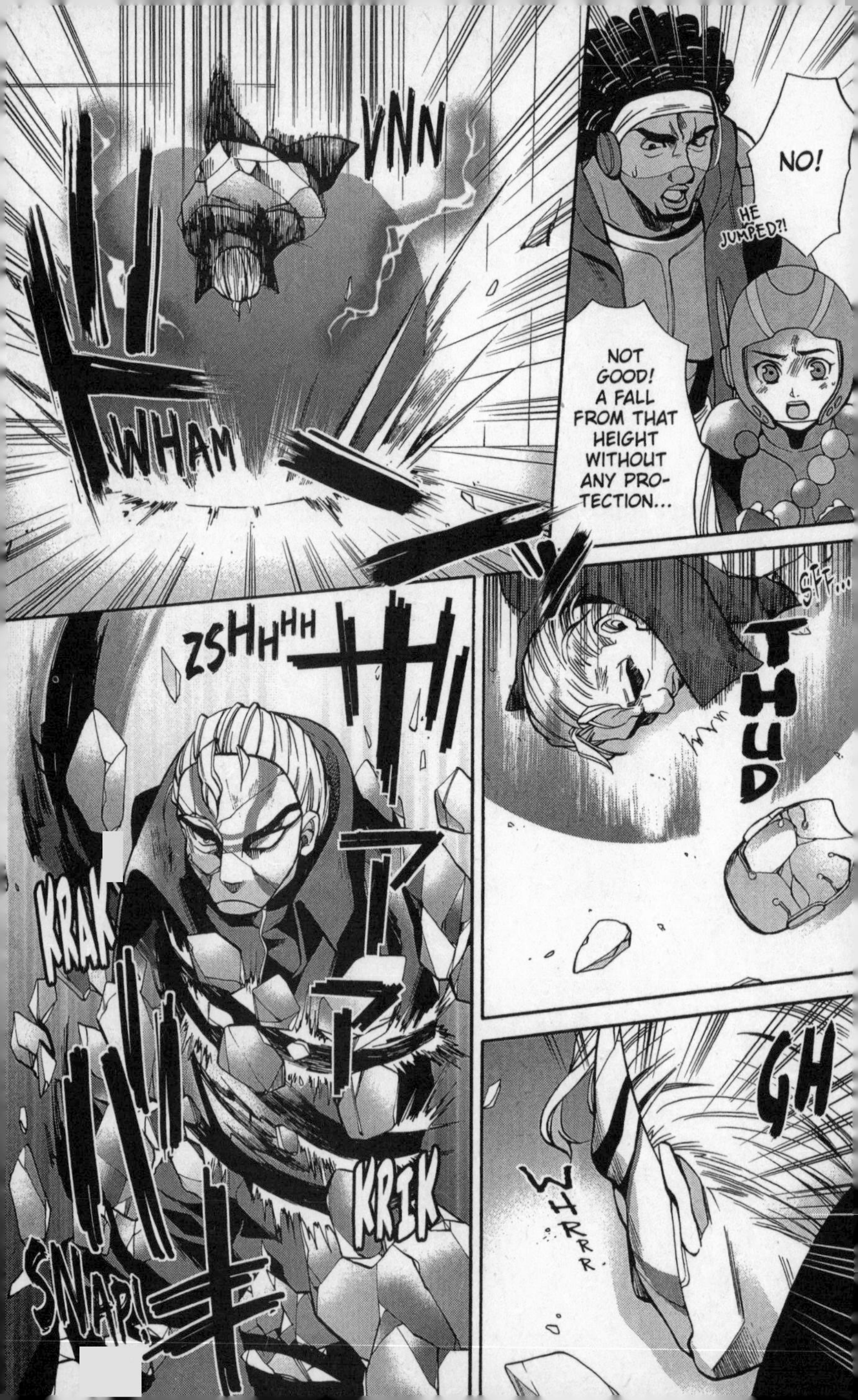
NO!
HE JUMPED?!
NOT GOOD! A FALL FROM THAT HEIGHT WITHOUT ANY PRO-TECTION...
VNN
WHAM
SFF...
THUD
GH
WHRRR
ZSHHHH
KRAK
KRIK
SNAP!

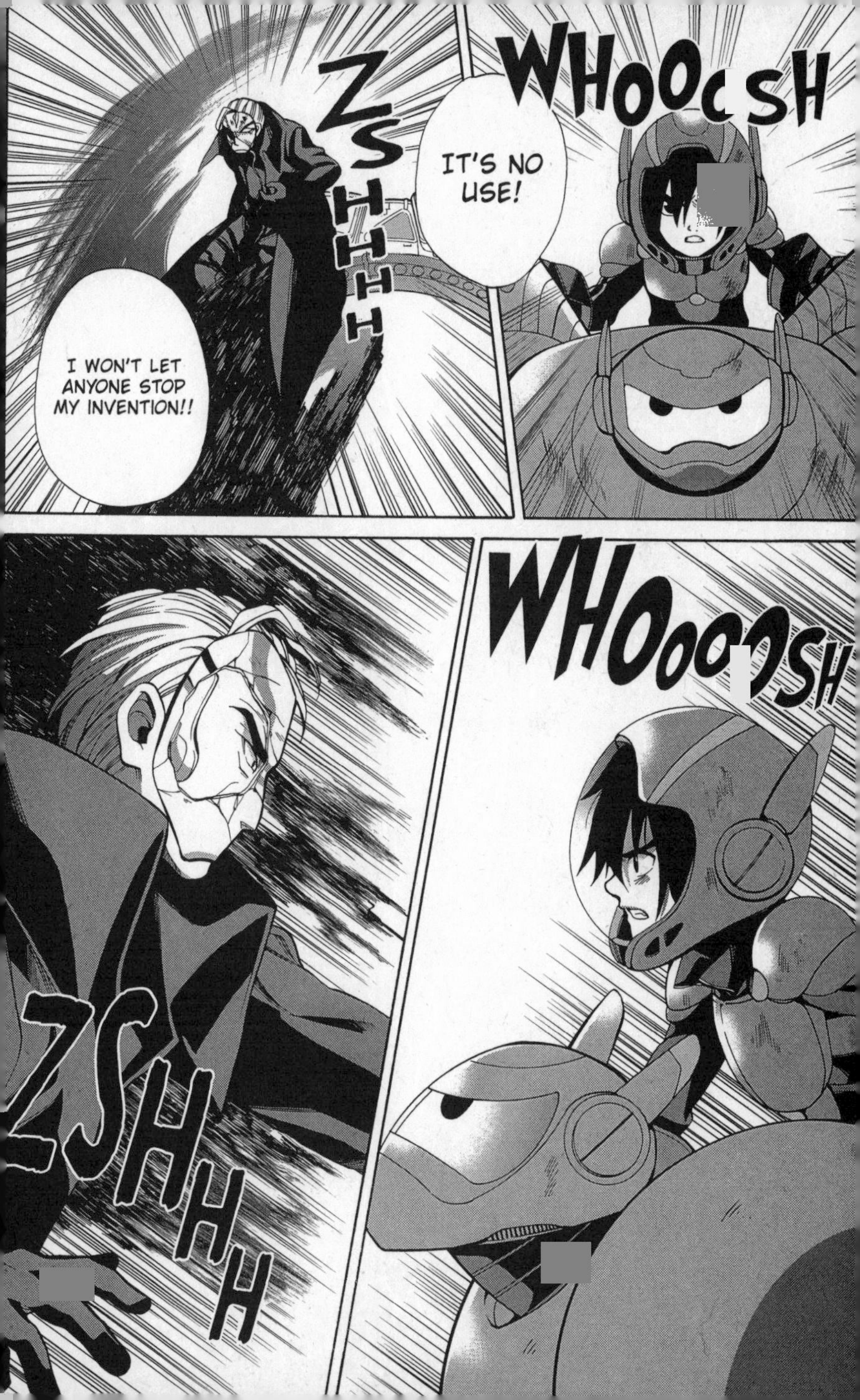
WHOOOSH
IT'S NO USE!
ZSHHHHH
I WON'T LET ANYONE STOP MY INVENTION!!
WHOOOOOSH
ZSHHHH

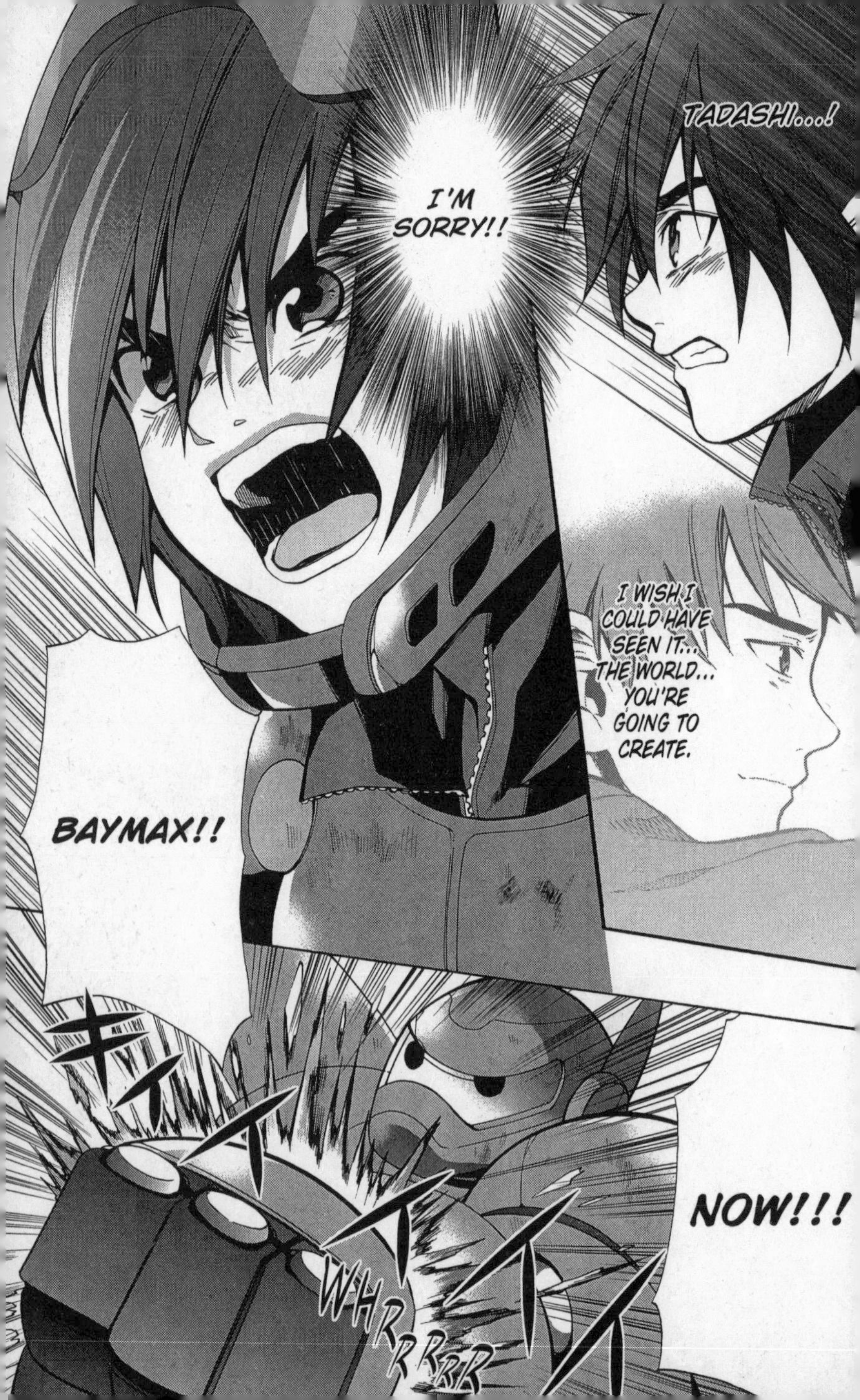
TADASHI...!
I'M SORRY!!
I WISH I COULD HAVE SEEN IT... THE WORLD... YOU'RE GOING TO CREATE.
BAYMAX!!
NOW!!!
WHRRRRRR

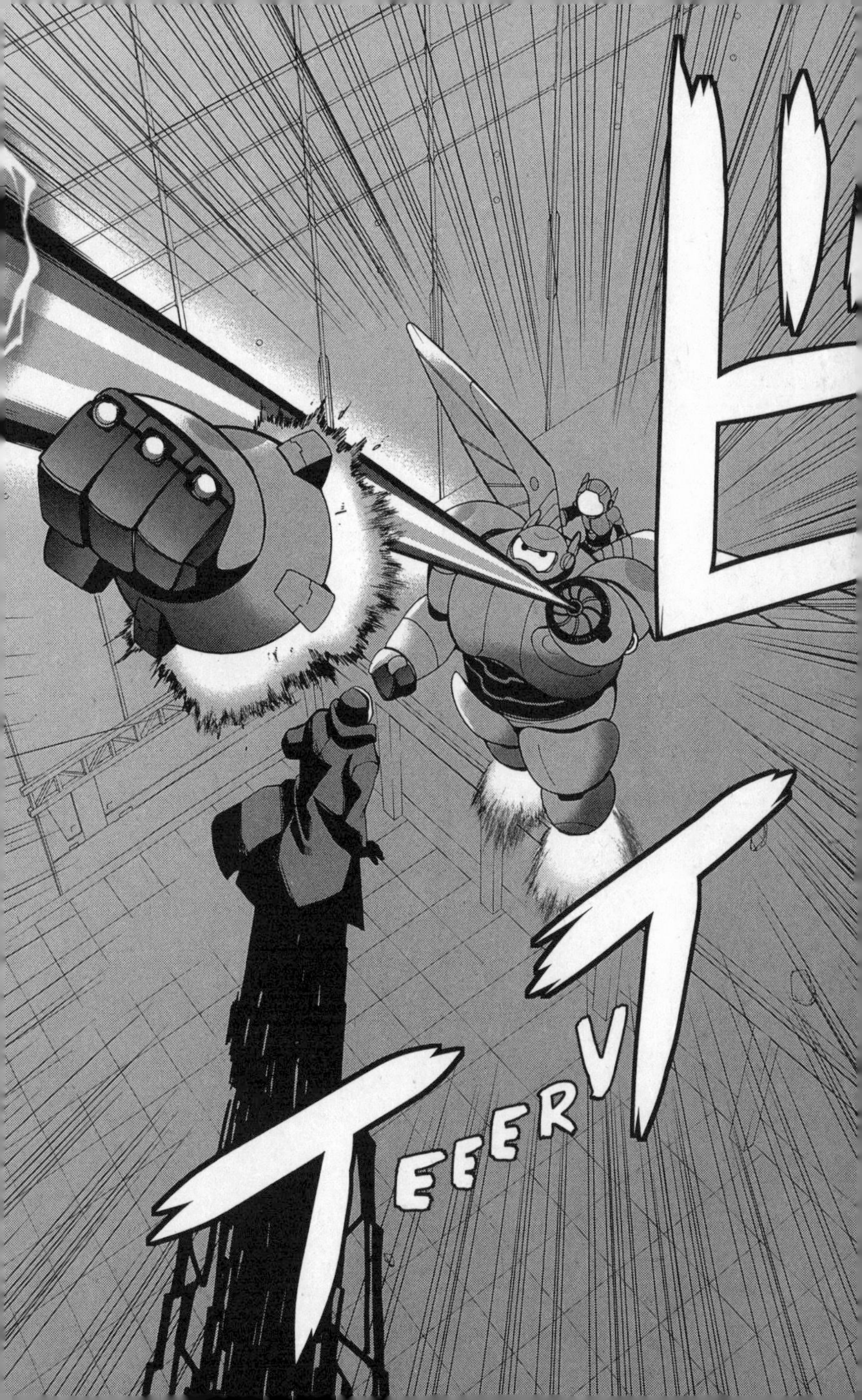

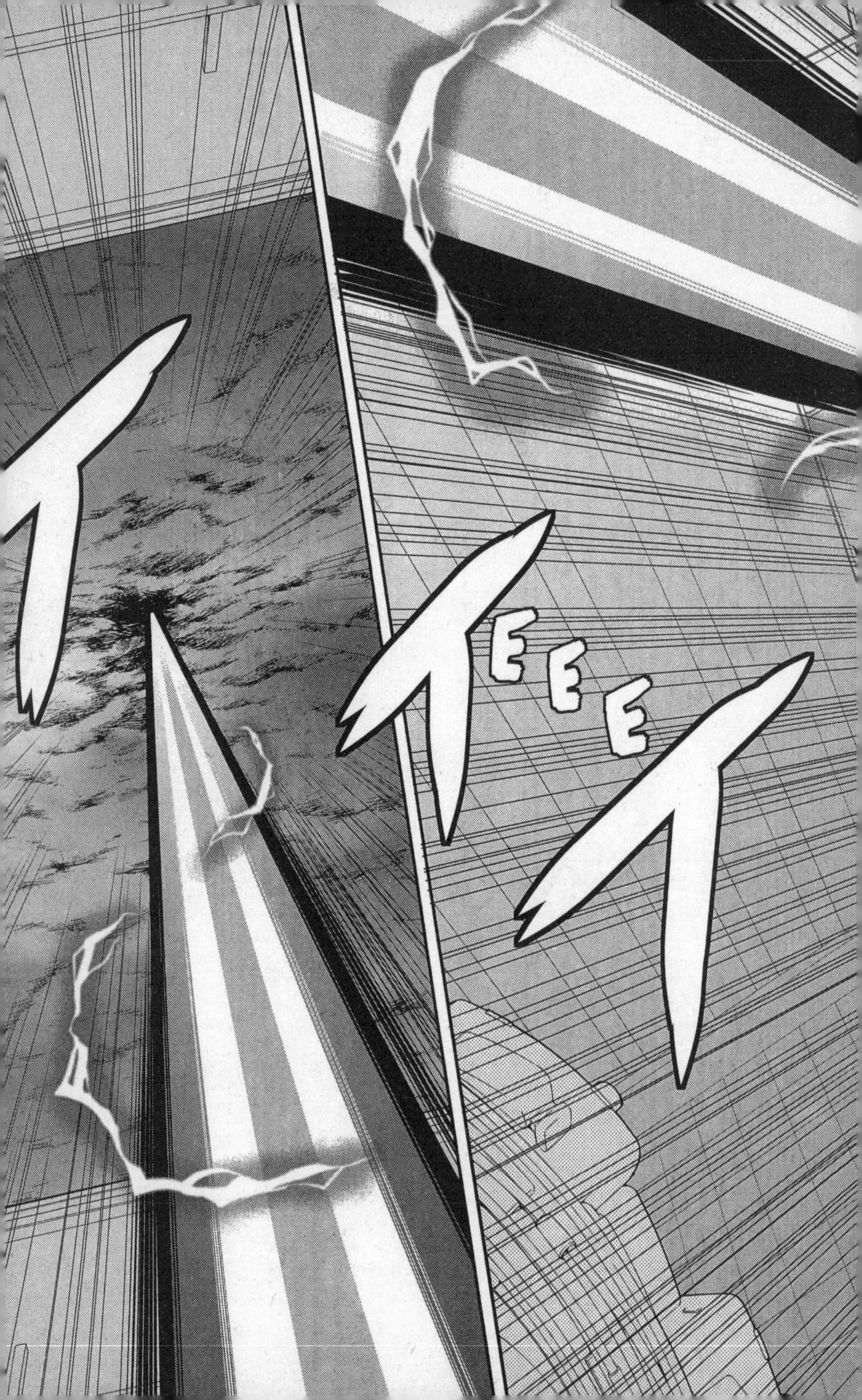
EEE

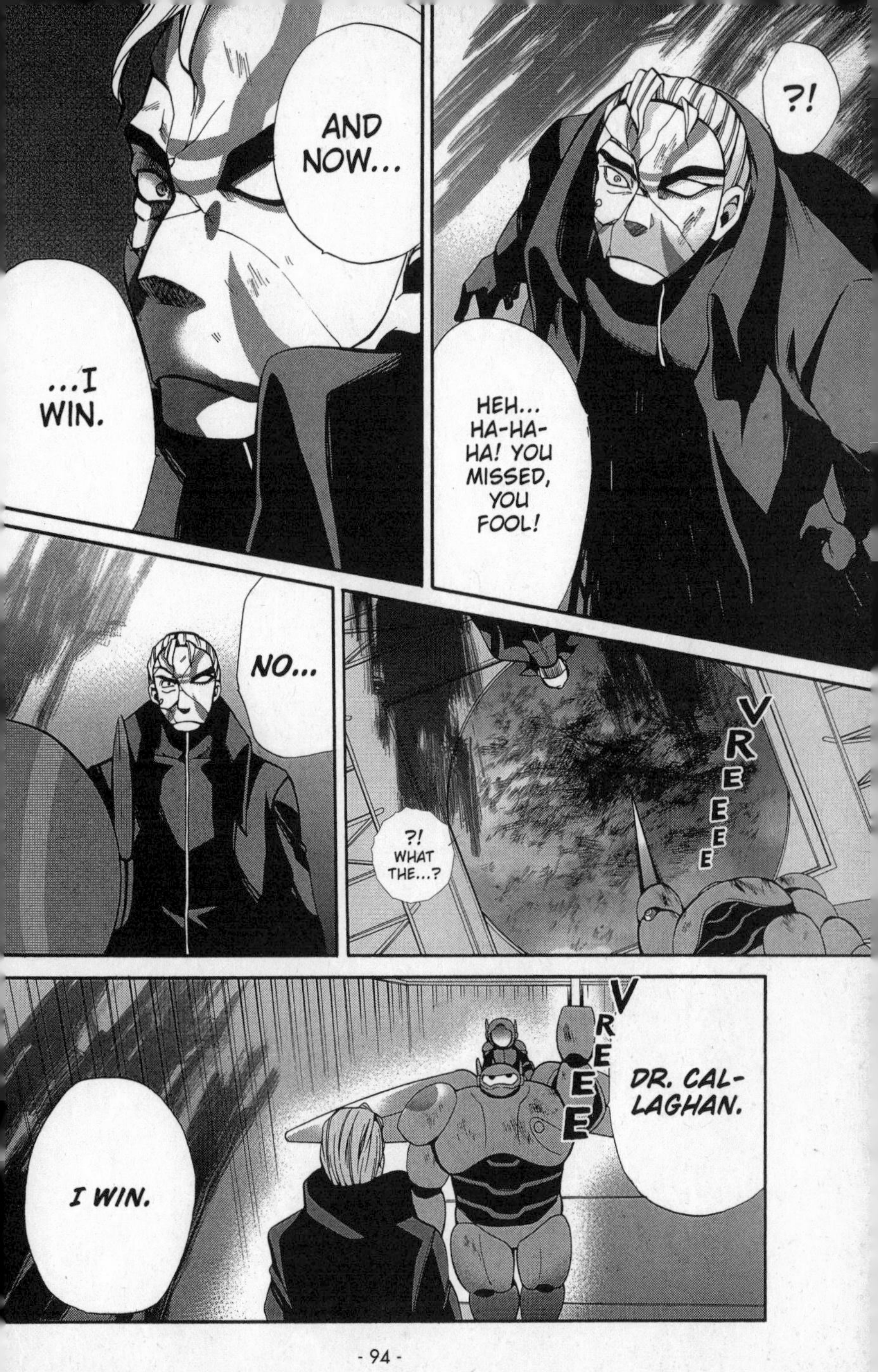
?!
HEH... HA-HA-HA! YOU MISSED, YOU FOOL!
AND NOW...
...I WIN.
VREEEEE
?! WHAT THE...?
NO...
VREEE
DR. CAL-LAGHAN.
I WIN.

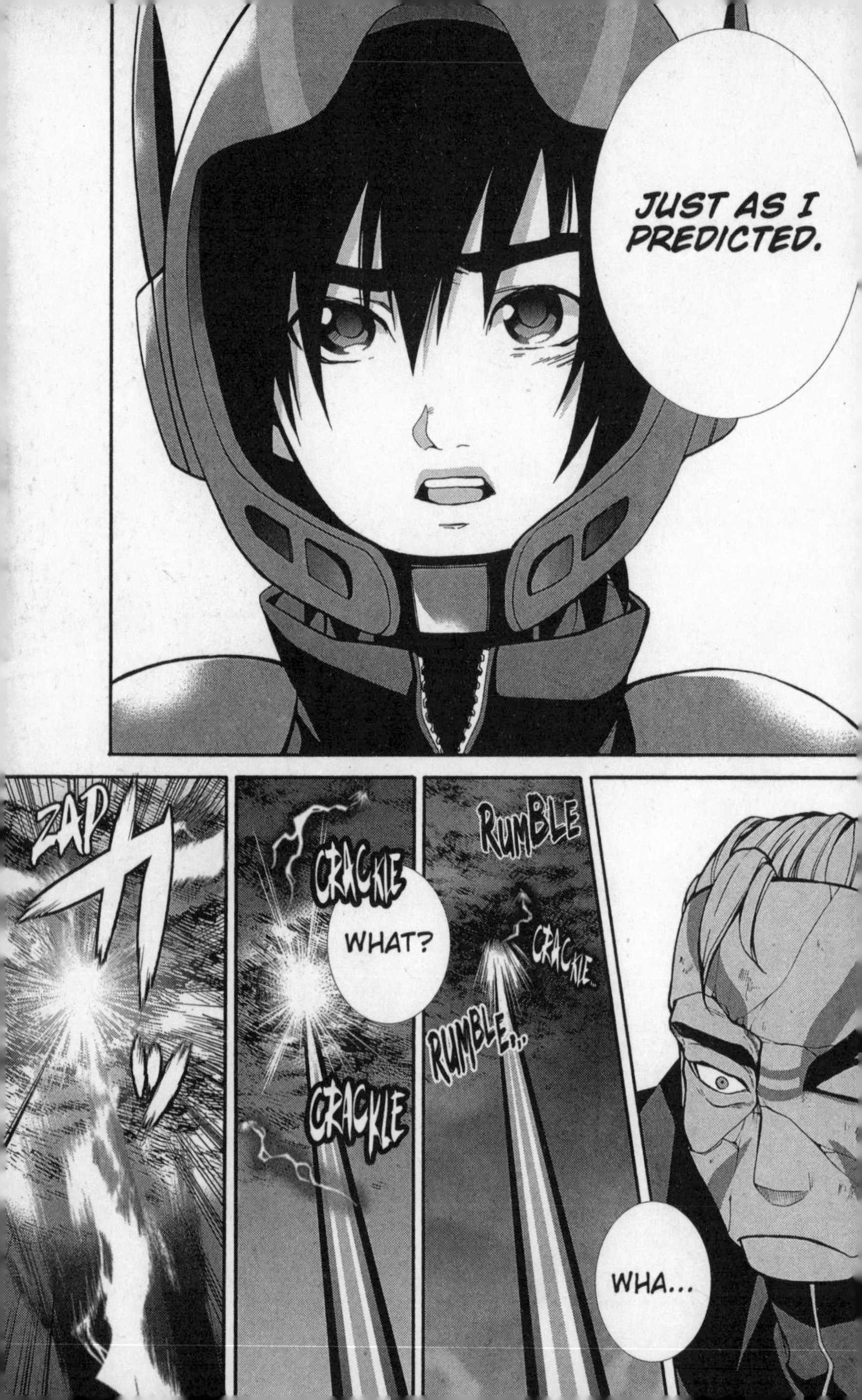
JUST AS I PREDICTED.
WHA...
RUMBLE
CRACKLE...
RUMBLE...
CRACKLE
WHAT?
CRACKLE
ZAP

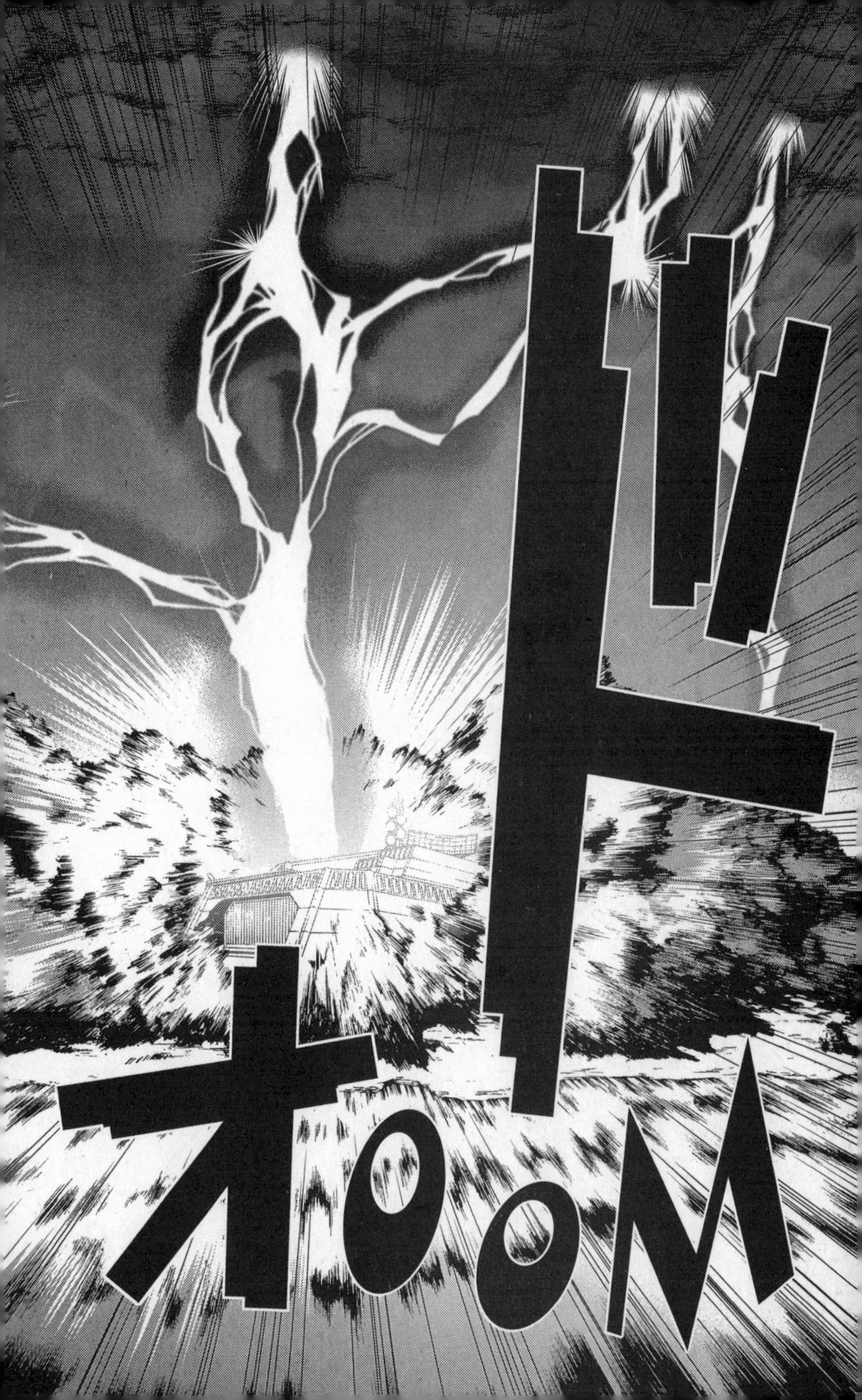

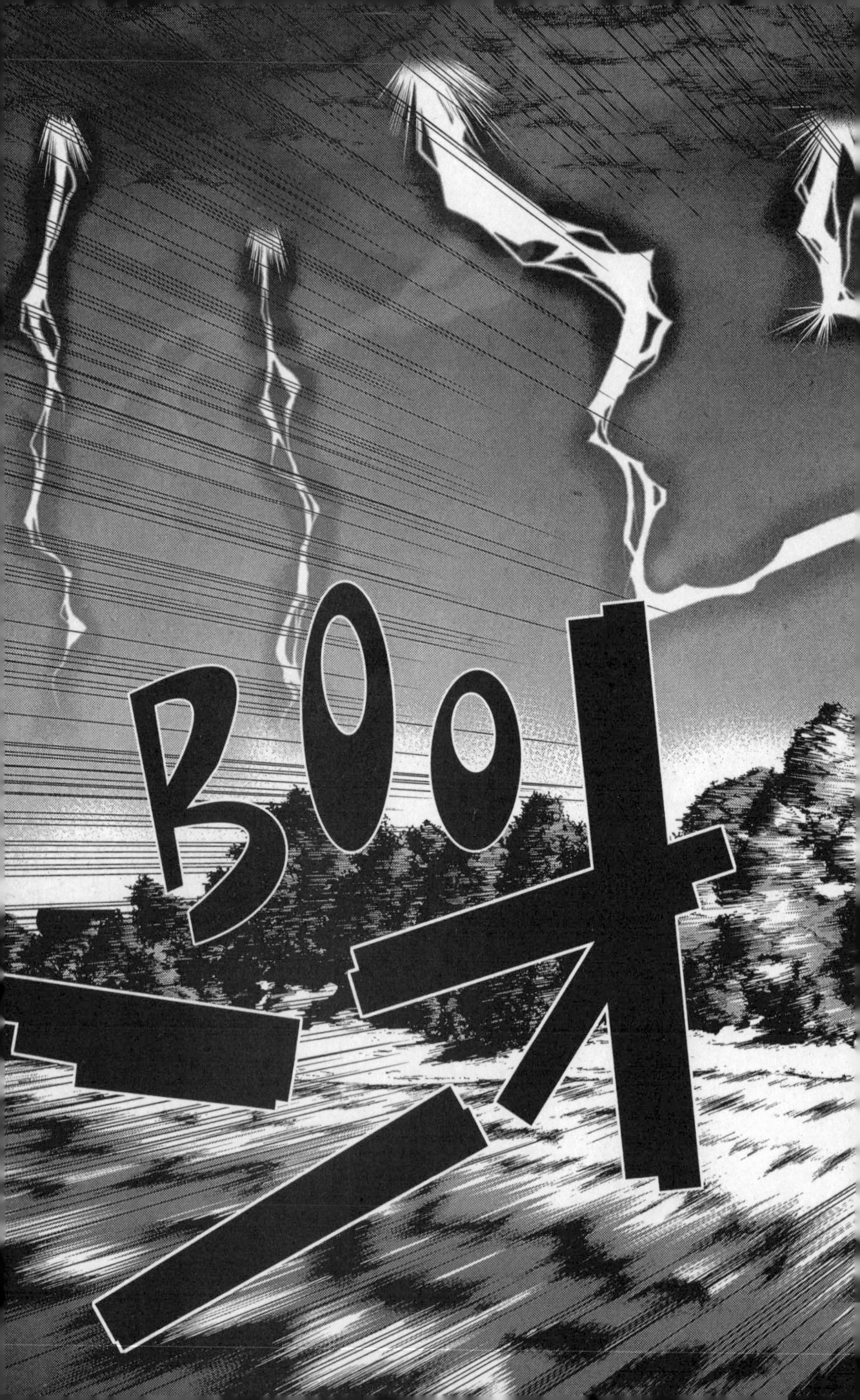
BOOOM

Disney

BIG HERO 6

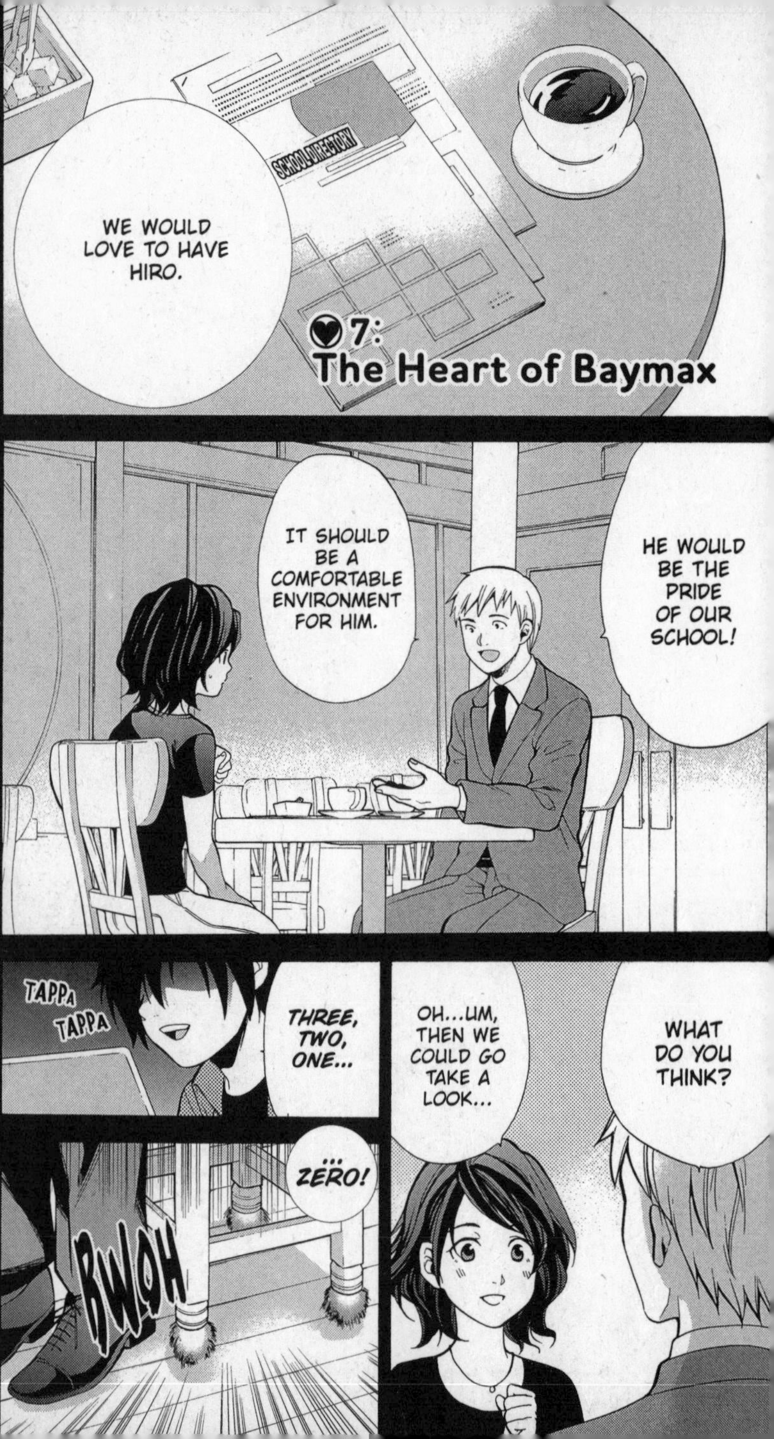
SCHOOL DIRECTORY
WE WOULD LOVE TO HAVE HIRO.
♥7: The Heart of Baymax
HE WOULD BE THE PRIDE OF OUR SCHOOL!
IT SHOULD BE A COMFORTABLE ENVIRONMENT FOR HIM.
WHAT DO YOU THINK?
OH...UM, THEN WE COULD GO TAKE A LOOK...
TAPPA TAPPA
THREE, TWO, ONE...
...ZERO!
BWOH

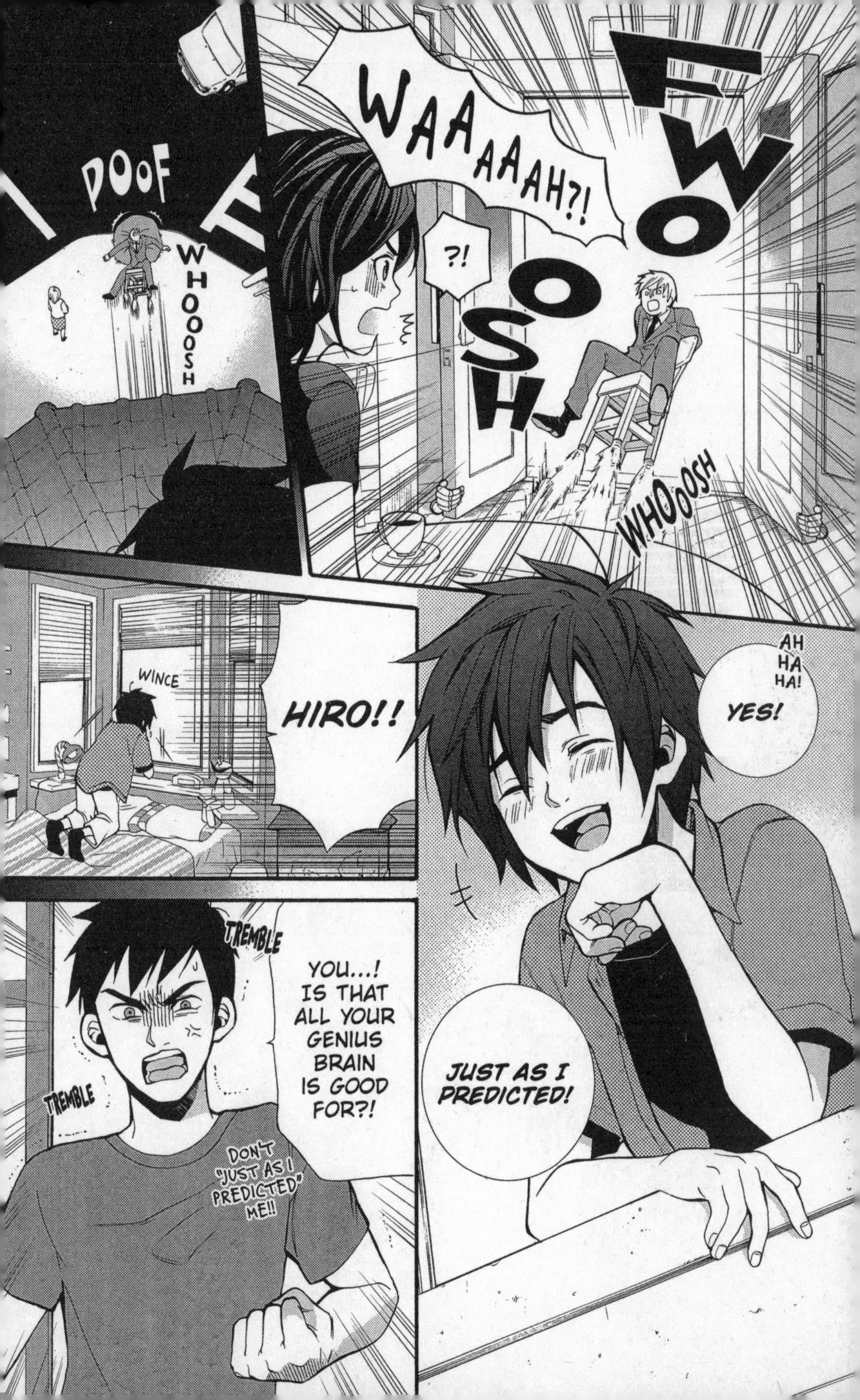
FWOOSH
WAAAAAAH?!
?!
WHOOOSH
DOOF
WHOOOOSH
AH HA HA!
YES!
JUST AS I PREDICTED!
WINCE
HIRO!!
TREMBLE
YOU...! IS THAT ALL YOUR GENIUS BRAIN IS GOOD FOR?!
TREMBLE
DON'T "JUST AS I PREDICTED" ME!!

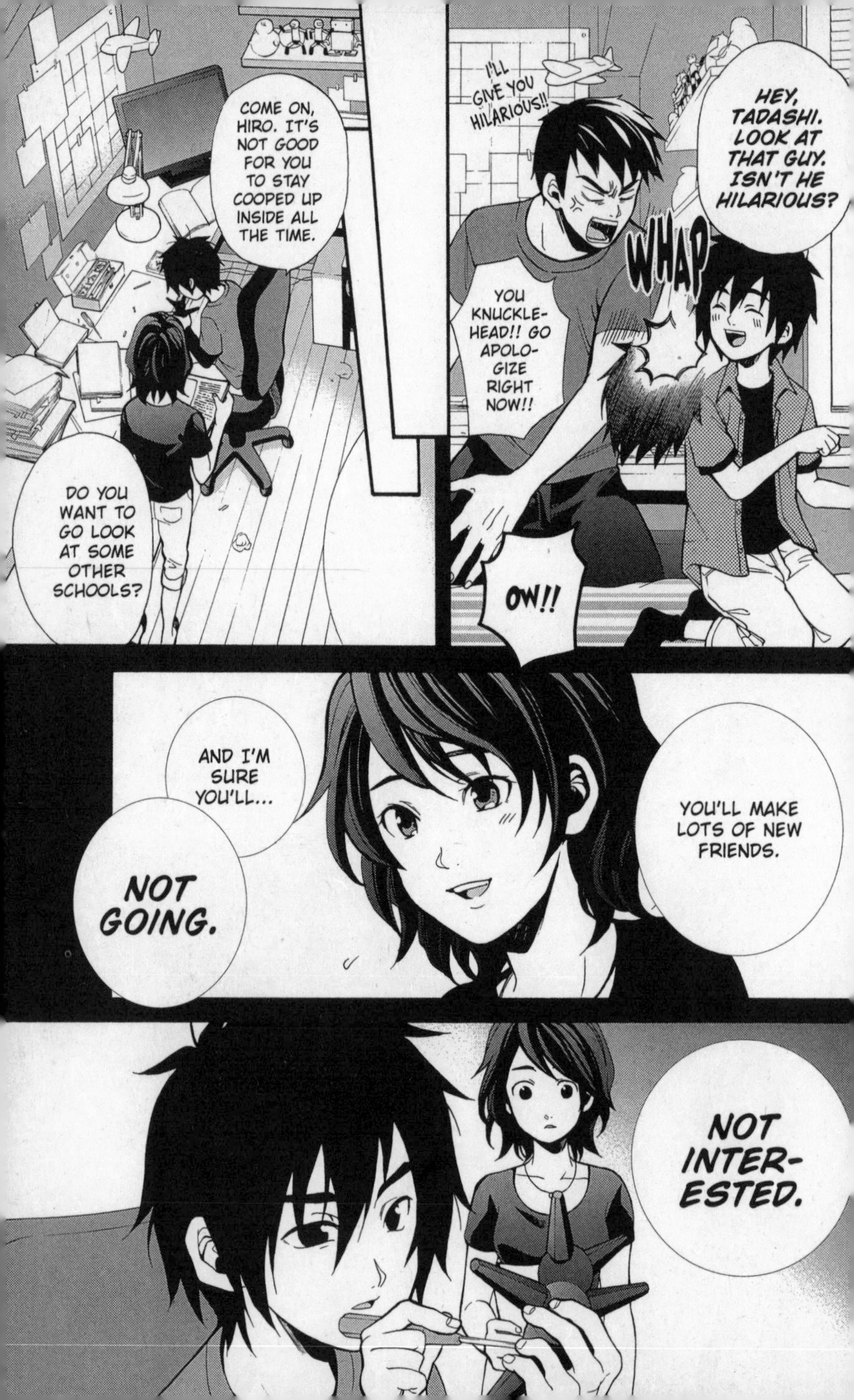
HEY, TADASHI. LOOK AT THAT GUY. ISN'T HE HILARIOUS?
I'LL GIVE YOU HILARIOUS!!
WHAP
YOU KNUCKLE-HEAD!! GO APOLO-GIZE RIGHT NOW!!
OW!!
COME ON, HIRO. IT'S NOT GOOD FOR YOU TO STAY COOPED UP INSIDE ALL THE TIME.
DO YOU WANT TO GO LOOK AT SOME OTHER SCHOOLS?
YOU'LL MAKE LOTS OF NEW FRIENDS.
AND I'M SURE YOU'LL...
NOT GOING.
NOT INTER-ESTED.

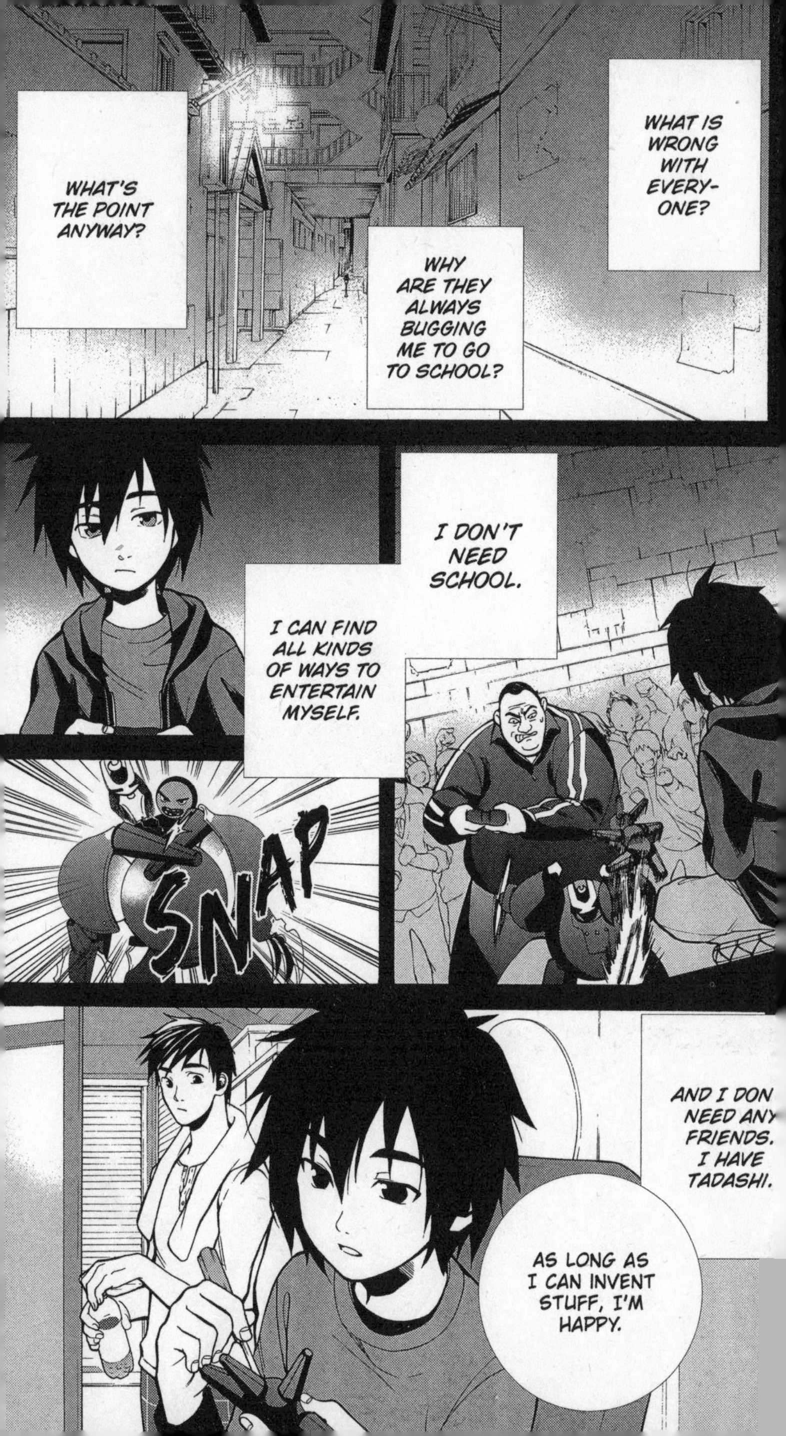
WHAT IS WRONG WITH EVERY-ONE?
WHY ARE THEY ALWAYS BUGGING ME TO GO TO SCHOOL?
WHAT'S THE POINT ANYWAY?
I DON'T NEED SCHOOL.
I CAN FIND ALL KINDS OF WAYS TO ENTERTAIN MYSELF.
SNAP
AND I DON NEED ANY FRIENDS. I HAVE TADASHI.
AS LONG AS I CAN INVENT STUFF, I'M HAPPY.

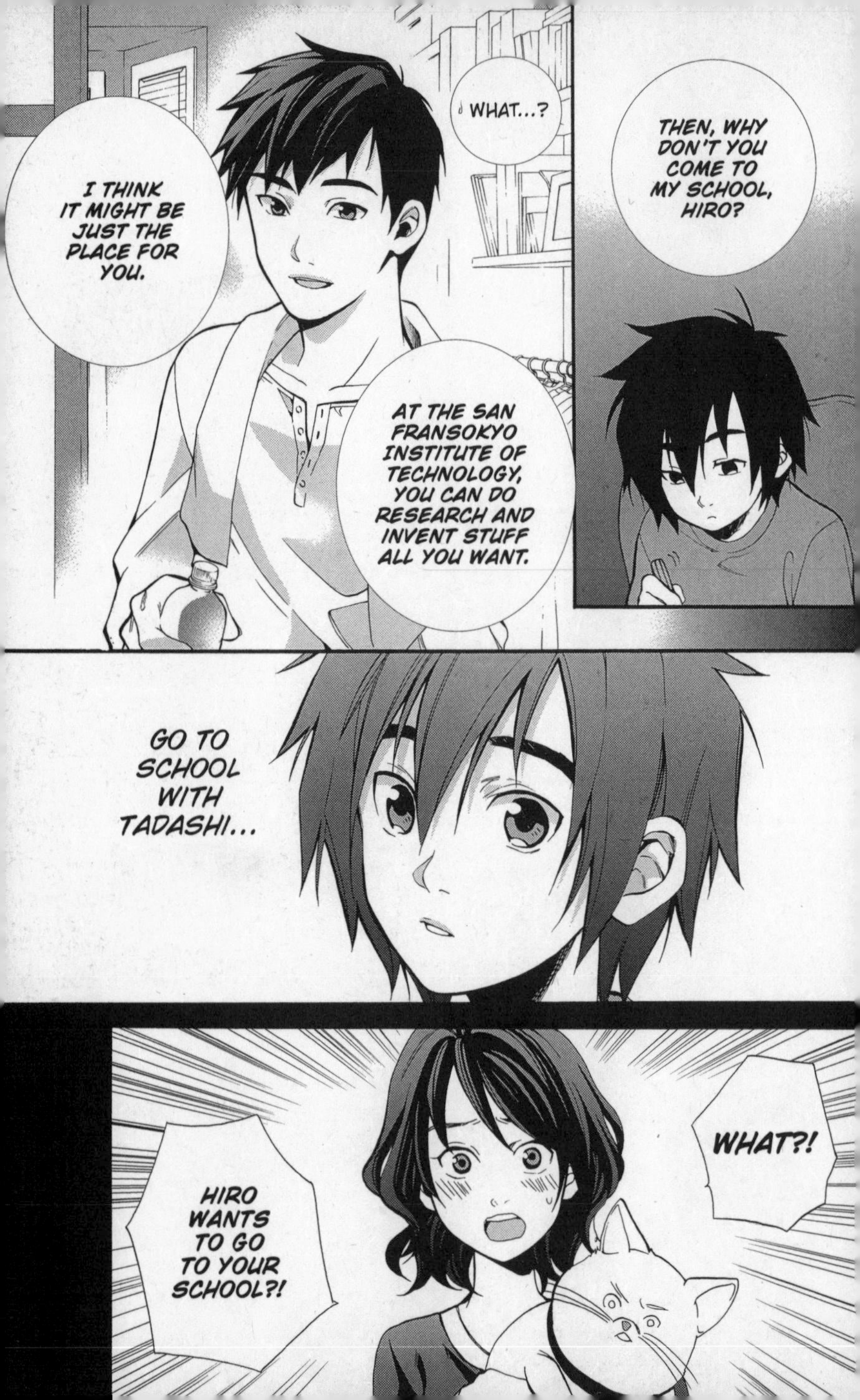
THEN, WHY DON'T YOU COME TO MY SCHOOL, HIRO?
WHAT...?
AT THE SAN FRANSOKYO INSTITUTE OF TECHNOLOGY, YOU CAN DO RESEARCH AND INVENT STUFF ALL YOU WANT.
I THINK IT MIGHT BE JUST THE PLACE FOR YOU.
GO TO SCHOOL WITH TADASHI...
WHAT?!
HIRO WANTS TO GO TO YOUR SCHOOL?!

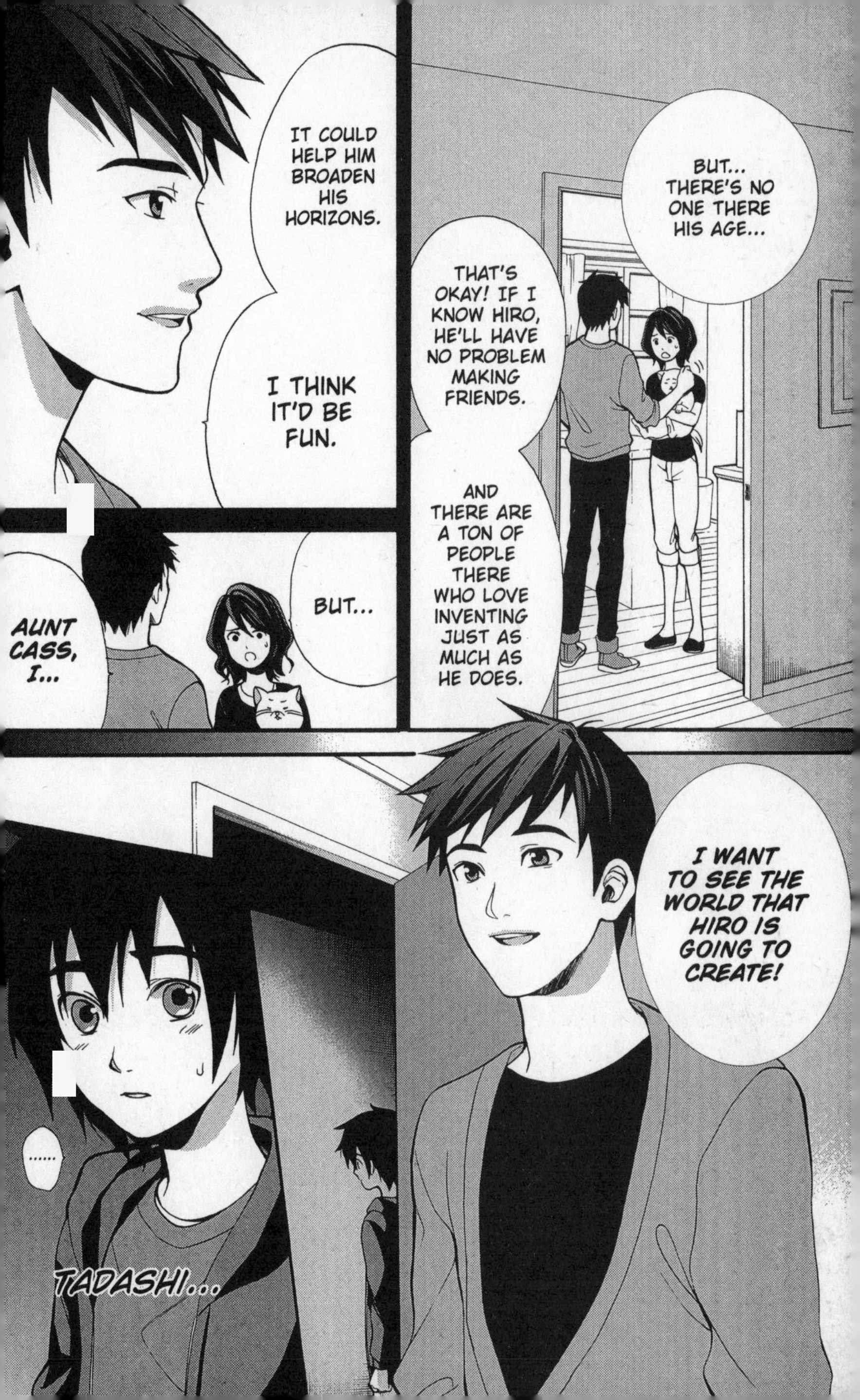
BUT... THERE'S NO ONE THERE HIS AGE...
THAT'S OKAY! IF I KNOW HIRO, HE'LL HAVE NO PROBLEM MAKING FRIENDS.
AND THERE ARE A TON OF PEOPLE THERE WHO LOVE INVENTING JUST AS MUCH AS HE DOES.
IT COULD HELP HIM BROADEN HIS HORIZONS.
I THINK IT'D BE FUN.
BUT...
AUNT CASS, I...
I WANT TO SEE THE WORLD THAT HIRO IS GOING TO CREATE!
......
TADASHI...

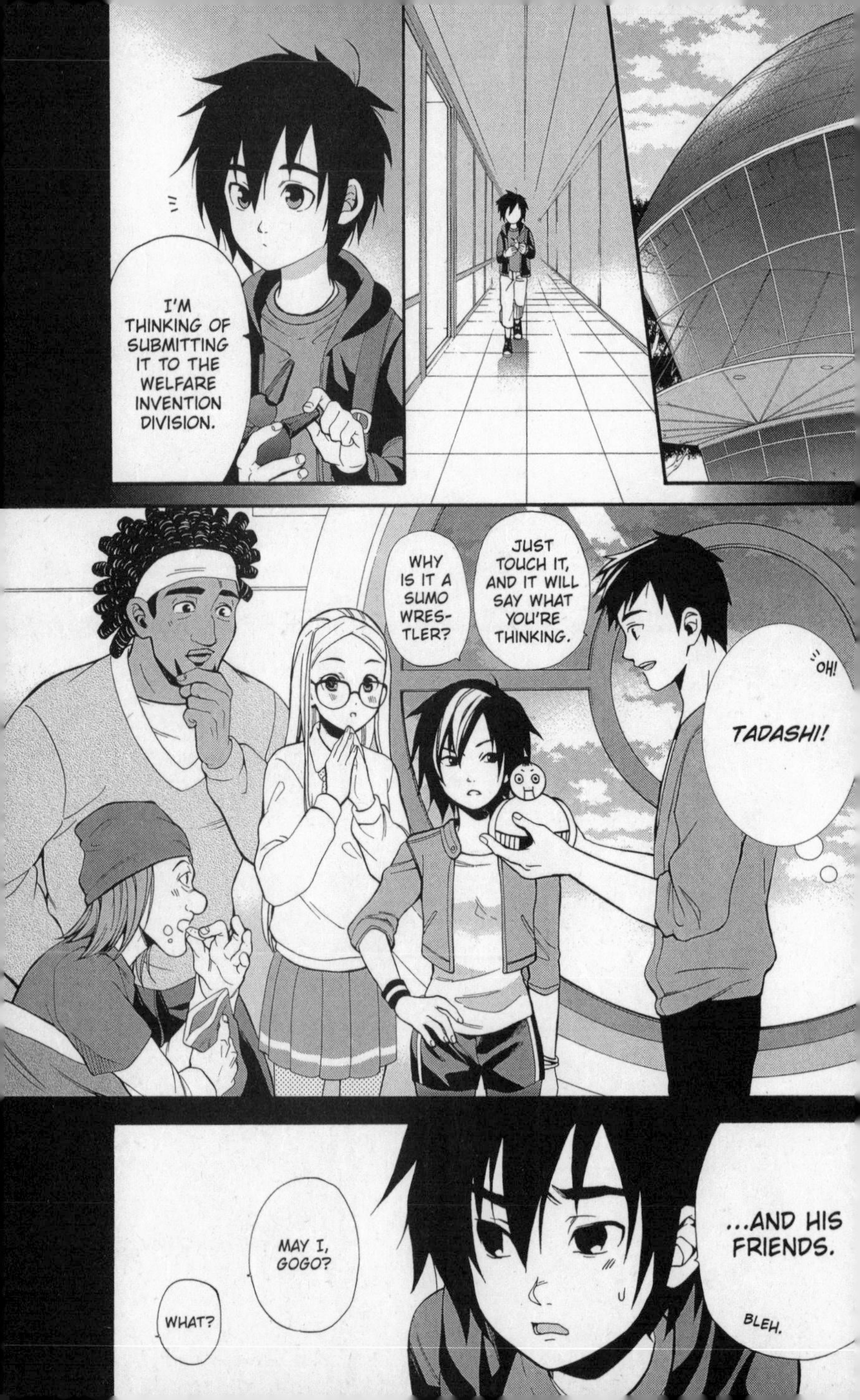
I'M THINKING OF SUBMITTING IT TO THE WELFARE INVENTION DIVISION.
OH!
TADASHI!
JUST TOUCH IT, AND IT WILL SAY WHAT YOU'RE THINKING.
WHY IS IT A SUMO WRES-TLER?
...AND HIS FRIENDS.
BLEH.
MAY I, GOGO?
WHAT?

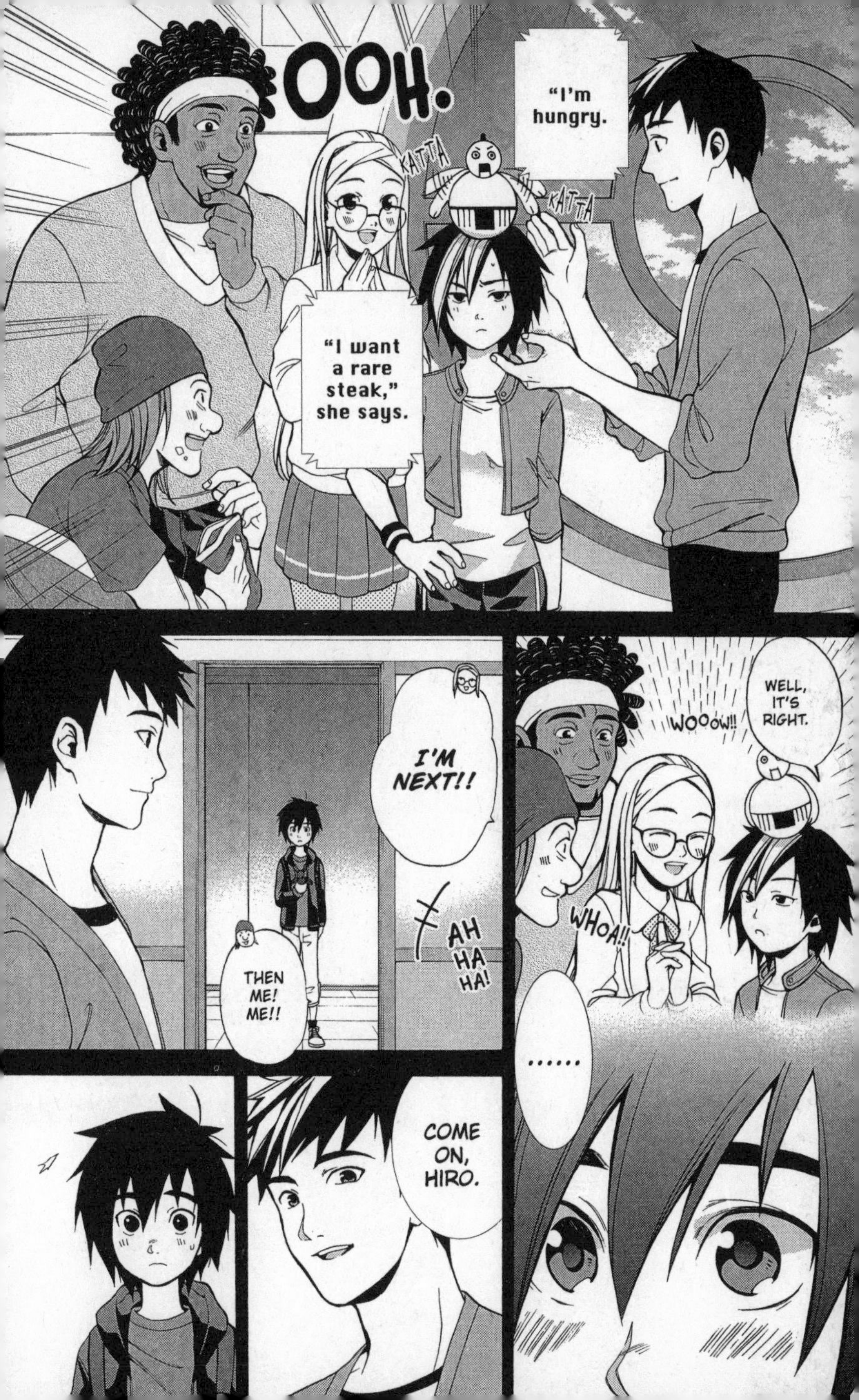
"I'm hungry.
KATTA
KATTA
OOH.
"I want a rare steak," she says.
WELL, IT'S RIGHT.
WOOOOW!!
WHOA!!
I'M NEXT!!
AH HA HA!
THEN ME! ME!!
......
COME ON, HIRO.

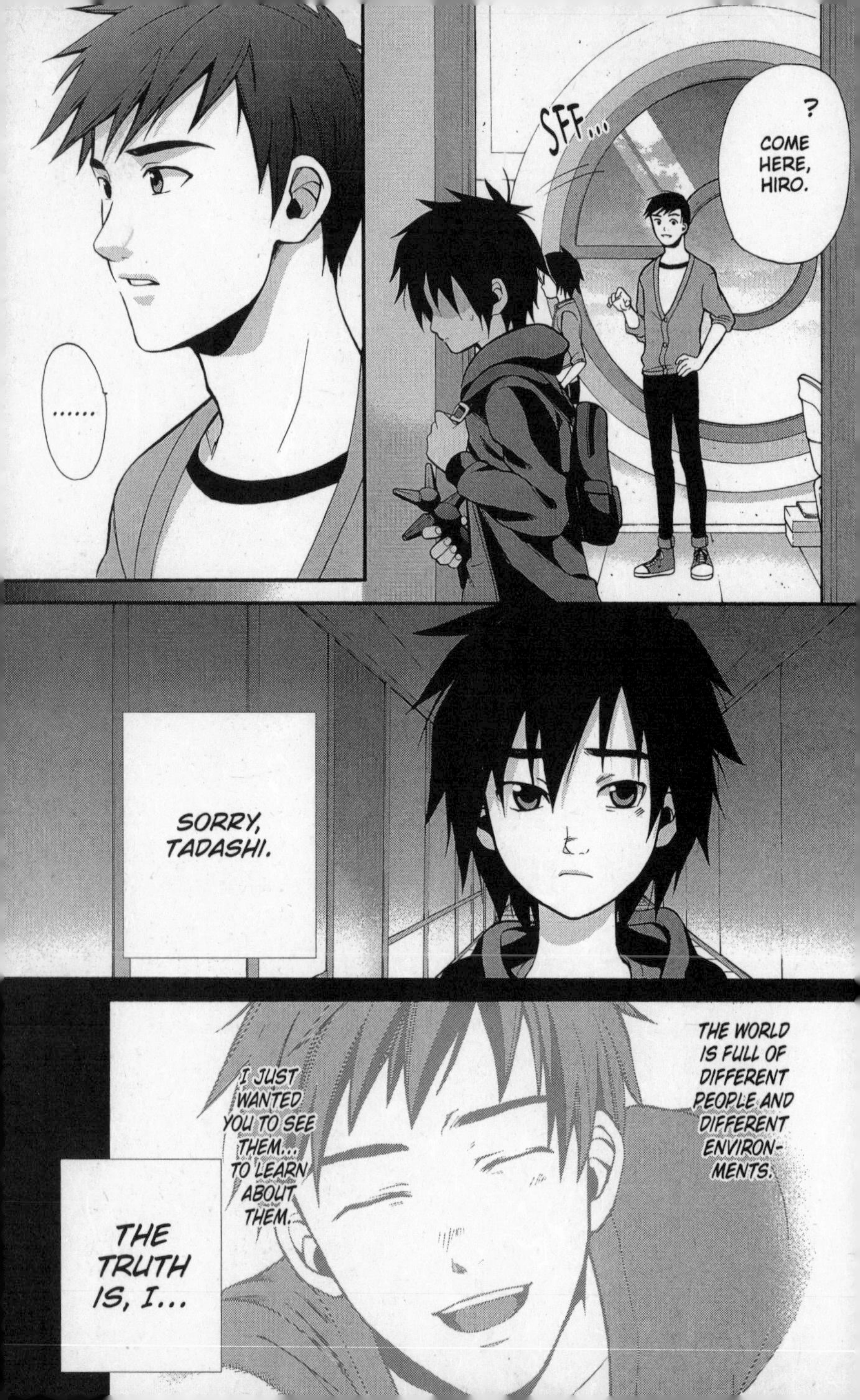
?
COME HERE, HIRO.
SFF...
......
SORRY, TADASHI.
THE WORLD IS FULL OF DIFFERENT PEOPLE AND DIFFERENT ENVIRON-MENTS.
I JUST WANTED YOU TO SEE THEM... TO LEARN ABOUT THEM.
THE TRUTH IS, I...

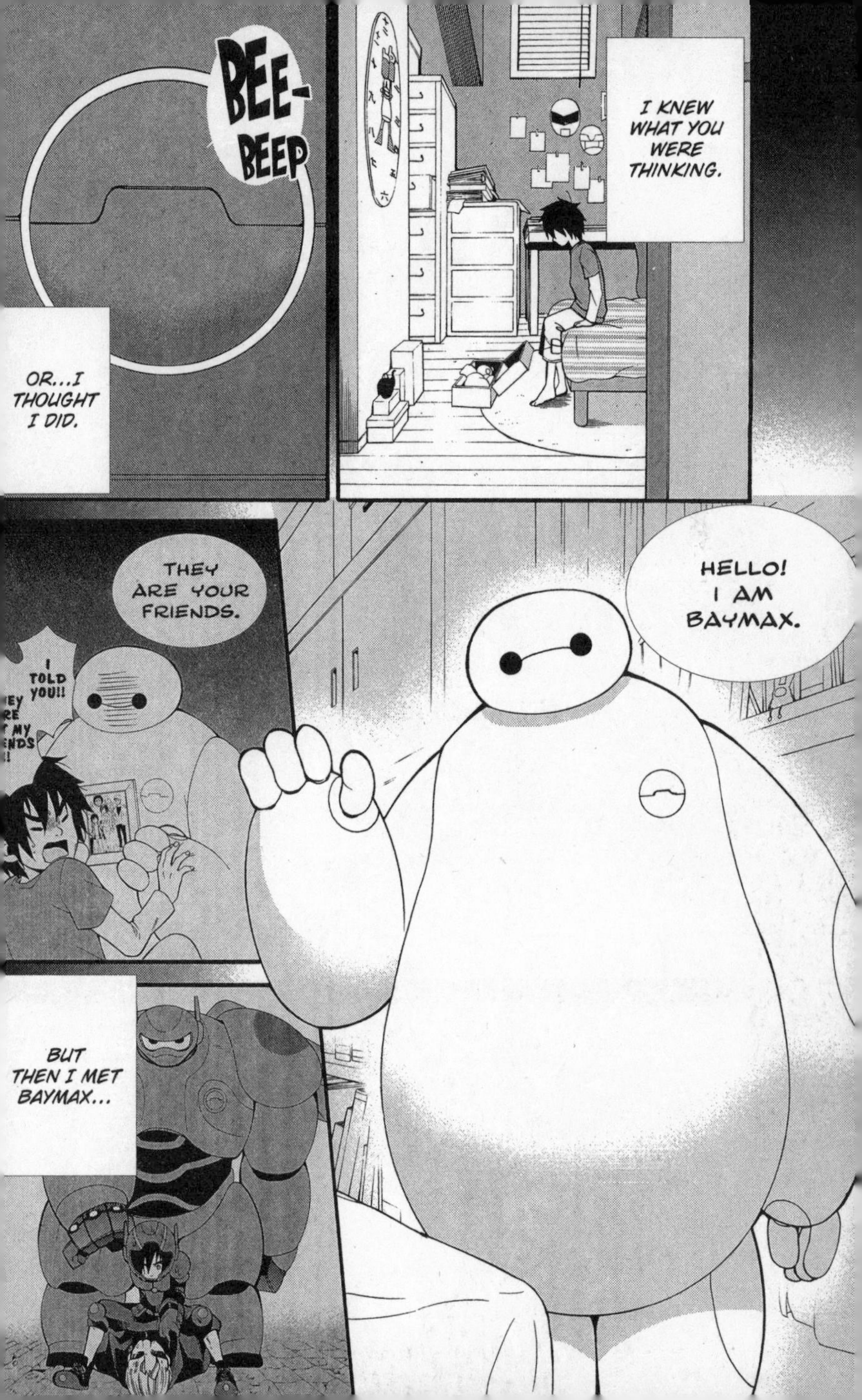
I KNEW WHAT YOU WERE THINKING.
BEE-BEEP
OR...I THOUGHT I DID.
HELLO! I AM BAYMAX.
THEY ARE YOUR FRIENDS.
I TOLD YOU!!
BUT THEN I MET BAYMAX...

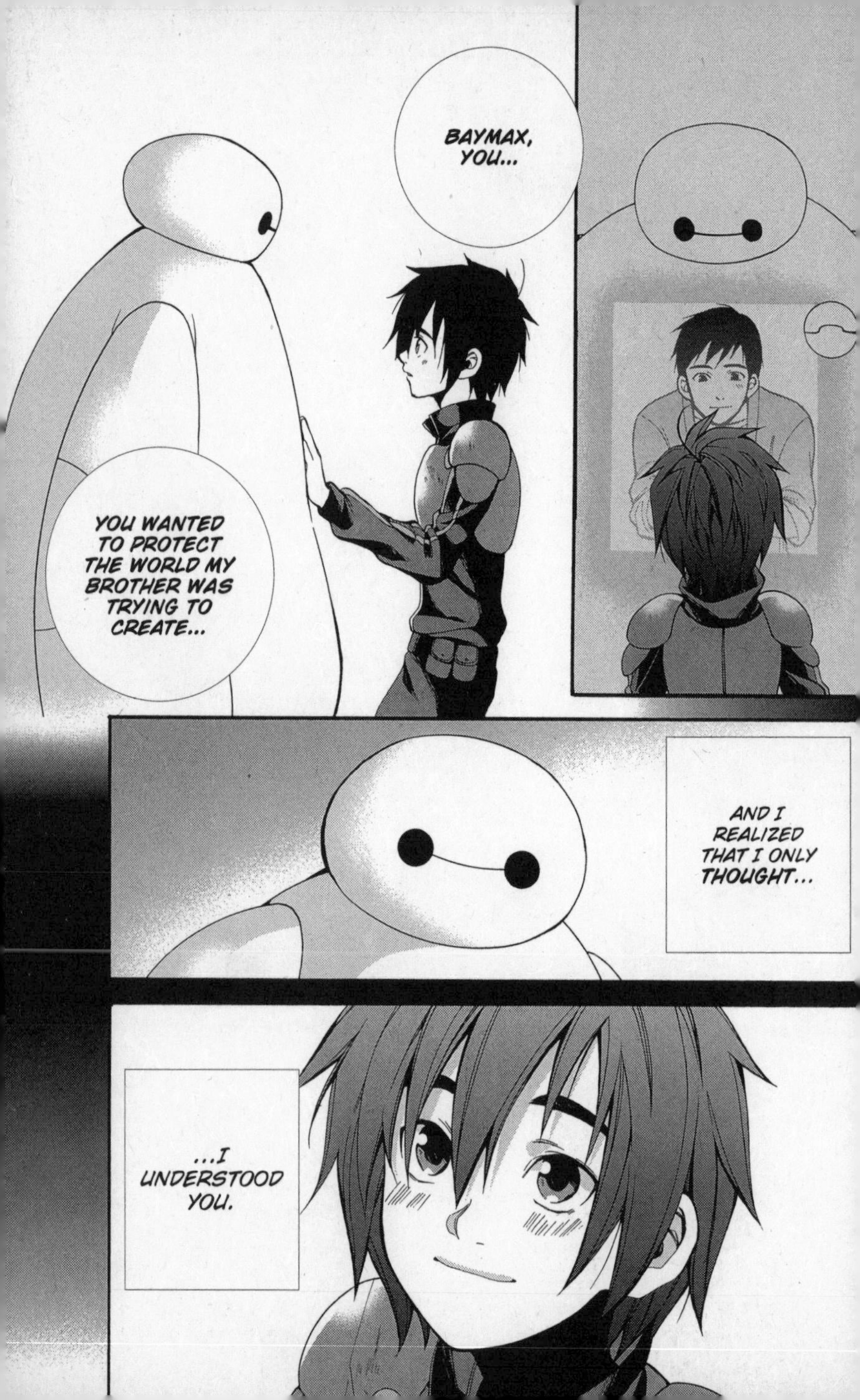
BAYMAX, YOU...
YOU WANTED TO PROTECT THE WORLD MY BROTHER WAS TRYING TO CREATE...
AND I REALIZED THAT I ONLY THOUGHT...
...I UNDERSTOOD YOU.

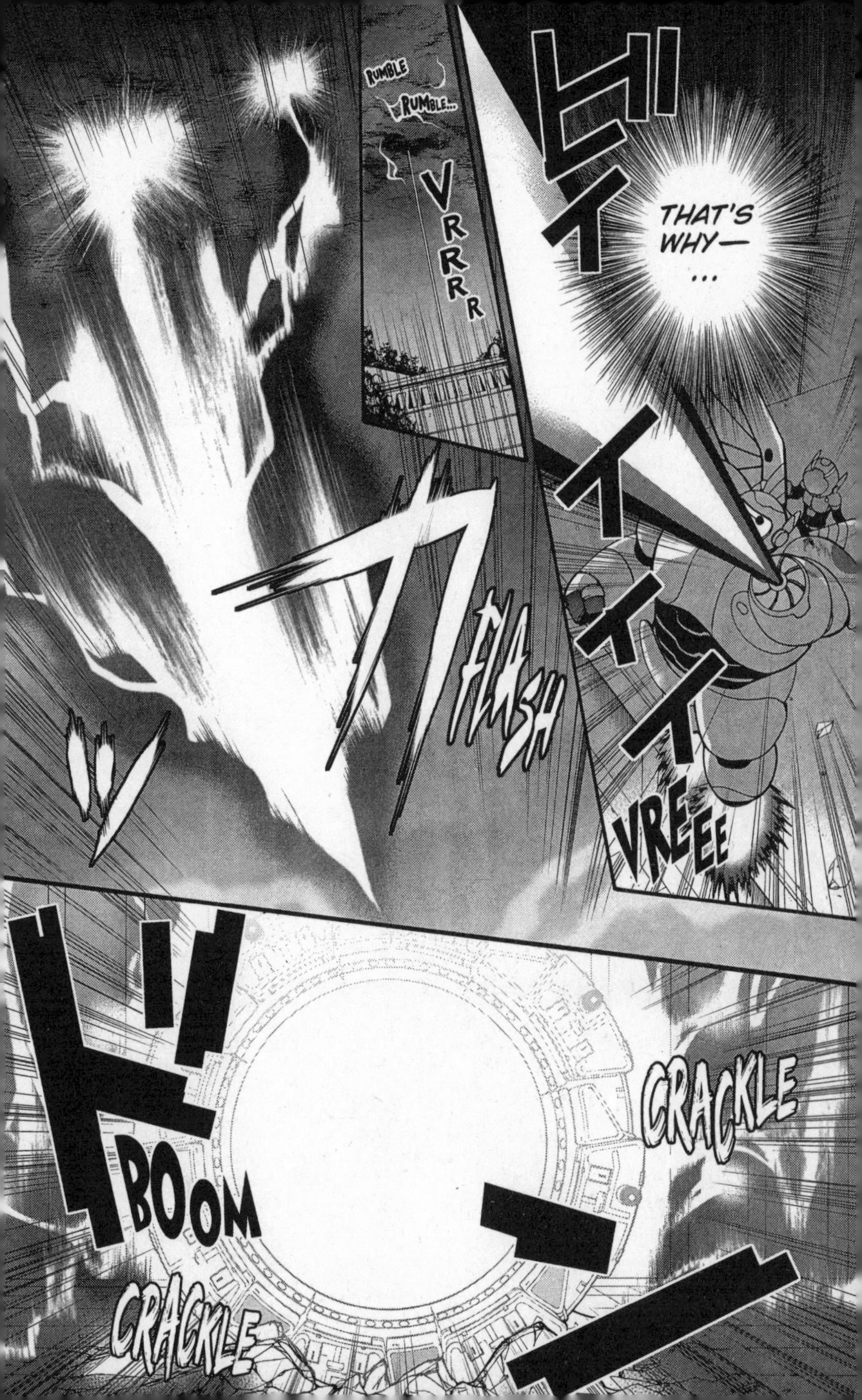
THAT'S WHY— ...
VREEE
RUMBLE
RUMBLE...
VRRRR
FLASH
CRACKLE
BOOM
CRACKLE

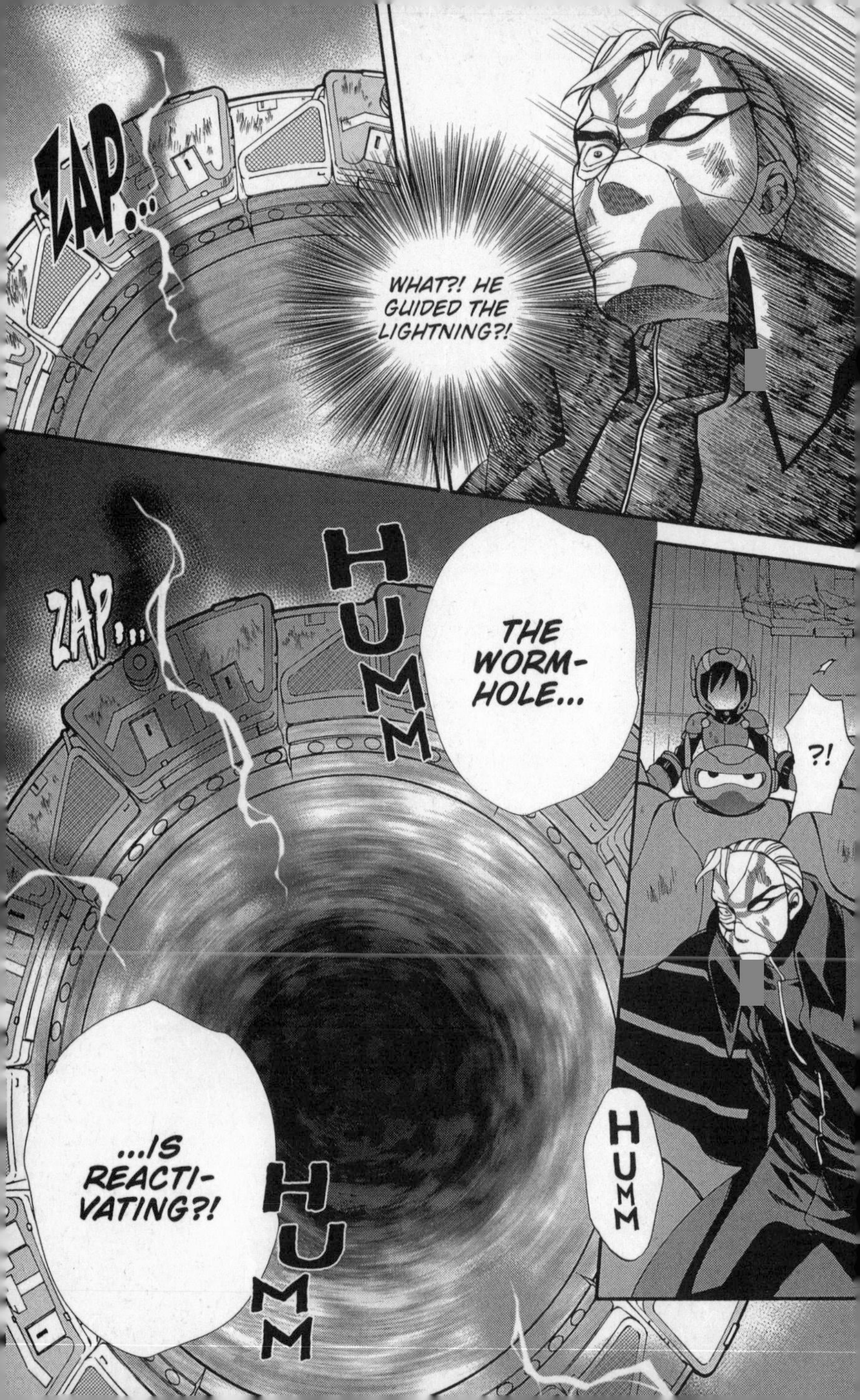
ZAP...
WHAT?! HE GUIDED THE LIGHTNING?!
?!
HUMM
HUMM
THE WORM-HOLE...
ZAP...
...IS REACTIVATING?!
HUMM

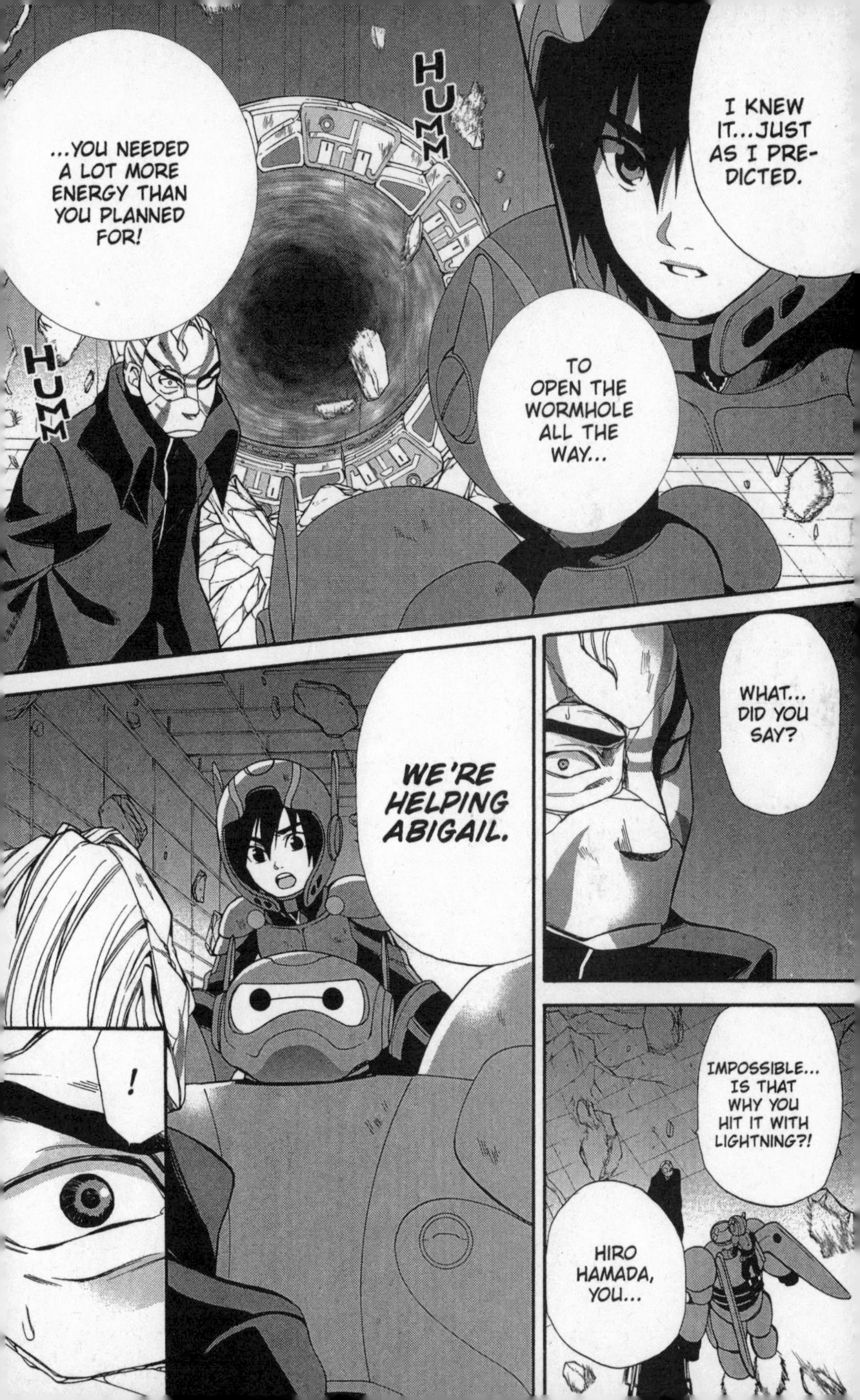
I KNEW IT...JUST AS I PREDICTED.
TO OPEN THE WORMHOLE ALL THE WAY...
HUMM
...YOU NEEDED A LOT MORE ENERGY THAN YOU PLANNED FOR!
HUMM
WHAT... DID YOU SAY?
IMPOSSIBLE... IS THAT WHY YOU HIT IT WITH LIGHTNING?!
HIRO HAMADA, YOU...
WE'RE HELPING ABIGAIL.
!

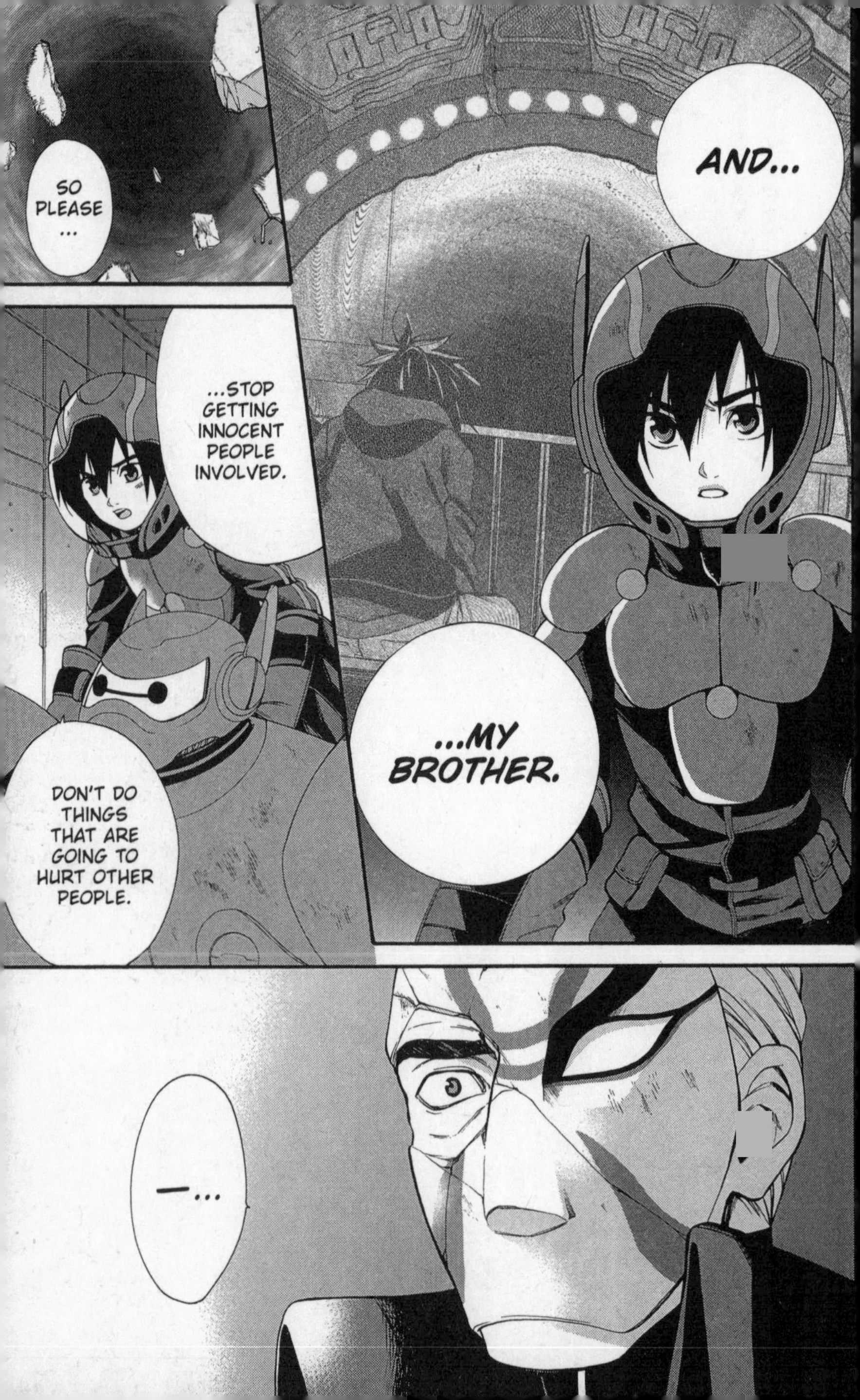
SO PLEASE ...
...STOP GETTING INNOCENT PEOPLE INVOLVED.
DON'T DO THINGS THAT ARE GOING TO HURT OTHER PEOPLE.
AND...
...MY BROTHER.
—...

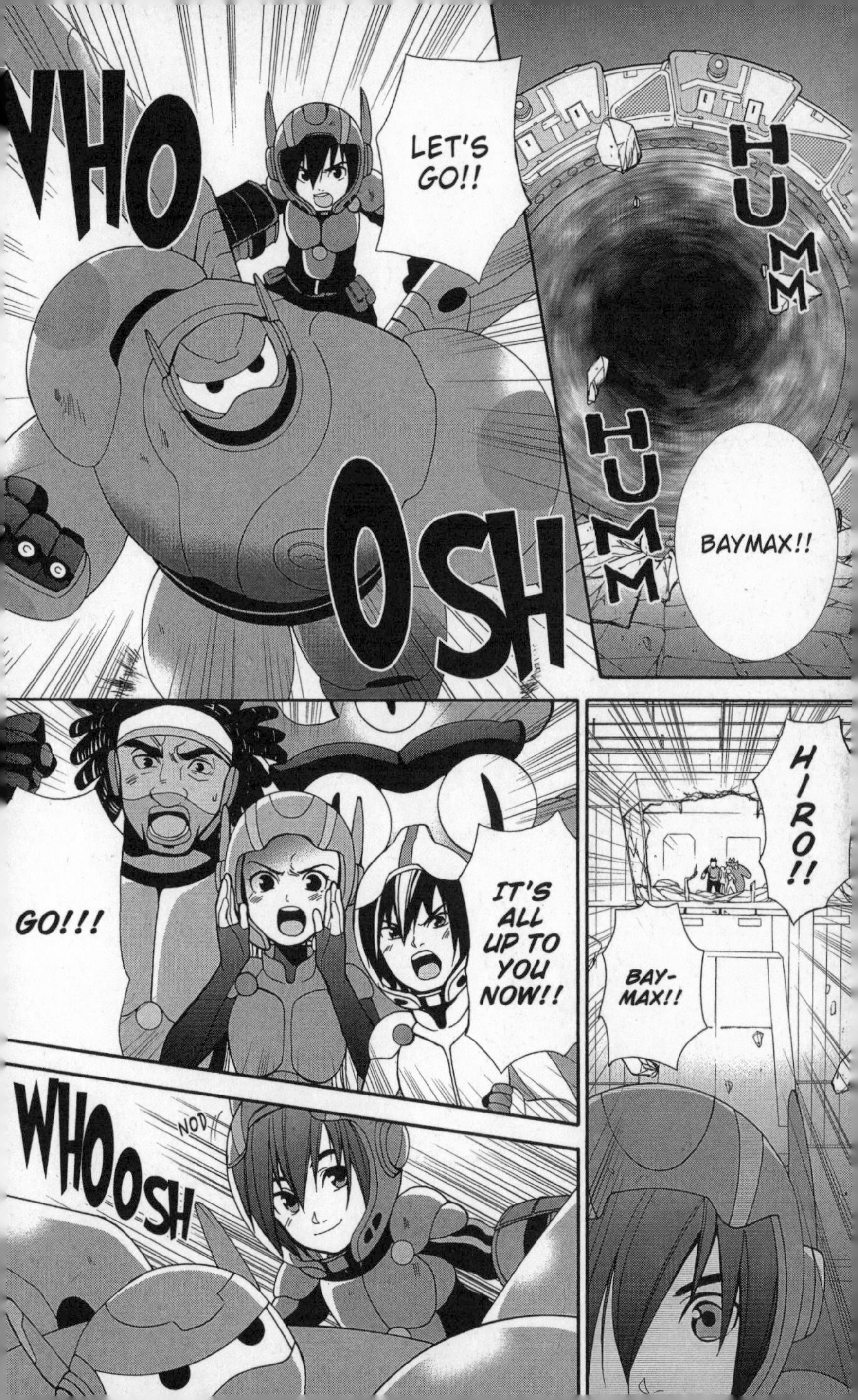
HUMM
HUMM
BAYMAX!!
LET'S GO!!
WHOOSH
HIRO!!
BAY-MAX!!
IT'S ALL UP TO YOU NOW!!
GO!!!
NOD
WHOOSH

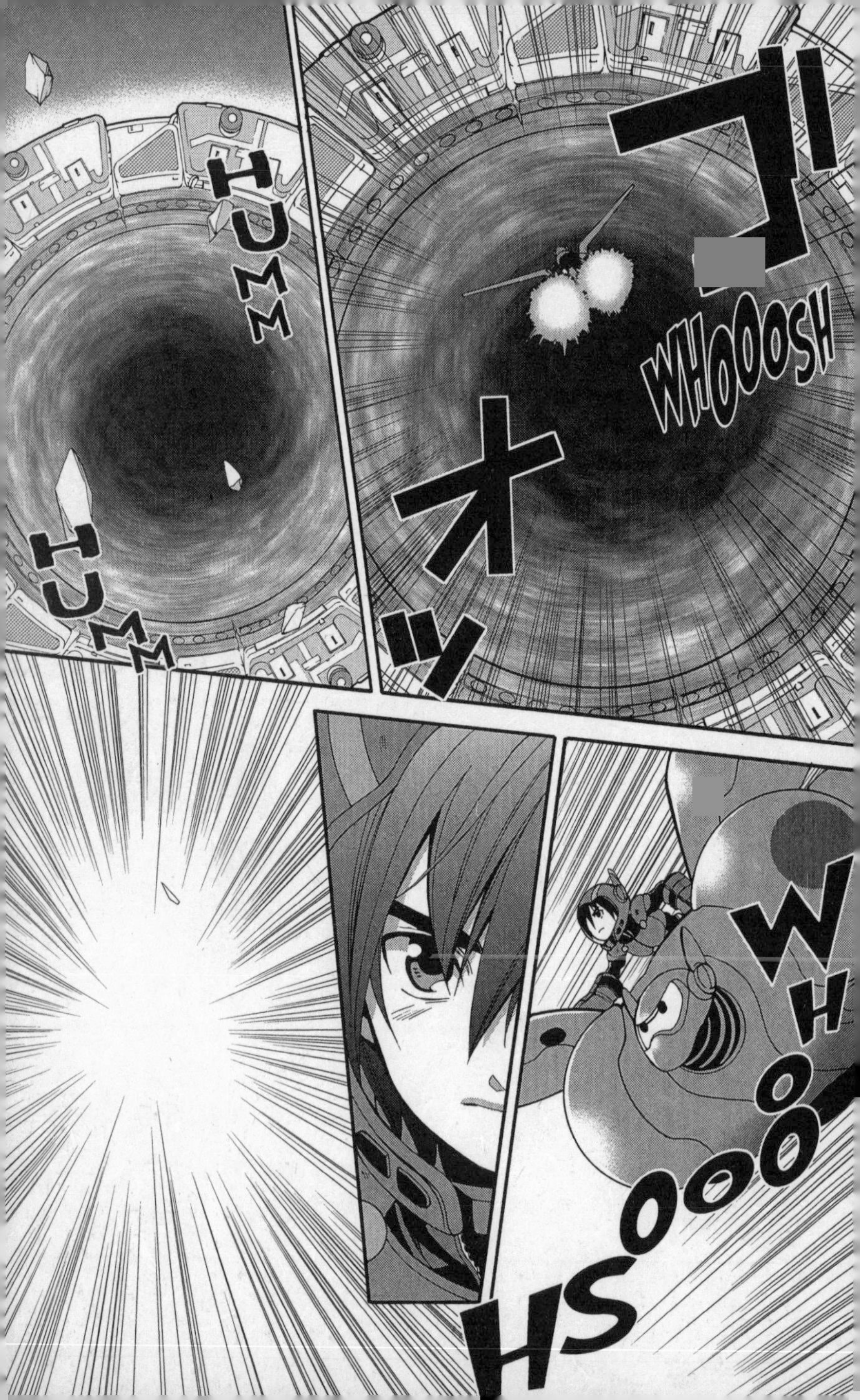

WHOOOSH
HUMM
HUMM
WHOOOOOSH

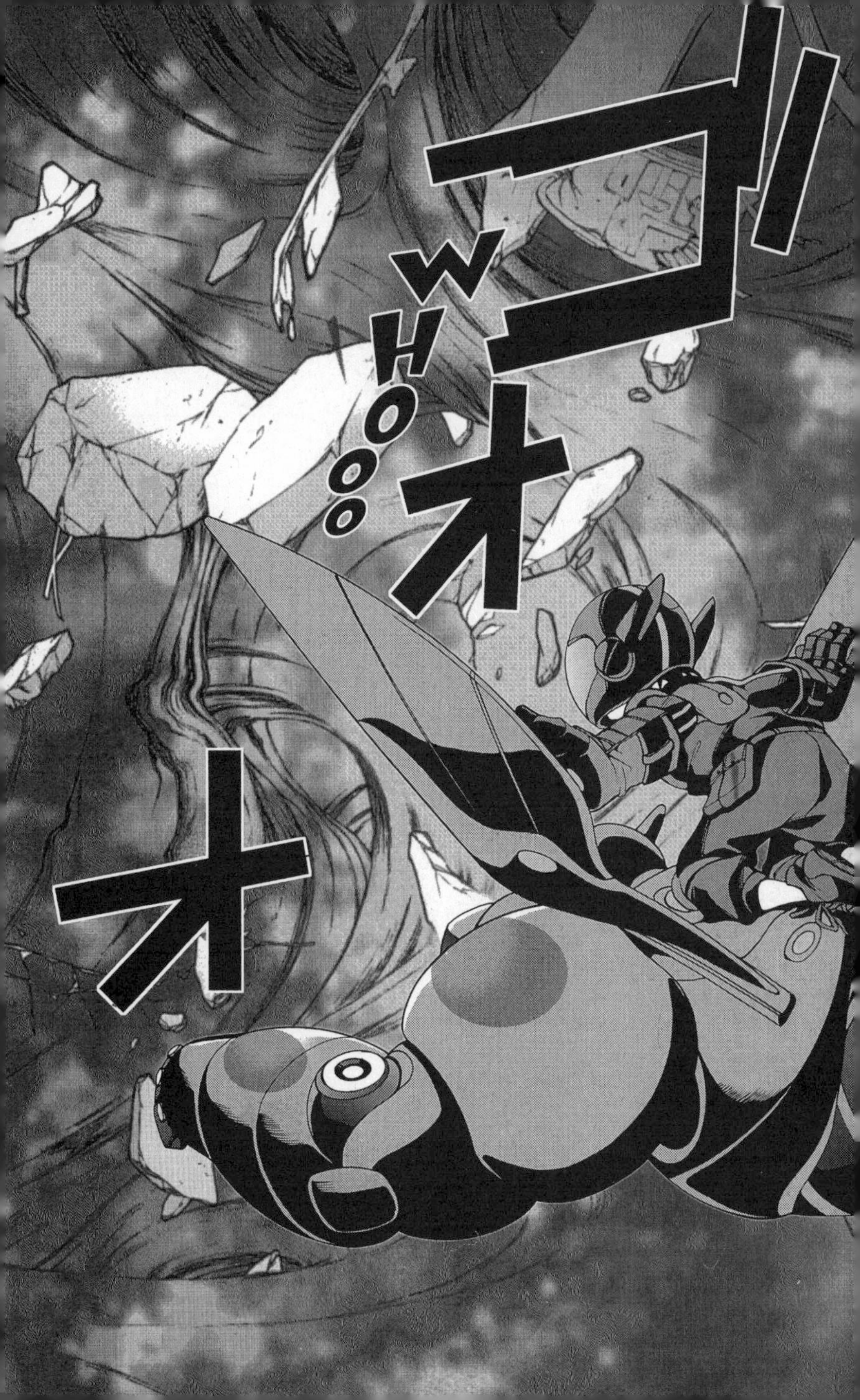

ゴオオ
WHOOO

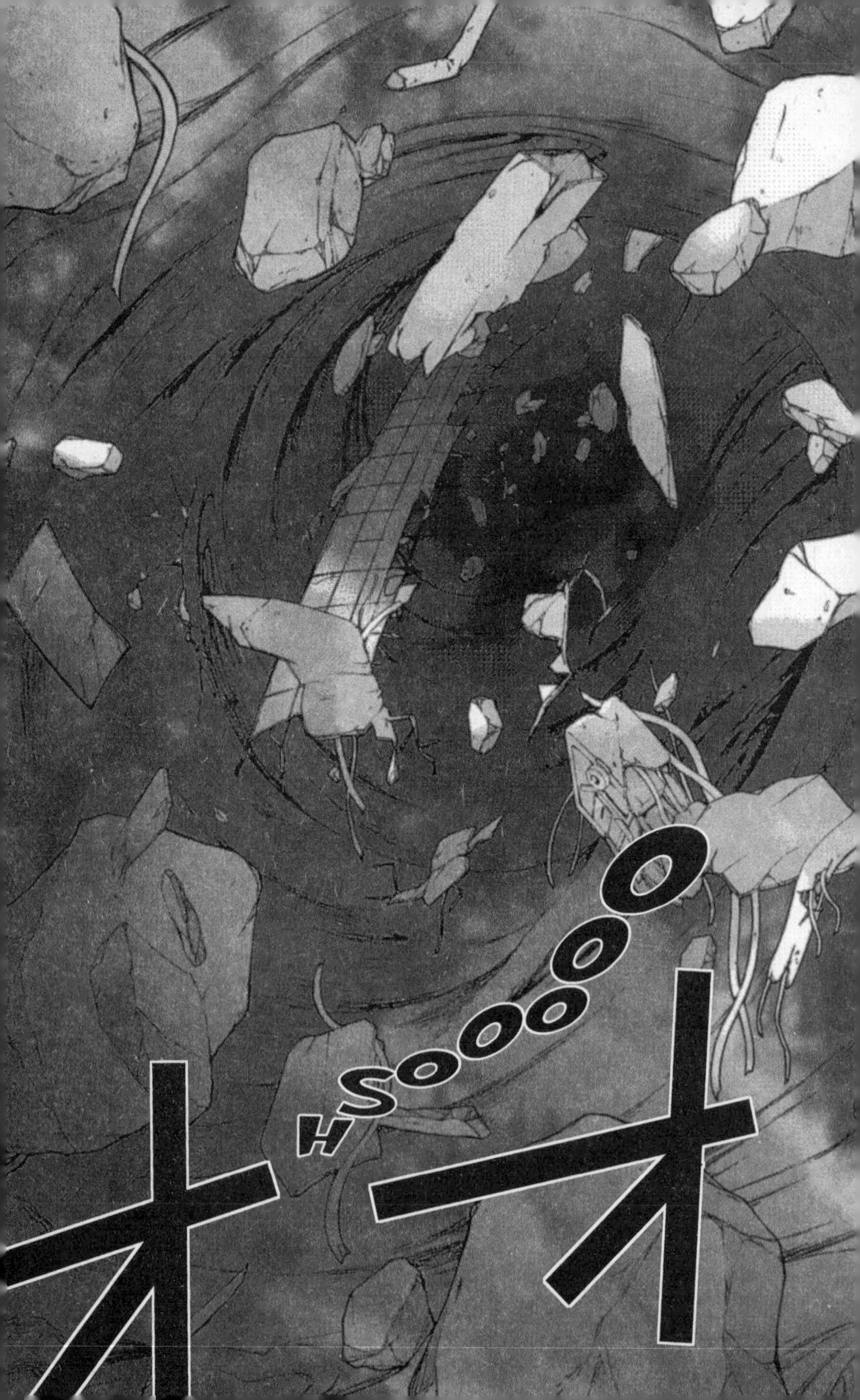
HSOOOOO

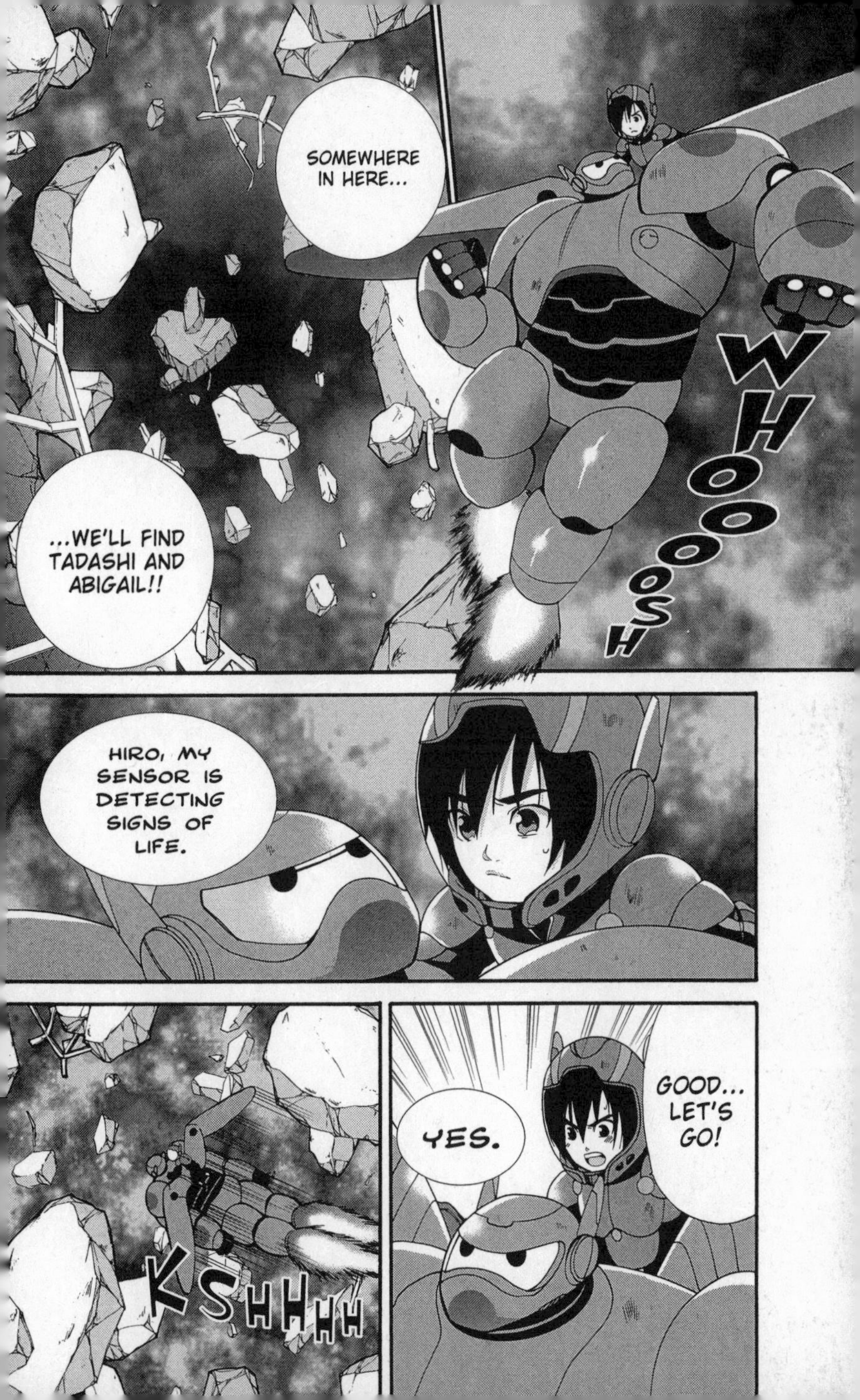
SOMEWHERE IN HERE...
WHOOOOOSH
...WE'LL FIND TADASHI AND ABIGAIL!!
HIRO, MY SENSOR IS DETECTING SIGNS OF LIFE.
GOOD... LET'S GO!
YES.
KSHHHH

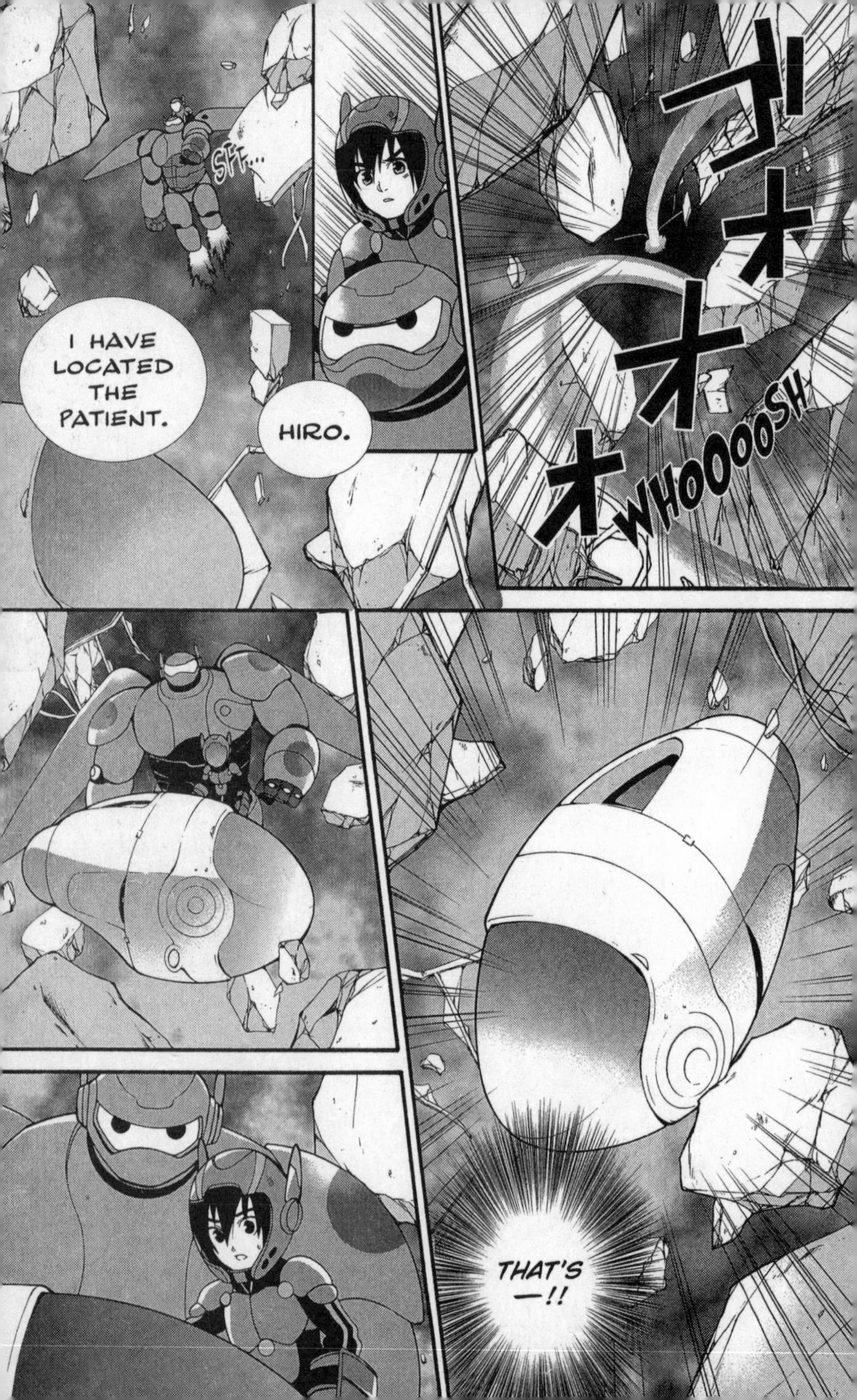
ゴオオオ
WHOOOOSH
HIRO.
SFF...
I HAVE LOCATED THE PATIENT.
THAT'S —!!

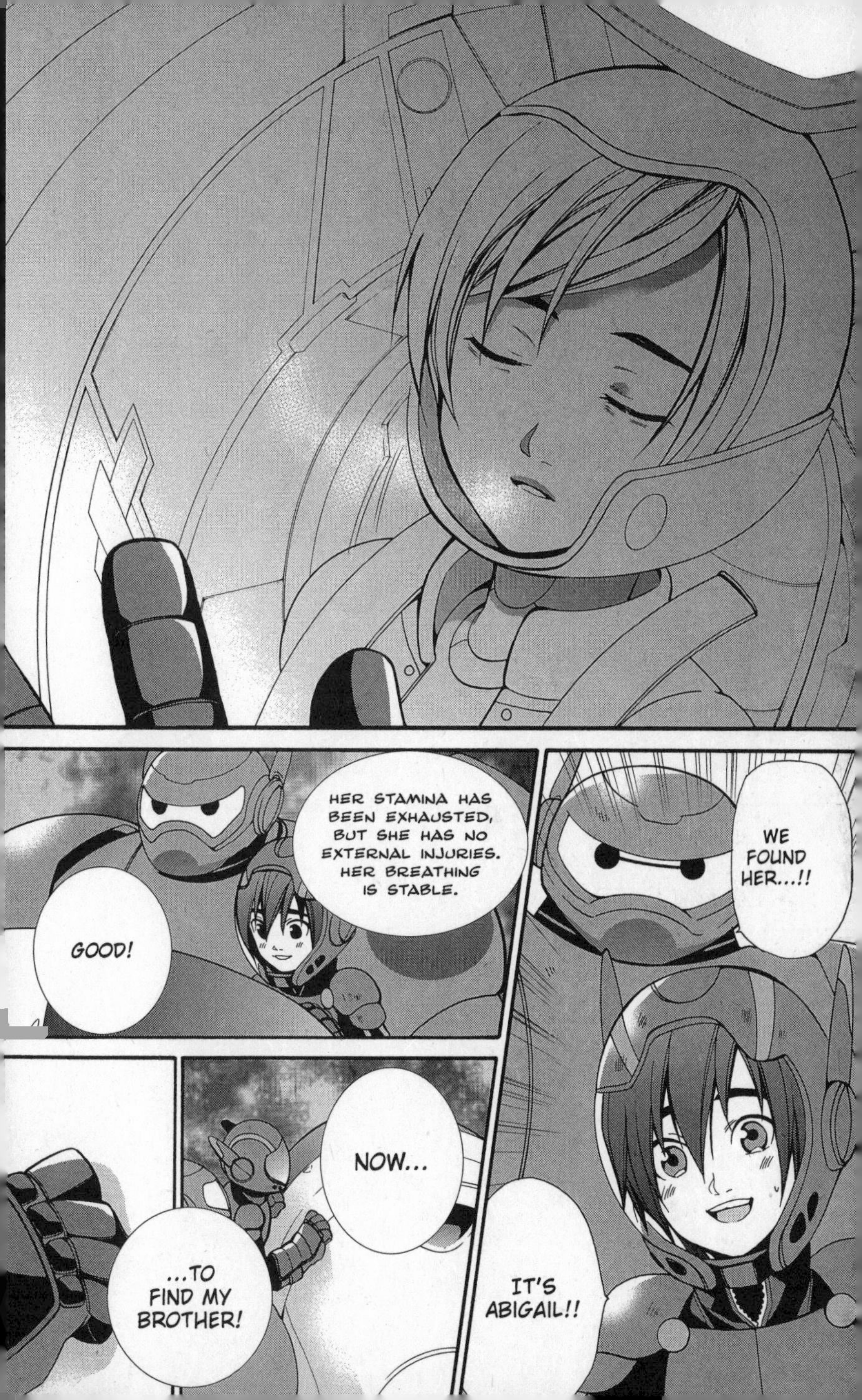
WE FOUND HER...!!
IT'S ABIGAIL!!
HER STAMINA HAS BEEN EXHAUSTED, BUT SHE HAS NO EXTERNAL INJURIES. HER BREATHING IS STABLE.
GOOD!
NOW...
...TO FIND MY BROTHER!

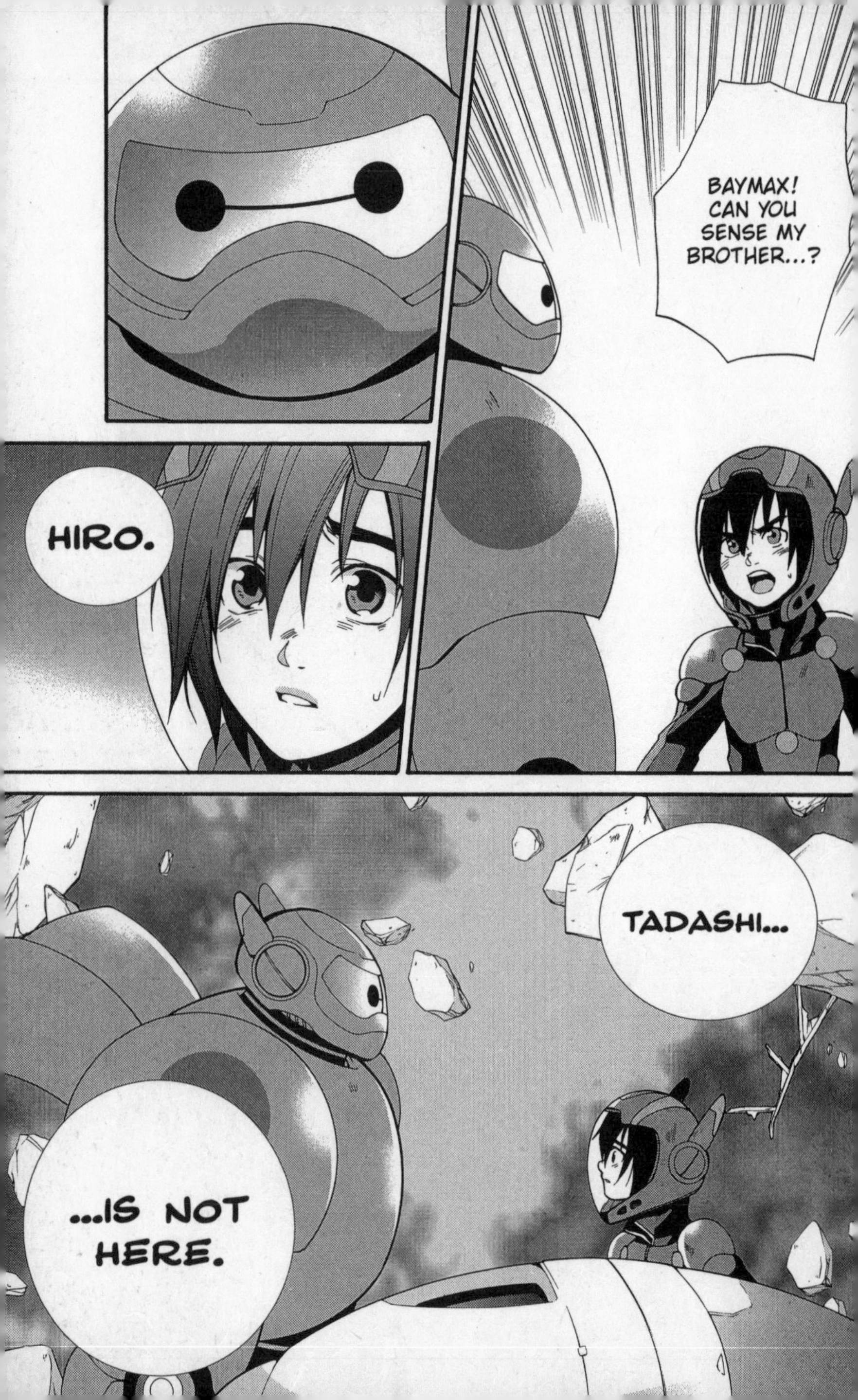
BAYMAX! CAN YOU SENSE MY BROTHER...?
HIRO.
TADASHI...
...IS NOT HERE.

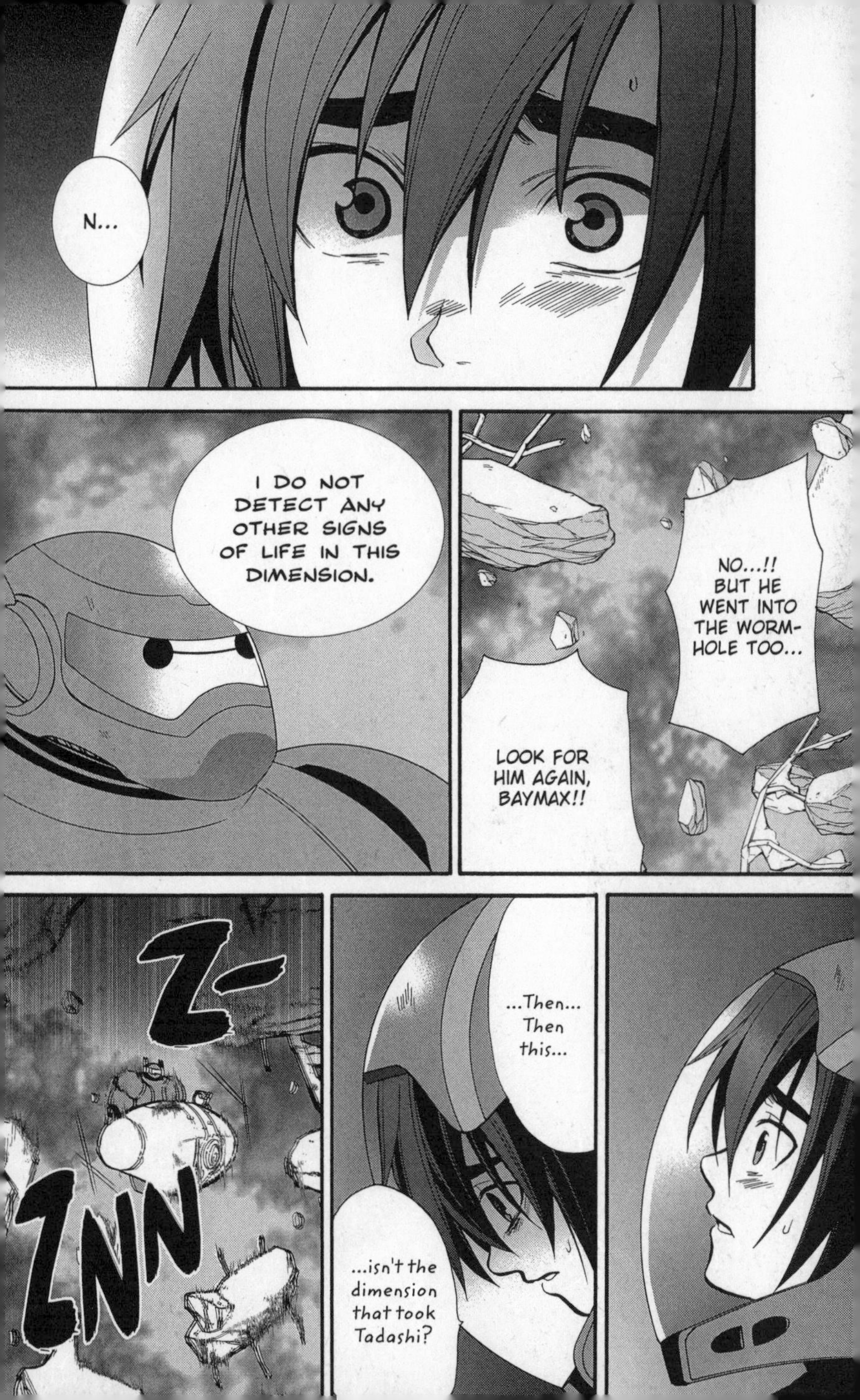
N...
NO...!! BUT HE WENT INTO THE WORM-HOLE TOO...
LOOK FOR HIM AGAIN, BAYMAX!!
I DO NOT DETECT ANY OTHER SIGNS OF LIFE IN THIS DIMENSION.
...Then... Then this...
...isn't the dimension that took Tadashi?
Z-
ZNN

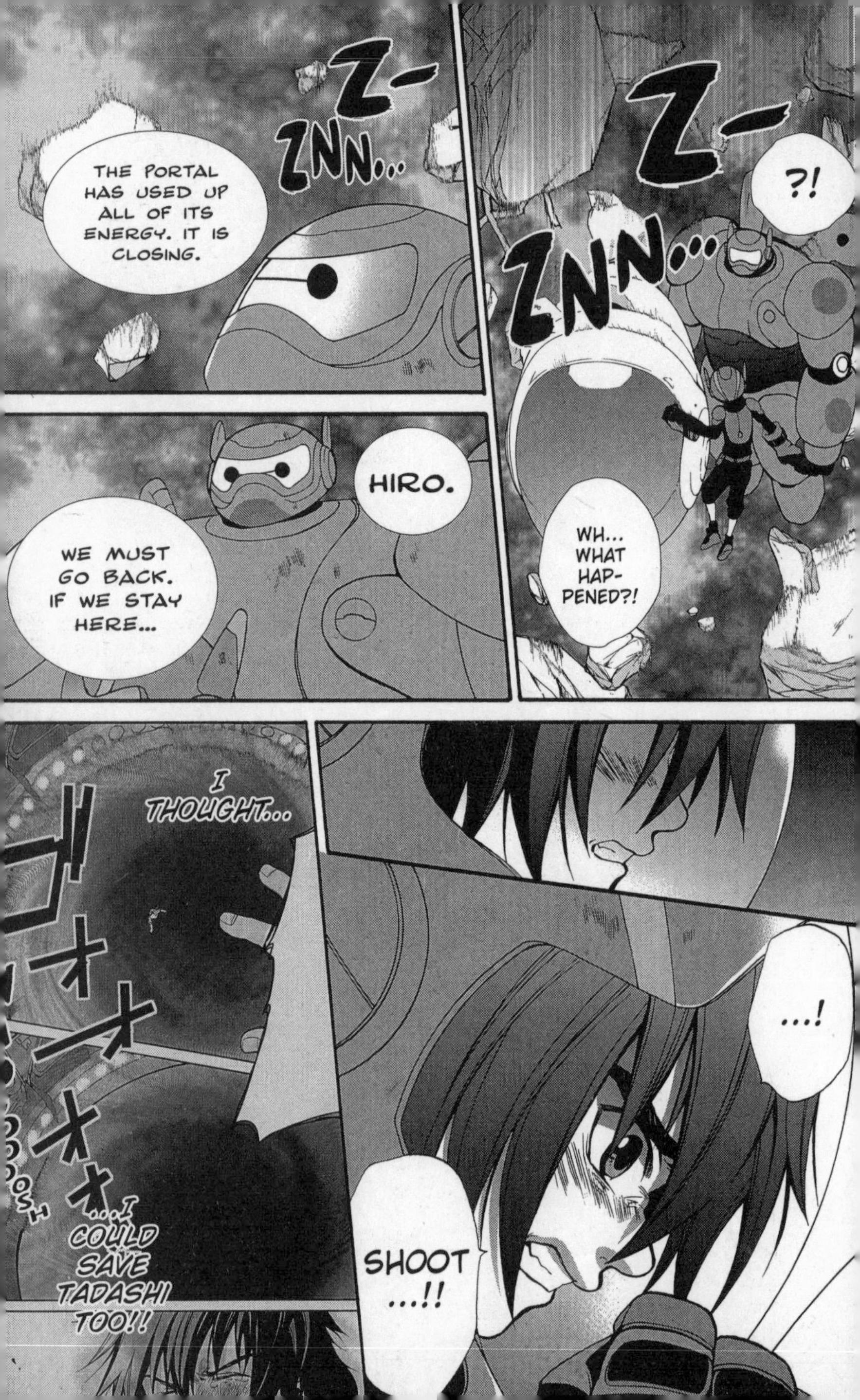
Z-
ZNN...
?!
WH... WHAT HAP-PENED?!
Z-
ZNN...
THE PORTAL HAS USED UP ALL OF ITS ENERGY. IT IS CLOSING.
HIRO.
WE MUST GO BACK. IF WE STAY HERE...
...!
SHOOT ...!!
I THOUGHT...
...I COULD SAVE TADASHI TOO!!

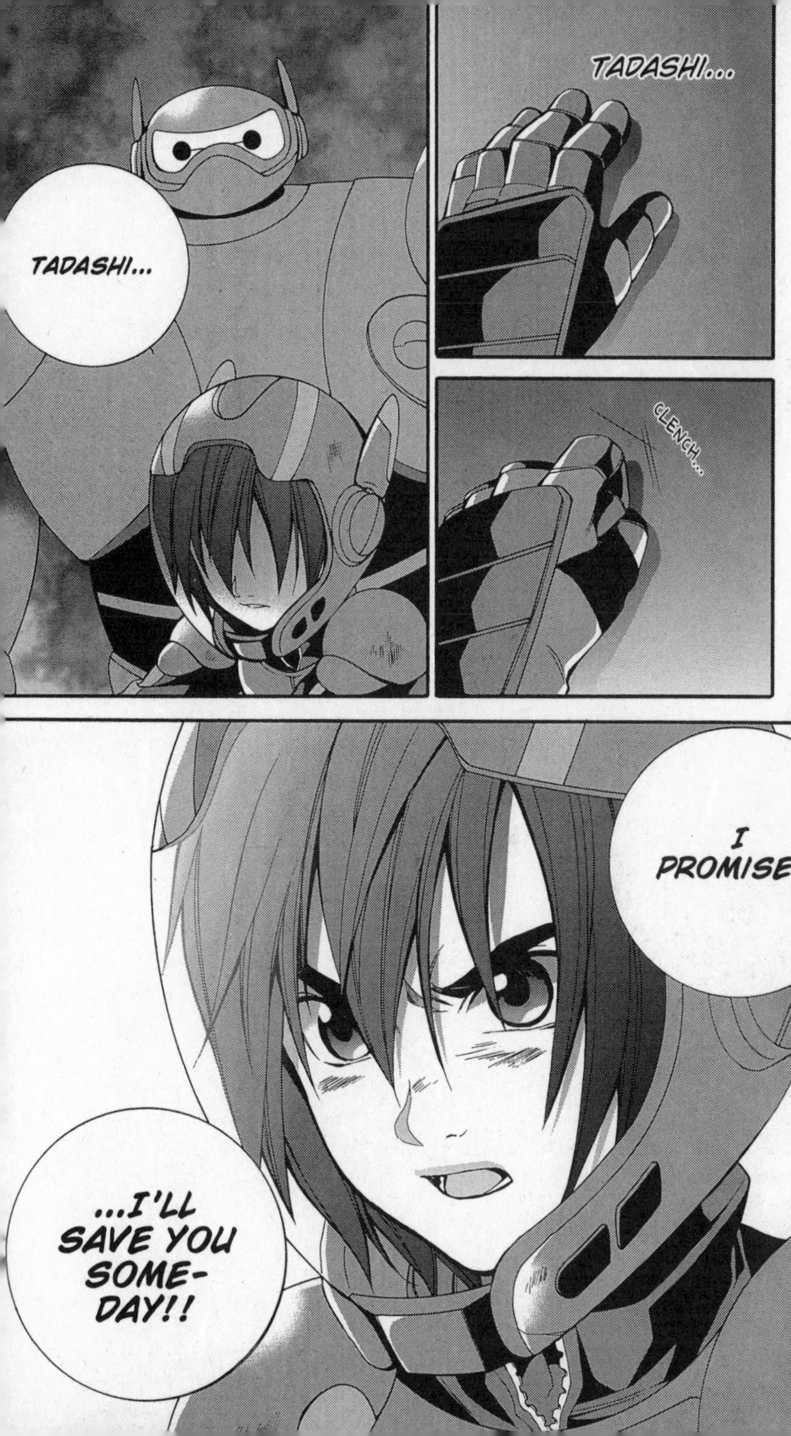
TADASHI...
CLENCH...
TADASHI...
I PROMISE...
...I'LL SAVE YOU SOME-DAY!!

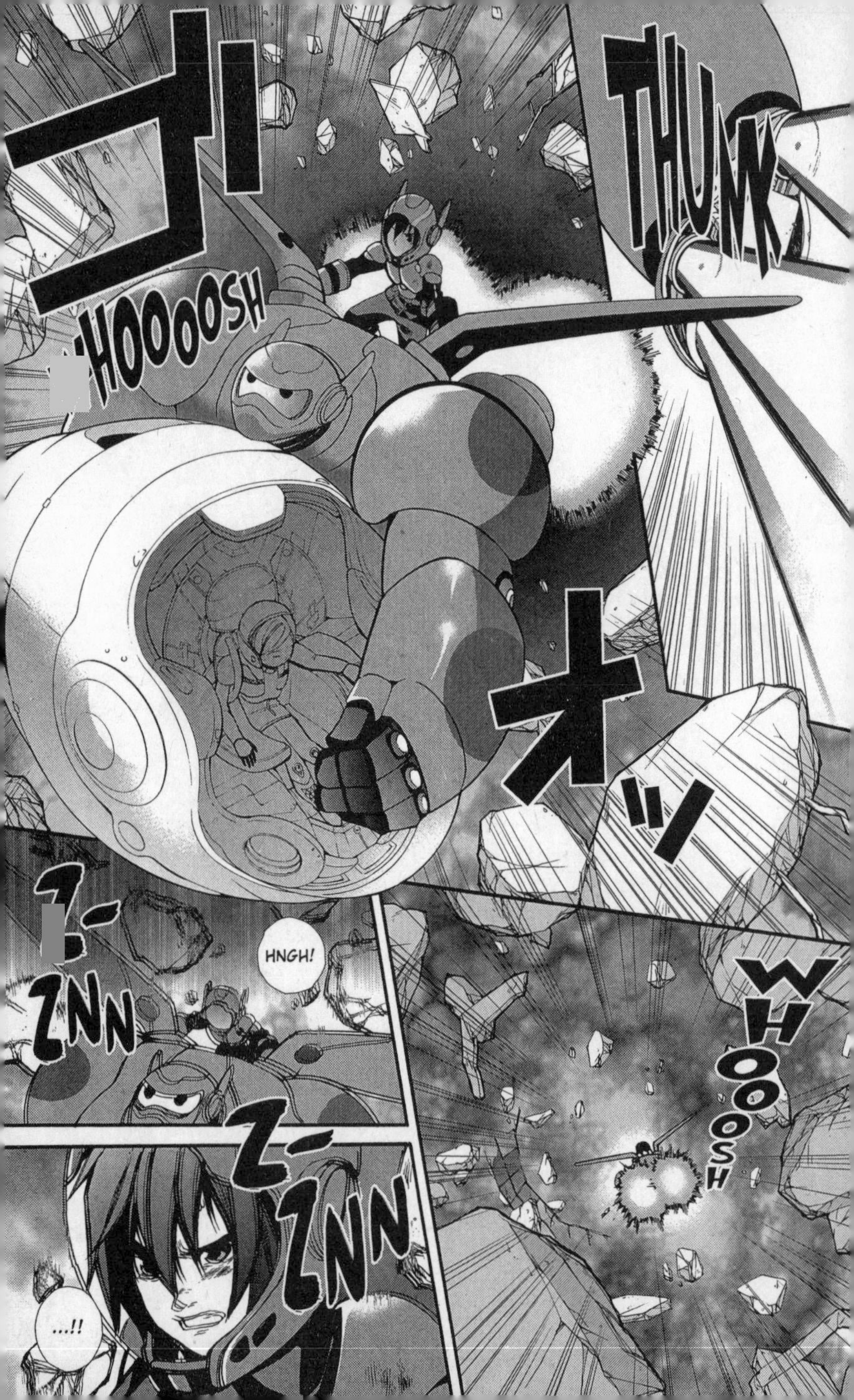
THUNK
HOOOOSH
オッ
WHOOOOSH
HNGH!
Z-ZNN
Z-ZNN
...!!

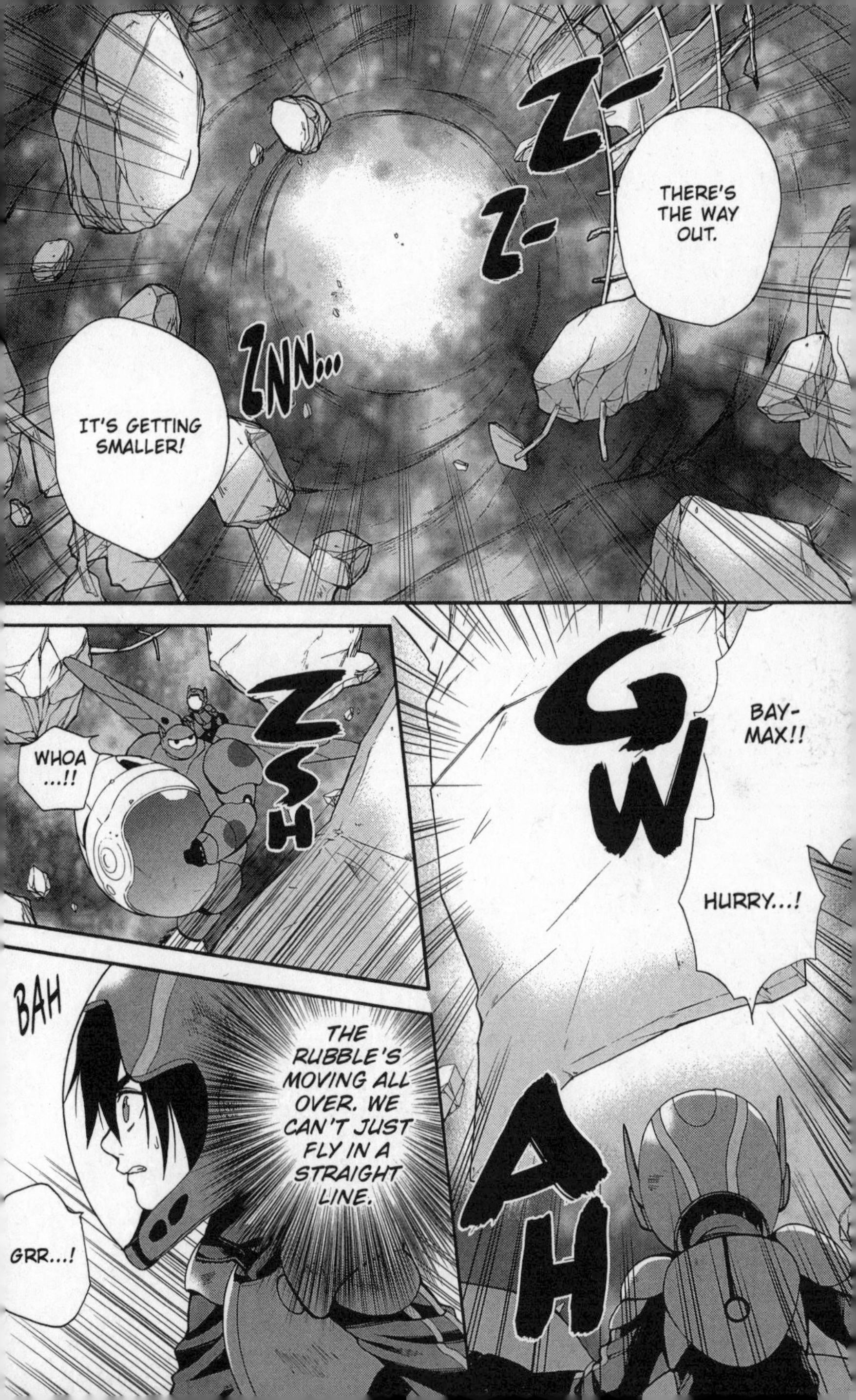
THERE'S THE WAY OUT.
Z-Z-
ZNN...
IT'S GETTING SMALLER!
BAY-MAX!!
GW
HURRY...!
AH
ZSH
WHOA...!!
THE RUBBLE'S MOVING ALL OVER. WE CAN'T JUST FLY IN A STRAIGHT LINE.
BAH
GRR...!

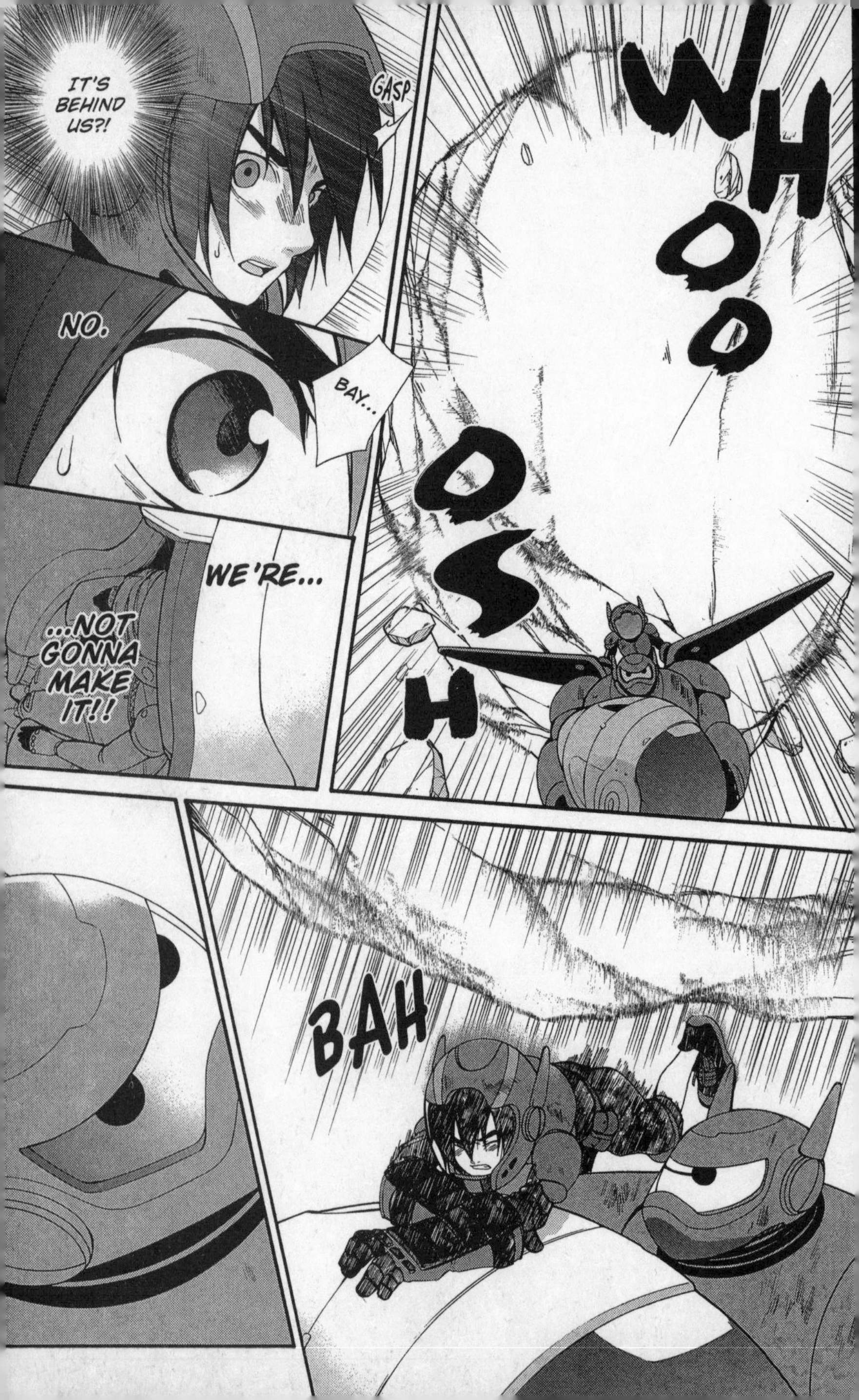
WHOOOSH
GASP
IT'S BEHIND US?!
NO.
BAY...
WE'RE...
...NOT GONNA MAKE IT!!
BAH

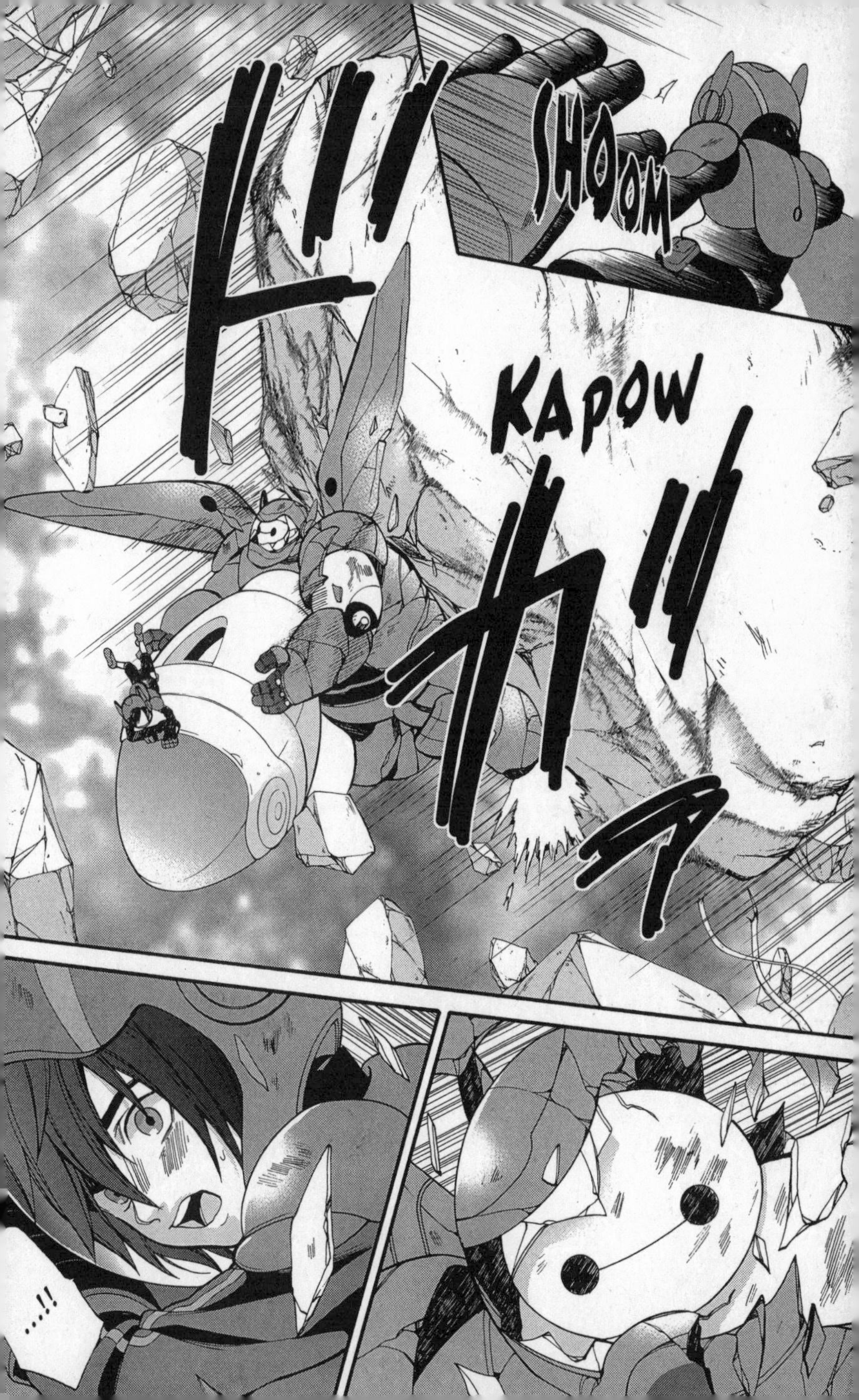
SHOOM
KAPOW
...!!

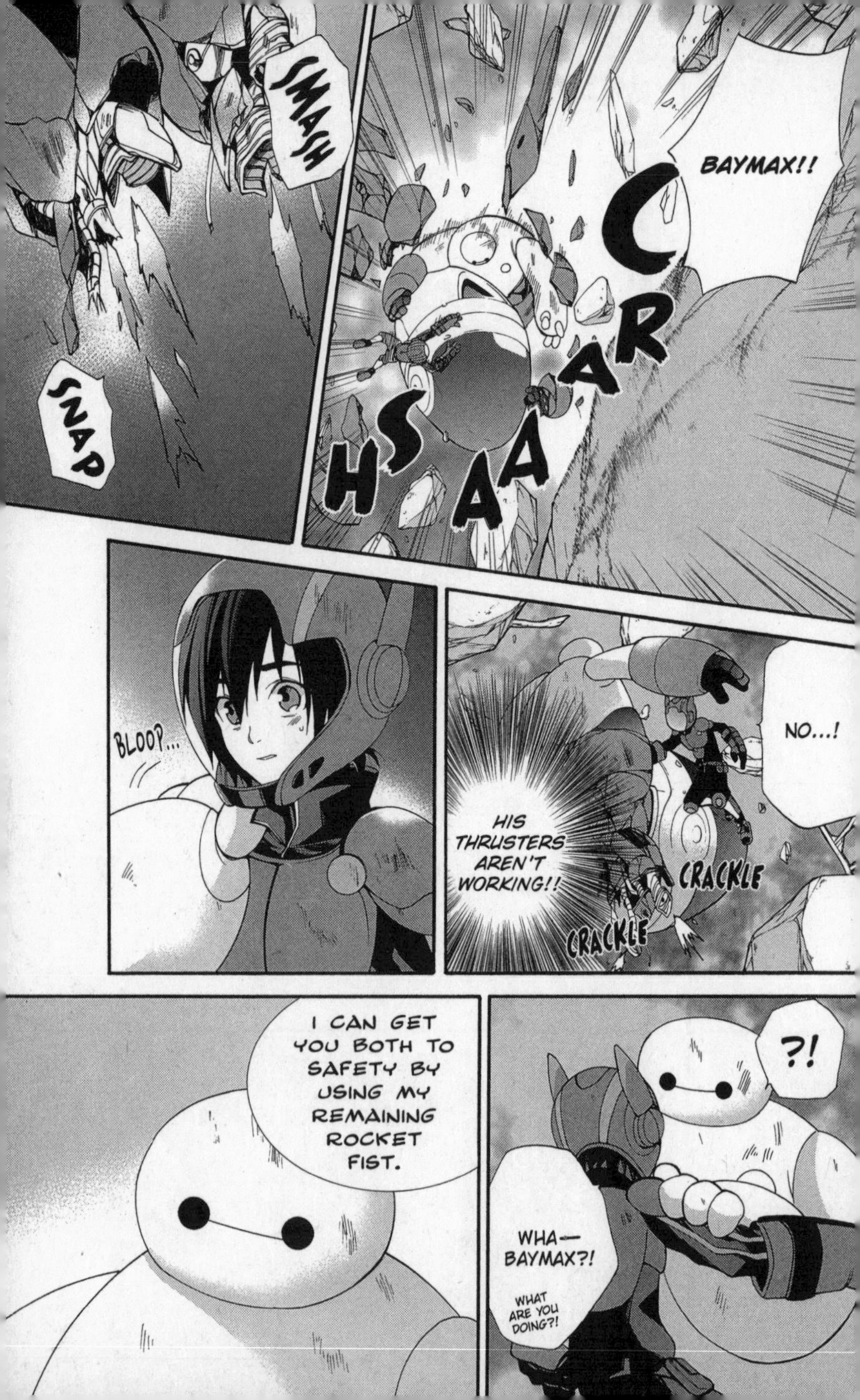
BAYMAX!!
CRAAASH
SMASH
SNAP
NO...!
HIS THRUSTERS AREN'T WORKING!!
CRACKLE
CRACKLE
BLOOP...
?!
WHA— BAYMAX?!
WHAT ARE YOU DOING?!
I CAN GET YOU BOTH TO SAFETY BY USING MY REMAINING ROCKET FIST.

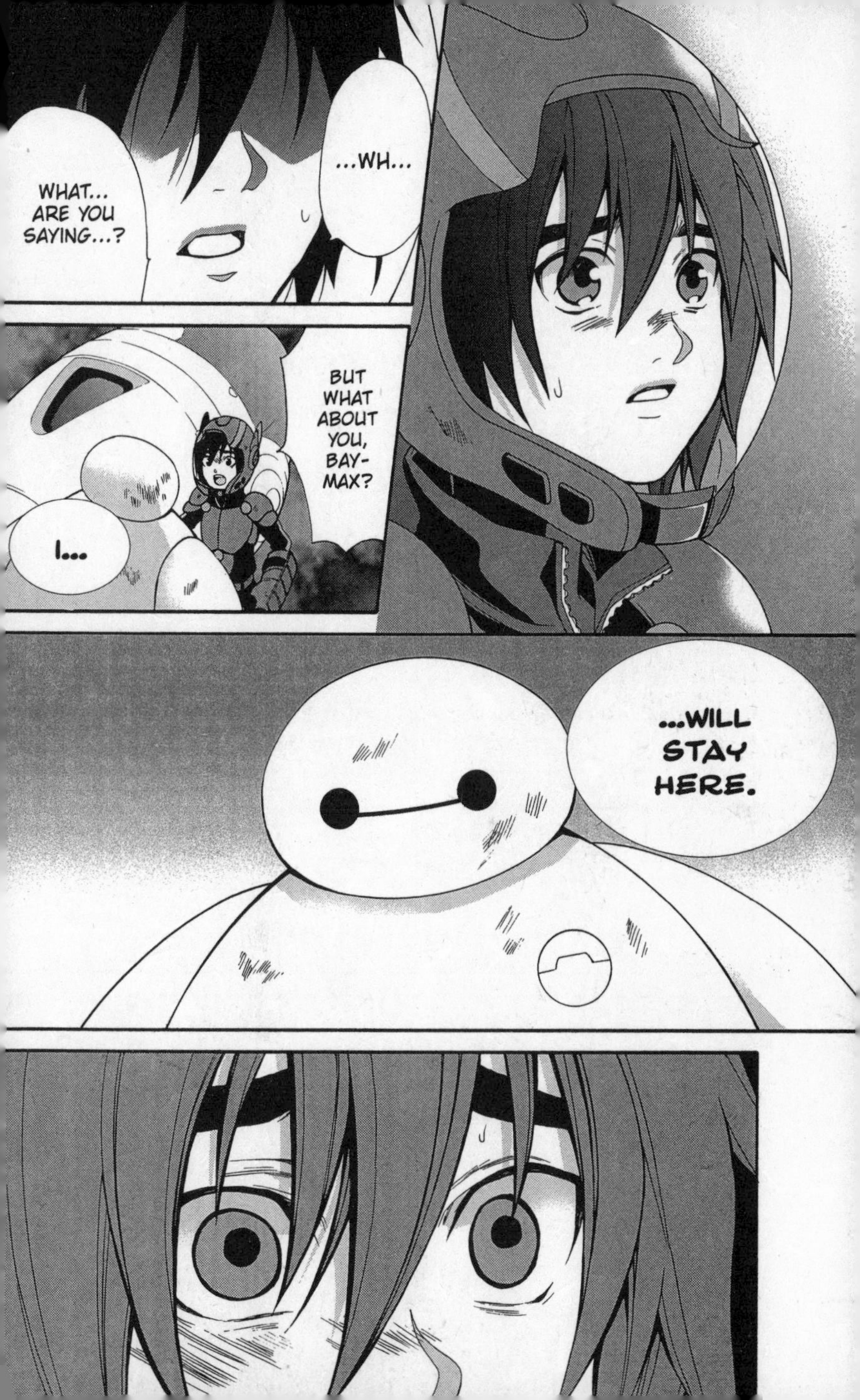
...WH...
WHAT... ARE YOU SAYING...?
BUT WHAT ABOUT YOU, BAY-MAX?
I...
...WILL STAY HERE.

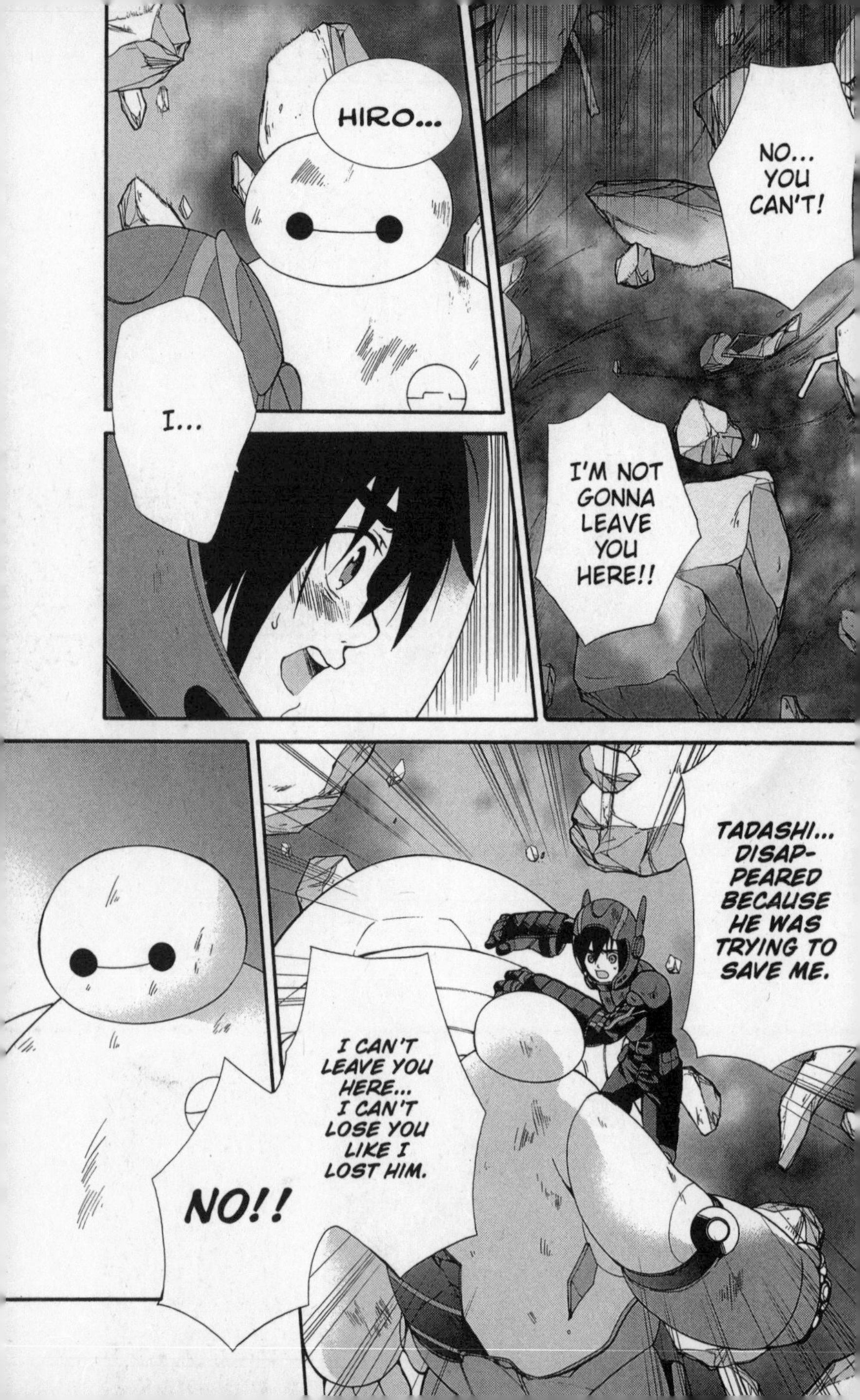
NO... YOU CAN'T!
I'M NOT GONNA LEAVE YOU HERE!!
HIRO...
I...
TADASHI... DISAPPEARED BECAUSE HE WAS TRYING TO SAVE ME.
I CAN'T LEAVE YOU HERE... I CAN'T LOSE YOU LIKE I LOST HIM.
NO!!

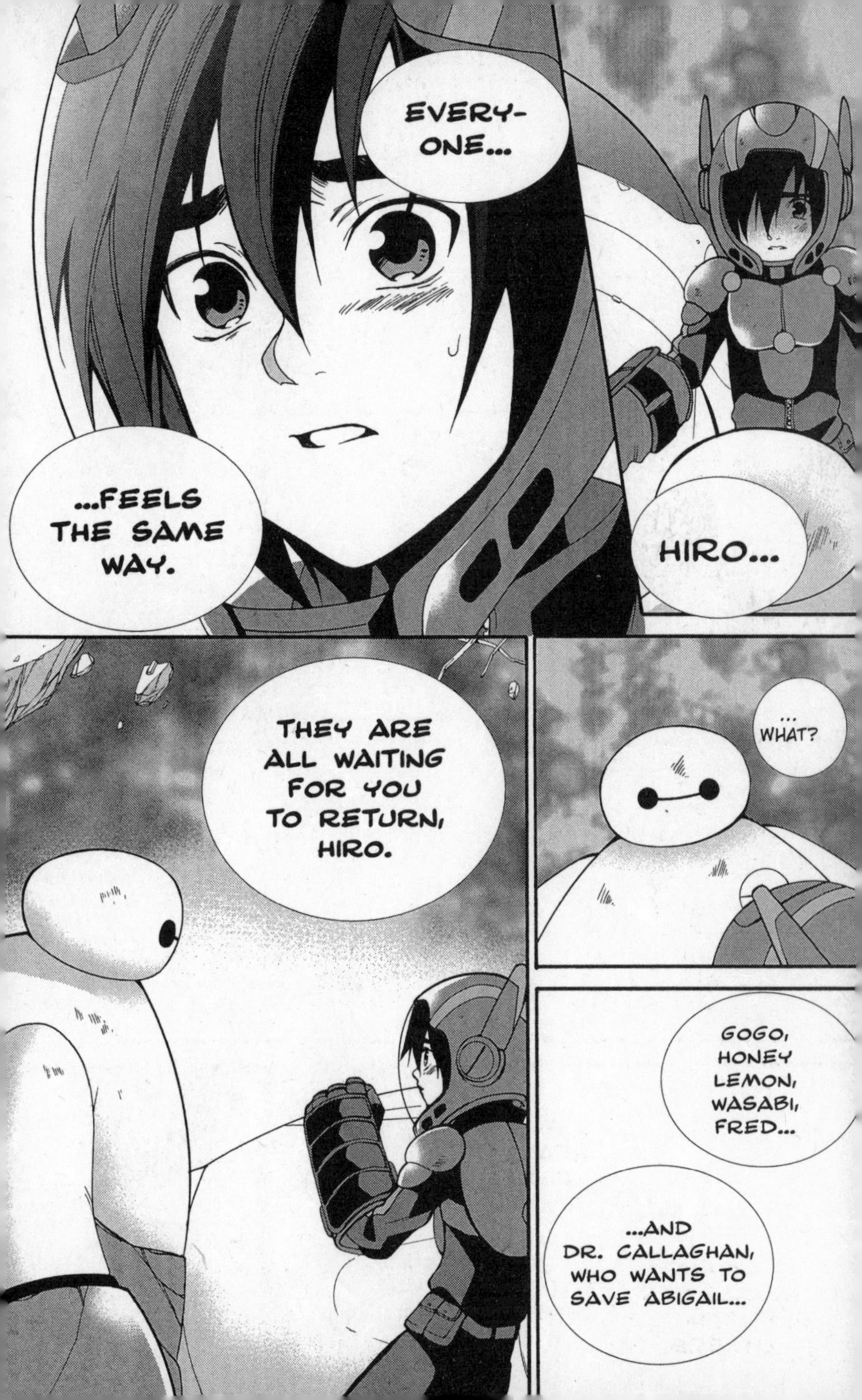
HIRO...
EVERY-ONE...
...FEELS THE SAME WAY.
...
WHAT?
GOGO, HONEY LEMON, WASABI, FRED...
...AND DR. CALLAGHAN, WHO WANTS TO SAVE ABIGAIL...
THEY ARE ALL WAITING FOR YOU TO RETURN, HIRO.

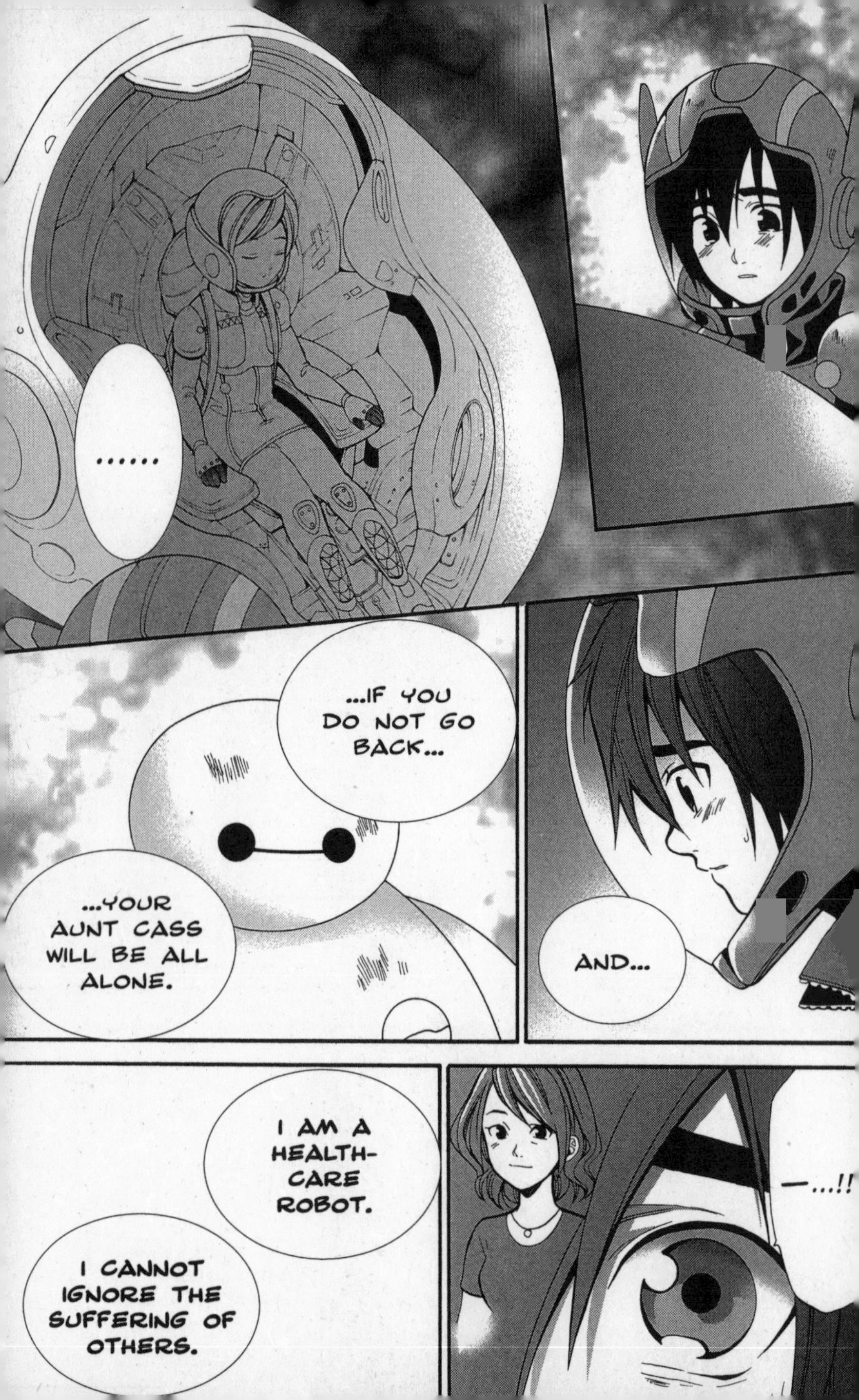
......
AND...
...IF YOU DO NOT GO BACK...
...YOUR AUNT CASS WILL BE ALL ALONE.
—...!!
I AM A HEALTH-CARE ROBOT.
I CANNOT IGNORE THE SUFFERING OF OTHERS.

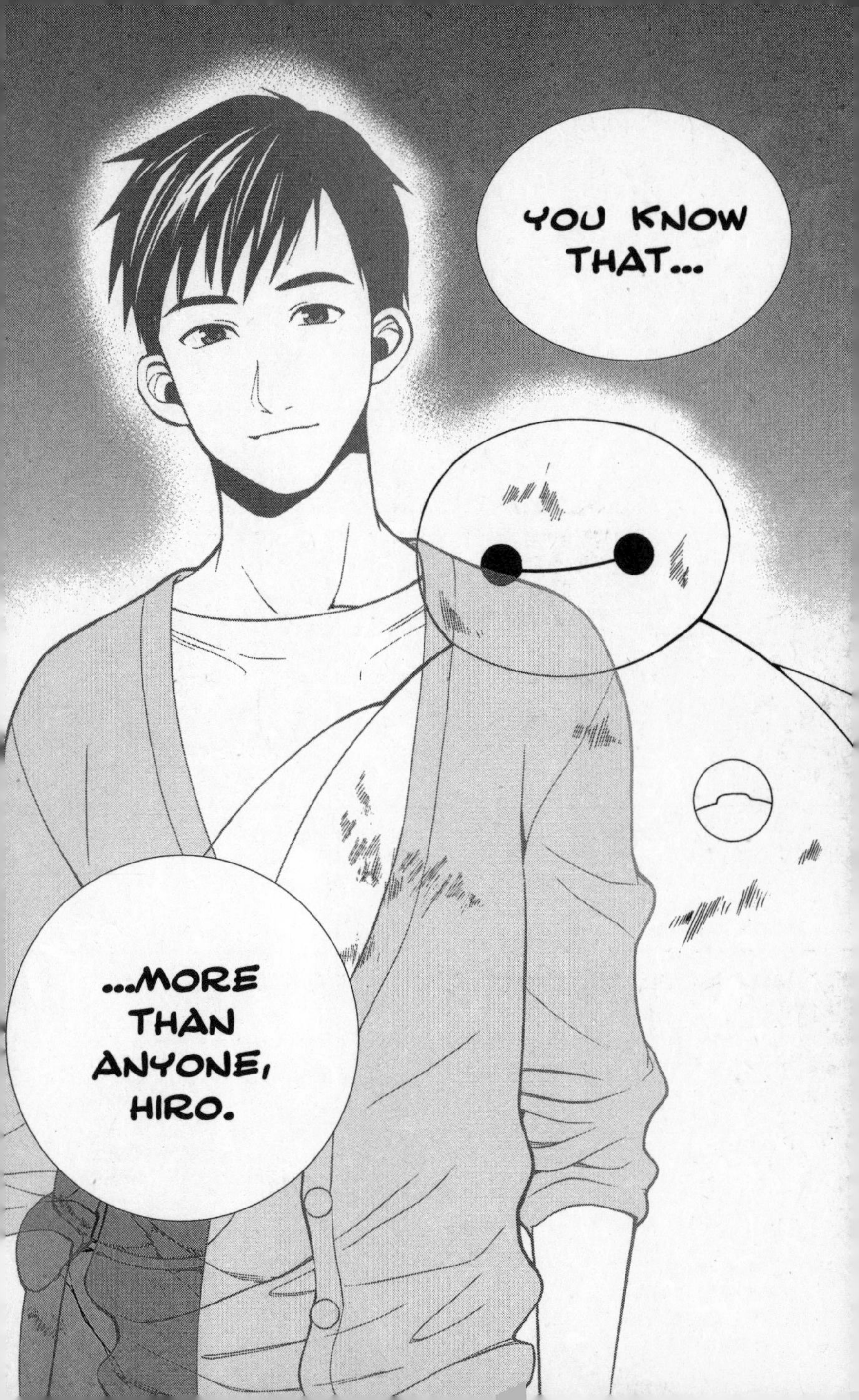
YOU KNOW THAT...
...MORE THAN ANYONE, HIRO.

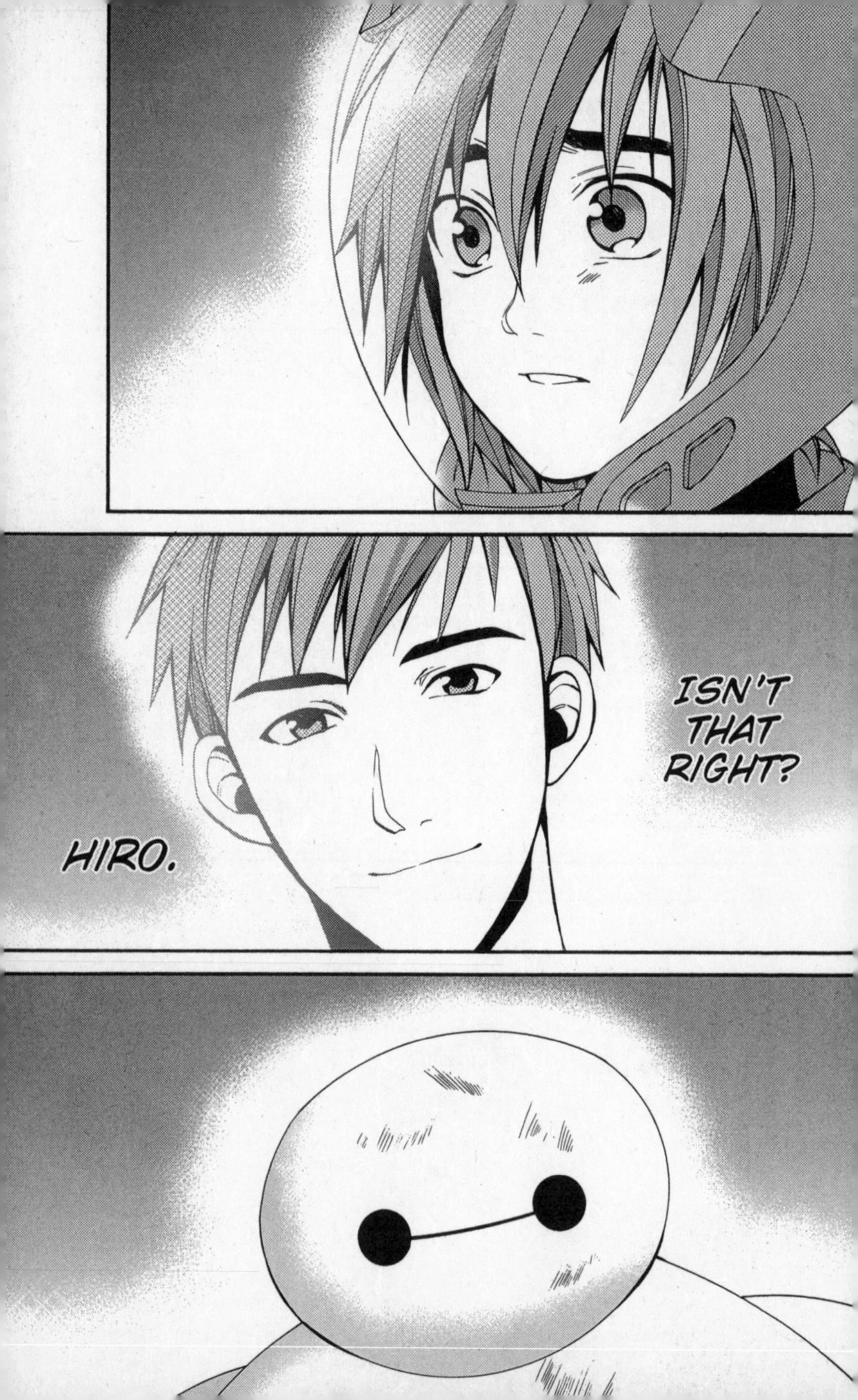
ISN'T THAT RIGHT?
HIRO.

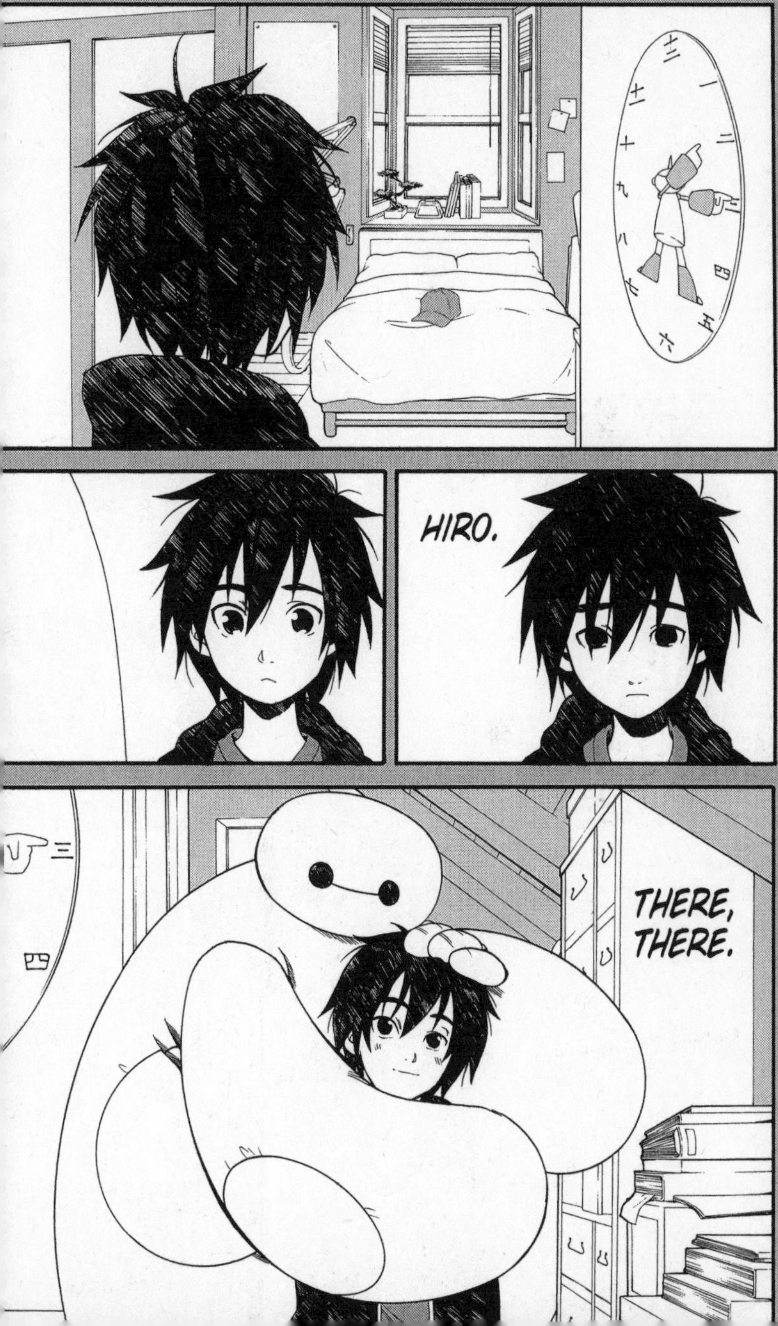
HIRO.
THERE, THERE.

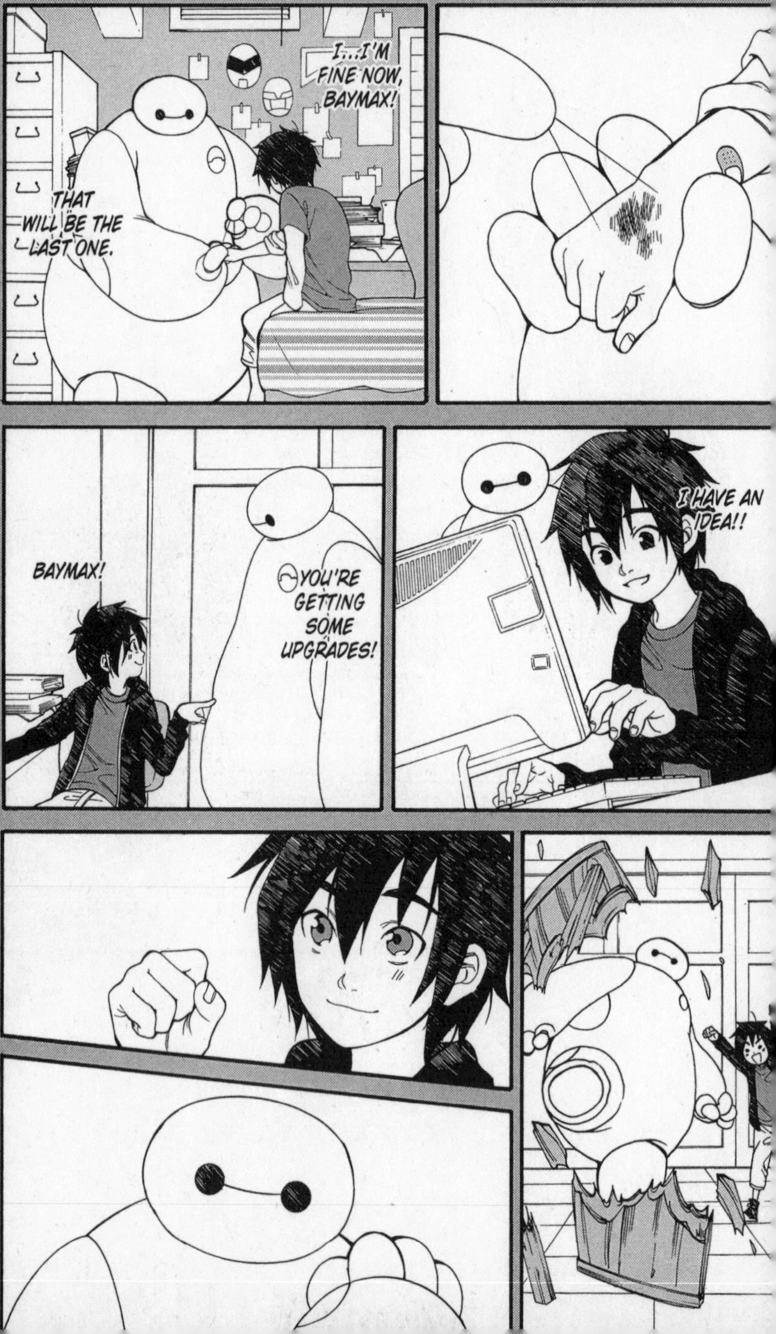
I...I'M FINE NOW, BAYMAX!
THAT WILL BE THE LAST ONE.
I HAVE AN IDEA!!
BAYMAX!
YOU'RE GETTING SOME UPGRADES!

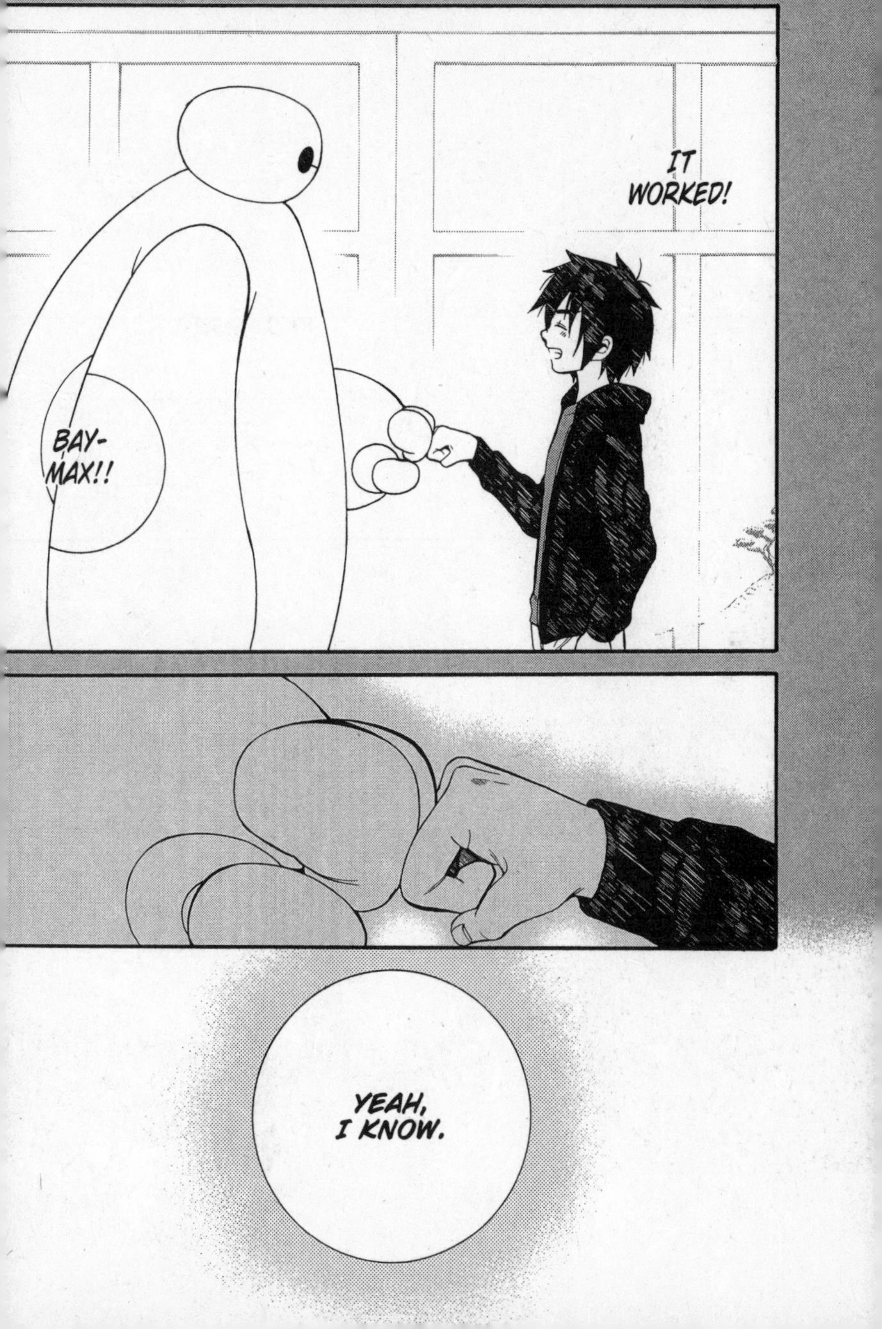
IT WORKED!
BAY-MAX!!
YEAH, I KNOW.

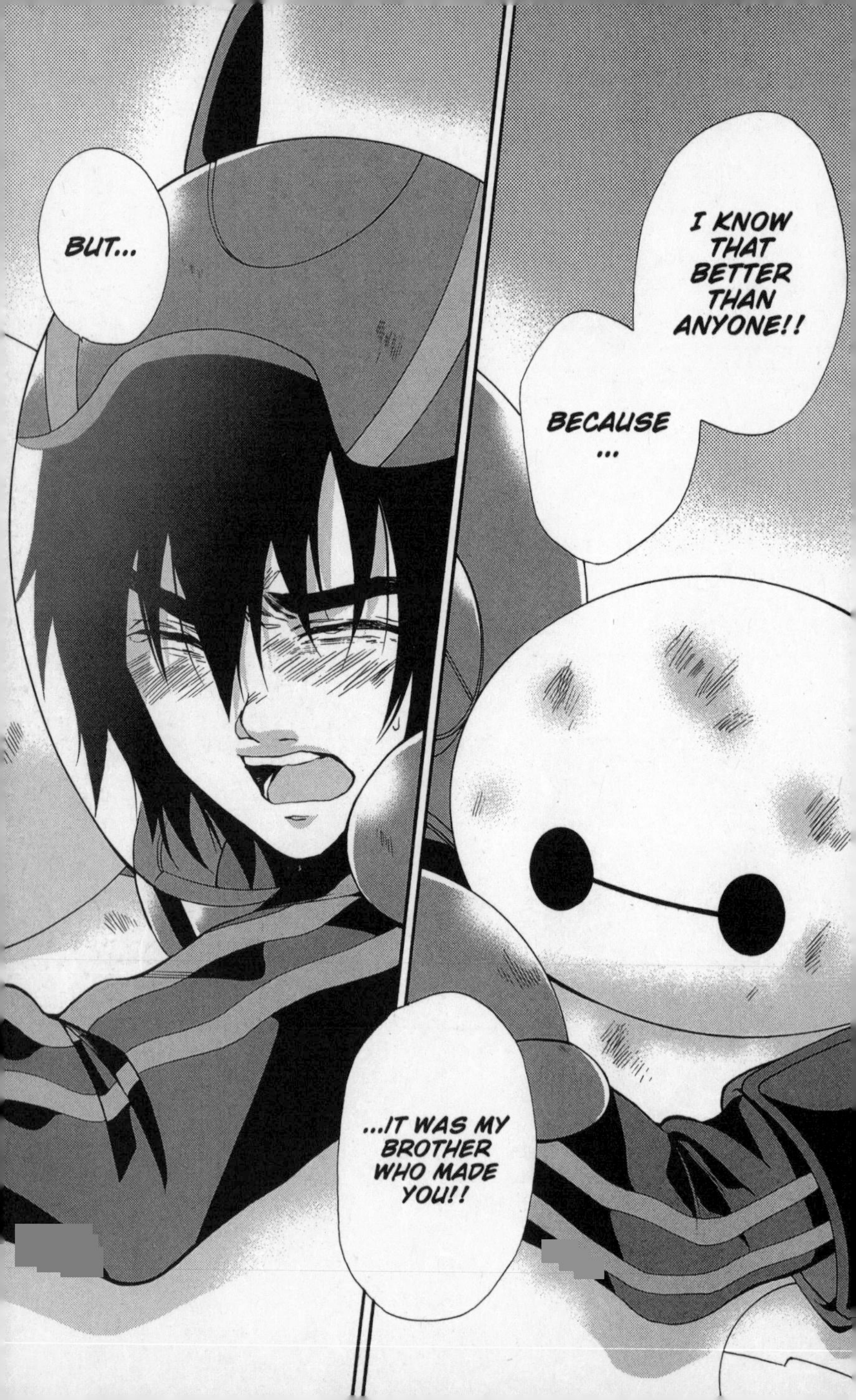
I KNOW THAT BETTER THAN ANYONE!!
BUT...
BECAUSE ...
...IT WAS MY BROTHER WHO MADE YOU!!

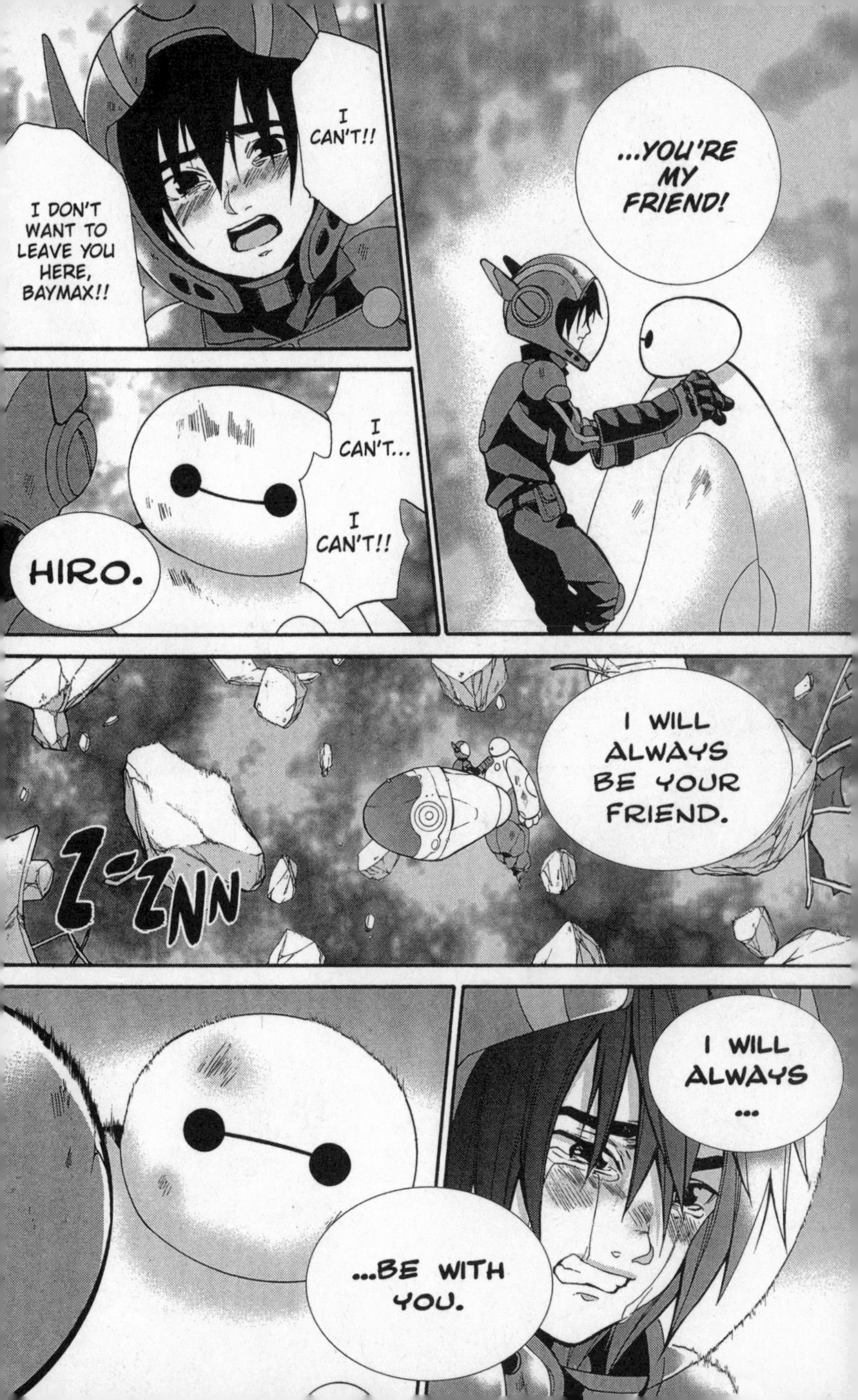
...YOU'RE MY FRIEND!
I CAN'T!!
I DON'T WANT TO LEAVE YOU HERE, BAYMAX!!
I CAN'T...
I CAN'T!!
HIRO.
I WILL ALWAYS BE YOUR FRIEND.
Z-ZNN
I WILL ALWAYS ...
...BE WITH YOU.

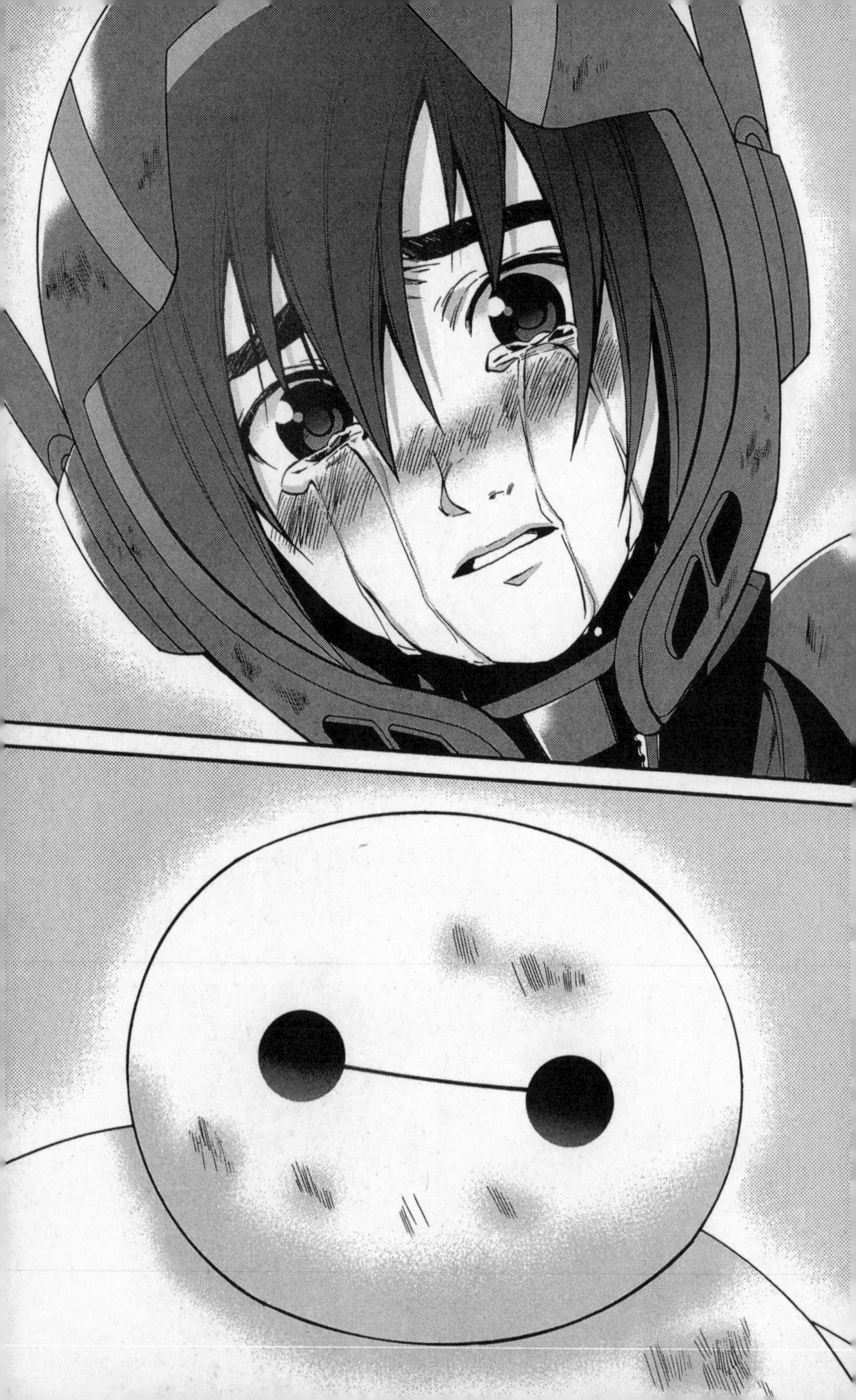

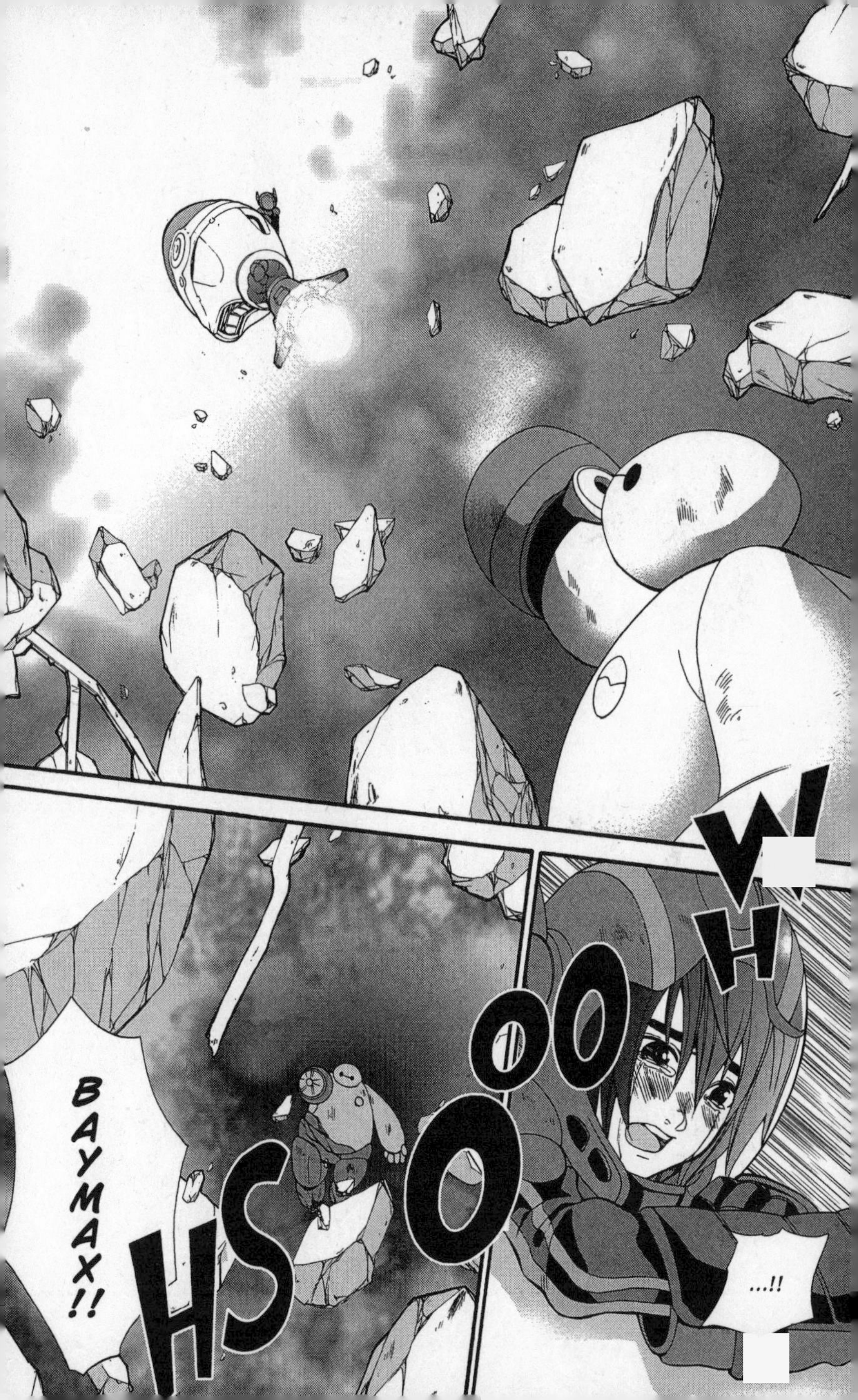
WHOOOOSH
...!!
BAYMAX!!

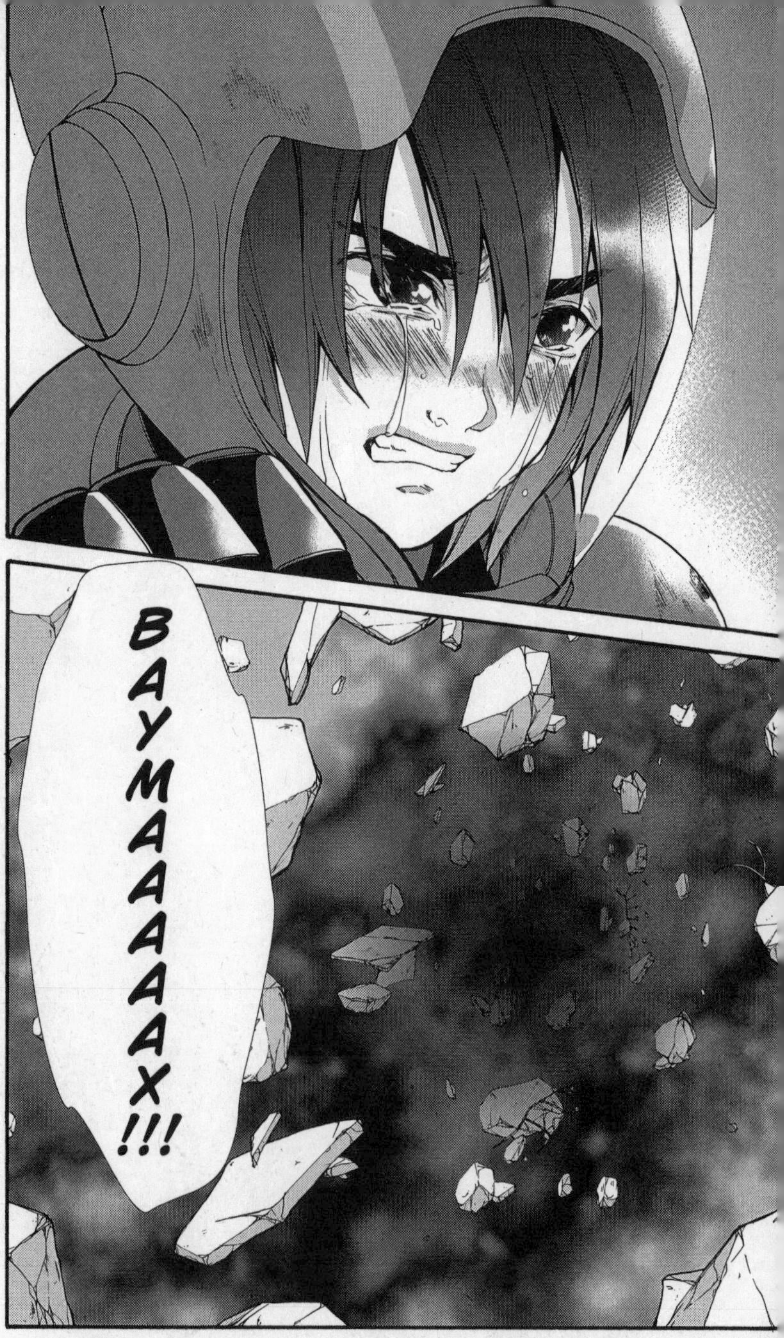
BAYMAAAAAAX!!!

Disney

BIG HERO 6

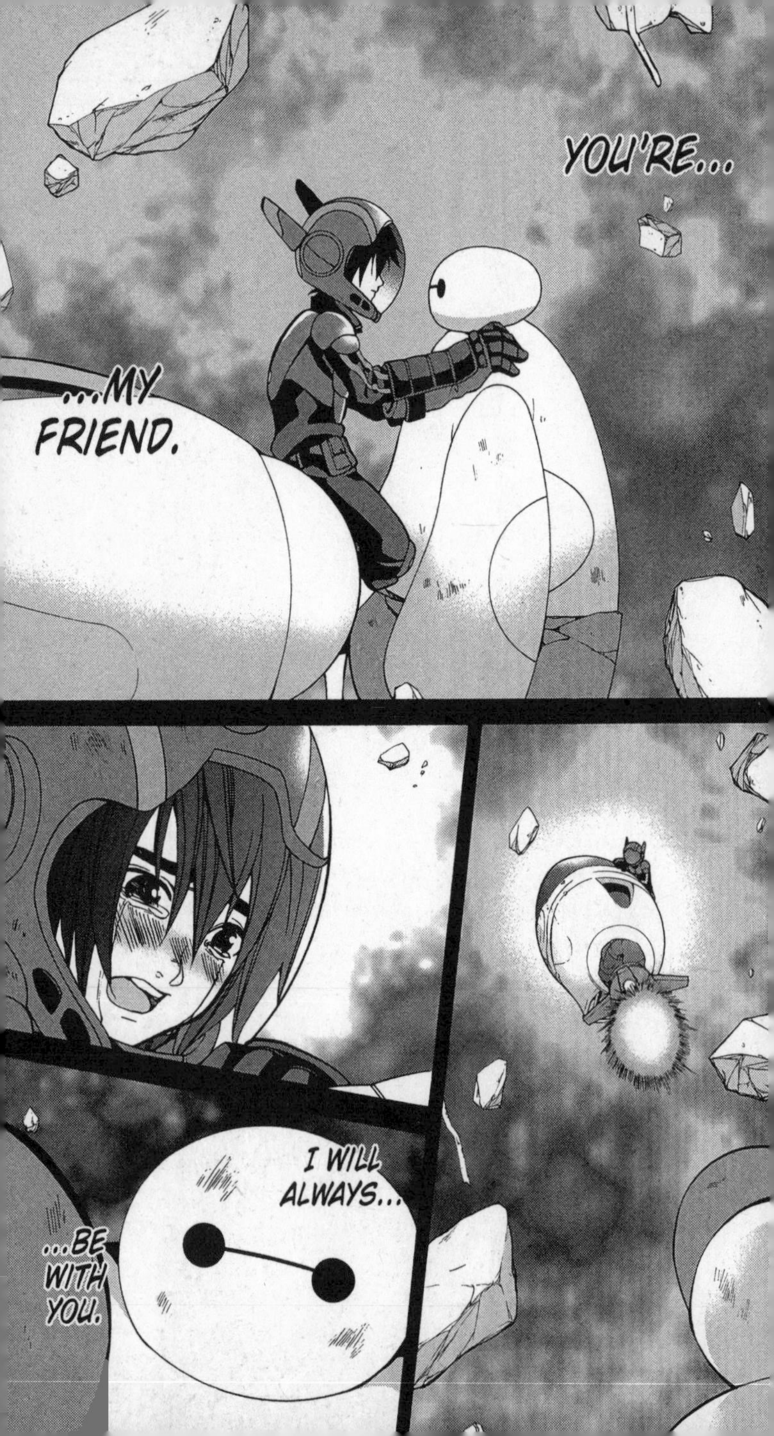
YOU'RE...
...MY FRIEND.
I WILL ALWAYS...
...BE WITH YOU.

Final Chapter: Hiro's Friends

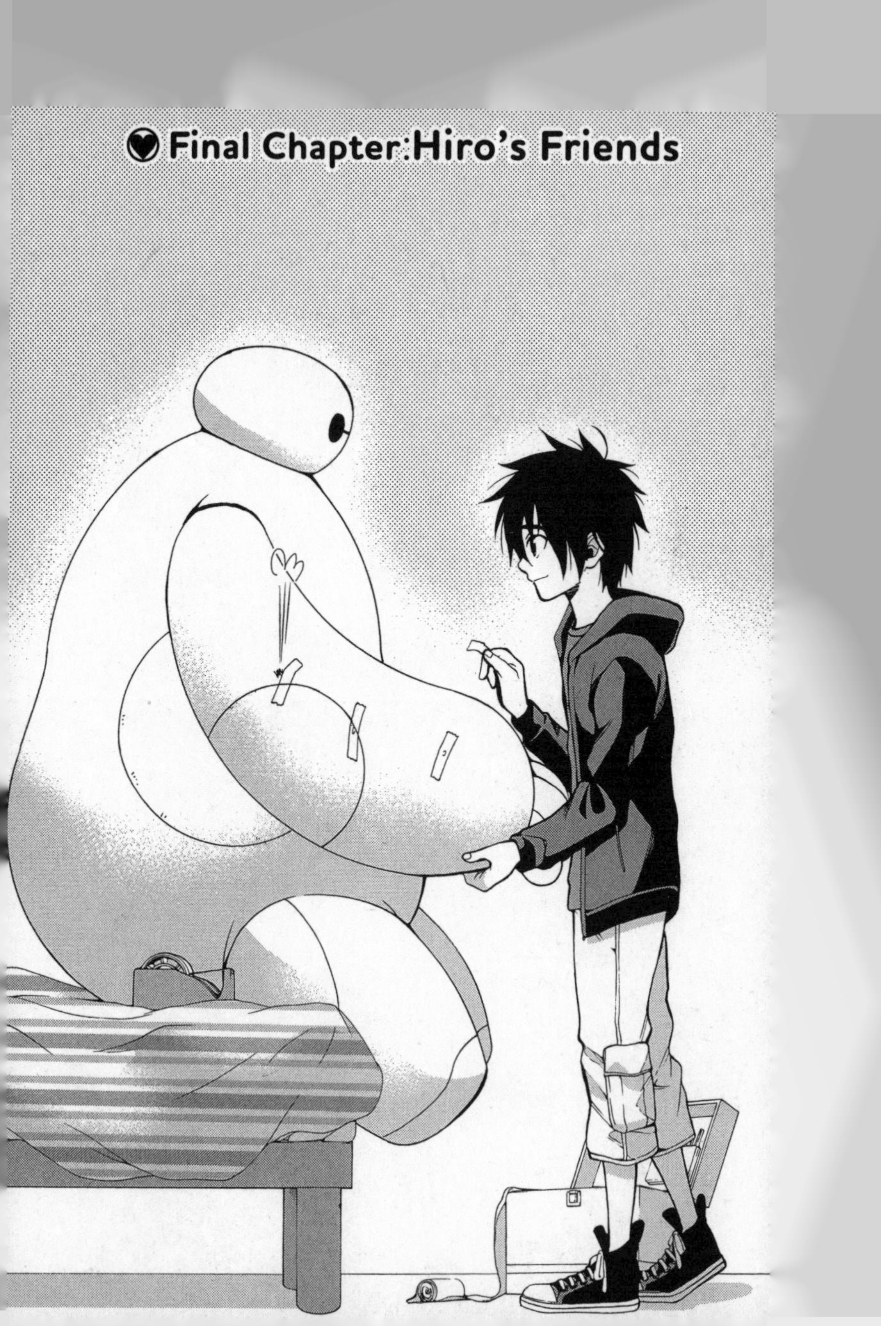

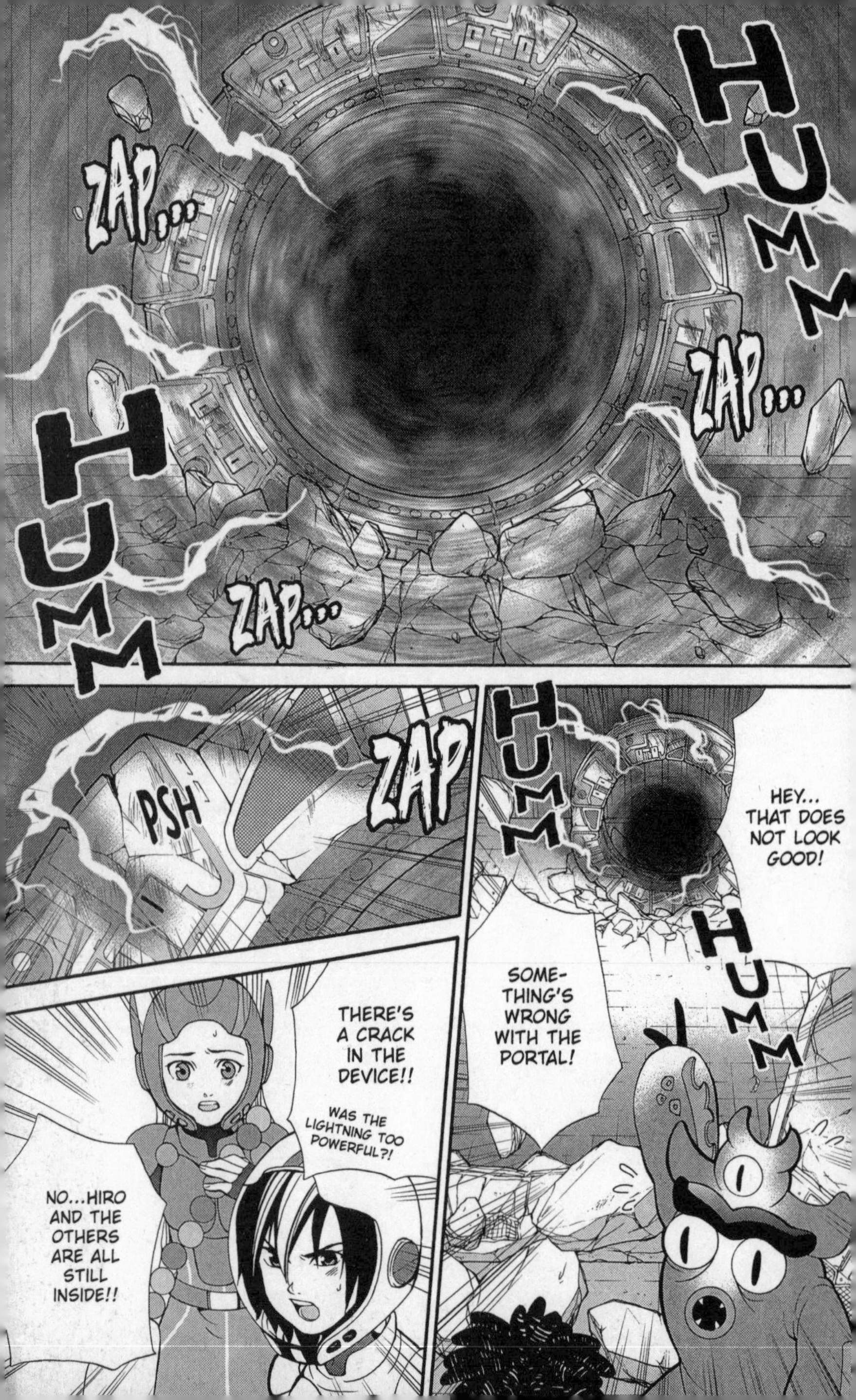
HUMM
ZAP...
ZAP...
HUMM
ZAP...
HEY... THAT DOES NOT LOOK GOOD!
HUMM
HUMM
HUMM
SOME-THING'S WRONG WITH THE PORTAL!
ZAP
PSH
THERE'S A CRACK IN THE DEVICE!!
WAS THE LIGHTNING TOO POWERFUL?!
NO...HIRO AND THE OTHERS ARE ALL STILL INSIDE!!

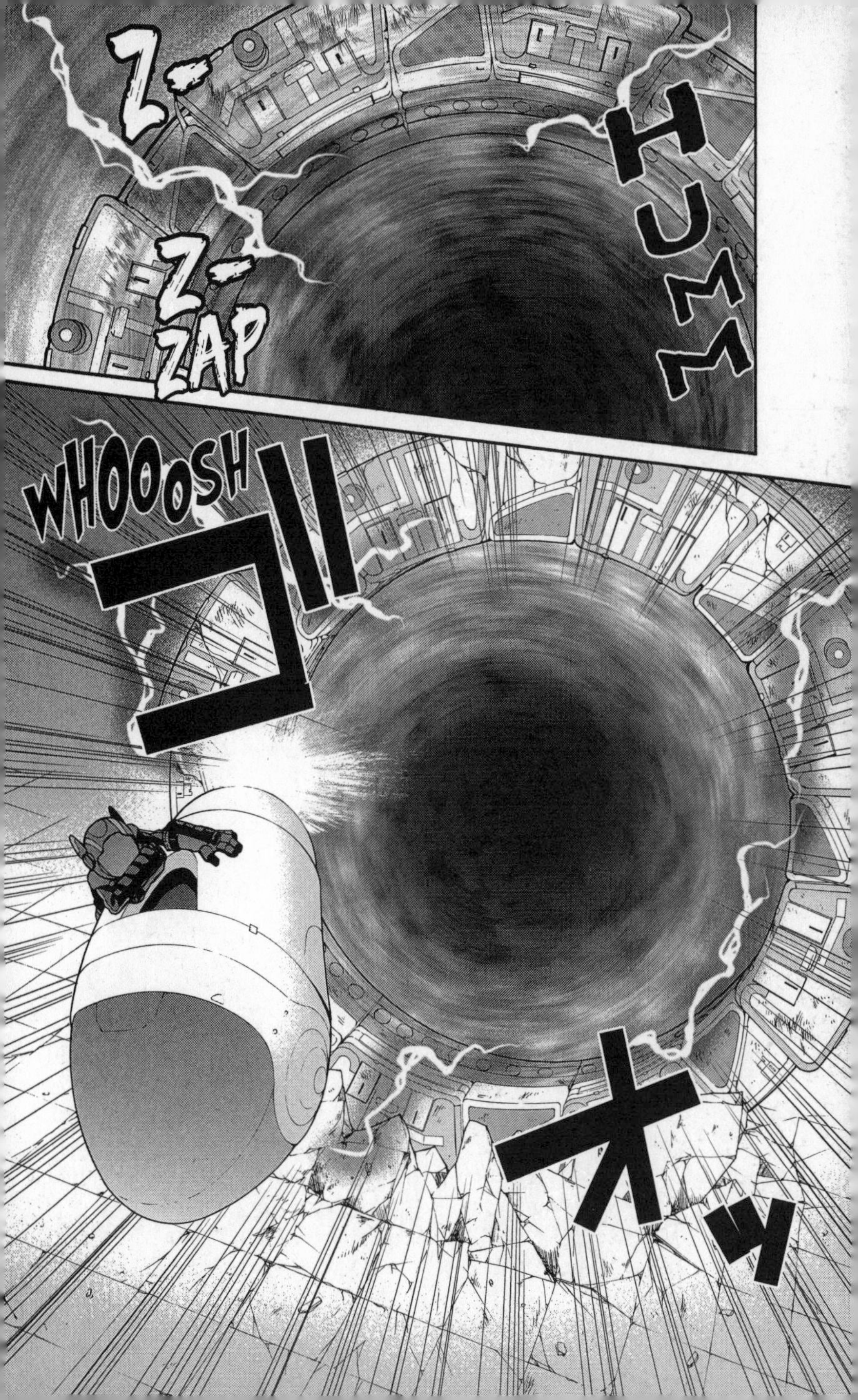
HUMM
Z- Z- ZAP
WHOOOSH

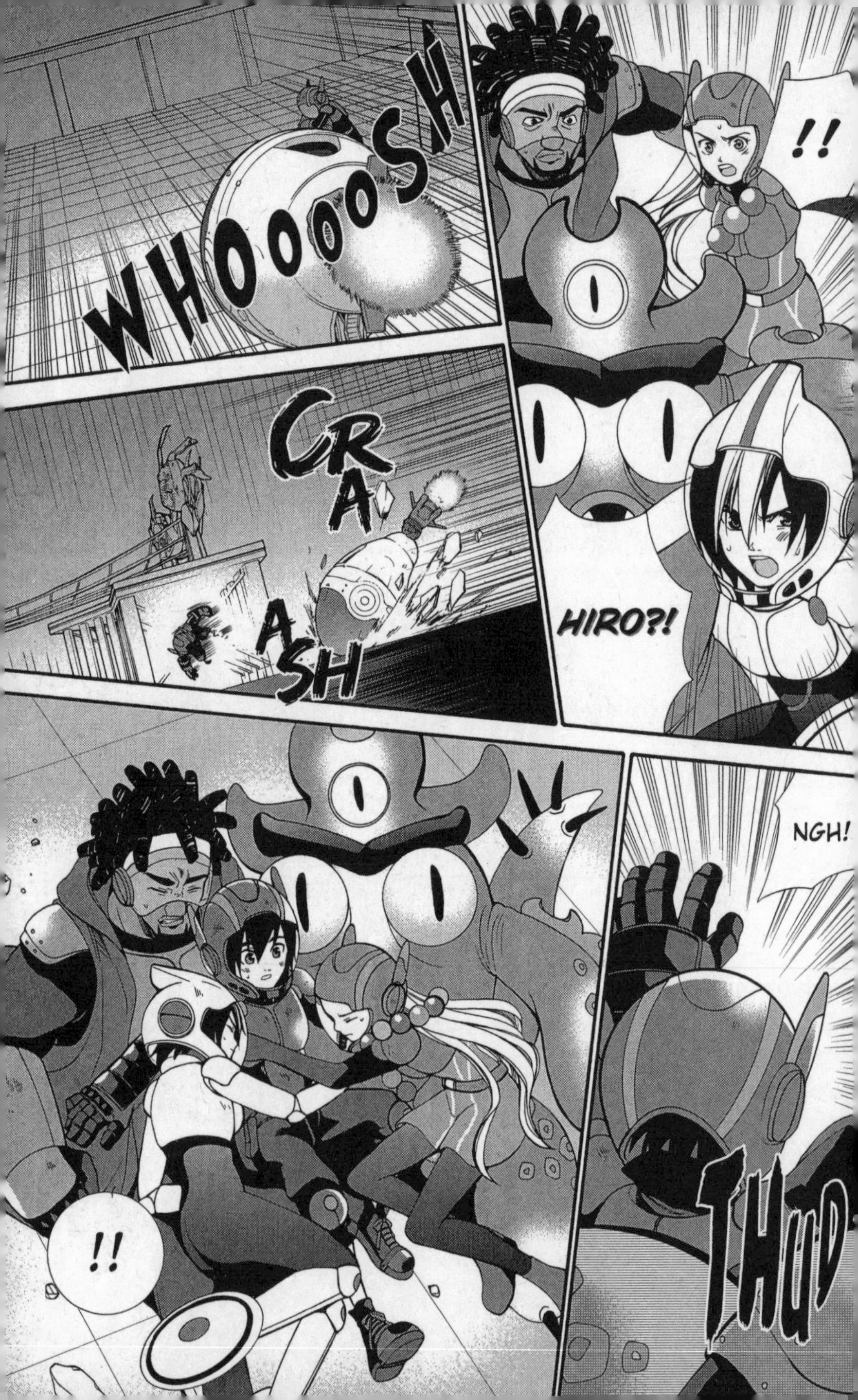
!!
WHOOOOSH
HIRO?!
CRASH
NGH!
THUD
!!

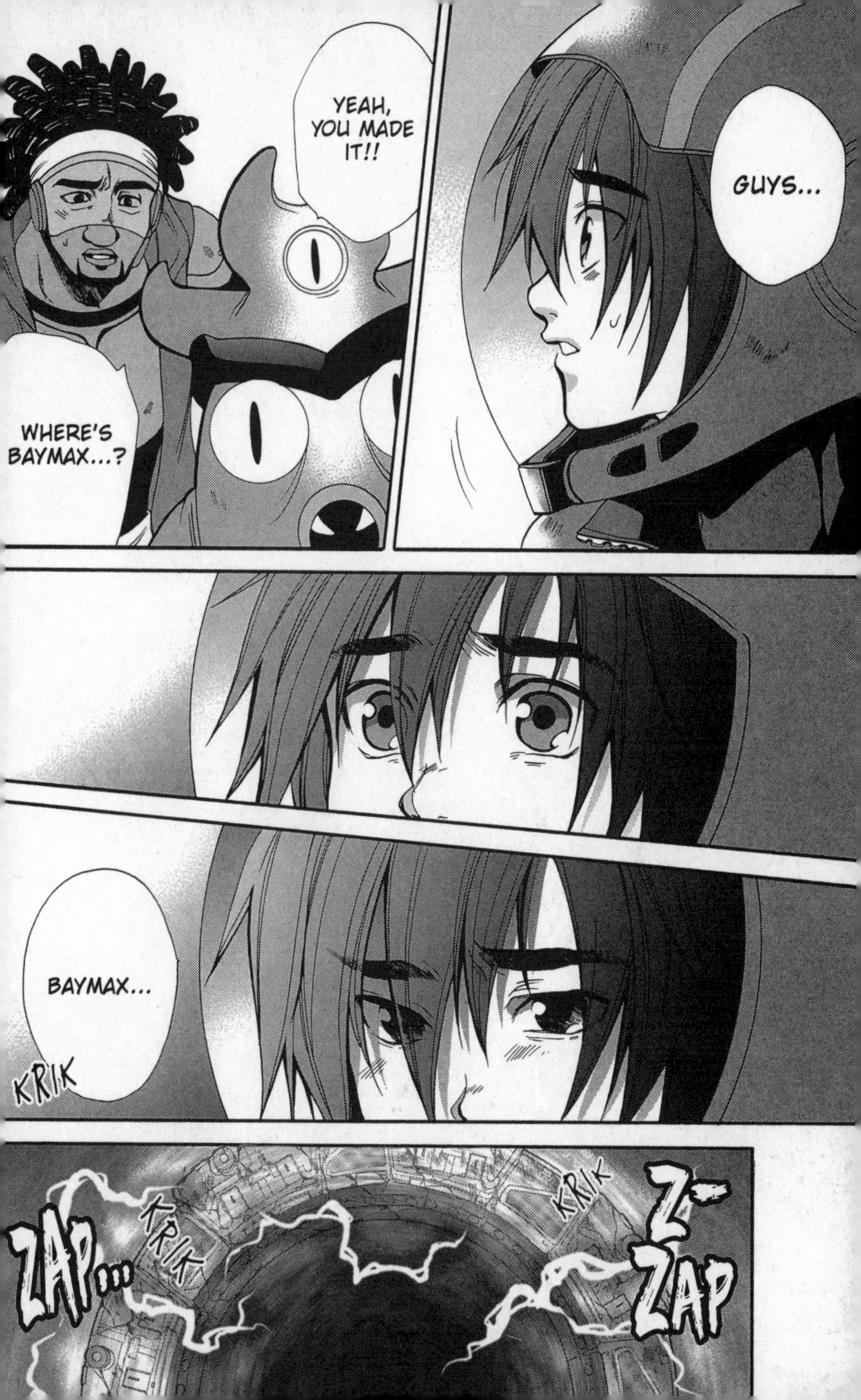
GUYS...
YEAH, YOU MADE IT!!
WHERE'S BAYMAX...?
BAYMAX...
KRIK
Z-ZAP
KRIK
KRIK
ZAP...

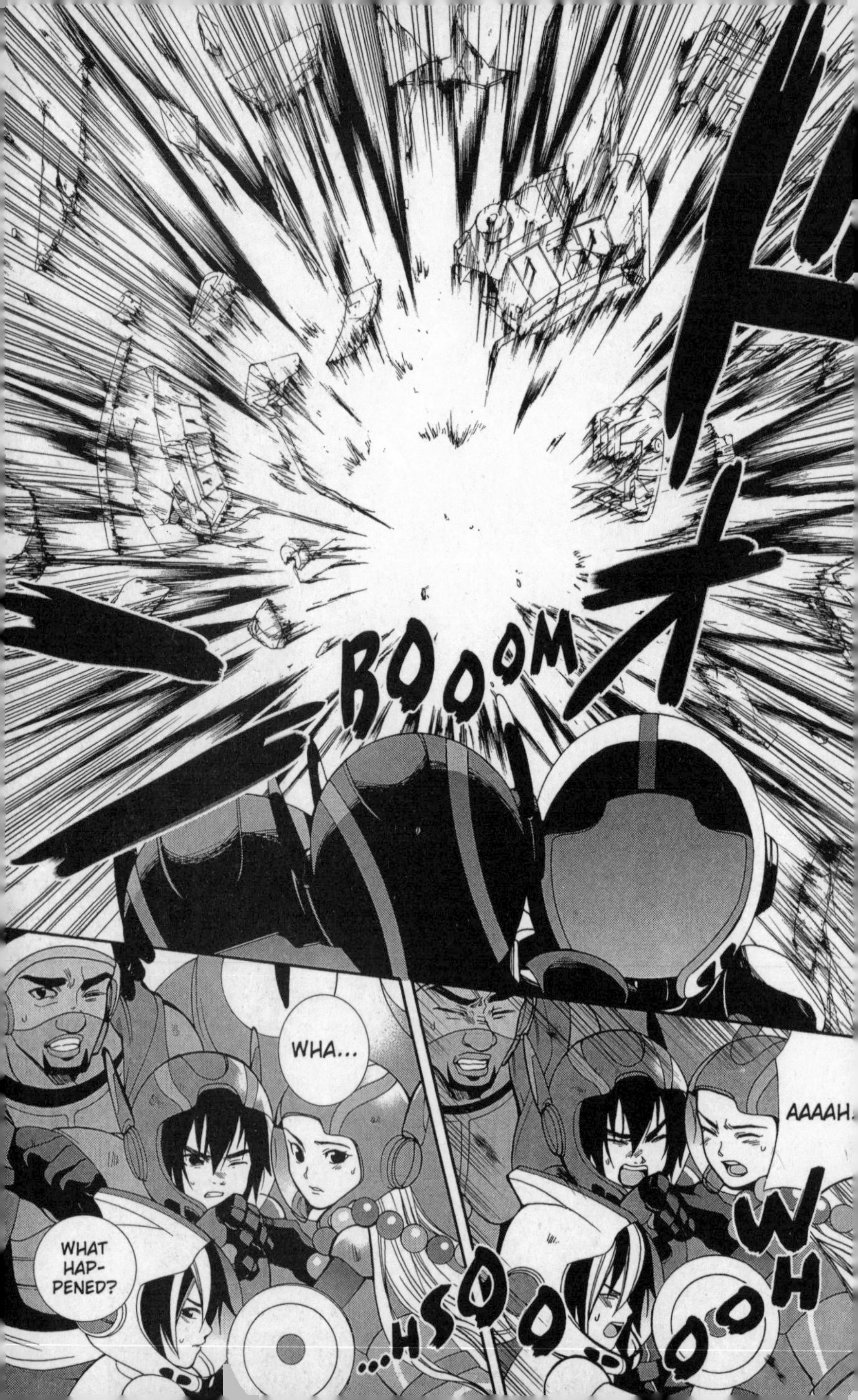
BOOOM
AAAAH.
WHOOOOSH...
WHA...
WHAT HAP-PENED?

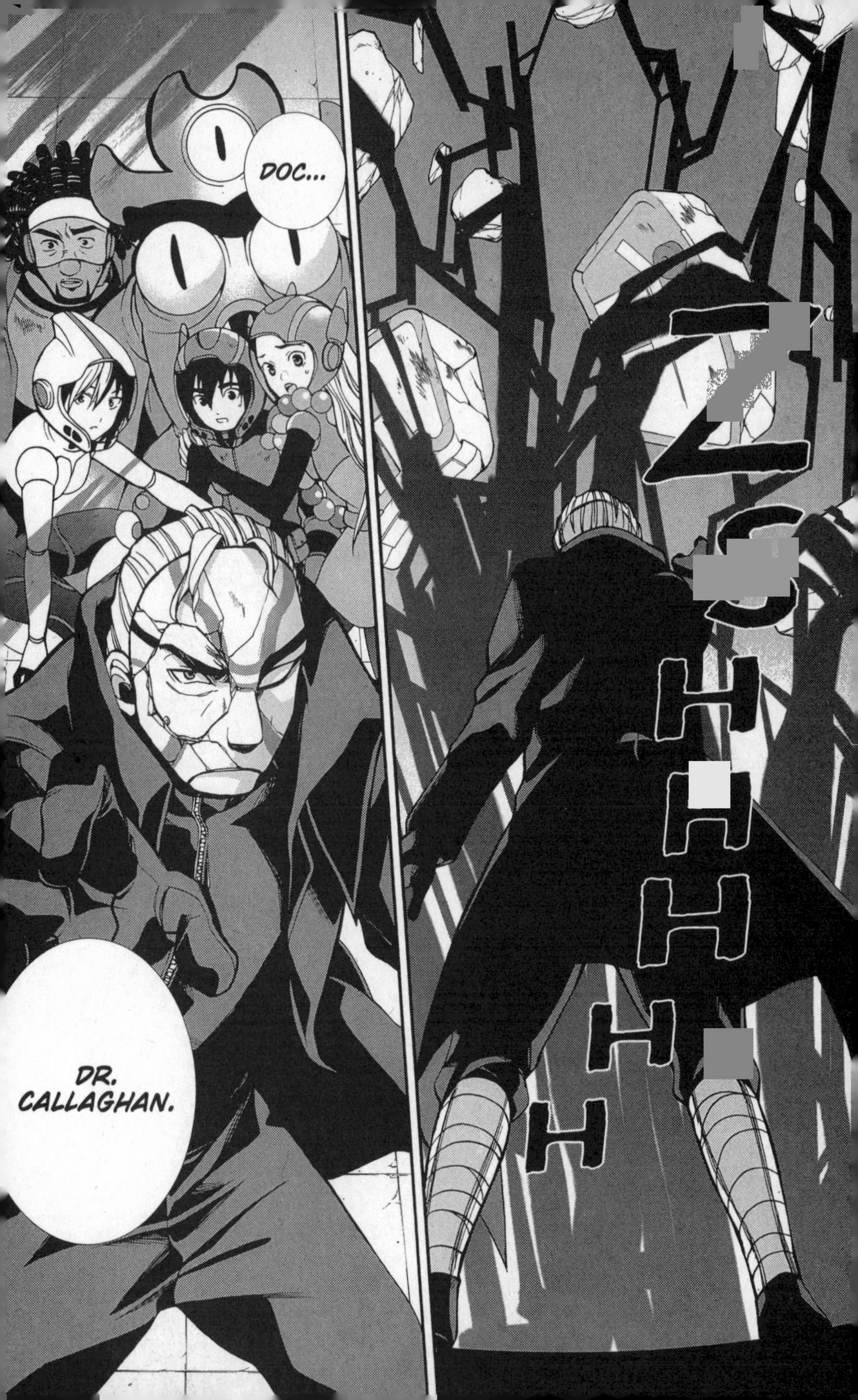
DOC...
DR. CALLAGHAN.

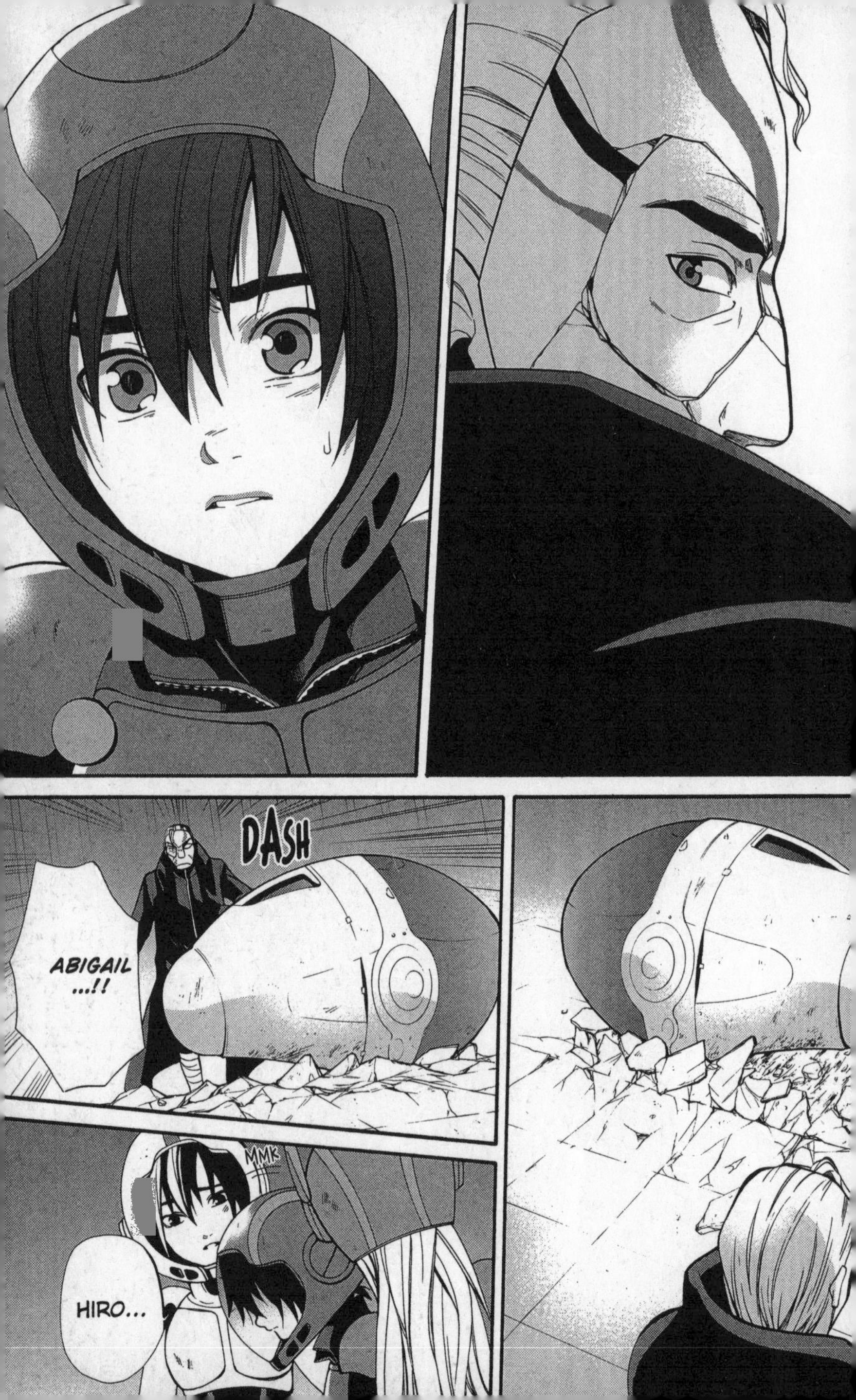
DASH
ABIGAIL ...!!
MMK
HIRO...

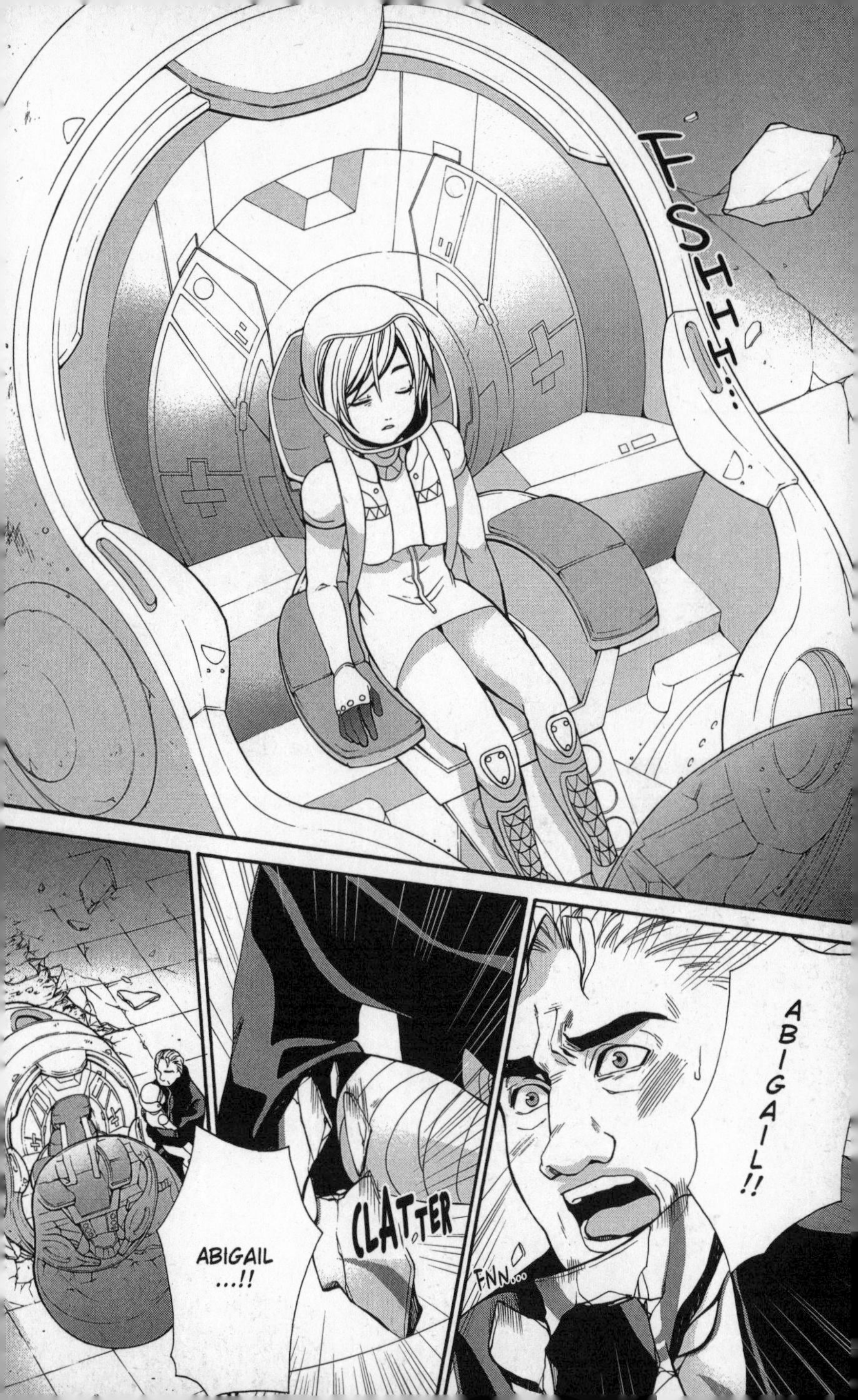
FSHHH...
ABIGAIL!!
FNN...
CLATTER
ABIGAIL
...!!

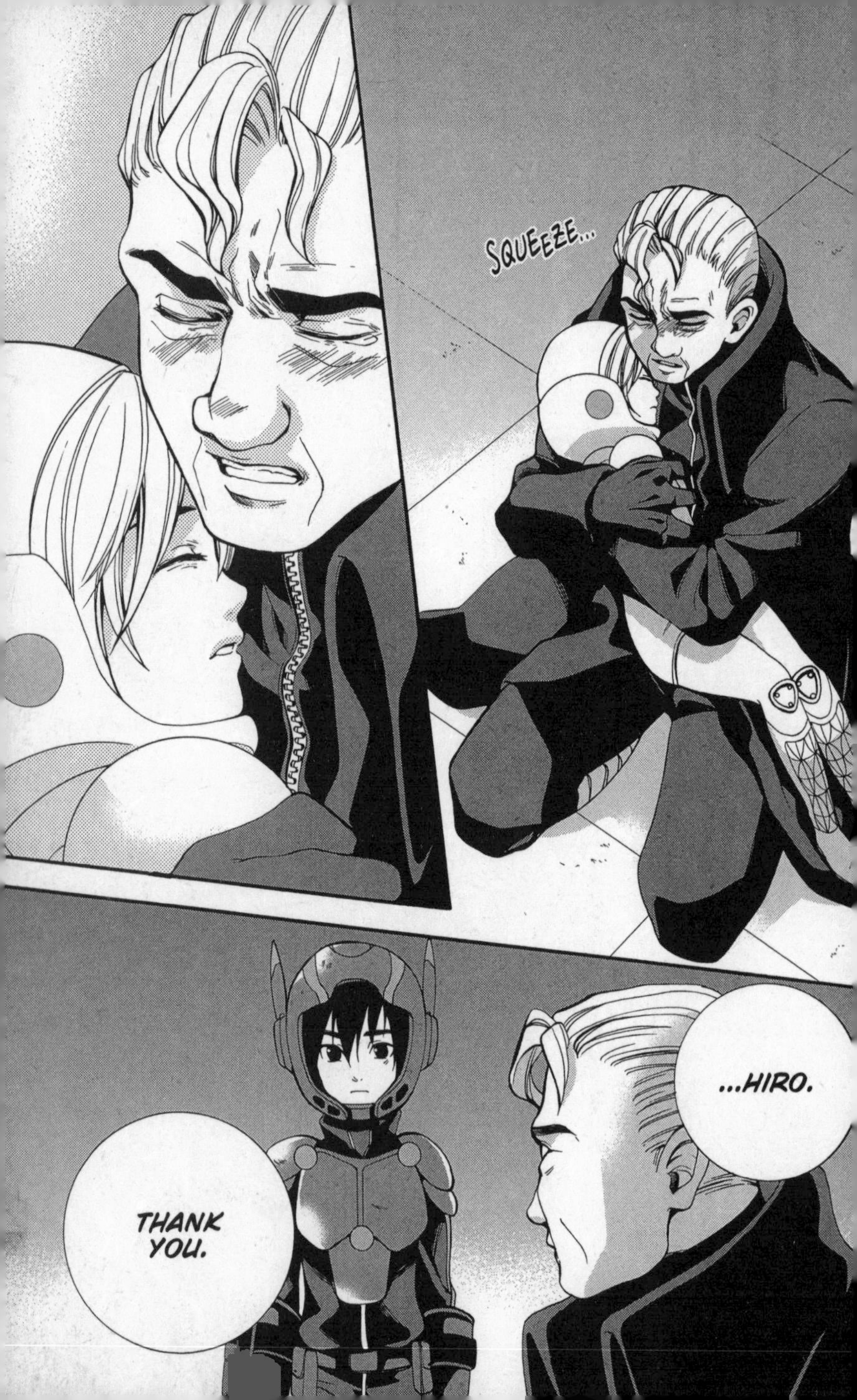
SQUEEZE...
...HIRO.
THANK YOU.

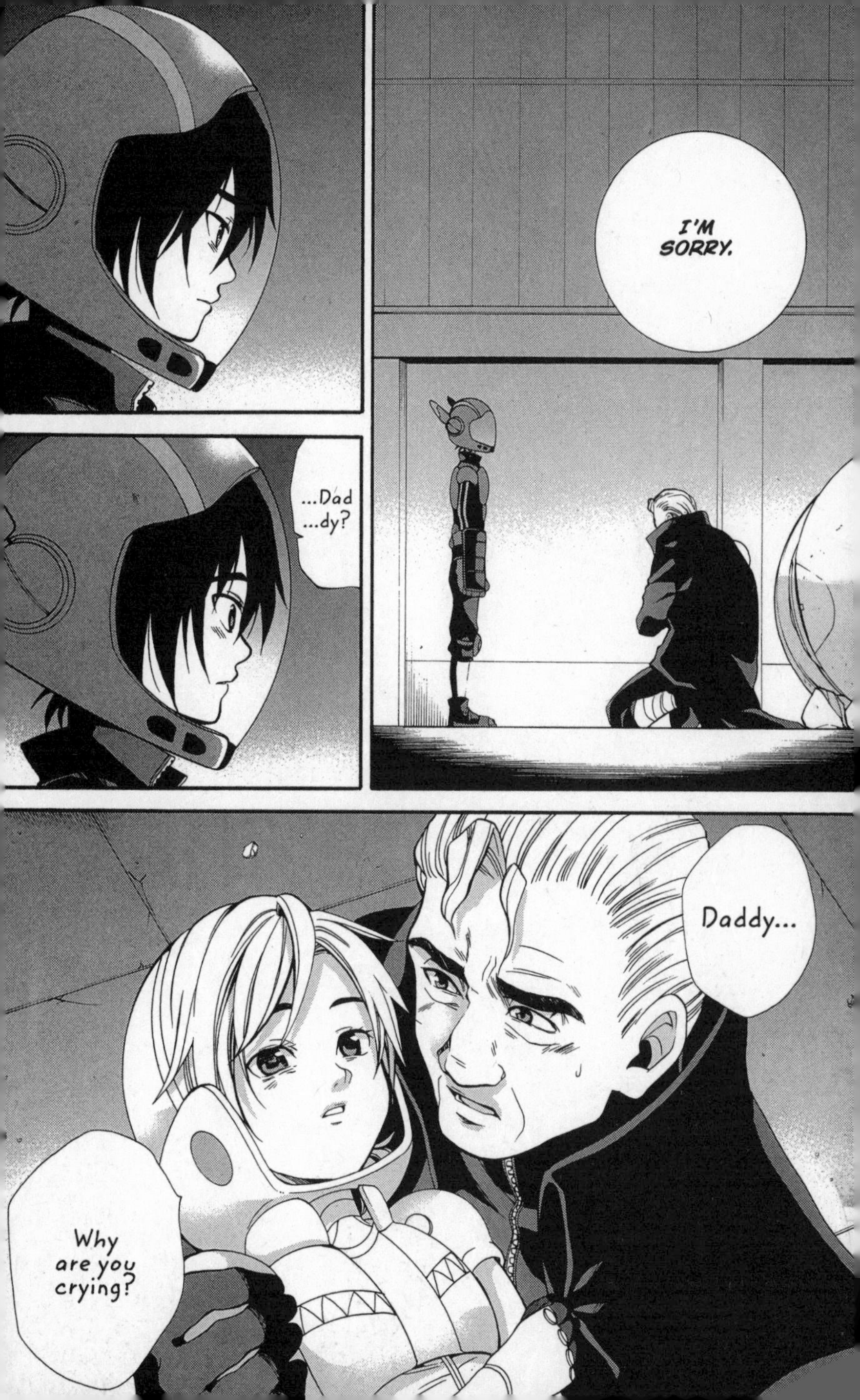
I'M SORRY.
...Dad ...dy?
Daddy...
Why are you crying?

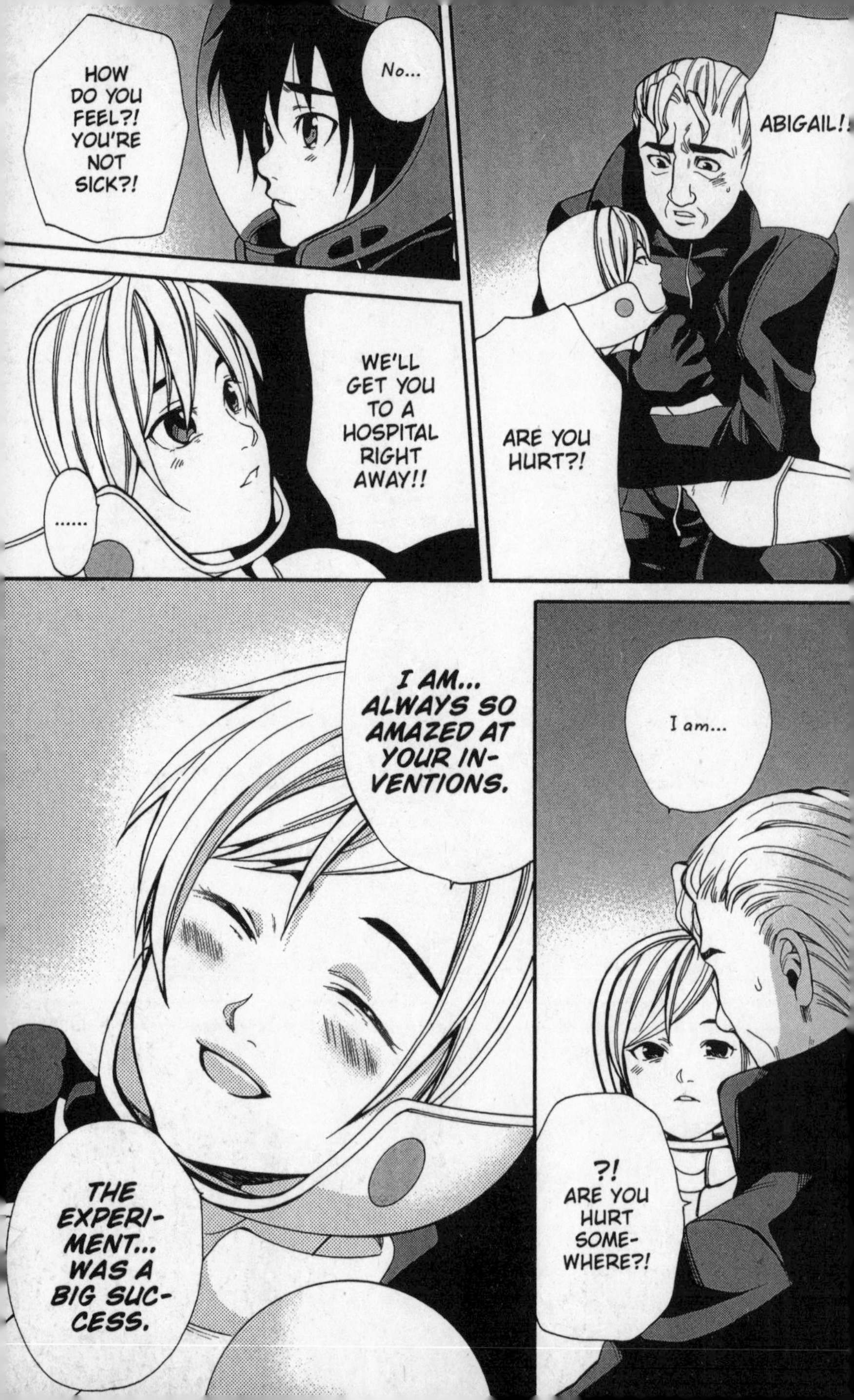
ABIGAIL!!
ARE YOU HURT?!
HOW DO YOU FEEL?! YOU'RE NOT SICK?!
No...
WE'LL GET YOU TO A HOSPITAL RIGHT AWAY!!
......
I am...
?! ARE YOU HURT SOME-WHERE?!
I AM... ALWAYS SO AMAZED AT YOUR IN-VENTIONS.
THE EXPERI-MENT... WAS A BIG SUC-CESS.

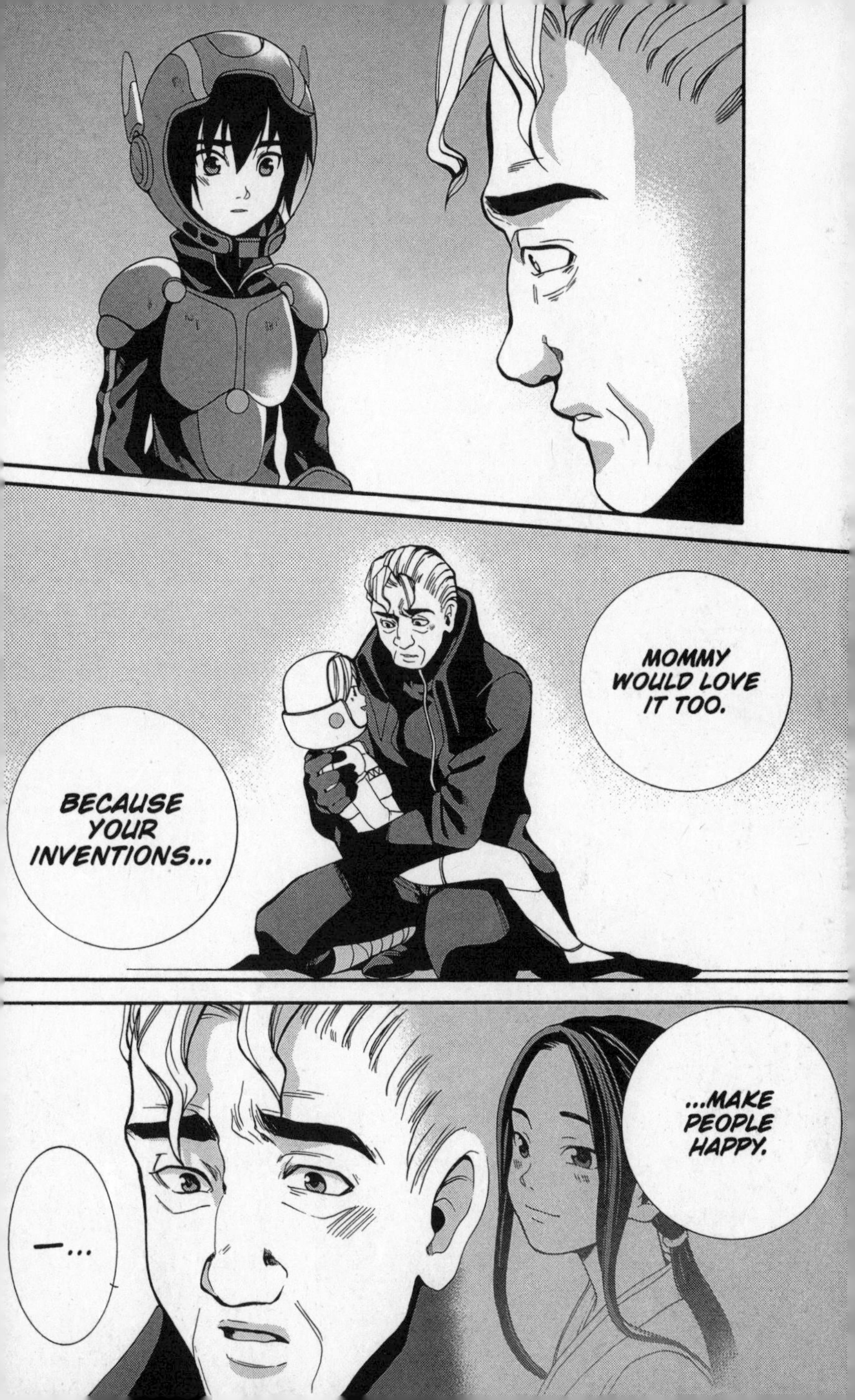
MOMMY WOULD LOVE IT TOO.
BECAUSE YOUR INVENTIONS...
...MAKE PEOPLE HAPPY.
—...

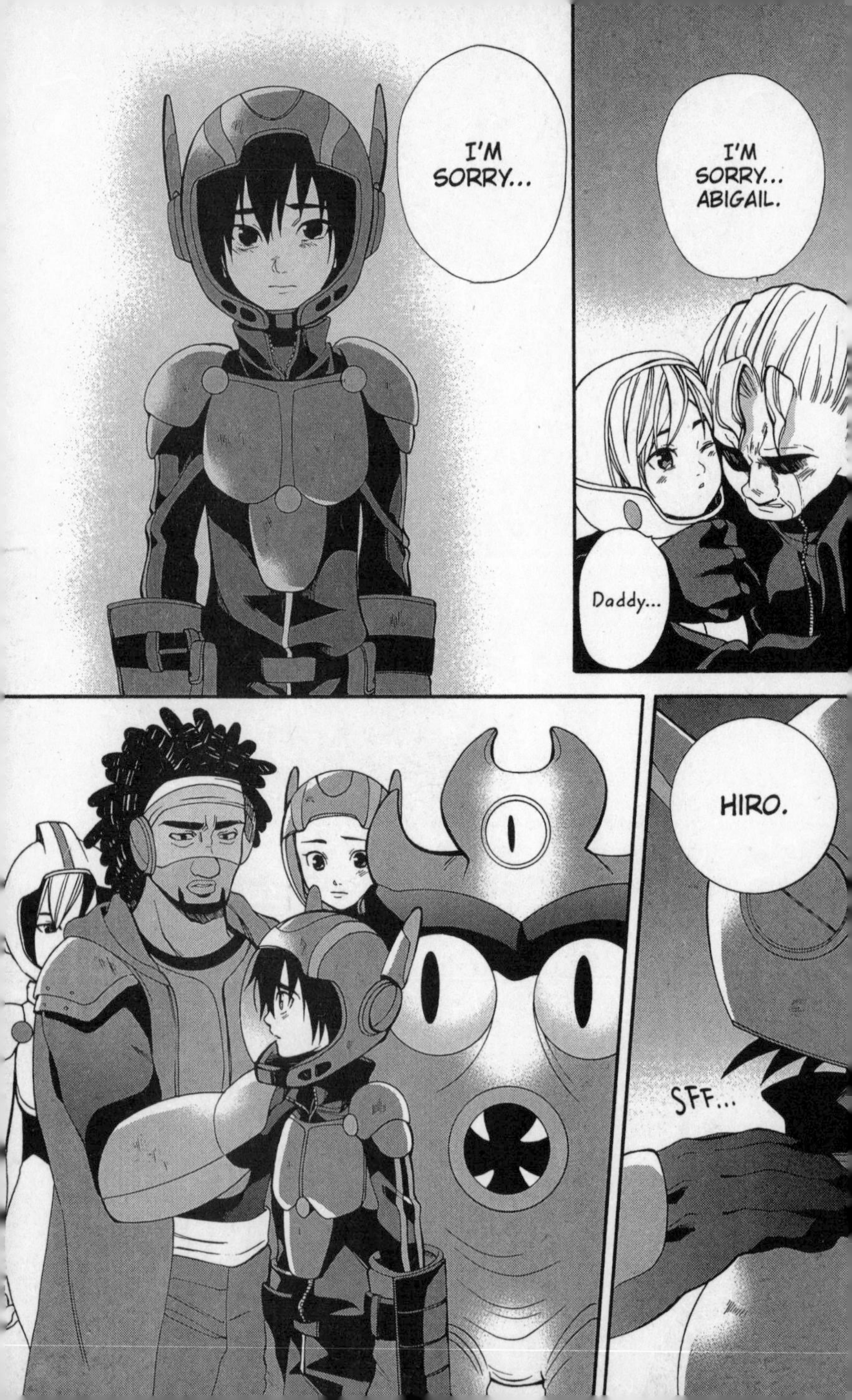
I'M SORRY... ABIGAIL.
Daddy...
I'M SORRY...
HIRO.
SFF...

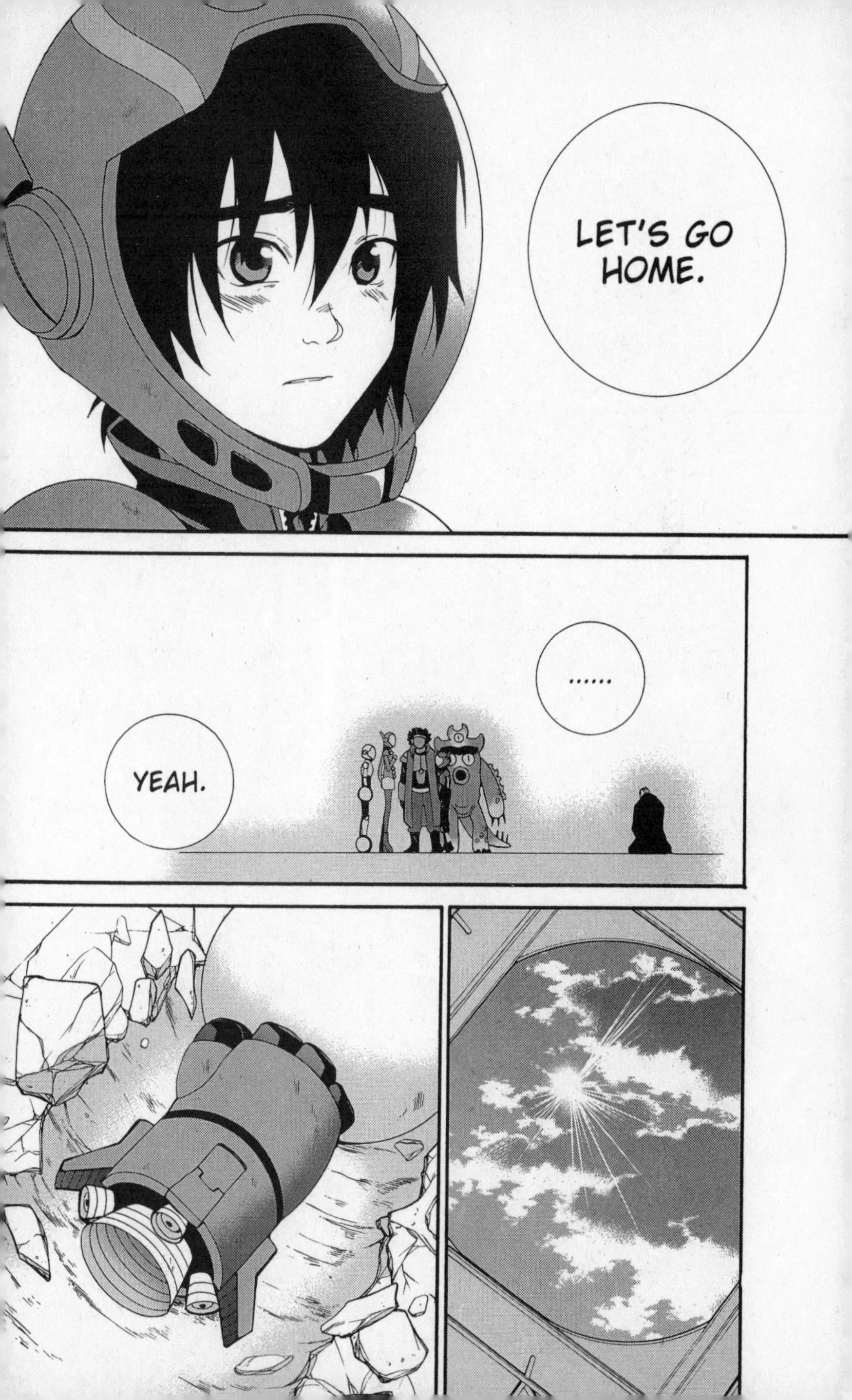
LET'S GO HOME.
......
YEAH.

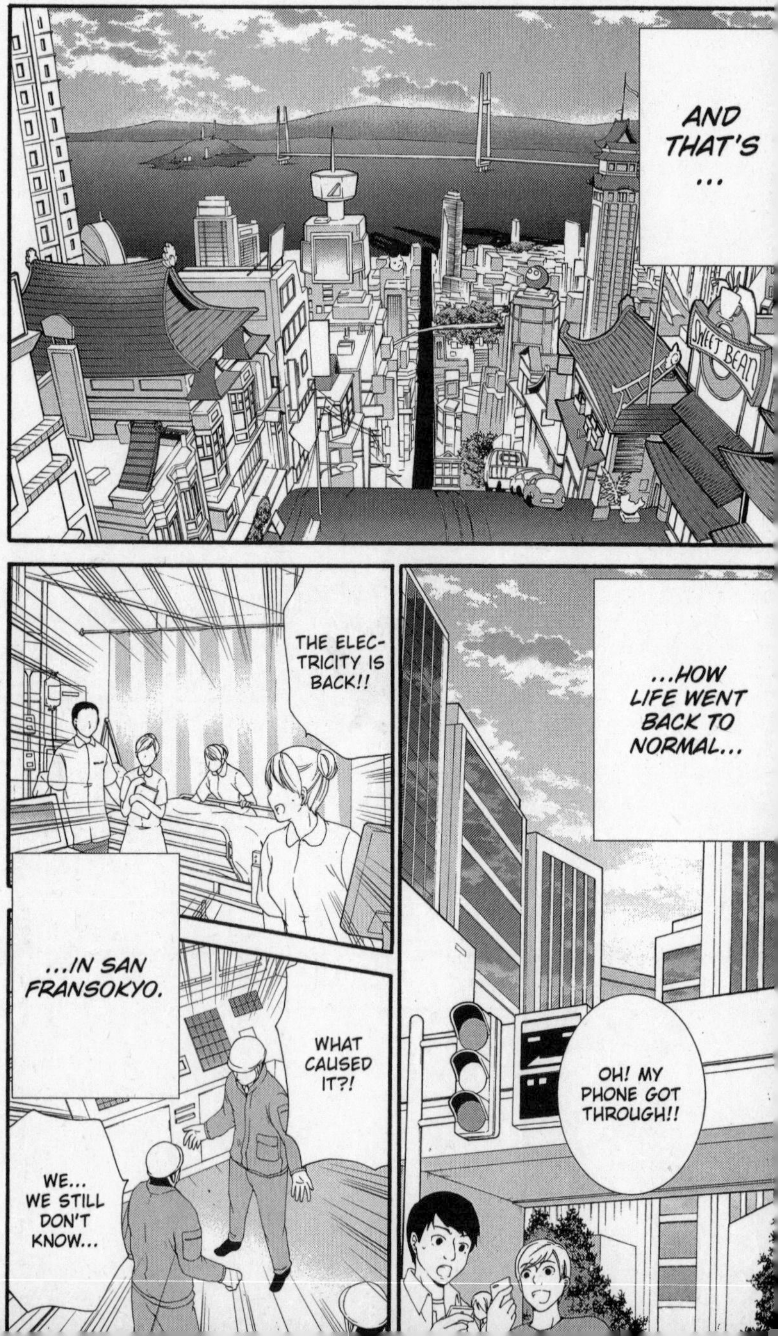
AND THAT'S ...
SWEET BEAN
...HOW LIFE WENT BACK TO NORMAL...
OH! MY PHONE GOT THROUGH!!
THE ELEC-TRICITY IS BACK!!
...IN SAN FRANSOKYO.
WHAT CAUSED IT?!
WE... WE STILL DON'T KNOW...

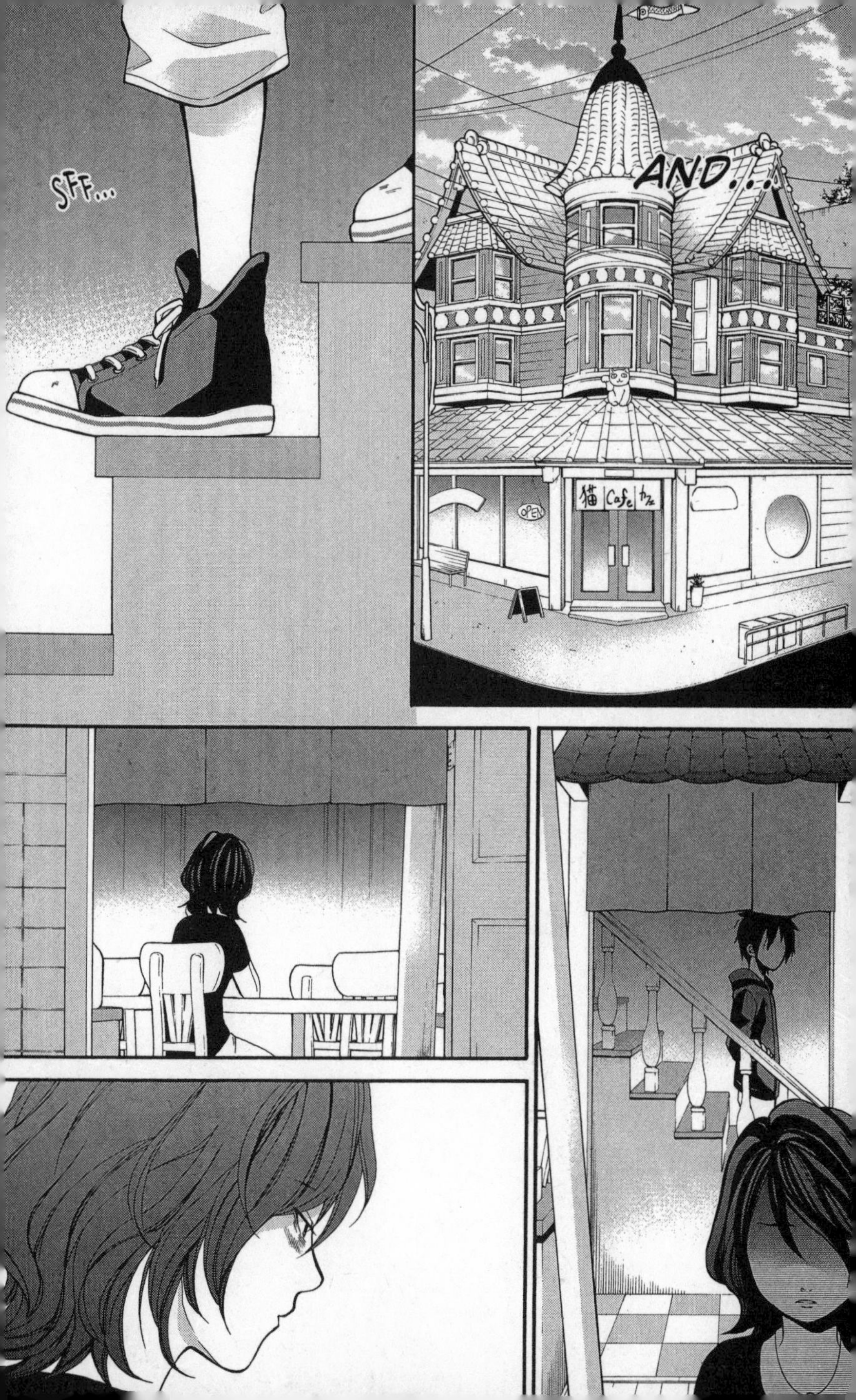
AND...
猫 Cafe カフェ
OPEN
SFF...

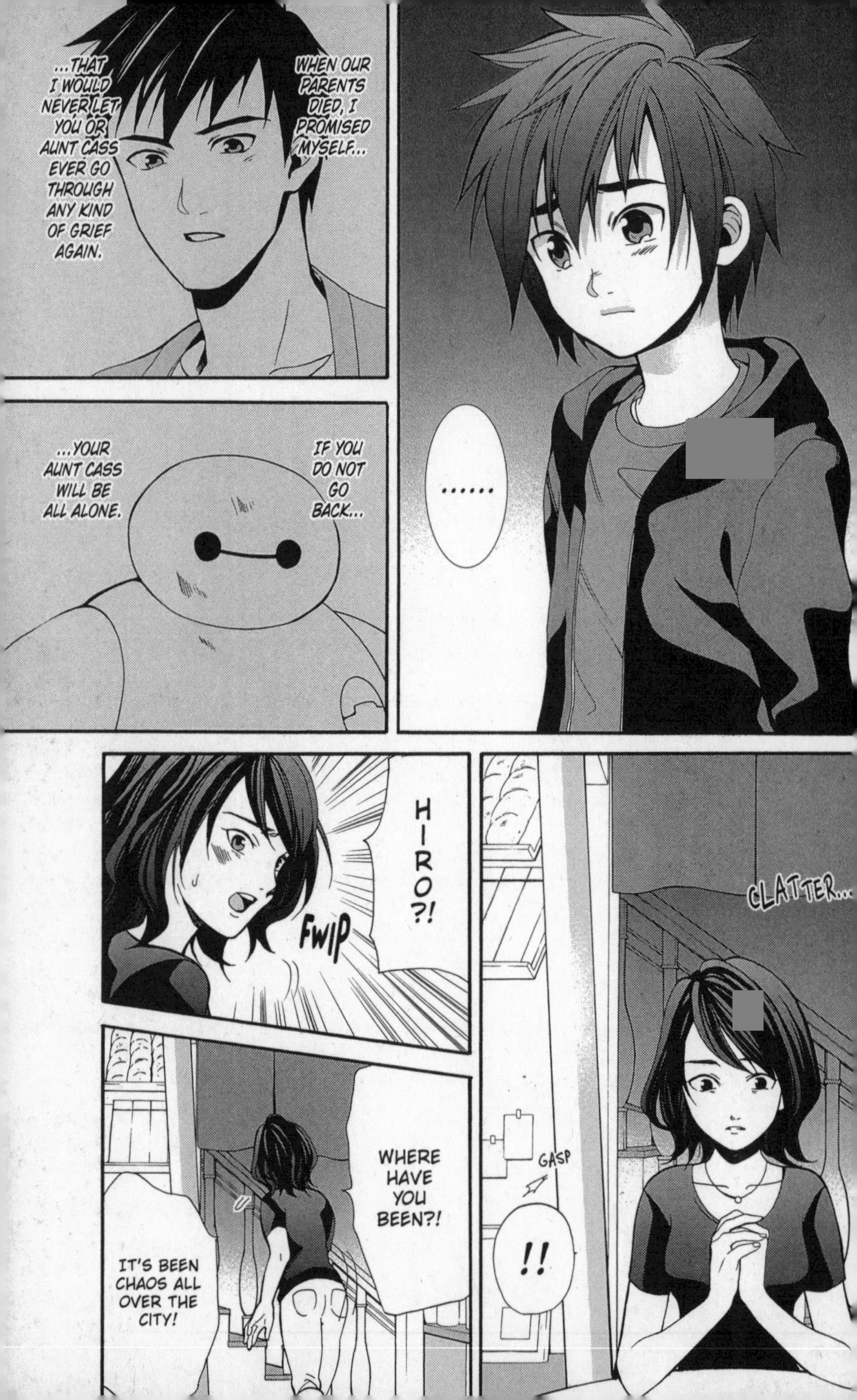
......
WHEN OUR PARENTS DIED, I PROMISED MYSELF...
...THAT I WOULD NEVER LET YOU OR AUNT CASS EVER GO THROUGH ANY KIND OF GRIEF AGAIN.
IF YOU DO NOT GO BACK...
...YOUR AUNT CASS WILL BE ALL ALONE.
CLATTER...
GASP
!!
HIRO?!
FWIP
WHERE HAVE YOU BEEN?!
IT'S BEEN CHAOS ALL OVER THE CITY!

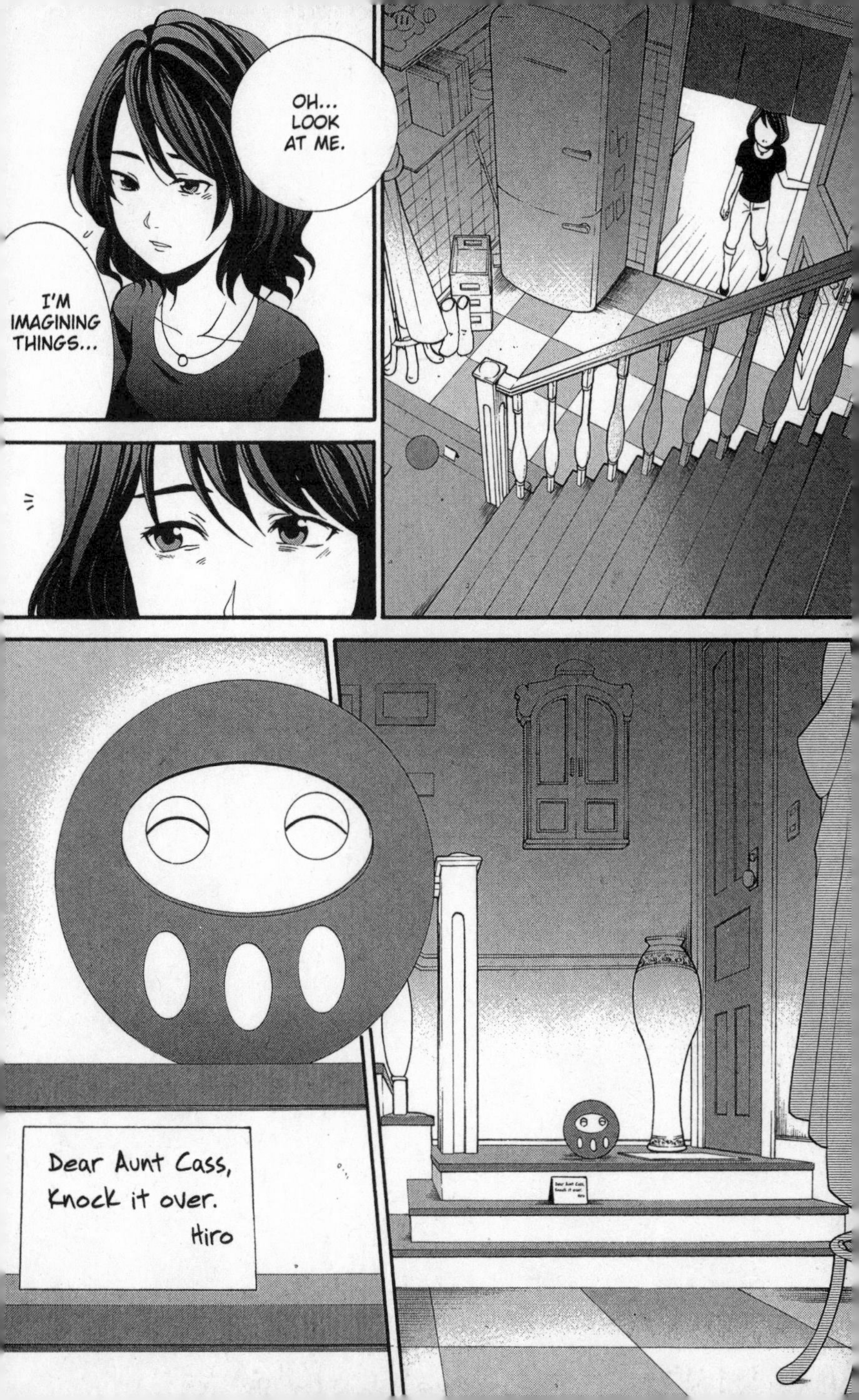
OH... LOOK AT ME.
I'M IMAGINING THINGS...
Dear Aunt Cass,
Knock it over.
Hiro

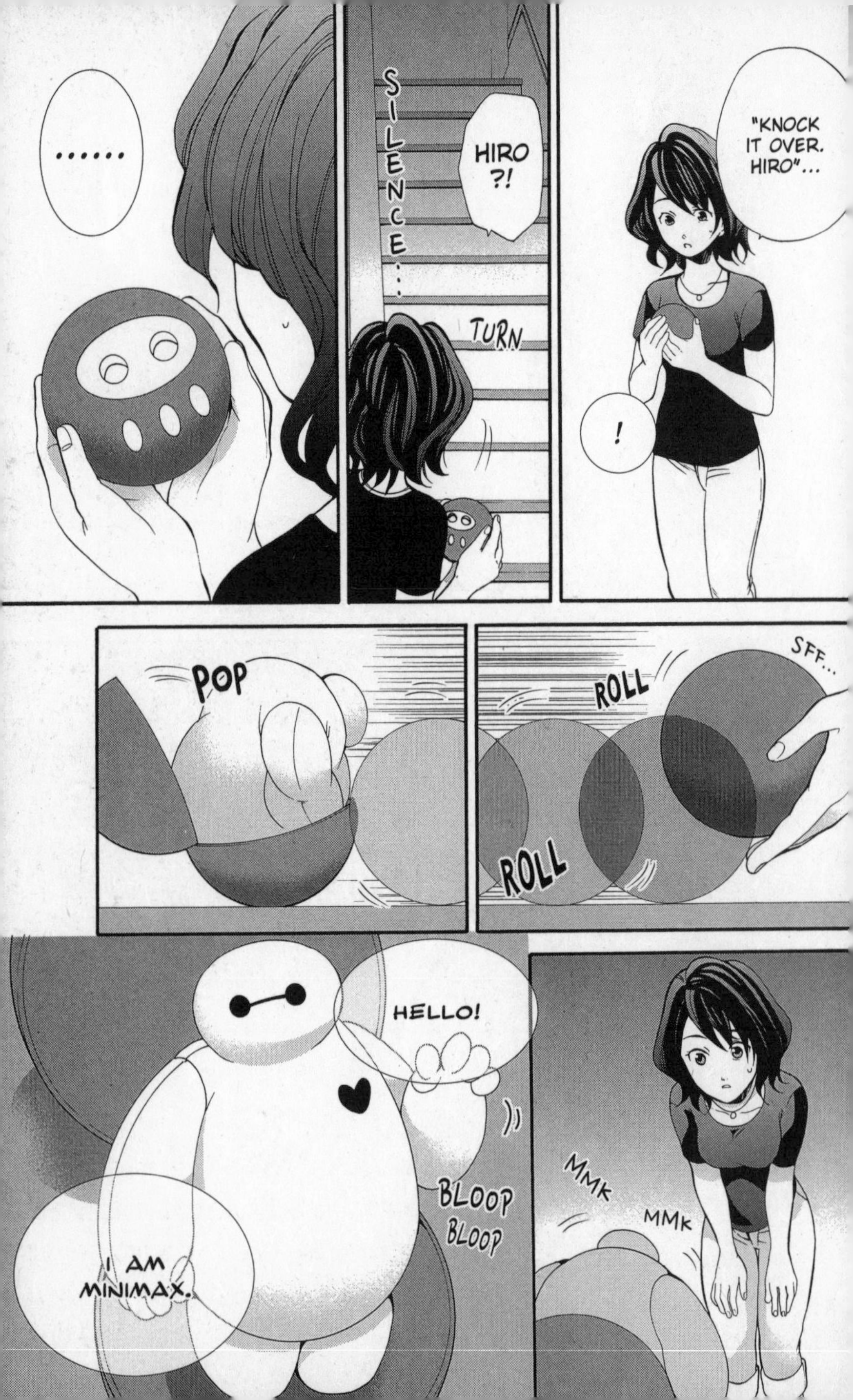
"KNOCK IT OVER. HIRO"...
!
HIRO ?!
SILENCE...
TURN
......
SFF...
ROLL
ROLL
POP
MMK
MMK
HELLO!
BLOOP BLOOP
I AM MINIMAX.

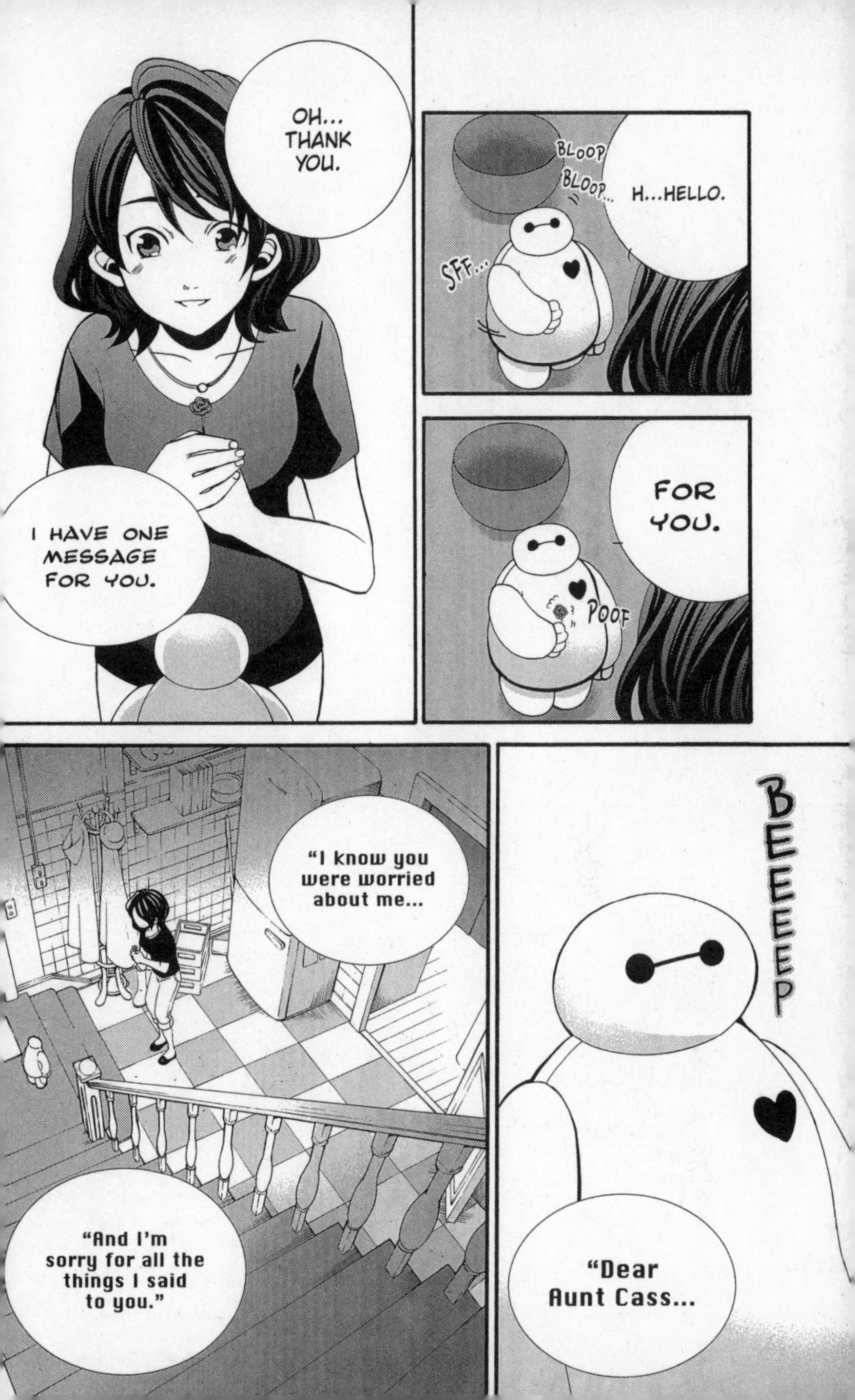
BLOOP
BLOOP...
H...HELLO.
SFF...
FOR YOU.
POOF
OH... THANK YOU.
I HAVE ONE MESSAGE FOR YOU.
BEEEEP
"Dear Aunt Cass...
"I know you were worried about me...
"And I'm sorry for all the things I said to you."

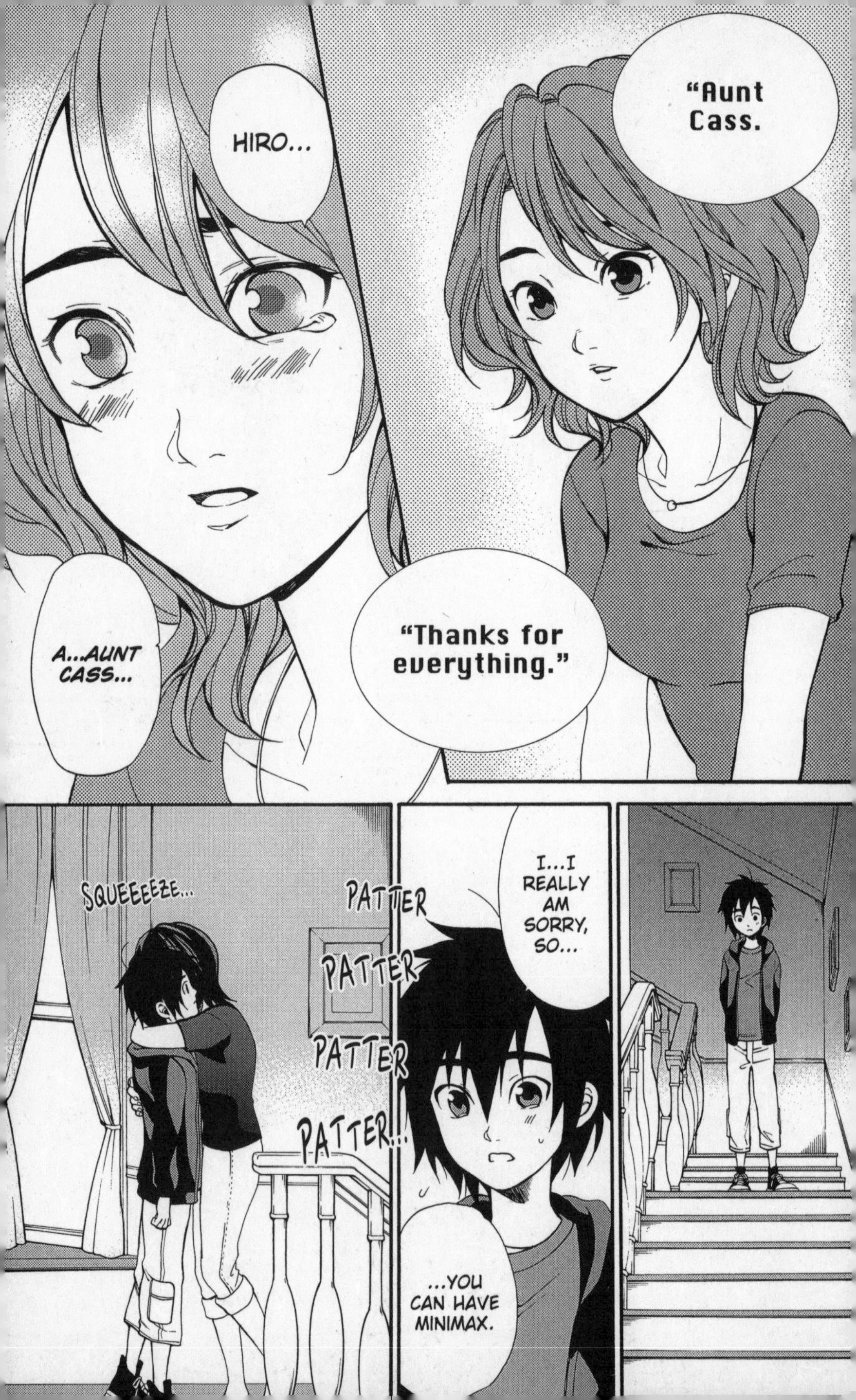

“Aunt Cass.
“Thanks for everything.”
HIRO...
A...AUNT CASS...
I...I REALLY AM SORRY, SO...
...YOU CAN HAVE MINIMAX.
PATTER
PATTER
PATTER
PATTER...
SQUEEEEZE...

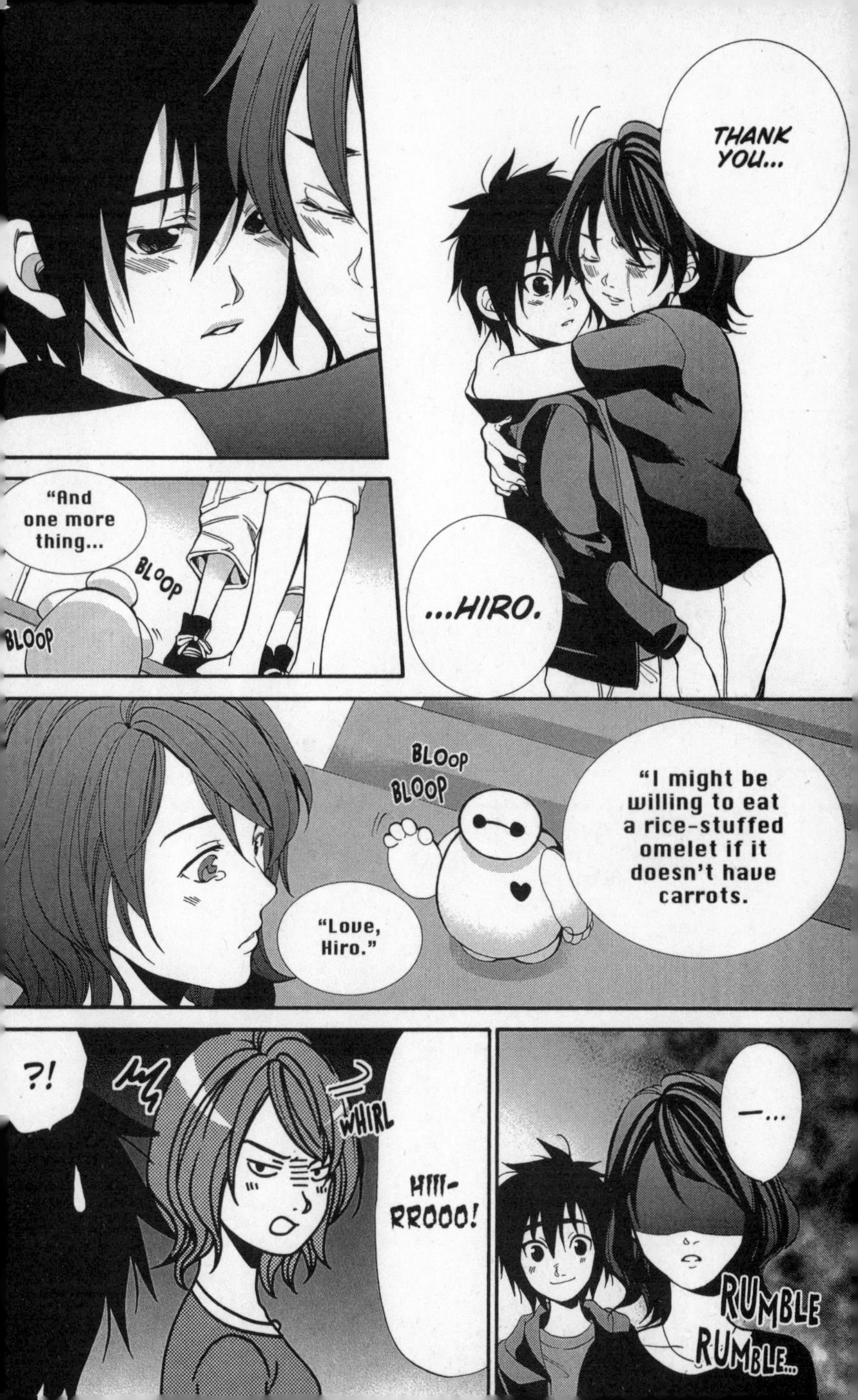
THANK YOU...
...HIRO.
"And one more thing...
BLOOP
BLOOP
"I might be willing to eat a rice-stuffed omelet if it doesn't have carrots.
BLOOP
BLOOP
"Love, Hiro."
—...
RUMBLE
RUMBLE...
HIII-RROOO!
WHIRL
?!

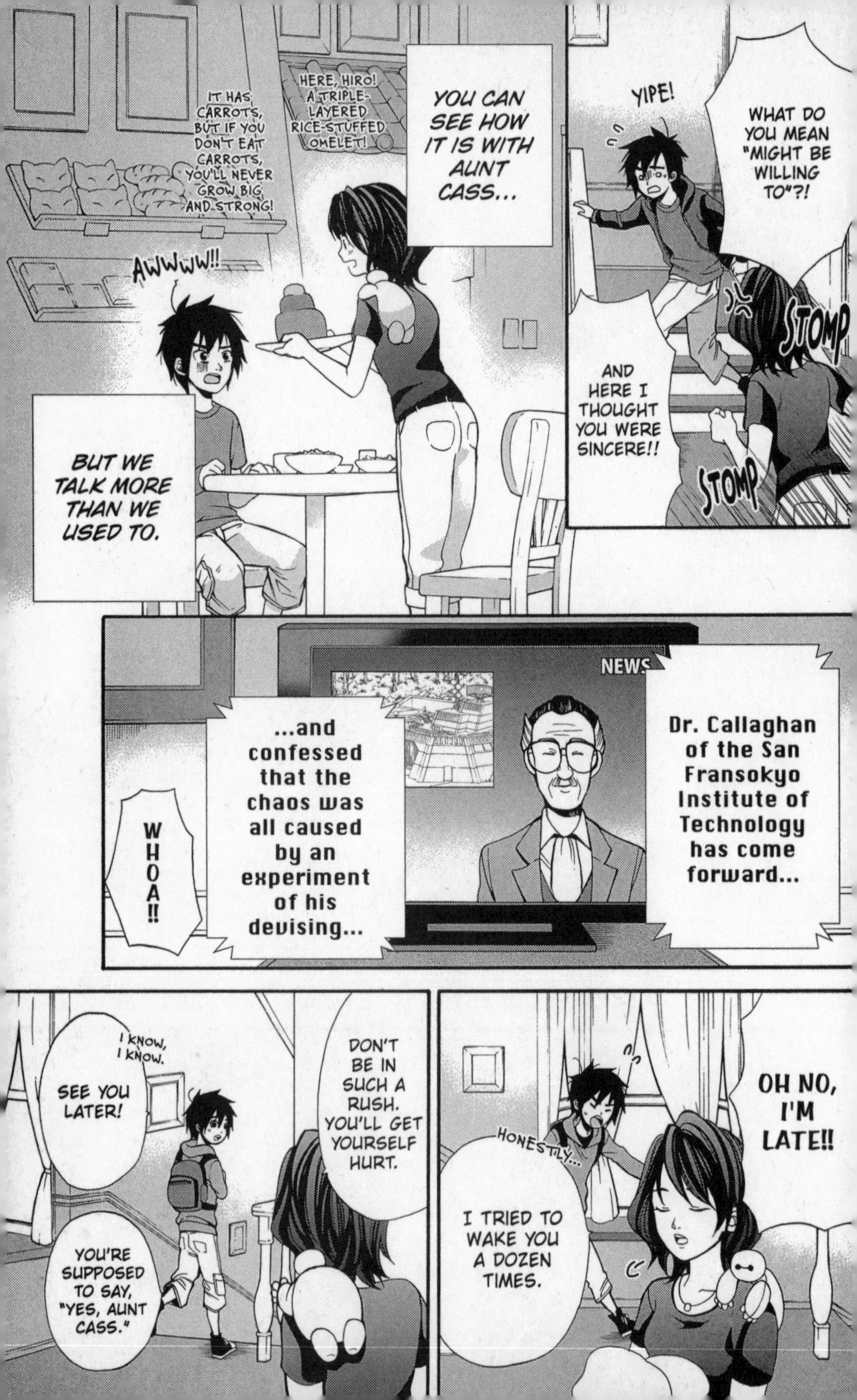
YIPE!
WHAT DO YOU MEAN "MIGHT BE WILLING TO"?!
AND HERE I THOUGHT YOU WERE SINCERE!!
STOMP
STOMP
YOU CAN SEE HOW IT IS WITH AUNT CASS...
HERE, HIRO! A TRIPLE-LAYERED RICE-STUFFED OMELET!
IT HAS CARROTS, BUT IF YOU DON'T EAT CARROTS, YOU'LL NEVER GROW BIG AND STRONG!
AWWWW!!
BUT WE TALK MORE THAN WE USED TO.
NEWS
Dr. Callaghan of the San Fransokyo Institute of Technology has come forward...
...and confessed that the chaos was all caused by an experiment of his devising...
WHOA!!
OH NO, I'M LATE!!
HONESTLY...
I TRIED TO WAKE YOU A DOZEN TIMES.
DON'T BE IN SUCH A RUSH. YOU'LL GET YOURSELF HURT.
I KNOW, I KNOW.
SEE YOU LATER!
YOU'RE SUPPOSED TO SAY, "YES, AUNT CASS."

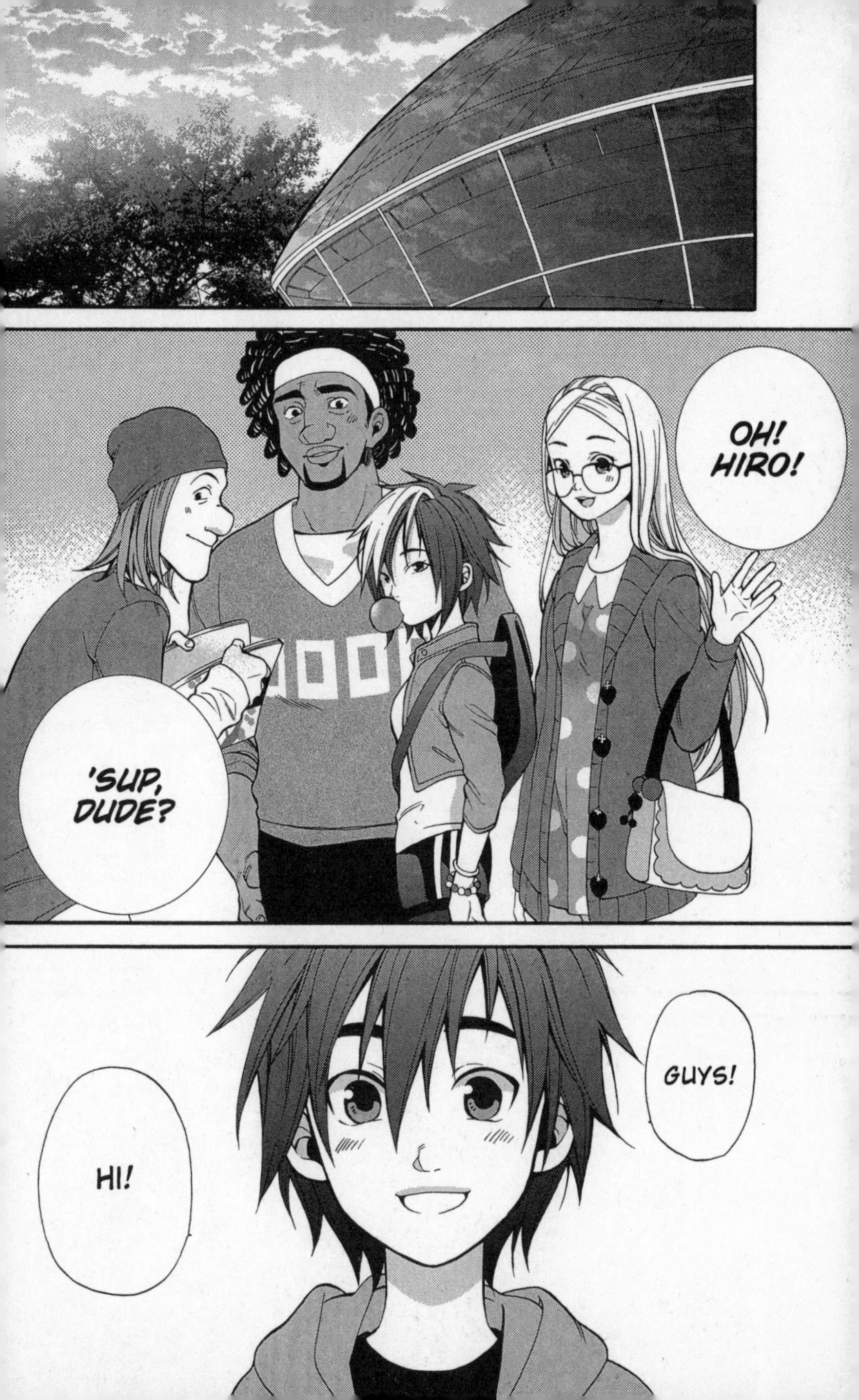
OH! HIRO!
'SUP, DUDE?
GUYS!
HI!

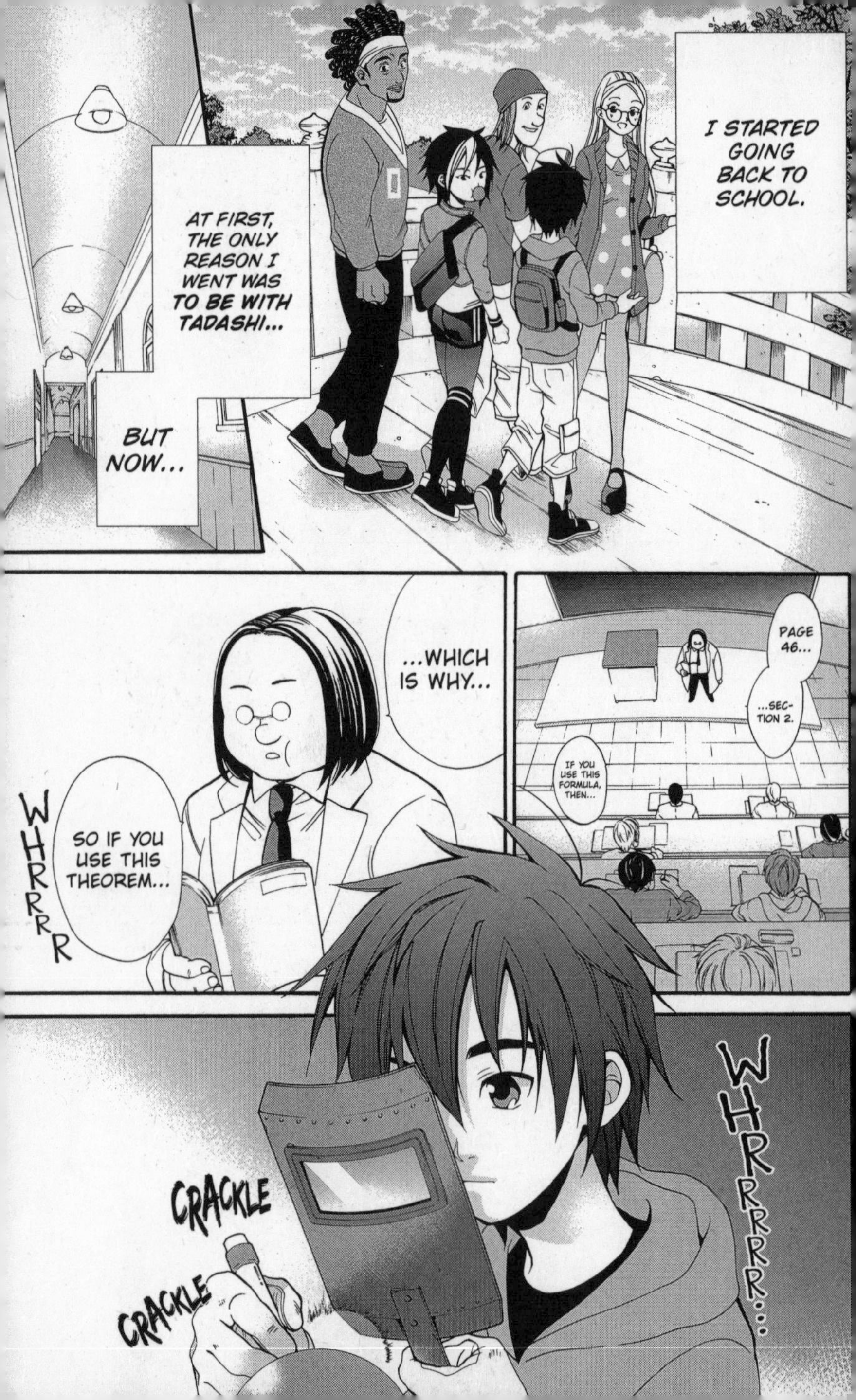
I STARTED GOING BACK TO SCHOOL.
AT FIRST, THE ONLY REASON I WENT WAS TO BE WITH TADASHI...
BUT NOW...
PAGE 46...
...SEC-TION 2.
IF YOU USE THIS FORMULA, THEN...
...WHICH IS WHY...
SO IF YOU USE THIS THEOREM...
WHRRRR
WHRRRRR...
CRACKLE
CRACKLE

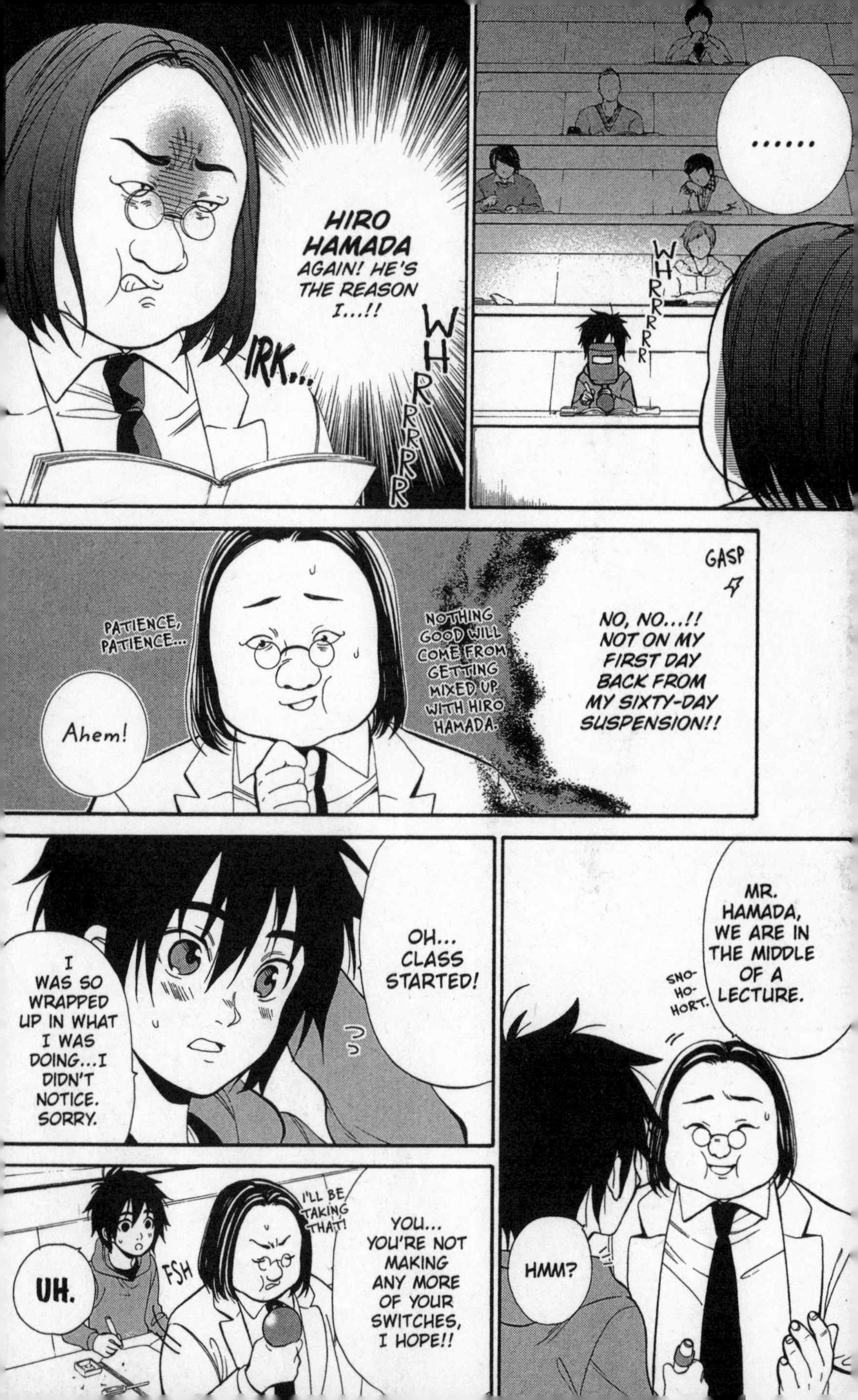
......
WHRRRRRR
HIRO HAMADA AGAIN! HE'S THE REASON I...!!
IRK...
WHRRRRRR
GASP
NO, NO...!! NOT ON MY FIRST DAY BACK FROM MY SIXTY-DAY SUSPENSION!!
NOTHING GOOD WILL COME FROM GETTING MIXED UP WITH HIRO HAMADA.
PATIENCE, PATIENCE...
Ahem!
MR. HAMADA, WE ARE IN THE MIDDLE OF A LECTURE.
SNO-HO-HORT.
HMM?
OH... CLASS STARTED!
I WAS SO WRAPPED UP IN WHAT I WAS DOING...I DIDN'T NOTICE. SORRY.
YOU... YOU'RE NOT MAKING ANY MORE OF YOUR SWITCHES, I HOPE!!
I'LL BE TAKING THAT!
FSH
UH.

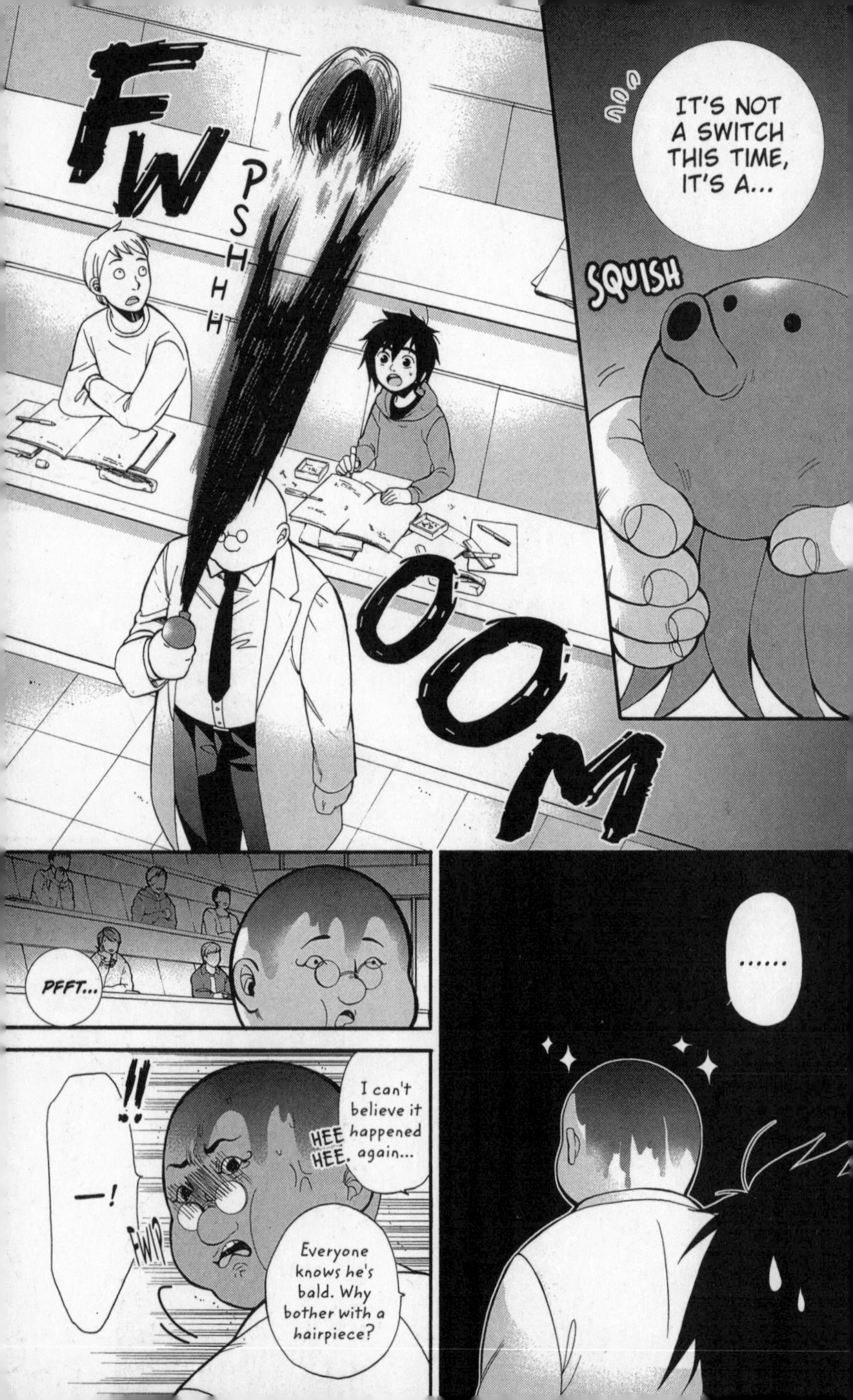
IT'S NOT A SWITCH THIS TIME, IT'S A...
SQUISH
FW
PSHHH
OOM
......
PFFT...
!!
—!
I can't believe it happened again...
HEE HEE.
Everyone knows he's bald. Why bother with a hairpiece?

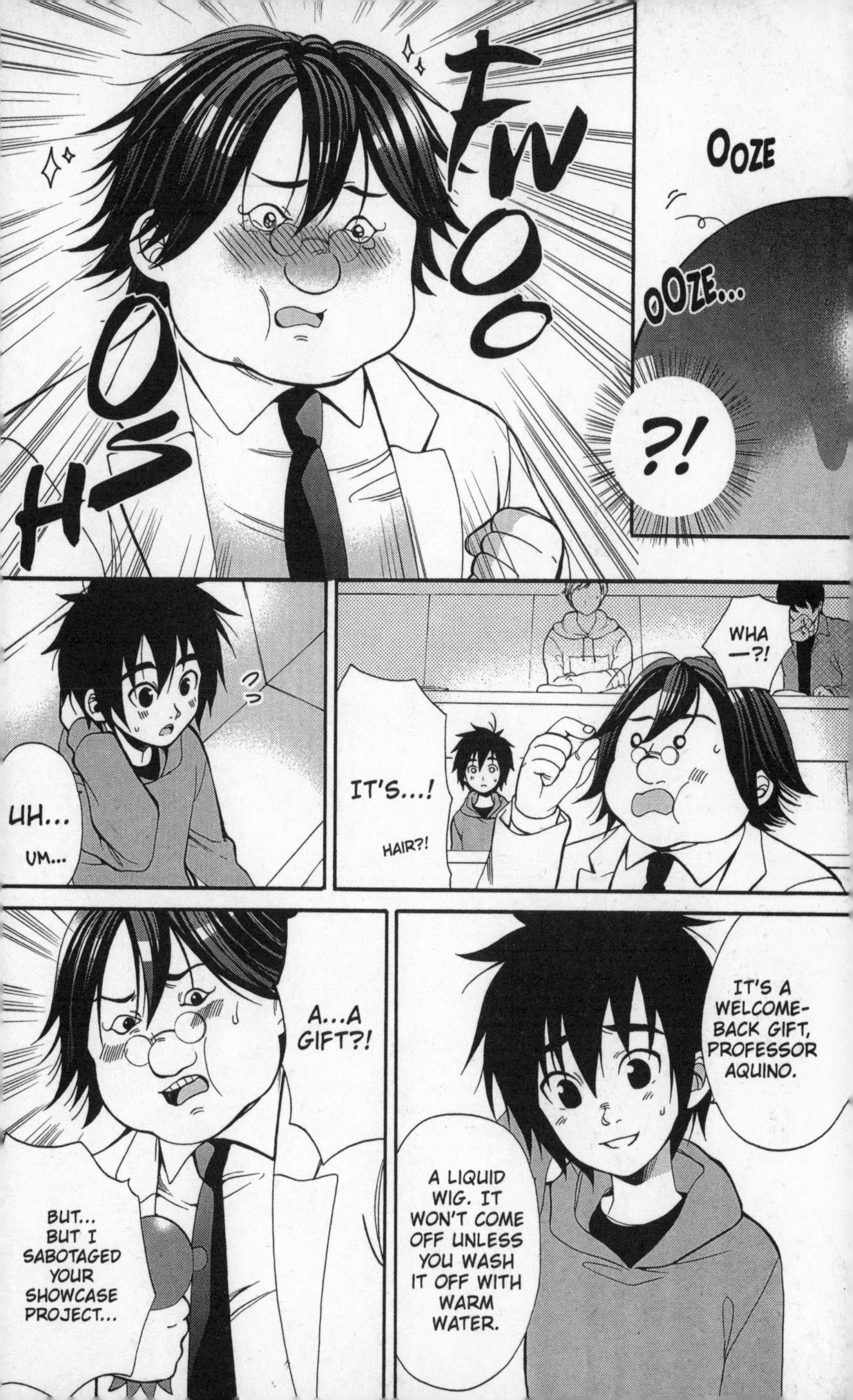
OOZE
OOZE...
?!
FWOOO
OOSH
WHA—?!
IT'S...!
HAIR?!
UH...
UM...
IT'S A WELCOME-BACK GIFT, PROFESSOR AQUINO.
A LIQUID WIG. IT WON'T COME OFF UNLESS YOU WASH IT OFF WITH WARM WATER.
A...A GIFT?!
BUT... BUT I SABOTAGED YOUR SHOWCASE PROJECT...

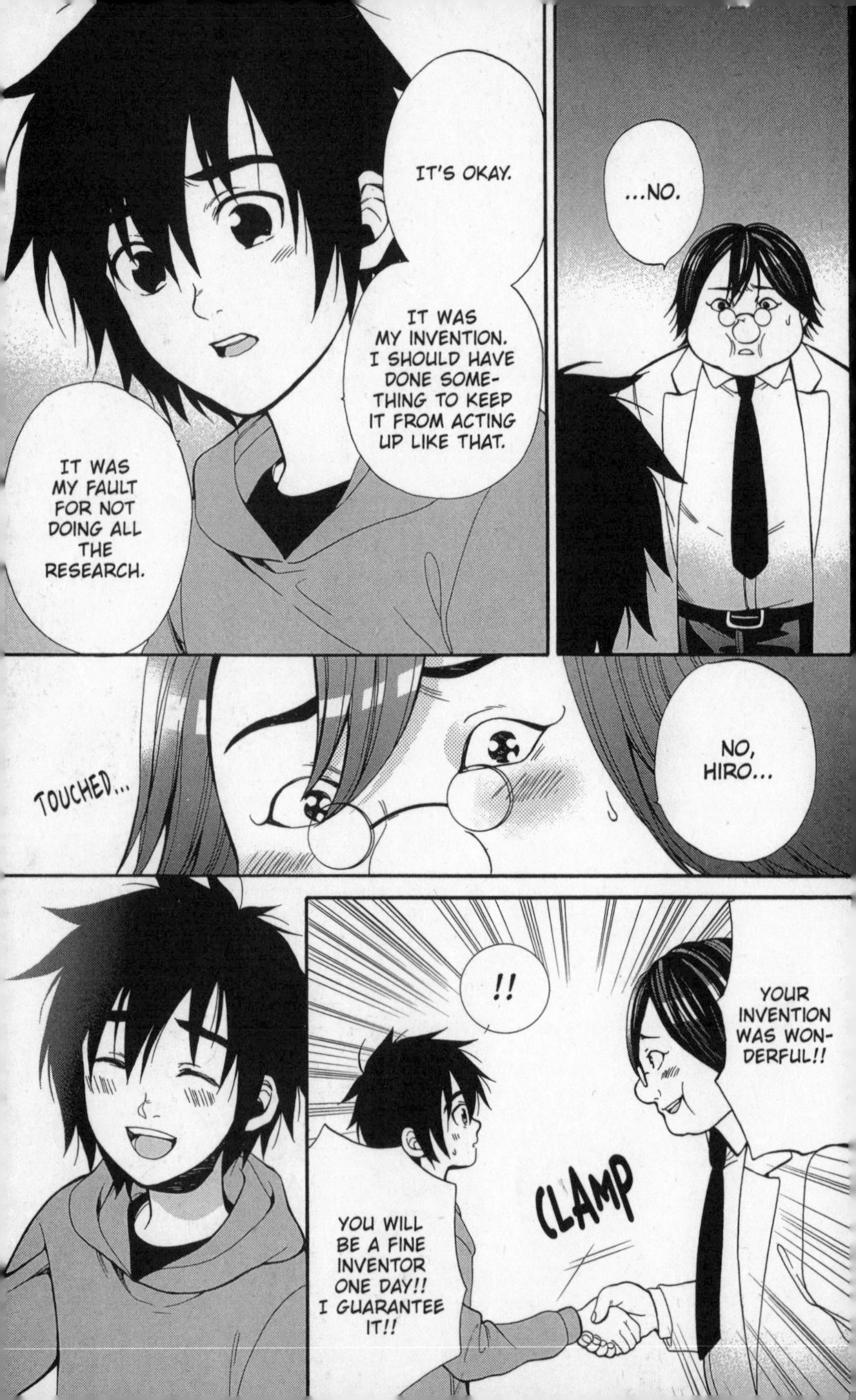
...NO.
IT'S OKAY.
IT WAS MY INVENTION. I SHOULD HAVE DONE SOME-THING TO KEEP IT FROM ACTING UP LIKE THAT.
IT WAS MY FAULT FOR NOT DOING ALL THE RESEARCH.
NO, HIRO...
TOUCHED...
YOUR INVENTION WAS WON-DERFUL!!
!!
CLAMP
YOU WILL BE A FINE INVENTOR ONE DAY!! I GUARANTEE IT!!

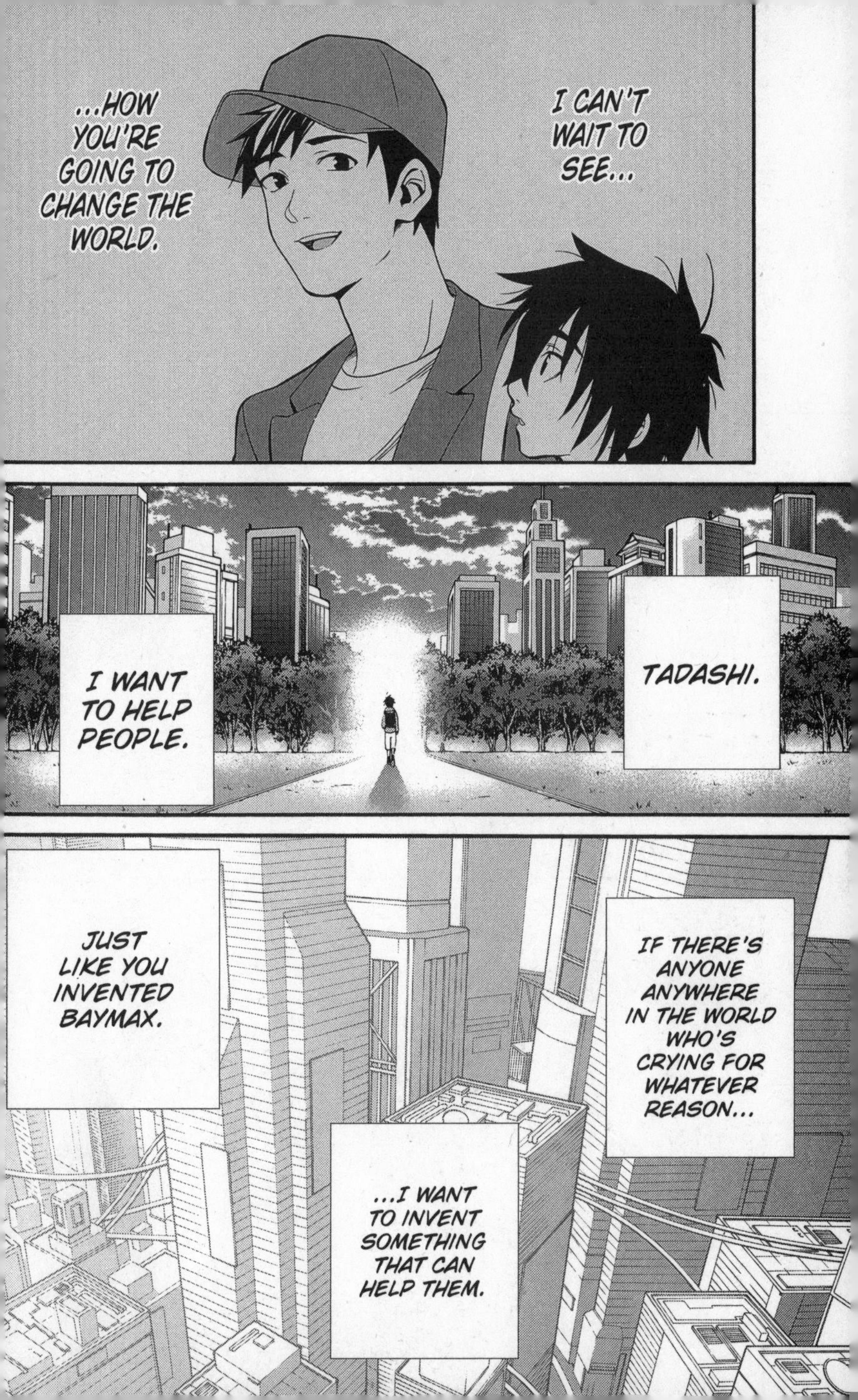
I CAN'T WAIT TO SEE...
...HOW YOU'RE GOING TO CHANGE THE WORLD.
TADASHI.
I WANT TO HELP PEOPLE.
IF THERE'S ANYONE ANYWHERE IN THE WORLD WHO'S CRYING FOR WHATEVER REASON...
...I WANT TO INVENT SOMETHING THAT CAN HELP THEM.
JUST LIKE YOU INVENTED BAYMAX.

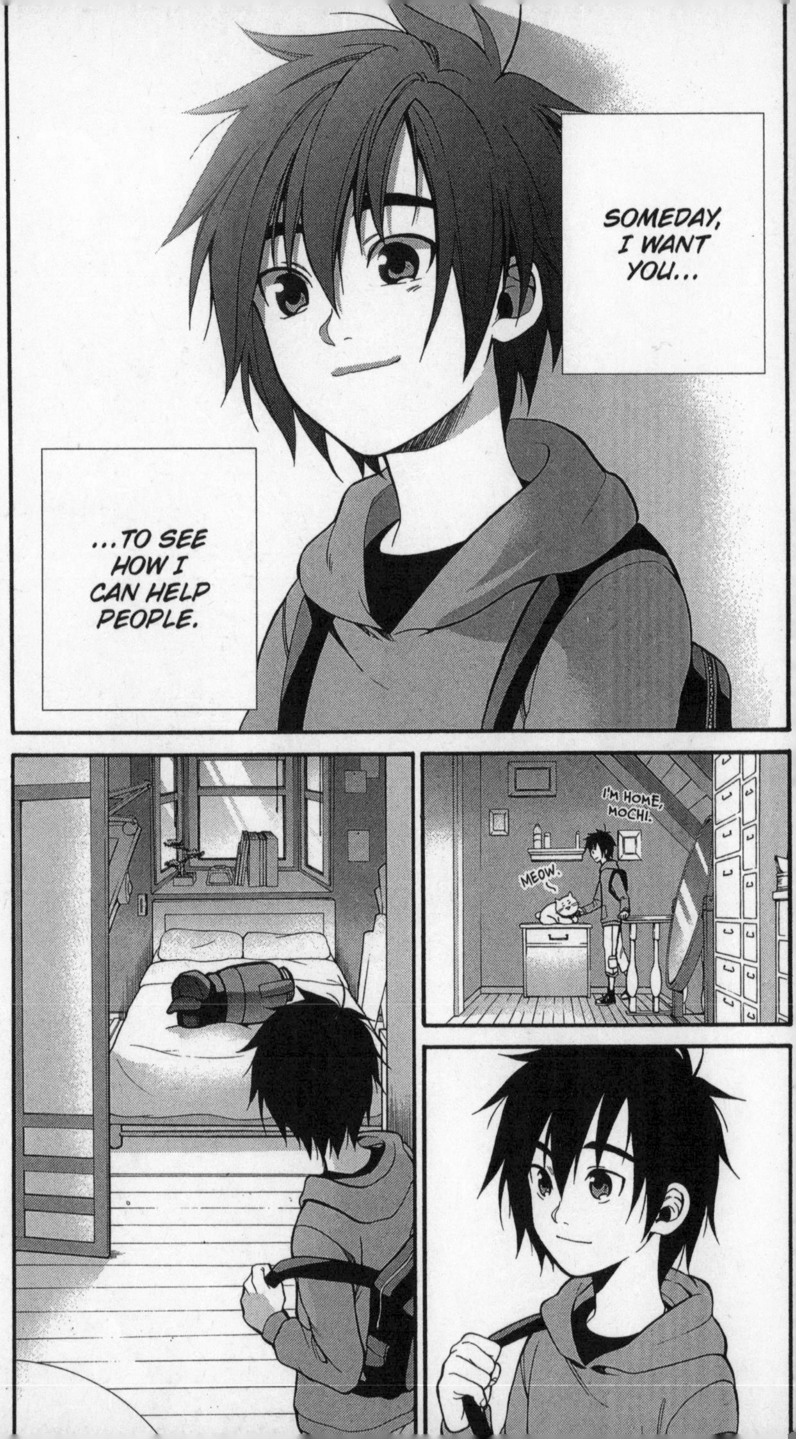
SOMEDAY, I WANT YOU...
...TO SEE HOW I CAN HELP PEOPLE.
I'M HOME, MOCHI!
MEOW.

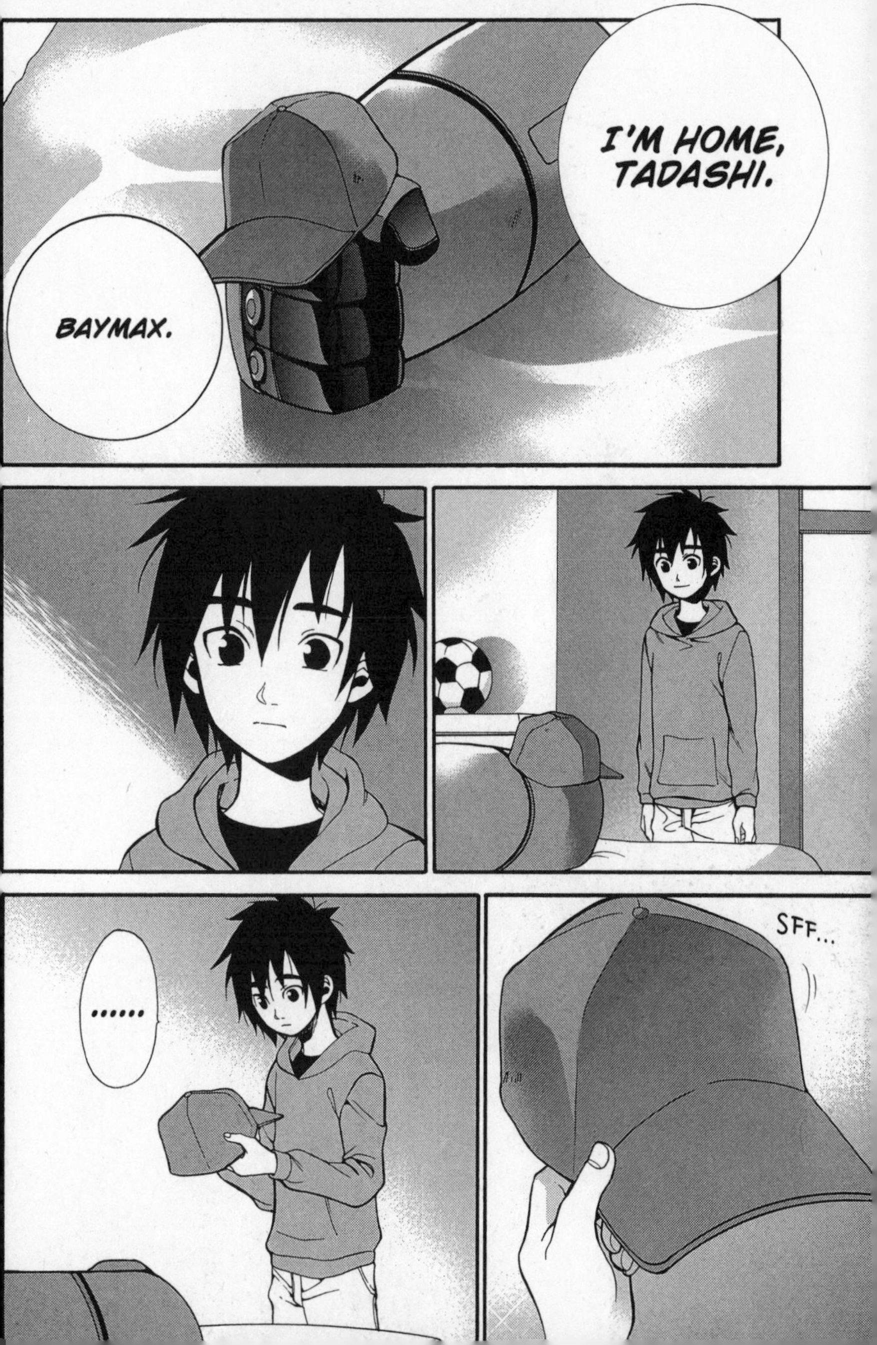
I'M HOME, TADASHI.
BAYMAX.
SFF...
......

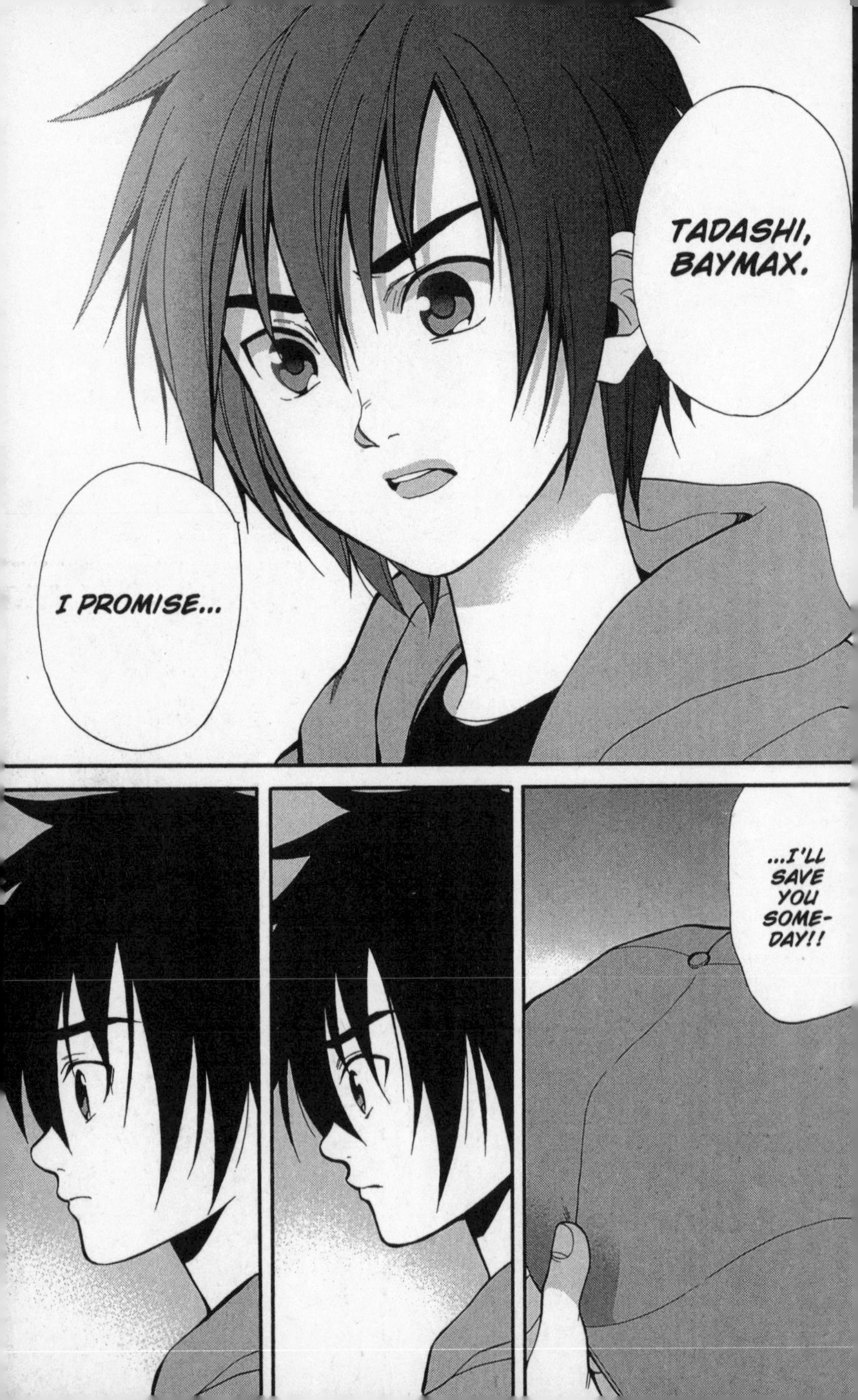
TADASHI, BAYMAX.
I PROMISE...
...I'LL SAVE YOU SOME-DAY!!

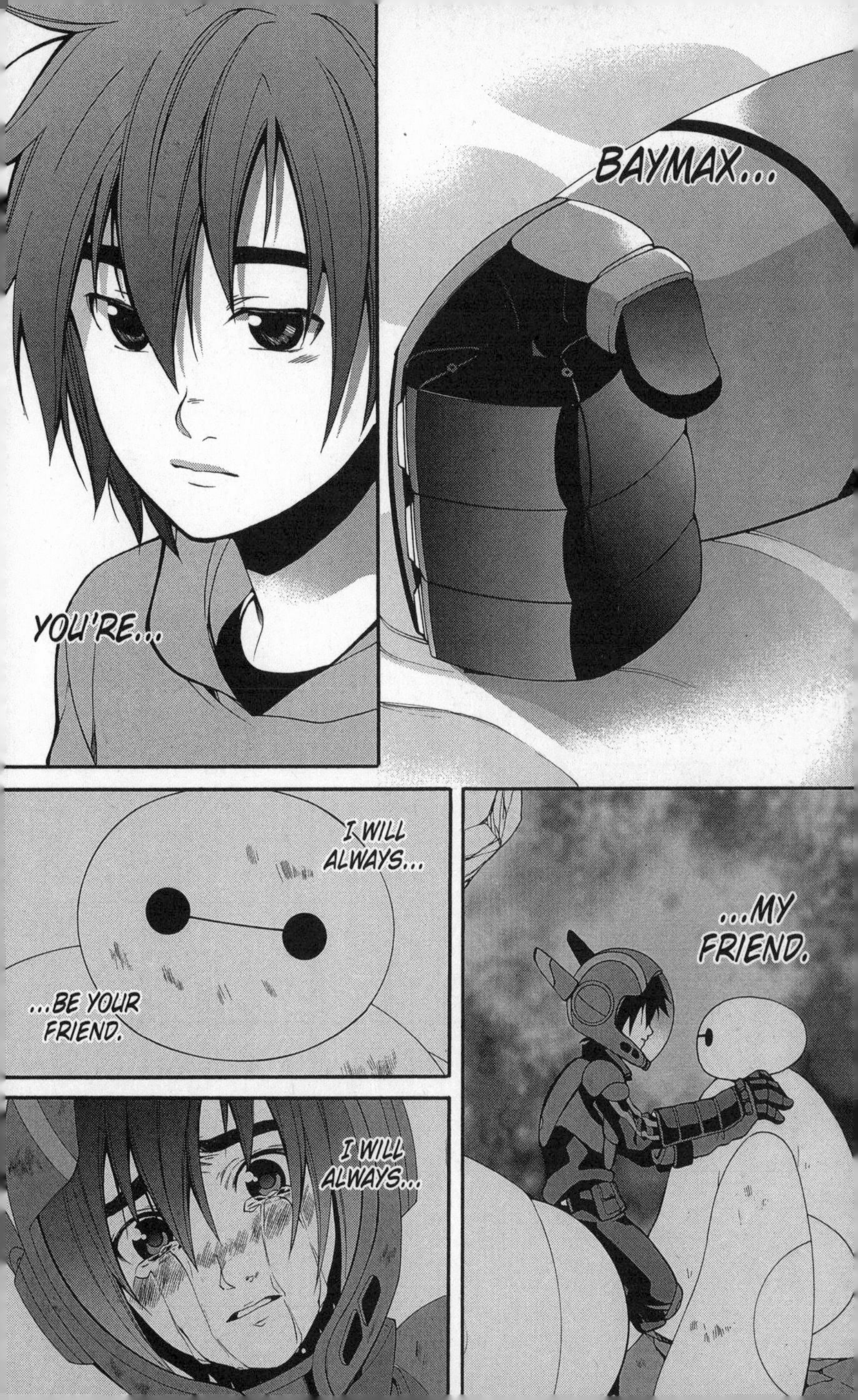
BAYMAX...
YOU'RE...
...MY FRIEND.
I WILL ALWAYS...
...BE YOUR FRIEND.
I WILL ALWAYS...

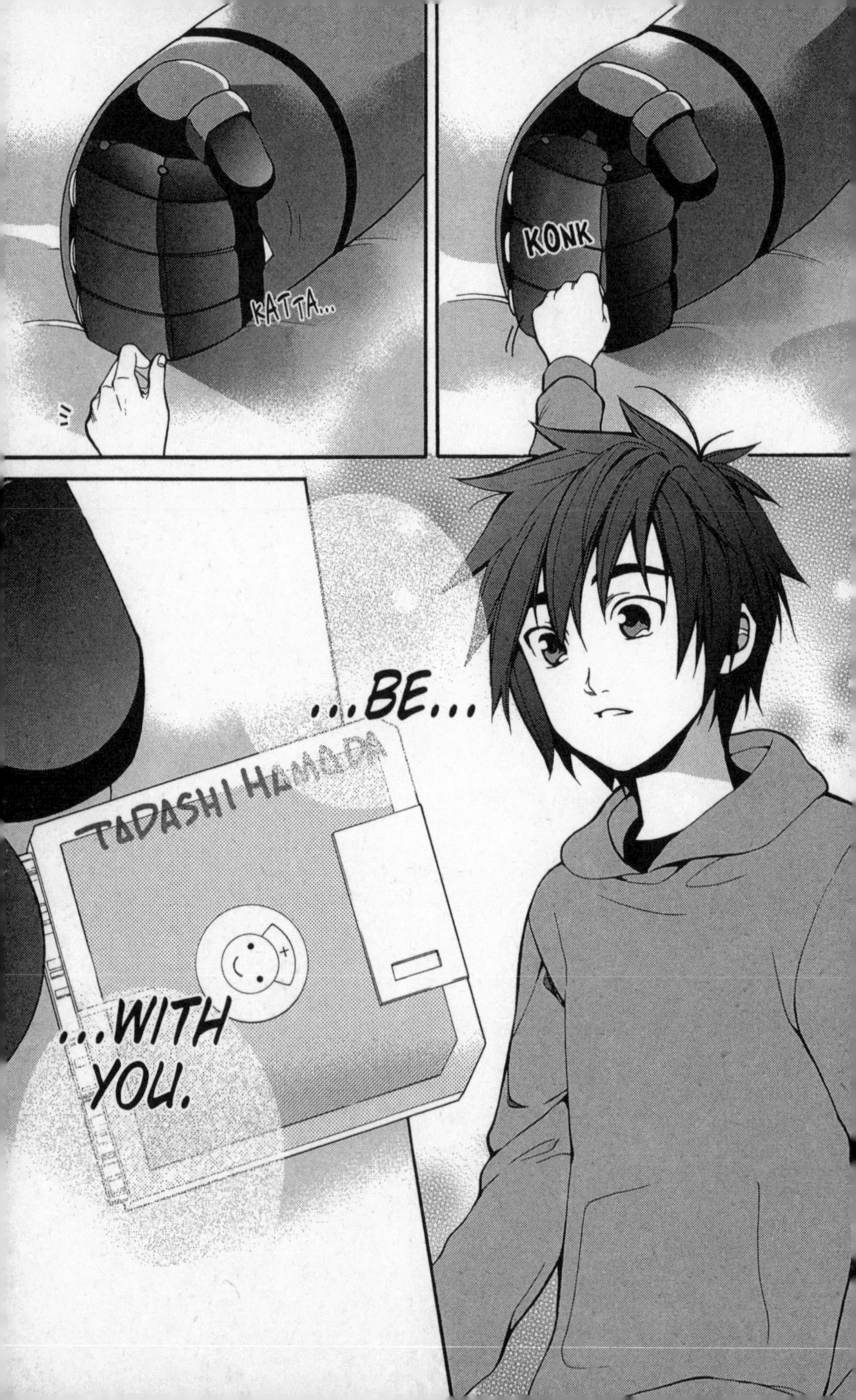
KONK
KATTA...
...BE...
TADASHI HAMADA
...WITH YOU.

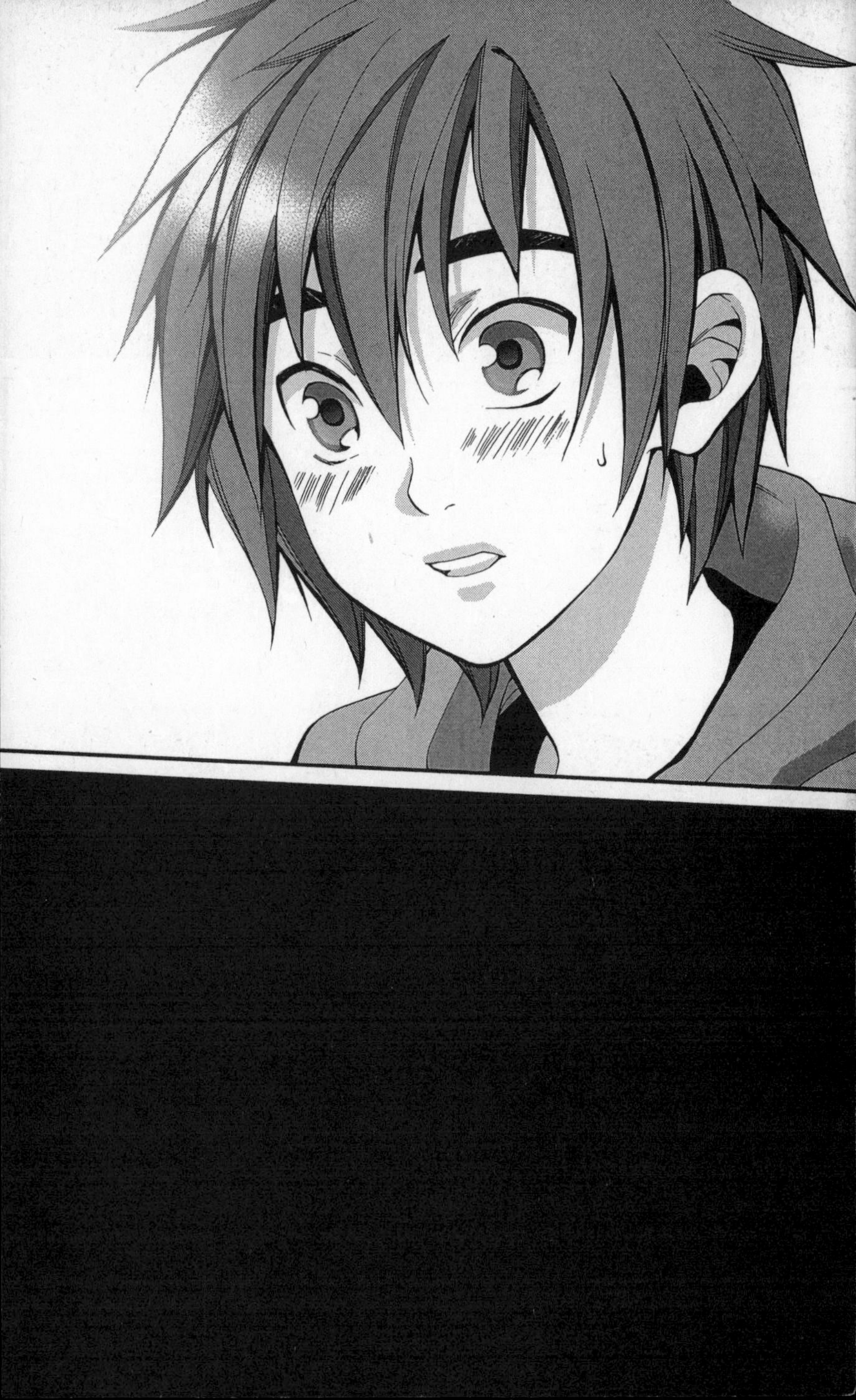

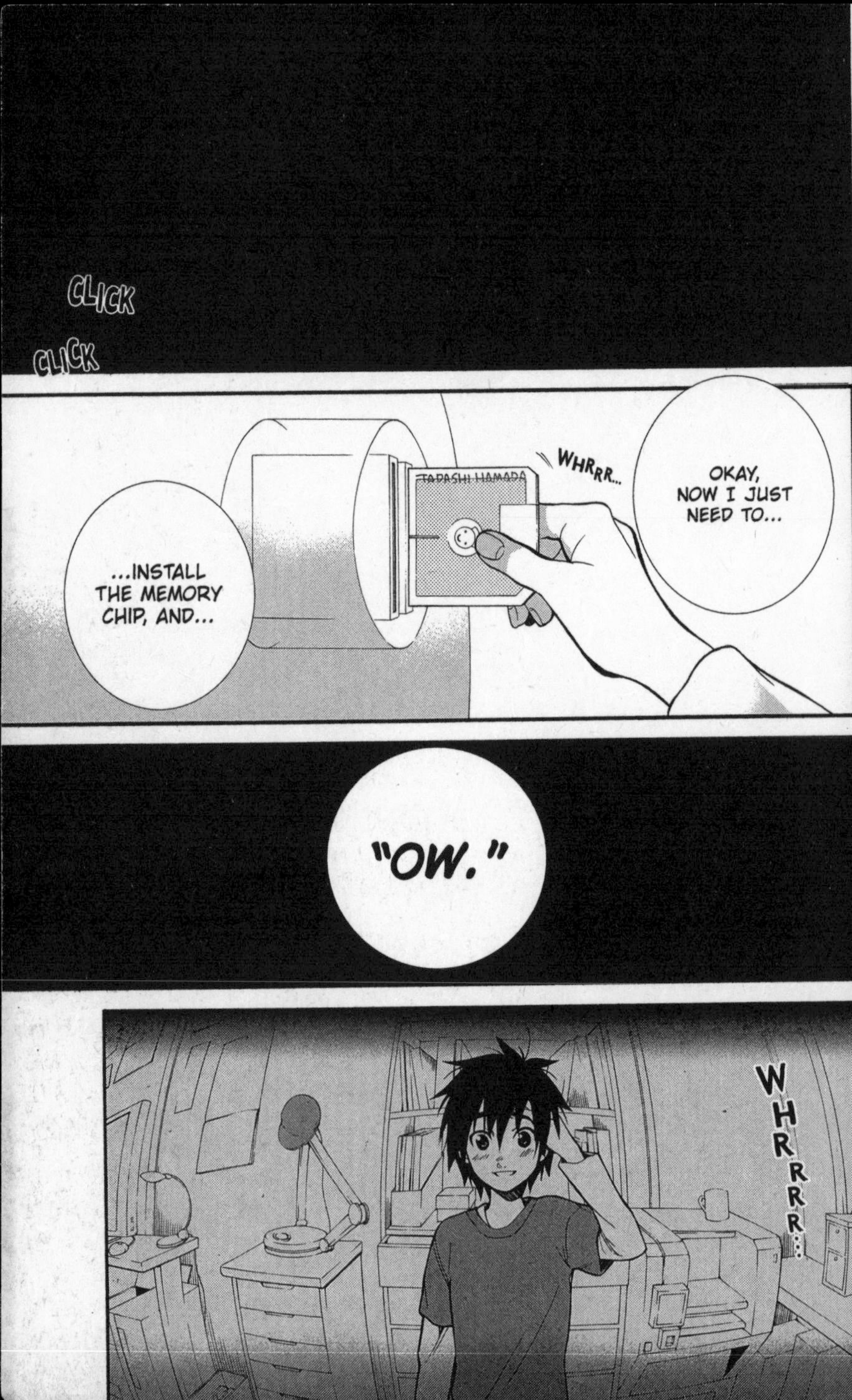
CLICK
CLICK
OKAY, NOW I JUST NEED TO...
WHRRR...
TADASHI HAMADA
...INSTALL THE MEMORY CHIP, AND...
"OW."
WHRRRR...

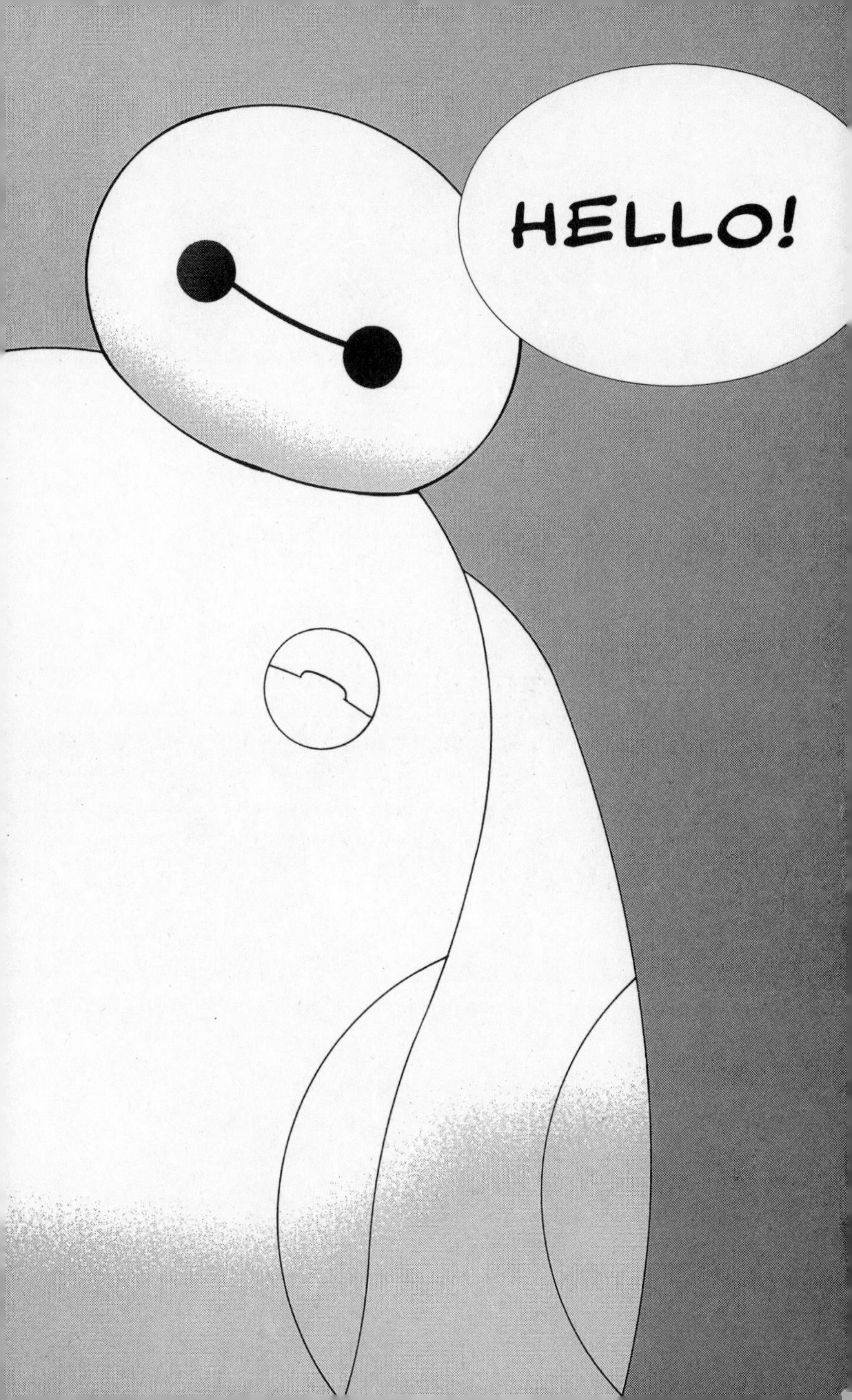
HELLO!

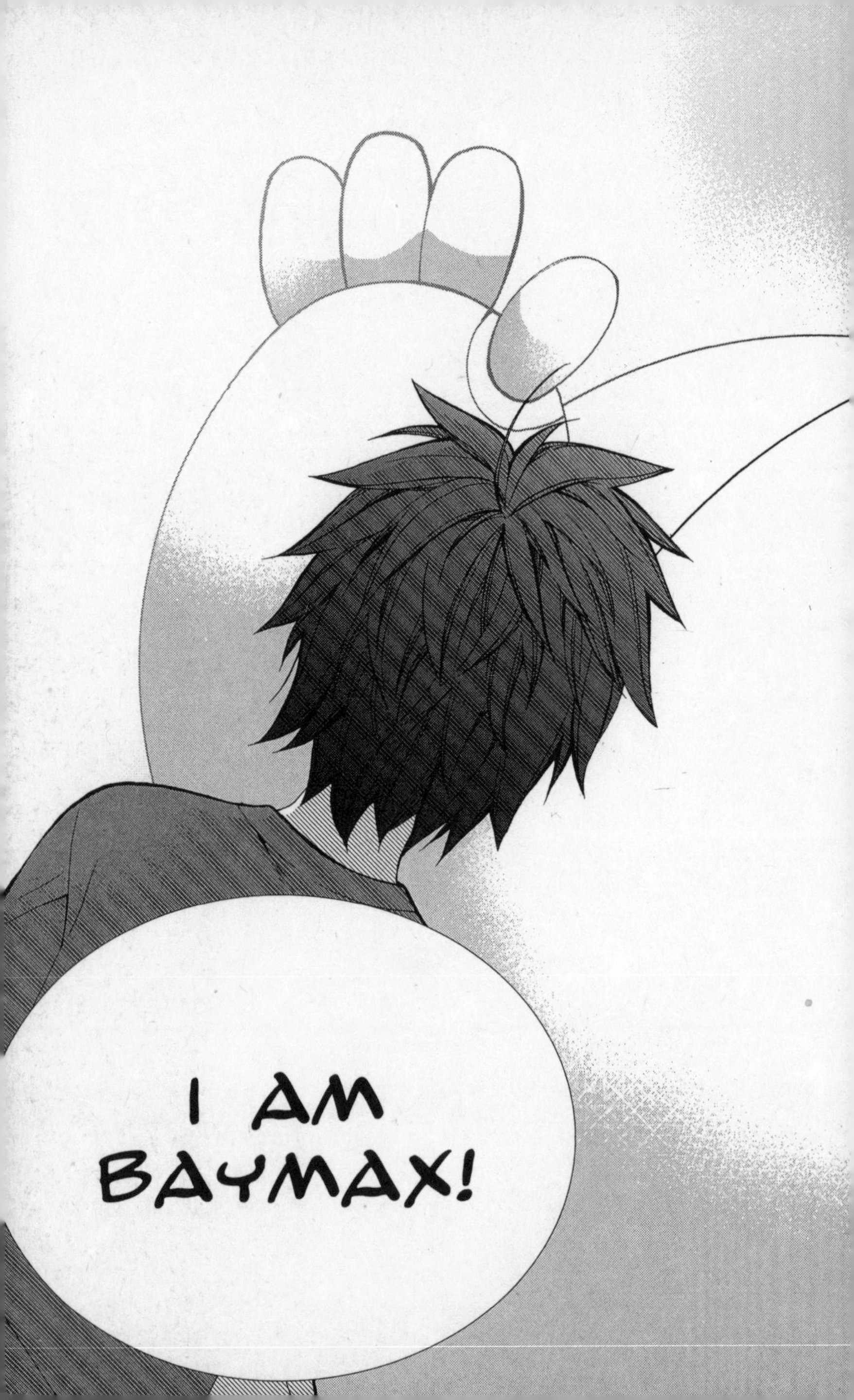
I AM BAYMAX!

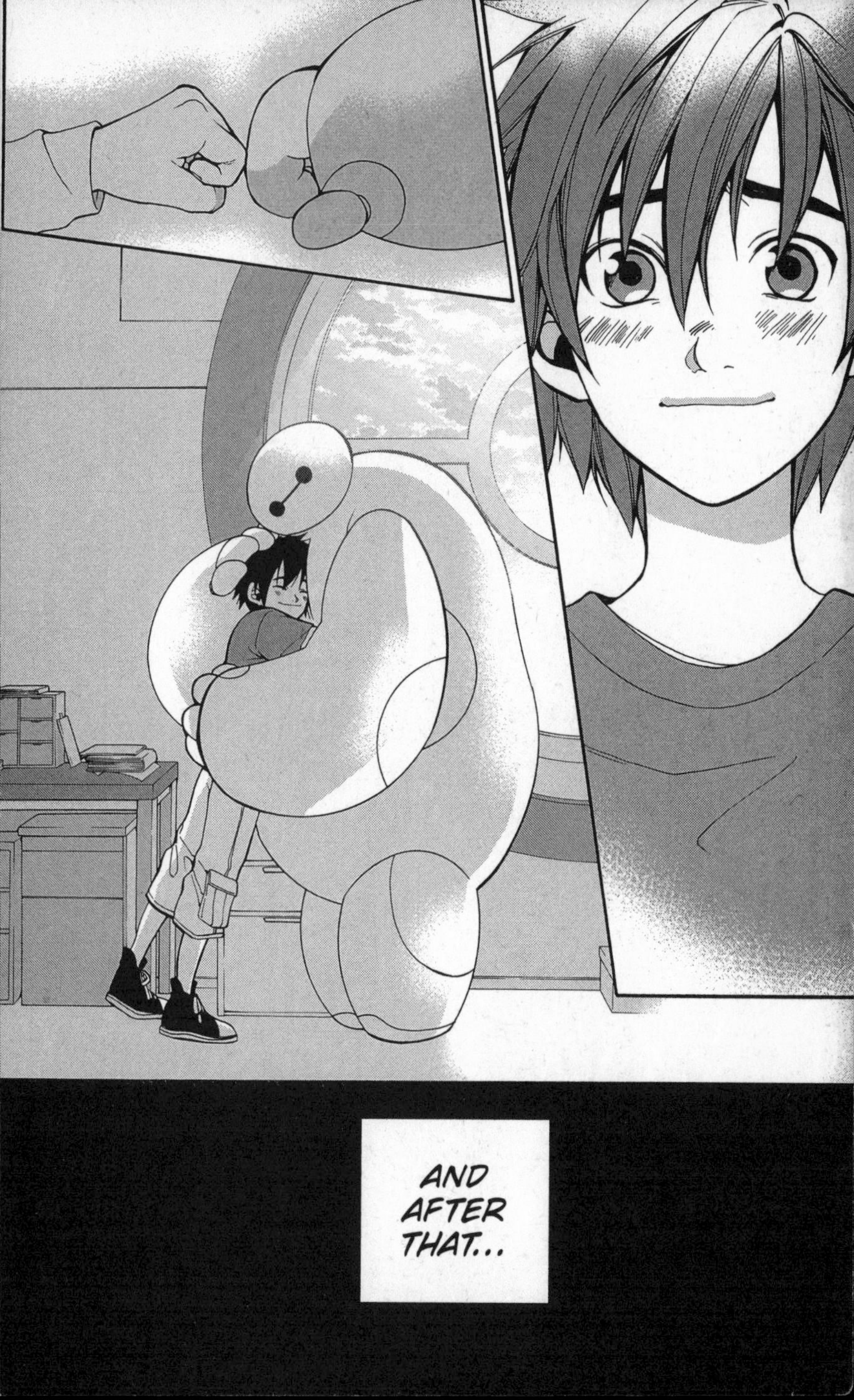
AND AFTER THAT...

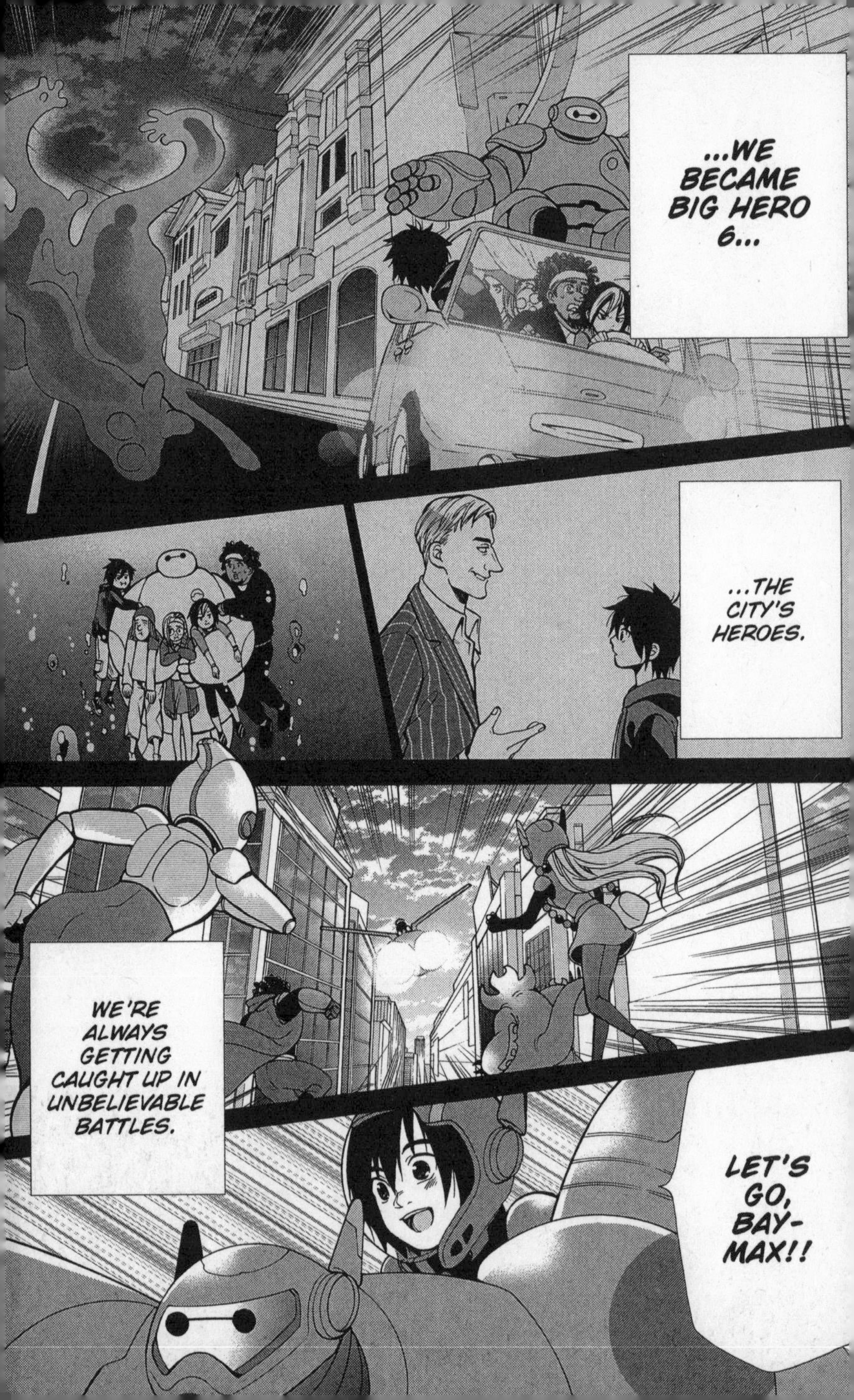
...WE BECAME BIG HERO 6...
...THE CITY'S HEROES.
WE'RE ALWAYS GETTING CAUGHT UP IN UNBELIEVABLE BATTLES.
LET'S GO, BAY-MAX!!

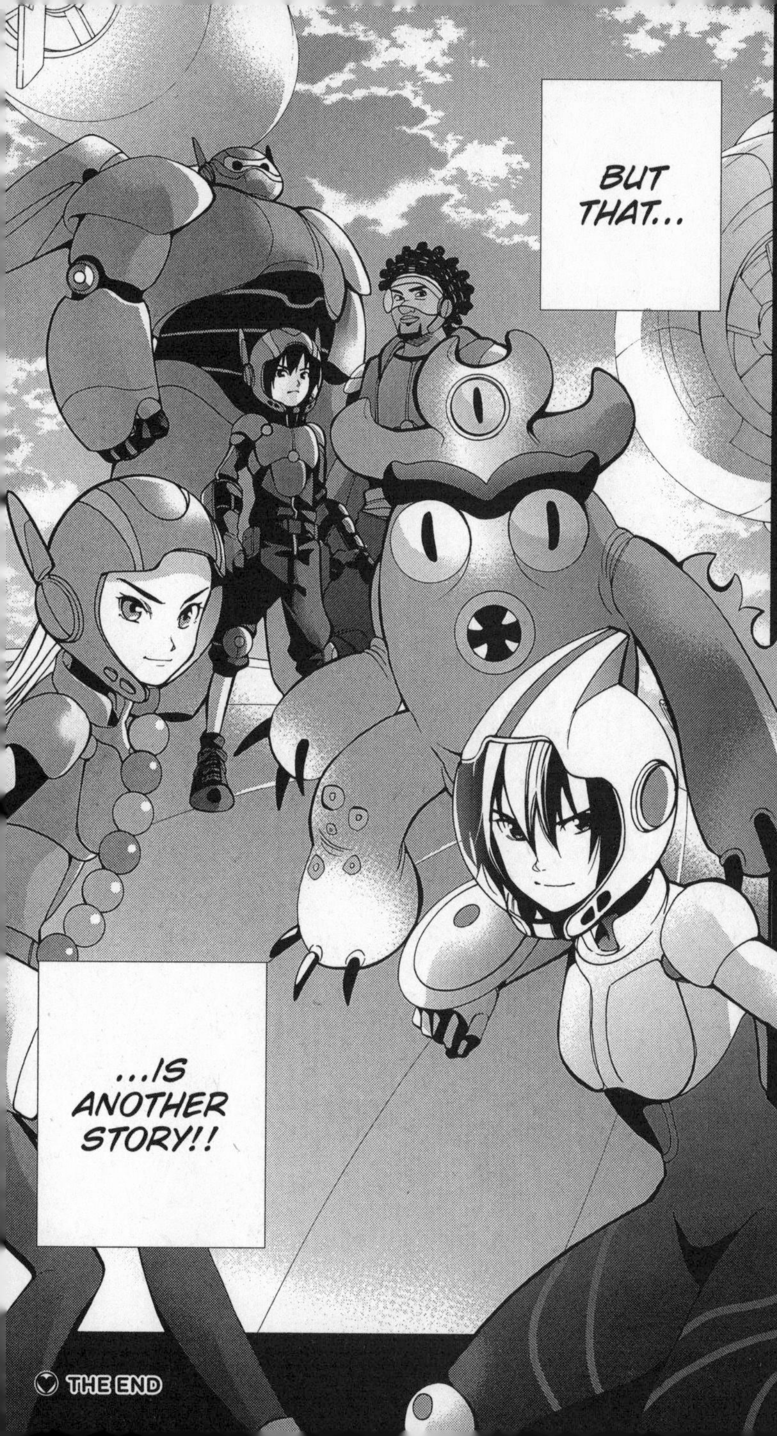
BUT THAT...
...IS ANOTHER STORY!!
THE END

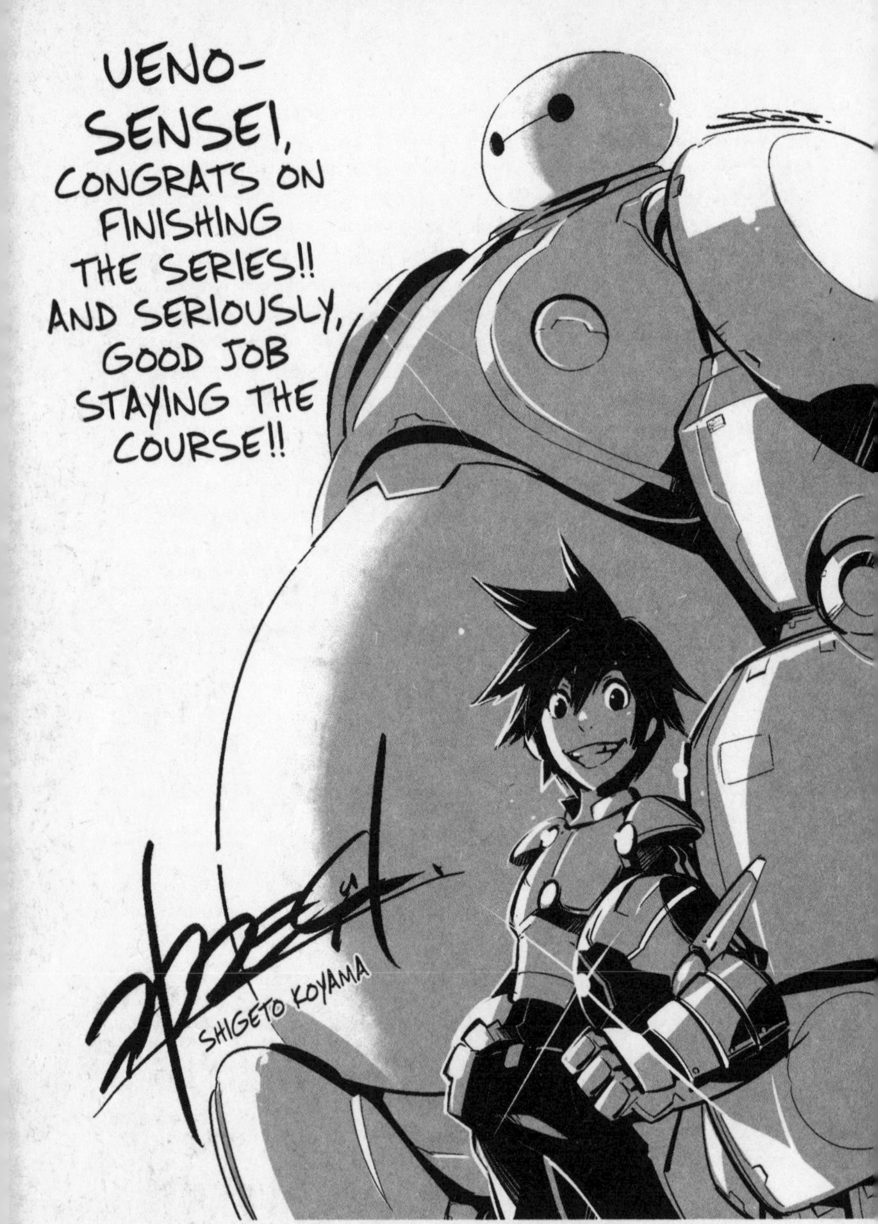
UENO-SENSEI, CONGRATS ON FINISHING THE SERIES!! AND SERIOUSLY, GOOD JOB STAYING THE COURSE!!
SHIGETO KOYAMA

Shigeto Koyama
Designer. Has contributed to a variety of projects, including design works for *Rebuild of Evangelion*, character designs for *Heroman*, art direction for *Kill la Kill*, design works for *Gundam Reconguista in G*, and more. Contributed to the concept design for Baymax in *Big Hero 6*.

Afterword

Hello! I am Haruki Ueno. I have loved Disney since I was a kid, but I never even dreamed I would get to draw a manga series for one of their movies. I was even invited to Disney Studios in the United States, and I worked out the details with a lot of people, trying to come up with something that would help the readers enjoy a story they would only see in the manga. I worked hardest on "Episode 0." It was a sixteen-page chapter that ran in *Weekly Shonen Magazine* before the series started in *Magazine Special*. I wasn't sure how to best convey the story of *Big Hero 6* in such a short chapter, so I drew lots of different versions of it. I had one where Hiro, Baymax, and friends save the city from a giant monster; one where we introduce Baymax and Hiro through the eyes of Cass's cat, Mochi; even one from the perspective of a manga-original character: a girl with a crush on Hiro...

This was an amazing opportunity. I wanted this to be a bonus story, the kind of story that when people read these sixteen pages, they would see more depth in the main story. And that's how I came up with the prequel, "Episode 0." Thank you to all you readers who read the bonus chapter, "Episode 0," and then read the *Big Hero 6* manga all the way through.

I hope we meet again!

Haruki Ueno

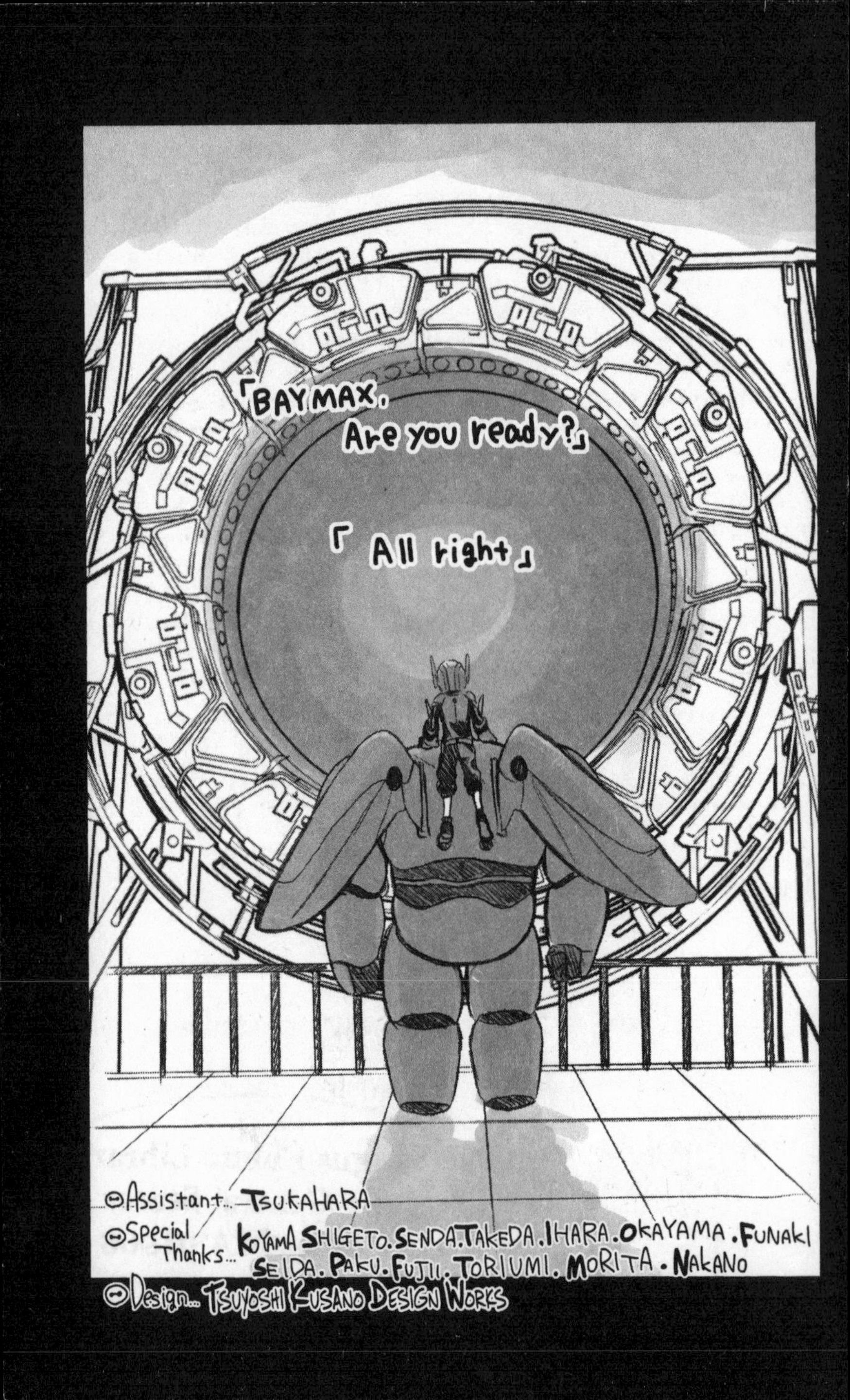
「BAYMAX, Are you ready?」
「All right」
Assistant... TSUKAHARA
Special Thanks... KOYAMA SHIGETO. SENDA. TAKEDA. IHARA. OKAYAMA. FUNAKI SEIDA. PAKU. FUJII. TORIUMI. MORITA. NAKANO
Design... TSUYOSHI KUSANO DESIGN WORKS

BIG HERO 6 ❷

HARUKI UENO

ORIGINAL CONCEPT:
MARVEL WORLDWIDE, INC.

Translation: Alethea and Athena Nibley • Lettering: Lys Blakeslee

This book is a work of fiction. Names, characters, places, and incidents are the product of the author's imagination or are used fictitiously. Any resemblance to actual events, locales, or persons, living or dead, is coincidental.

Yen Press
Hachette Book Group
1290 Avenue of the Americas
New York, NY 10104

www.HachetteBookGroup.com
www.YenPress.com

Yen Press is an imprint of Hachette Book Group, Inc. The Yen Press name and logo are trademarks of Hachette Book Group, Inc.

The publisher is not responsible for websites (or their content) that are not owned by the publisher.

First Yen Press Edition: September 2015

ISBN: 978-0-316-26390-0

10 9 8 7 6 5 4 3 2 1

BVG

Printed in the United States of America